FRENCH GRAMMAR

Jon Balserak

May 27, 1978

On my first trip home from Edinburgh!!

HARCOURT BRACE JOVANOVICH COLLEGE OUTLINE SERIES

FRENCH GRAMMAR

Thomas J. Cox

San Diego State University

Books for Professionals
Harcourt Brace Jovanovich, Publishers
San Diego   New York   London

LIBRARY OF CONGRESS CATALOGING IN PUBLICATION DATA

Cox, Thomas J.
    French grammar
    (Harcourt Brace college outline series)
(Books for professionals)
    Includes index.
    1. French language—Grammar—1950-   . 2. French language—Text-books for foreign speakers—English. I. Title.
II. Series. III. Series: Books for professionals.
PC2112.C68 1986   448.2′421   85-16417
ISBN 0-15-601611-7

First Edition

45678 074 8765432

PREFACE

The purpose of this book is to present a complete introductory course in French grammar in the clear, concise format of an outline. It is comprehensive enough to be used by itself for independent study, or as a supplement to college courses and textbooks on the subject. In the case of independent study, regular features of the book are specially designed to build your skills in a logical sequence of study. If used as a supplement to your course work, these regular features are easily located and structured to give extra practice in all areas of French grammar.

ORGANIZATION The book is organized according to the parts of speech: that is, nouns and articles, adverbs and adjectives, verbs, and so forth. Each rule of grammar and of syntax (word order) is explained, and such explanation is followed by one or more examples. All examples are translated into English so that you do not need to look up vocabulary. If you do not understand a grammar explanation, study the example.

EXERCISES Once you understand each grammar explanation and the corresponding examples, do the exercise or exercises relating to that section. *Do not skip the exercises and go to the next point of grammar.* Each exercise should be completed immediately following the corresponding grammar point for reinforcement of learning. Try to finish the exercise before you turn to the answers. If you are unable to complete an item within the exercise, go to the next item, completing as many as you can.

SUMMARY This feature consists of a brief restatement of the main grammatical points in each chapter. The summary is presented in the efficient form of a numbered list, so that you can use it to refresh your memory quickly before an exam.

RAISE YOUR GRADES This feature consists of more exercises provided at the end of each chapter that offer comprehensive application of or extra practice in the major grammatical points covered in each chapter. Should you have trouble completing any of these exercises, section references are provided so that you can locate and review the relevant information.

ANSWERS The answers to all of the exercises, including the Raise Your Grades exercises, are provided at the end of each chapter and translated into English. Because the answers are translated, the vocabulary of the exercises is slightly more varied than is usual in a book of this kind. This enables you to use the answers as a tool in building vocabulary. Once you have completed and checked the exercises, you can use the English translations to further reinforce your vocabulary by translating them back into French and checking them against the completed exercises.

The author wishes to thank all those whose knowledge and hard work made this book possible. Special thanks, however, go to Francoise Demerson-Baker, for her expert editing throughout.

CONTENTS

FRENCH GRAMMAR

1 NOUNS AND ARTICLES

THIS CHAPTER IS ABOUT

☑ **Definite Articles**
☑ **Nouns**
☑ **More About Definite Articles**
☑ **Indefinite Articles**
☑ **Partitive Articles**

1-1. Definite Articles

In English, the definite article *the* has only one form which we use with any noun, regardless of whether the noun is singular or plural. BUT, in French you must change the form of the definite article according to the *number*, *gender* and *form* of the noun it introduces.

A. Agreement of the definite article

In French, all nouns are either masculine or feminine, as well as singular or plural—there are no neuter nouns! So, you must always use a form of the definite article that corresponds with the noun it modifies—that is, the definite article must *agree* with the noun.

1. The definite article must *agree in gender* with the noun it introduces.

   • use a masculine form of the definite article before a masculine noun
   • use a feminine form of the definite article before a feminine noun

2. The definite article must *agree in number* with the noun it introduces.

   • use a singular form of the definite article before a singular noun
   • use a plural form of the definite article before a plural noun

B. Forms of the definite article

1. The definite article has four forms. Study carefully the following chart and examples.

	Singular	Plural
Masculine	**le**	**les**
	(l' + vowel)	
Feminine	**la**	**les**
	(l' + vowel)	

M–sing	le pied	*the foot*	M–pl	**les** pieds	*the feet*
F–sing	la rue	*the street*	F–pl	**les** rues	*the streets*
F–sing	l'anniversaire	*the birthday*	F–pl	**les** anniversaires	*the birthdays*

> *REMEMBER:* The masculine and feminine plural definite articles are the same—**les**. So, you can't tell the gender of a plural noun from its definite article.

EXERCISE 1-1: Write the gender (**M** or **F**) and the number (**sing** or **pl**) of the article and noun in the space provided. Then translate the noun into English. If you don't know the gender of a noun, look it up in your dictionary. Don't guess. Answers and translations are at the end of the chapter.

Example: le livre <u>M, sing, book</u>

les fenêtres F, pl, windows

1. la pluie	_____	6. les skieurs	_____
2. les plantes	_____	7. la cuisine	_____
3. les rhumes	_____	8. le chocolat	_____
4. le loup	_____	9. les télévisions	_____
5. le magasin	_____	10. la femme	_____

2. If the singular definite article **le** or **la** precedes a noun that begins with a vowel, change the definite article to **l'**. Do not change the plural definite article **les** before a vowel.

<u>M–sing</u> **l'**animal *the animal* <u>M–pl</u> **les a**nimaux *the animals*
<u>F–sing</u> **l'**année *the year*   <u>F–pl</u> **les a**nnées *the years*

3. You must change **le** or **la** to **l'** before a *silent h*—called **h muet**. BUT do not change the definite article before a noun that begins with an *h that is not silent*—called **h aspiré**.

       h muet   h aspiré

<u>M–sing</u>	**l'**homme	*the man*	<u>M–sing</u>	**le h**avre	*the haven*
<u>F–sing</u>	**l'**habitude	*the habit*	<u>F–sing</u>	**la h**aine	*the hatred*
<u>F–sing</u>	**l'**histoire	*the history, story*	<u>M–sing</u>	**le h**ibou	*the owl*

EXERCISE 1-2: Write the gender of the noun in the first blank. Then determine the number of the noun and choose the correct article—**le, la, l', or les**—and write it in the blank following the noun. If you don't know the gender of a noun, look it up in your dictionary. Don't guess. Answers and translations are at the end of the chapter.

Example: <u>**M**</u> 1. **le** parc

    <u>**F**</u> 2. **les** églises

___ 1. ___ ski	___ 8. ___ Etats-Unis	___ 15. ___ éléphant
___ 2. ___ air	___ 9. ___ sucre	___ 16. ___ valise
___ 3. ___ verres	___ 10. ___ bijouterie	___ 17. ___ océan
___ 4. ___ motocyclette	___ 11. ___ tante	___ 18. ___ trains
___ 5. ___ restaurants	___ 12. ___ papillons	___ 19. ___ horde
___ 6. ___ lapin	___ 13. ___ fleur	___ 20. ___ lampes
___ 7. ___ huile	___ 14. ___ marché	

1-2. Nouns

All French nouns are either masculine or feminine. You can learn the gender of each new French noun by looking it up in a dictionary or by noticing the gender of the article or adjectives that modify it. There are also some general patterns of meaning and spelling which will help you determine the gender of some French nouns.

A. Natural gender nouns

1. Nouns that refer to males are usually masculine, and nouns that refer to females are usually feminine. Study the following examples of nouns that have natural gender.

Feminine		Masculine	
la femme	*woman*	**l'homme**	*man*
la jeune fille	*girl*	**le garçon**	*boy*
l'actrice	*actress*	**l'acteur**	*actor*
l'étudiante	*student*	**l'étudiant**	*student*
la cousine	*cousin*	**le cousin**	*cousin*
la vache	*cow*	**le taureau**	*bull*
la lionne	*lioness*	**le lion**	*lion*
la chatte	*cat*	**le chat**	*cat*
la chienne	*dog*	**le chien**	*dog*

2. Nouns referring to a group that includes at least one male are masculine.

les grands-parents	*grandparents*
les gens	*people*
les jeunes gens	*young people*

> *NOTE:* Nouns referring to certain professions which were once restricted to men remain masculine.

le professeur	*professor, teacher*
le médecin	*doctor*
l'écrivain	*writer*
le pilote	*pilot*

B. Categories of masculine nouns

1. Most nouns ending with the suffixes **-ment**, **-eur**, **-oir**, **-acle**, **-isme**, **-ose**, and **-age** are masculine.

le dans**eur**	*dancer*	**le** chant**eur**	*singer*
le commenc**ement**	*beginning*	**le** capit**alisme**	*capitalism*
l'admir**ateur**	*admirer*	**le** gluc**ose**	*glucose*
le compt**oir**	*counter*	**le** jardin**age**	*gardening*
le spect**acle**	*show*		

> *NOTE:* Some feminine nouns end in **-eur** or **-age**—which is part of the stem.

la fav**eur**	*favor*	**la** p**age**	*page*
la douc**eur**	*sweetness*	**la** c**age**	*cage*
la sav**eur**	*flavor*		

2. Compound nouns that begin with a verb or a preposition are masculine—even when the noun is feminine.

le gagne-pain	*livelihood*	**le portemonnaie**	*change purse*
l'en-tête	*heading* (of a letter)	**le portefeuille**	*wallet*
le passe-partout	*master key*	**le tournevis**	*screwdriver*

3. Most words borrowed from languages in which nouns have no gender—like English—are masculine.

le whiskey	*whiskey*	**le jazz**	*jazz*
le sandwich	*sandwich*		

C. Categories of feminine nouns

1. Nouns ending with the suffixes **-ion**, **-aison**, **-té**, **-tude**, **-ale**, **-ole**, **-ure**, **-ie**, and **-esse** are feminine.

l'invit**ion**	*invitation*	**la** casser**ole**	*pan*
la combin**aison**	*combination*	**la** pein**ture**	*painting*
la beau**té**	*beauty*	**la** bourgeois**ie**	*middle class*
la soli**tude**	*solitude*	**la** jeun**esse**	*youth*
la capit**ale**	*capital*		

2. Adding the endings **-ée**, **-ette**, **-elle**, or **-ille** to nouns of either gender makes them feminine.

l'an	**l'**ann**ée**	*year*
le cigare	**la** cigar**ette**	*cigarette*
la passe	**la** pass**erelle**	*gangplank*

3. Most nouns that end in **-ce**, **-che**, **-sse**, and **-se** are feminine.

la pelouse	*lawn*	**la** fiche	*index card, form*
la fraise	*strawberry*	**l'**église	*church*

la chose	*thing*	la quiche	*quiche, custard pie*
la chance	*chance, luck*	la crèche	*cradle, nursery*
la patience	*patience*	la classe	*class*

BUT

le vice	*vice*
le négoce	*business, trade*

4. Nouns referring to the sciences and to most academic disciplines are feminine.

la chimie	*chemistry*	la physique	*physics*
l'histoire	*history*	la biologie	*biology*
la médecine	*medicine*	la psychologie	*psychology*

BUT nouns referring to languages are masculine.

le français	*French*	l'anglais	*English*
l'allemand	*German*		

NOTE: Do not capitalize the names of languages in French.

5. Most names for machines and mechanical devices are feminine.

la machine	*machine*	la cuisinière	*stove*
la voiture	*car, carriage*	la guillotine	*guillotine*
l'auto	*automobile*		

BUT names of machines using masculine suffixes are masculine.

le séchoir	*dryer*	l'ordinateur	*computer*
le moteur	*motor*		

D. Homonyms

Homonyms are nouns that have identical spellings and pronunciation. The article before a homonym tells you which meaning to use.

le livre	*book*	la livre	*pound*
le somme	*nap*	la somme	*sum*
le tour	*turn, rotation*	la tour	*tower*
le vase	*vase*	la vase	*slime*
le mode	*method*	la mode	*fashion*
le manche	*handle*	la manche	*sleeve*

REMEMBER: Learn the gender of each new noun as you learn its meaning, spelling, and pronunciation.

EXERCISE 1-3: Identify the gender of the following nouns by placing an **M** or **F** in the blank preceding the number. Then translate the noun. Answers and translations are at the end of the chapter.

Example: <u>**M**</u> chapeau *hat*

<u>**F**</u> cousine *cousin*

_____ 1. soeur _____
_____ 2. peinture _____
_____ 3. question _____
_____ 4. maison _____
_____ 5. train _____
_____ 6. tasse _____
_____ 7. professeur _____
_____ 8. salle de classe _____
_____ 9. petite amie _____
_____ 10. tante _____
_____ 11. oncle _____

_____ 12. chat _____
_____ 13. pianiste _____
_____ 14. chaise _____
_____ 15. traduction _____
_____ 16. fiancée _____
_____ 17. machine à écrire _____
_____ 18. fourchette _____
_____ 19. promesse _____
_____ 20. pension _____
_____ 21. carton _____
_____ 22. feuille _____

_____	23. serviette _____	_____	27. famille _____
_____	24. langue maternelle _____	_____	28. propriété _____
_____	25. feu _____	_____	29. chance _____
_____	26. portefeuille _____	_____	30. cocktail _____

E. Plural of nouns

Several different spelling patterns form the plurals of French nouns—even though the plural noun usually has the same pronunciation as the singular.

1. Add an unpronounced final **-s** to the singular to form the plural of most nouns.

Singular	Plural	
la voiture	**les** voitures	*car(s)*
le comité	**les** comités	*committee(s)*
le son	**les** sons	*sound(s)*

2. The spelling of a noun does not change in the plural if the singular form ends in **-s**, **-x**, or **-z**.

Singular	Plural	
le fils	**les** fils	*son(s)*
le bras	**les** bras	*arm(s)*
le prix	**les** prix	*price(s)*
le gaz	**les** gaz	*gas(es)*

3. Add an unpronounced final **-x** to form the plural of nouns ending in **-eau** or **-eu**, and some nouns ending in **-ou**.

Singular	Plural	
le tabl**eau**	**les** tabl**eaux**	*picture(s)*
le f**eu**	**les** f**eux**	*fire(s)*
le bij**ou**	**les** bij**oux**	*jewel(s)*
le caill**ou**	**les** caill**oux**	*pebble(s)*
le gen**ou**	**les** gen**oux**	*knee(s)*

BUT

le clou	**les** clous	*nail(s)*
le fou	**les** fous	*madman(men)*
le verrou	**les** verrous	*bolt(s)*

4. Most nouns ending in **-al** have plurals ending in **-aux**.

Singular	Plural	
l'anim**al**	**les** anim**aux**	*animal(s)*
le chev**al**	**les** chev**aux**	*horse(s)*
le journ**al**	**les** journ**aux**	*newspaper(s)*

BUT

le bal	**les** bals	*dance(s)*
le carnaval	**les** carnavals	*carnival(s)*
le festival	**les** festivals	*festival(s)*

5. Some nouns ending in **-l** preceded by more than one vowel have plurals ending in **-x**.

Singular	Plural	
l'aïeul	**les** aïeux	*ancestor(s)*
le ciel	**les** cieux	*sky, skies*
l'émail	**les** émaux	*enamel(s)*
le travail	**les** travaux	*work(s)*
le vitrail	**les** vitraux	*stained glass window(s)*

6. You form the plural of a compound noun according to its composition.

- If a compound noun consists of two nouns in which one noun identifies or explains the other, make *both* nouns plural.

Singular	Plural	
le chou-fleur	**les** choux-fleurs	*cauliflower(s)*
le chef-lieu	**les** chefs-lieux	*county seat(s)*

- If a compound noun consists of two nouns in which one noun completes the meaning of the other, make *only* the first noun plural.

Singular	Plural	
le timbre-poste	**les** timbres-poste	*stamp(s)*
le chef-d'oeuvre	**les** chefs-d'oeuvre	*masterpiece(s)*

- If a compound noun consists of a noun and an adjective, make *both* parts plural.

Singular	Plural	
la grand-mère	**les** grands-mères	*grandmother(s)*
le procès-verbal	**les** procès-verbaux	*official report(s)*

- If a compound noun consists of a noun and a verb, a preposition, or an adverb, make *only* the noun plural.

Singular	Plural	
le casse-**noisette**	**les** casse-noisettes	*nutcracker(s)*
le chemin de fer	**les** chemins de fer	*railroad(s)*

7. Do not make proper names or family names plural.

Madame Hérault vient dîner ce soir.   *Mrs. Hérault is coming to dinner this evening.*

Les Hérault viennent dîner ce soir.   *The Héraults are coming to dinner this evening.*

EXERCISE 1-4: Change the singular form of the noun to its plural form. Then write the correct plural translation of the noun. Don't forget to change the definite article from singular to plural. Answers and translations are at the end of the chapter.

Example: la faute   **les**   **fautes**   *mistakes*
              le château   **les**   **châteaux**   *castles*

1. la croix _____ _____ _____

2. le bureau _____ _____ _____

3. le chandail _____ _____ _____

4. le pardessus _____ _____ _____

5. la bicyclette _____ _____ _____

6. le gâteau _____ _____ _____

7. le tour de force _____ _____ _____

8. le parapluie _____ _____ _____

9. le chapeau _____ _____ _____

10. le cheval _____ _____ _____

11. le matelas _____ _____ _____

12. le festival _____ _____ _____

13. le plateau _____ _____ _____

14. le fils _____ _____ _____

15. l'arc-en-ciel _____ _____ _____

16. la cheminée _____ _____ _____

17. le tire-bouchon _____ _____ _____

18. le vitrail _____ _____ _____

19. le journal _____ _____ _____

20. le hors-d'oeuvre _____ _____ _____

1-3. More About Definite Articles

The definite article has many similar uses in French and English, but you'll use it much more frequently in French.

A. Use of the definite article

1. Use a definite article before a specific noun.

Le sel est dans **la cuisine**. *The salt is in the kitchen.*
Donnez-moi **les assiettes** jaunes. *Give me the yellow plates.*
Où sont **les enfants**? *Where are the children?*
Il veut **le livre** qui est sur **la table**. *He wants the book that is on the table.*

> *NOTE:* Unlike English, a French definite article comes before each noun in a series—not just before the first noun.

Passez-moi **le sel** et **le poivre**, *Pass the salt and pepper, please.*
  s'il vous plait.

2. Use a definite article before collective or generic nouns, and before nouns used in an abstract sense.

Collective Nouns
J'aime **le pain**. *I like bread (all bread).*
Les enfants adorent **le chocolat**. *Children love chocolate.*
Les skieurs préférent **l'hiver**. *Skiers prefer winter.*
Les Français abhorrent **la** mauvaise *The French abhor bad cooking.*
  cuisine.

> *NOTE:* Do capitalize a noun referring to a nationality when you are speaking about the people.

Abstract Nouns
Les hommes adorent **la liberté**. *Mankind adores liberty.*
L'alcool détruit **la santé**. *Alcohol destroys health.*

3. Use a definite article instead of a possessive adjective (see Sec. 3-1) before parts of the body.

Il a **le nez** grand et **la bouche** *His nose is big and his mouth is small.*
  petite.
Elle s'est lavé **les cheveux**. *She washed her hair.*

4. Here are some rules governing the use of the definite article with days, months, and seasons.

- Use a definite article before days *only* when you speak about something done generally. Days are masculine—do not capitalize them when they come after a definite article.

Je fais du footing **le lundi**.	*I jog on Monday(s) (every Monday).*
Les banques ne sont ouvertes ni **le samedi** ni **le dimanche**.	*Banks aren't open Saturdays or Sundays.*
La femme d'à côté garde les enfants tous **les mercredis**.	*The woman next door babysits every Wednesday.*

- Do not use a definite article with days of the week to tell about a single event or occurrence.

Lundi prochain, je vais chez le dentiste.	*Next Monday, I'm going to the dentist.*
Grâce à Dieu, c'est **vendredi**.	*Thank God, it's Friday.*

- Never use a definite article before the name of a month. Capitalize names of months only at the beginning of a sentence.

Mai est toujours un très joli mois.	*May is always a pretty month.*
Nous prenons nos vacances en **juillet**.	*We are going on vacation in July.*

- Always use a definite article before a season of the year. Do not capitalize the names of seasons.

L'hiver est très froid.	*Winter is very cold.*
L'automne est la saison que je préfère.	*Autumn is the season (that) I prefer.*

NOTE: Use the preposition **en**, *in*, *to*, or *during*, before seasons and months to tell when something happened or happens. Use **au** instead of **en** before **le printemps**, *spring*.

Va en Alaska **en juin**.	*Go to Alaska in (during) June.*
Il n'y va jamais **en été**.	*He never goes in (during) summer.*
Il fait très froid **en hiver**.	*It's very cold in (during) winter.*
Il fait très bon **au printemps**.	*It's very agreeable in (during) spring.*

5. Use a definite article before most geographic names. Study the following list carefully.

Continents:	l'Europe, l'Asie
Countries:	la France, **les** Etats-Unis
Provinces:	la Franche-Comté, **la** Bourgogne
Rivers:	la Seine, **la** Loire
Mountains:	le Mont-Blanc, **les** Alpes
Bodies of Water:	la Méditerranée, l'Atlantique
Islands:	le Japon, **la** Corse

NOTE: Do not use a definite article before the name of a city unless the definite article is part of the name or an adjective modifies the name.

Paris est la cité des lumières.	*Paris is the city of lights.*
Je vais souvent à **Berlin**.	*I often go to Berlin.*

BUT

Je suis allé à **la Nouvelle Orléans** pour le Mardi Gras.	*I went to New Orleans for Mardi Gras.*
Le Paris que j'adore est le Paris des **quartiers populaires**.	*The Paris I love is the Paris of neighborhoods.*

6. Use a definite article before expressions of quantity to mean *per*.

Les oeufs coûtent dix francs **la douzaine**.	*Eggs cost ten francs a dozen.*
Le prix est trente francs **le kilo**.	*The price is thirty francs a kilo.*

7. Use a definite article before the names of languages.

L'italien est une très belle langue.   *Italian is a very pretty language.*
Il est très difficile d'apprendre   *It's very difficult to learn German.*
   l'allemand.

> *NOTE:* Do not use a definite article with the name of a language after the verb **parler**, *to speak*, or after the preposition **en**—unless the name of the language is modified.

Il **parle** français.   *He speaks French.*
Il **parle bien le** français.   *He speaks French well.*
Le roman *Le Rouge et le Noir* est   *The novel* The Red and The Black *is*
   traduit **en** anglais.   *translated in English.*
Le *Chanson de Roland* est en   *The Song of Roland is in*
   ancien français.   *old French.*

EXERCISE 1-5: Fill in the blank with the correct form of the definite article—if one is needed. Then translate the sentence into English. Look back to the appropriate section to refresh your memory. Answers and translations are at the end of the chapter.

1. _____ fille achète _____ robe verte.

2. _____ lait coûte cinq francs _____ litre.

3. _____ bouteilles sont dans _____ réfrigérateur.

4. _____ Madame Rhéault, aimez-vous _____ café avec ou

   sans _____ sucre?

5. Où sont _____ femmes?

6. _____ Président vit à _____ Maison Blanche.

7. _____ homme mange _____ pommes.

8. Je travaille tous _____ vendredis.

9. Je suis allé à _____ montagne _____ année dernière.

10. _____ soupe est dans _____ cuisine.

11. Où sont _____ nouveaux livres?

12. _____ eau est meilleure que _____ bière.

13. Mon frère vit à _____ Nouvelle-Orléans.

14. J'aime bien _____ sport.

15. _____ garçon se fait couper _____ cheveux.

16. Nous allons visiter _____ galerie _____ mardi prochain.

17. _____ huile coûte 200 francs _____ barrel.

18. Lille est une grand ville au _____ Nord de _____

   France.

EXERCISE 1-6: Translate the following sentences into French. Nouns and verbs that you might not know are in parentheses. Answers are at the end of the chapter.

1. I like bread.

2. He works on Mondays.

3. She speaks Italian well.

4. The children are going to (vont en) China.

5. Miss Delmotte isn't here (n'est pas là).

6. The children washed (se sont lavé) their hands.

7. Houses are expensive.

8. Tomatoes (tomates) cost forty (quarante) francs a pound.

9. I like baseball (base-ball).

10. He writes well in English.

11. Students like a vacation.

12. Do you want the newspaper, Mr. Favre?

13. His beard (barbe) is blond.

14. Today is Tuesday.

15. Truth (verité) is relative.

B. Contractions of the definite article

1. **Le** or **les** with **à**

- When the preposition **à**, *to, toward, at, in*, precedes the singular definite article **le**, contract the two words to form **au**.

Le théâtre? Je ne vais jamais **au** théâtre.	*The theater? I never go to the theater.*
Le magasin? Je n'achète rien **au** magasin.	*The store? I never buy anything at the store.*

  > *NOTE:*   Do not contract **à** with **la** or **l'**.

La plage? J'adore aller **à la** plage.	*The beach? I love to go to the beach.*
L'université? Il n'est pas **à l'**université.	*The university? He's not at the university.*

- When the preposition **à** precedes the plural definite article **les**, contract the two words to form **aux**.

Les insultes? Je ne réponds jamais **aux** insultes.	*Insults? I never respond to insults.*

- If the definite article **le** is part of the name of a city, contract **le** with the preceding preposition **à** to form **au**.

Le Havre? Nous arrivons **au** Havre dimanche prochain.	*Le Havre? We arrive at Le Havre next Sunday.*
Le Caire? **Au** Caire, il fait très chaud.	*Cairo? In Cairo, it's very hot.*

- Do not contract the preposition **à** with the names of cities that begin with **la**.

Le carnaval a lieu **à la Nouvelle-Orléans**.	*The carnival takes place in New Orleans.*

EXERCISE 1-7:   Complete the following sentences, using the preposition **à** and the correct definite article or contraction. Answers and translations are at the end of the chapter.

> Example: Louis va souvent _____ bistros.   *Louis often goes to bars.*
> Louis va souvent aux bistros.

1. Anne–Marie va souvent _____ école.
2. J'ai conseillé _____ garcon de finir ses études.
3. Le vendeur propose _____ acheteur un nouveau modèle.

4. La petite Simone veut aller _____ parc.
5. Les Lamant défendent _____ invités de fumer dans la maison.
6. Ma mère a donné l'argent _____ vendeur.
7. Claudine et Régis demandent _____ chauffeur d'aller plus vite.
8. Paul a dit _____ élèves de se taire.
9. Nous allons _____ Londres.
10. Françoise va inviter les Dupont, mais elle ne vas pas envoyer d'invitation _____ Mitterand.

2. **Le** or **les** with **de**

- When the preposition **de**, *of*, *from*, *belonging to*, precedes the definite article **le**, contract the two words to form **du**.

Le parc? Il revient **du** parc.	*The park? He just came back from the park.*
Le professeur? Elle parle **du** professeur.	*The professor? She is speaking of the professor.*

> *NOTE:* Again, do not form a contraction when **de** precedes **la** or **l'**.

Ils parlent **de l'**économie.	*They are speaking of the economy.*
Il vient **de la** montagne.	*He comes from the mountain.*

- When the preposition **de** precedes the plural definite article **les**, contract the two words to form **des**.

Les hauteurs? Je n'ai pas peur **des** hauteurs.	*Heights? I'm not afraid of heights.*
Les enfants? Ils ne savent rien **des** enfants.	*Children? They don't know anything about children.*

EXERCISE 1-8: Complete the following sentences, using the preposition **de** and the correct form of the definite article or a contraction. Answers and translations are at the end of the chapter.

Example:	Elle a honte _____ manières de son fils.	*She is ashamed of her son's manners.*
	Elle a honte **des** manières de son fils.	

1. J'ai les devoirs _____ élèves.
2. Les passagers dèbarquent _____ bateau.
3. Je viens _____ gare.
4. Monsieur Duval arrive _____ hôtel.
5. Le sénateur n'est pas informé _____ événements.
6. On ne parle que _____ pollution.
7. L'élève a besoin _____ livres de classe.
8. Le banquier s'occupe _____ finances.
9. Je parle _____ France.
10. Elle s'occupe _____ appartement.

3. **Le** or **les** with **en**

- When the preposition **en**, *in*, *into*, precedes the definite article **le** used with seasons or place names, contract the two words to form **au**.

Le Japon? Taiwan n'est pas **au** (*instead of* **en le**) Japon.	*Japan? Taiwan isn't in Japan.*
Le Texas? J'ai deux fils **au** Texas.	*Texas? I have two sons in Texas.*
Le printemps? Il pleut beaucoup **au** printemps.	*Springtime? It rains a lot in spring.*

- When the preposition **en** precedes the plural definite article **les**, contract the two words to form **aux**.

Les Etats-Unis? Qui va **aux** Etats-Unis?	The United States? Who's going to the United States?

- When **en** precedes **la** or **l'** used with seasons or place names, **la** and **l'** are completely absorbed and disappear.

La France? Il ne va jamais **en France**.	*France? He never goes to France.*
L'Alaska? Ne va pas **en Alaska** en hiver!	*Alaska? Don't go to Alaska in the winter!*
L'automne? Je suis occupé **en automne**.	*Autumn? I'm busy in autumn.*

EXERCISE 1-9: Answer the questions affirmatively, using the season in the parentheses in your answer. Answers and translations are at the end of the chapter.

Example:	La France? (Le printemps?)	*France? (spring)*	
	Oui, nous allons en France au printemps.	*Yes, we're going to France in the spring.*	

1. La Russie? (L'été?)
2. Le Danemark? (Le printemps?)
3. L'Arizona? (L'automne?)
4. Le Mexique? (L'hiver?)
5. La Chine? (Le printemps?)
6. L'Israël? (L'hiver?)
7. Le Pérou? (L'automne?)
8. Les Etats-Unis? (L'été?)
9. Le Canada? (L'automne?)
10. L'Angleterre? (Le printemps?)

1-4. Indefinite Articles

Use an indefinite article before a noun to indicate *a* or *an* in the singular and *some* or *any* in the plural. The indefinite article *must agree* in *number* and *gender* with the noun it precedes. There are no special forms to use before vowels.

A. Forms of the indefinite article

The indefinite article has three forms. Study the following chart and examples.

<u>M–sing</u>	**un**	*a, an*	<u>M–pl</u>	**des**	*some, any*
<u>F–sing</u>	**une**	*a, an*	<u>F–pl</u>	**des**	*some, any*
	un livre	*a book*		**des** livres	*some books*
	une chaise	*a chair*		**des** chaises	*some chairs*

EXERCISE 1-10: Translate the definite article and noun in the first column into English. Then write the correct indefinite article before the noun in the second column and translate both into English. Use your dictionary to look up the correct translation of the nouns. Answers and translations are at the end of the chapter.

Example:	la plume	<u>the pen</u>	**une**	plume	<u>a pen</u>
	les japonais	<u>the Japanese people</u>	**des**	japonais	<u>some Japanese people</u>
1.	l'homme	_____	____	homme	_____
2.	les chaussures	_____	____	chaussures	_____
3.	le tableau	_____	____	tableau	_____
4.	la ville	_____	____	ville	_____
5.	les idées	_____	____	idées	_____
6.	le vase	_____	____	vase	_____
7.	les mères	_____	____	mères	_____

8. l'arbre	_____	_____ arbre	_____
9. les étoiles	_____	_____ étoiles	_____
10. la gare	_____	_____ gare	_____
11. le traducteur	_____	_____ traducteur	_____
12. les repas	_____	_____ repas	_____

B. Use of the indefinite article

1. In its singular form—**un/une**—the indefinite article may mean *a*, *an*, or *one*. You must determine its meaning from the context of the sentence.

> J'ai **une** jolie maison.   *I have a pretty house.*
> J'ai **un** chien et deux chats.   *I have one dog and two cats.*

2. In its plural form—**des**—the indefinite article may mean *some* or *any*. Again, you'll have to determine its meaning from the context of the sentence.

> Il y a **des** messages pour vous.   *There are some messages for you.*
> Est-ce que vous prenez **des** carottes?   *Are you having any carrots?*

3. Use an indefinite article before each noun in a series.

> Je voudrais **un sandwich** et   *I would like a sandwich and*
> **des pommes** frites.   *some french fries.*
> J'ai acheté **une chemise** et   *I bought a shirt and a pair*
> **un pantalon**.   *of pants.*

4. Omit the indefinite article before an unmodified noun that follows the verb **être**, *to be*.

> Je **suis écrivain**.   *I am a writer.*
> Ma soeur **est médecin**.   *My sister is a doctor.*
> Ils sont fiers d'**être américains**.   *They are proud to be Americans.*

> BUT you must use the indefinite article before a modified noun that follows the verb **être**.

> Je suis **un bon écrivain**.   *I am a good writer.*
> Ma soeur est **un médecin savant**.   *My sister is a well-trained doctor.*
> Ils sont fiers d'être **des**   *They are proud to be patriotic*
> **américains patriotes**.   *Americans.*

5. Omit the indefinite article after the exclamation **quel(le)**, *what a . . .* !

> Quel toupet!   *What (a) nerve!*
> Quelle pagaille!   *What a mess!*

EXERCISE 1-11:   Translate the following sentences into French. Use the correct form of the indefinite article—if one is necessary. Answers are at the end of the chapter.

1. I am a sailor.

2. I would like a small salad, please.

3. She is English.

4. What a pity!

5. He has one knife and some apples.

6. I want a beer, please.

7. I need a new car.

8. I have one American dollar and some French francs.

9. She is a lawyer.

10. I have a hundred dollars.

11. I want some new shoes.

12. I have a house.

13. She buys some bread, a kilo of meat, and a bottle of milk.

14. He is eating a sandwich and some carrots.

15. This is a long exercise.

1-5. Partitive Articles

Use the partitive article before a noun to express the idea of *some* or *any* in both the singular and the plural.

A. Forms of the partitive article

The partitive article has four forms. Study the following chart and examples.

M–sing	**du** (de + le) **de l'** (before a vowel)	M–pl	**des** (de + les)
F–sing	**de la** **de l'** (before a vowel)	F–pl	**des** (de + les)

du gâteau	*some cake*	**des** gâteaux	*some cakes*
de la confiture	*some jam*	**des** confitures	*some jams*

B. Use of the partitive article

You must use a partitive article before a noun referring to an **undetermined** quantity of something to express the idea of *some* or *any*. Many singular nouns such as *sugar, water, energy, enthusiasm,* or *patience* refer to things that cannot be counted. In English we don't need an article before these nouns, but in French you must use a partitive article.

Il y a **du vin** dans le réfrigérateur.	*There is (some) wine in the refrigerator.*
Avez-vous encore **de la glace**?	*Do you still have (any) ice?*
Elle a certainement de **l'ambition**.	*She certainly has (some) ambition.*

EXERCISE 1-12: Supply the correct form of the partitive article. Then translate the sentence into English. Answers and translation are at the end of the chapter.

Example:	J'aimerais avoir _____ haricots.	*I would like to have some beans.*
	J'aimerais avoir des haricots.	
	Voulez-vous _____ confiture?	*Do you want some jam?*
	Voulez-vous de la confiture?	

1. Il y a _____ papier dans le tiroir.

2. Tous les après-midi, je bois _____ café.

3. Avez-vous _____ monnaie?

4. Veut-il _____ billets de théâtre?

5. Vois-tu _____ fumée sur le toit?

6. J'ai acheté _____ fleurs pour ma mère.

7. On mange _____ pommes frites avec les hamburgers.

8. Je veux _____ beurre pour le petit déjeuner.

9. Il y a _____ miel sur la table.

10. Elle a vraiment _____ patience.

C. Omission of the partitive article

1. When a **plural** noun is preceded by an adjective, use **de** alone—do not use an article.

Elle porte **de jolies robes**.	*She wears pretty dresses.*
La maison a **de grands tableaux**.	*The house has large paintings.*
Elles préparent **de bonnes salades**.	*They prepare good salads.*

BUT when a **single** noun has a preceding adjective, use **du, de la,** or **de l'**.

| Elle m'a donné **de l'excellente soupe**. | *She gave me (some) excellent soup.* |
| Les invités ont mangé **de la bonne viande**. | *The guests ate (some) good meat.* |

2. When the statement expresses a general negation, use **de** alone—do not use an article.

| Je **n'ai pas d'**argent. | *I don't have any money.* |

- Study the following list and examples of general negations which indicate that something isn't available or wanted or eaten or . . .

ne . . . **pas de**	*not any*
ne . . . **jamais de**	*never any*
ne . . . **plus de**	*no more, no longer any*
ne . . . **guère de**	*hardly any*

De la musique? Nous **n'avons pas de** musique.	*Music? We don't have any music.*
Du vin? Je **n'ai plus de** vin.	*Wine? I don't have any more wine.*
Des examens? Il **n'a guère d'**examens.	*Exams? He has hardly any exams.*
Des frères et **des soeurs?** Tu as des frères mais tu **n'as pas de** soeurs.	*Brothers and sisters? You have some brothers but you don't have any sisters.*
Des enfants? On **ne voit plus d'**enfants qui sont bien-élevés.	*Children? You no longer see any children who are well-bred.*

BUT when the nouns in a negative statement are specific, you must use a partitive article.

De la musique? Nous **n'avons pas de la** musique **que vous avez demandé**.	*Music? We don't have any of the music that you requested.*
Du vin? Je **n'ai plus du** vin **que vous m'avez donné**.	*Wine? I don't have any of the wine that you gave me.*
Des enfants? On **ne voit jamais** ici **des** enfants **qui sont malades**.	*Children? You never see any sick children here.*

- You may use either a partitive article or an indefinite article after the negetive form of
- the verbs **être**, *to be*, **devenir**, *to become*, or **rester**, *to stay*—in these cases, the negative is specific, not general.

| Ce sont des olives? Non, ce **ne sont pas des** olives. | *Are these olives? No, they're not olives.* |
| Est-ce que le cidre devient du cognac? Non, le cidre **ne devient jamais du** cognac. | *Does cider become cognac? No, cider never becomes cognac.* |

NOTE: A definite article is not affected by a preceding negative verb.

J'aime **les** escargots.	*I like snails.*
Je **n'aime pas les** escargots.	*I don't like snails.*
J'ai **le** billet.	*I have the ticket.*
Je **n'ai pas le** billet.	*I don't have the ticket.*

NOTE: Do not omit the singular indefinite article—**un/une**—after the preposition **de** which is part of the verbal expression.

Un somme? Nous **n'avons pas** besoin
d'un somme.

A nap? We don't need a nap.

Une promenade? Je **n'ai pas** envie
d'une promenade.

A walk? I don't feel like a walk.

EXERCISE 1-13: Fill in the blank with the correct form of the article—if one is needed. If you have to, refer to the preceding rules. Answers and translations are at the end of the chapter.

1. Il achete _____ petits pains.
2. Elles ne mangent pas _____ pain.
3. Ils n'aiment pas _____ pain que je leur ai donné.
4. Ce ne sont pas _____ professeurs d'université.
5. Il n'a pas _____ ambition mais il a _____ enthousiasme.
6. Nous n'avons pas _____ paquet, mais deux.
7. Elles préparent _____ bons gâteaux.
8. Vous n'avez pas _____ amis.
9. Il n'a pas mangé _____ confiture que vous avez préparée.
10. Les erreurs corrigées ne deviennent pas _____ habitudes.
11. Je ne vois pas _____ fumée.
12. Les grands-parents ne fument pas _____ cigarettes.

3. When a noun or an adverb of quantity (see Sec. 2-5) modifies a noun, use **de** alone—do not use an article before the noun.

Nous avons mangé **un morceau
de fromage** et avons bu
une bouteille de vin pour le
déjeuner.

*We ate a piece of cheese and drank
a bottle of wine for lunch.*

On a besoin de **plus de
chauffage** en hiver.

We need more heat in winter.

BUT do use a definite article before a noun used with the following expressions of quantity.

bien de	*a lot of*
la plupart de	*most of*
la majorité de	*the majority of*

Il s'est donné **bien du mal** pour
faire cela.

He took great pains in doing that.

La plupart des passagers
descendent à Londres.

*Most of the passengers are getting
off in London.*

La majorité de la classe a
réussi.

The majority of the class passed.

NOTE: Whenever you would use *of the* in English, use **de
plus the definite article** in French.

4. When a noun modifies another noun, use **de** alone—do not use an article before the modifying noun.

Ills ont construit un **chemin de fer.**

They built a railroad.

Jerôme a préparé une **salade de riz.**

Jerome made a rice salad.

5. When a noun that expresses an undetermined quantity follows an expression ending with the preposition **de**, do not use an article before the noun. Study the following list and examples of some of these common expressions.

être couvert de	*to be covered with*	**se passer de**	*to get along without*
être débordé de	*to be up to one's ears in*	**s'occuper de**	*to take care of*
		se régaler de	*to feast on*
être entouré de	*to be surrounded by*		
être rempli de	*to be filled with*		

La maison **est couverte de neige**.	*The house is covered with snow.*
Il **est débordé de travail**.	*He is up to his ears in work.*
Elle **se passe de sommeil**.	*She gets along without sleep.*

6. When another word in a sentence specifies a quantity (see Sec. 2-1B, you don't need **de** or an article.

Des erreurs? Je vois **quelques erreurs**.	*Mistakes? I see a few mistakes.*
Des livres? Nous avons **cinquante livres**.	*Books? We have fifty books.*
Des exceptions? Il y a **plusieurs exceptions**.	*Exceptions? There are several exceptions.*
Du papier? Je compte **plusieurs feuilles** de **papier**.	*Paper? I count several pieces of paper.*

EXERCISE 1-14: Fill in the blank in the sentence with the correct word(s) to express the partitive—if needed. Answers and translations are at the end of the chapter.

Example: Ils boivent assez _____ vin.
Ils boivent assez _____ de _____ vin.   *They drink enough wine.*

1. Vous m'offrez quelques _____ bonnes suggestions.
2. C'est une salle _____ études.
3. Il ne voulait pas un verre _____ eau.
4. La majorité _____ électeurs est ignorante.
5. Voici un bon morceau _____ viande.
6. Je vois plusieurs _____ joueurs de football.
7. Elle a besoin _____ une bicyclette.
8. Le jardin est entouré _____ fleurs.
9. La plupart _____ oignons étaient abimés.
10. C'est une robe _____ soie.
11. Vous faites trop _____ bruit.
12. Il s'occupe _____ bagages.

SUMMARY

1. The definite articles **le, la, l'**, and **les** must agree in gender and number with the noun they introduce.
2. French nouns are masculine or feminine. There are no neuter nouns.
3. An unpronounced final **-s** added to the singular forms the plural of most nouns.
4. A definite article introduces a) a specific noun; b) collective or generic nouns and nouns used in an abstract sense; c) parts of the body; (d) most geographic names; e) expressions of quantity; and f) names of languages.
5. The indefinite article **un/une** introduces singular nouns of undetermined quantity. **Des**, *some, any,* must be used with plural nouns of undetermined quantity.
6. The partitive articles **du, de la**, or **de l'** must be used with singular nouns that refer to an indefinite amount of something.
7. Indefinite and partitive articles are not used after expressions of quantity or after negatives indicating there isn't any of something.

RAISE YOUR GRADES

Gender of nouns

Determine the gender of the noun preceding the parentheses in each of the following sentences, and write **M** or **F** in the parentheses. Then choose the reason for your answer from the following list, and write the corresponding letter in the blank before the sentence number. You may use the same letter more than once. Answers and translations are at the end of the chapter.

A Male(s) or mixed group
B Masculine article
C Masculine ending
D Foreign word
E. Former male profession
G Contains verb or preposition

H No feminine indicators
I Female(s)
J Feminine article
K Feminine ending
L Mechanical device
N Academic field

_____ 1. Les cigarettes ( ) sont chères en France.

_____ 2. Beaucoup de choses ( ) m'intéressent ici.

_____ 3. L'adresse ( ) n'est pas sur la liste.

_____ 4. Où a-t-il mis l'autre calendrier ( )?

_____ 5. Les églises ( ) datent du XIIe siècle.

_____ 6. Quelle est la date ( ) de l'examen?

_____ 7. Quelques garçons ( ) doivent rester dehors.

_____ 8. Le bureau ( ) est au deuxième etage.

_____ 9. Prenez l'autre chaise ( ), s'il vous plaît.

_____ 10. Les hommes ( ) adorent la liberté.

_____ 11. Etudiez la leçon ( ) avant la prochaine classe.

_____ 12. Je lui ai écrit une carte ( ) de Paris.

_____ 13. Les enfants ( ) l'adorent!

_____ 14. Tout le monde ( ) le trouve amusant.

_____ 15. C'est une école ( ) privée.

_____ 16. L'autre mur ( ) est couvert de tableaux.

_____ 17. La belle fleur ( ) a un nom bizarre.

_____ 18. Prenez un stylo ( ) et écrivez!

_____ 19. Qu'est-ce que vous voyez par la fenêtre?

_____ 20. Des élèves ( ) vous attendent à la porte.

_____ 21. Ecrivez cela au tableau ( ).

_____ 22. A quelle heure est ton autre classe ( )?

_____ 23. L'exercice ( ) est trop facile.

_____ 24. Les pages ( ) expliquent le problème.

_____ 25. Les meilleurs élèves vont au lycée ( ).

_____ 26. Notre prononciation ( ) est authentique.

_____ 27. Vos études ( ) vous aideront à l'avenir.

_____ 28. L'instrument qu'il préfère, c'est le violon ( ).

_____ 29. Son livre est plein de sarcasmes ( ).

_____ 30. Nous apprenons en étudiant les autres cultures ( ).

_____ 31. L'incroyable beauté ( ) de cet enfant me fascine.

_____ 32. Ces tableaux sont des chefs-d'oeuvre ( ).

_____ 33. Comme médecin ( ) elle est formidable.

_____ 34. Mes grands-parents ( ) habitent à Philadelphie.

_____ 35. Les vacances arrivent à la fin de l'année. ( )

_____ 36. Qui sont les membres de ces comités ( )?

_____ 37. Le coeur a ses raisons ( ).

_____ 38. Les chats ( ) sont plus amusants que les chiens.

_____ 39. Je gare ma bicyclette dans notre garage ( ).

_____ 40. Qui a étudié l'anthropologie ( )?

_____ 41. Je désire toujours votre bien ( ).

_____ 42. Où avez-vous passé l'autre week-end ( )?

_____ 43. Il travaille comme infirmier ( ) dans cet hôpital.

_____ 44. Les aide-mémoire ( ) sont souvent utiles.

_____ 45. Il faut apporter votre nourriture ( ) si vous y allez.

Definite articles

Replace the words in parentheses in the following sentences with the appropriate form of the definite article. Be sure to give the correct contracted forms. Answers and translations are at the end of the chapter.

46. (Leurs) parents vont venir à (leur) lycée.
47. (Cet) hotel ne plaît pas à (sa) mère.
48. (Quelques) employés de (cet) homme sont à ses ordres.

49. En (ce) printemps il pleut beaucoup.
50. En (ces) Etats-Unis nous avons (nos) élections en novembre.

51. (Plusieurs) élèves de (ce) professeur assistent à (son) autre classe.
52. Quelle proportion de (ces) femmes participe à (ces) activités?
53. (Son) oncle, (sa) tante et (ses) cousins habitent (cette) ville.
54. (Votre) auto ne marche pas, mais vous avez (votre) bicyclette dans (votre) garage.
55. Tu vas avoir quelques lettres de (tes) amis et (ce) cadeau de (ton) grand-père à (ton) prochain anniversaire.

Indefinite and partitive articles

Replace the nouns in parentheses in the following sentences with the nouns following the sentence. Use an appropriate indefinite or partitive article—if one is needed. Answers and translations are at the end of the chapter.

     Example: Tout le monde a besoin   *Everyone needs a friend.*
                d'un (ami). (amis)

                Tout le monde a besoin d'amis.   *Everyone needs (some) friends.*

56. Jacques n'a pas de (voiture). (skis)
57. Cette fille a du (talent). (admirateurs)
58. Pourquoi ne prends-tu pas de (carottes)? (soupe)
59. Je suis contente de voir tant de (monde). (gens)
60. Les explorateurs ont des (projets). (courage)
61. Ce tableau-là n'est pas un (chef-d'oeuvre). (original)
62. L'italien a un article partitif. (articles partitifs)
63. Nos vendeurs ne font jamais d'(erreurs). (promesses)
64. Quand leurs enfants ont-ils des (vacances)? (travail)
65. Qui n'a plus d'(espoir)? (illusions)
66. J'ai très envie d'une (glace). (bonbons)
67. Dans ce dessert il y a beaucoup de (sucre). (oeufs)
68. Cet acteur joue dans une (comédie). (tragédies)
69. Elle s'occupe d'un (enfant). (enfants)
70. Je ne prends que du (lait). (eau)
71. Au printemps il fait souvent de la (brume). (soleil)
72. Ce n'est pas du (cristal). (porcelaine)
73. Pour faire une omelette il faut du (sel). (oeufs)
74. Quand j'ai soif, je bois un verre d'(eau). (jus de fruit)
75. Est-ce que tu manges du (poisson)? (viande)
76. Votre essai est plein d'(imagination). (fautes)
77. Il a plus de (chance) que moi. (idées)
78. Elle n'a plus de (fiancé). (amis)
79. Il prend toujours trop de (vin). (risques)
80. Nous ne connaissons pas la majorité des (élèves). (classe)

CHAPTER ANSWERS

EXERCISE 1-1:

1. F, sing, *rain*
2. F, pl, *plants*
3. M, pl, *colds*
4. M, sing, *wolf*
5. M, sing, *store*
6. M, pl, *skiers*
7. F, sing, *kitchen*
8. M, sing, *chocolate*
9. F, pl, *televisions*
10. F, sing, *woman*

EXERCISE 1-2:

1. M, le, *ski*
2. M, l', *air*
3. M, les, *glasses*
4. F, la, *motorcycle*
5. M, les, *restaurants*
6. M, le, *rabbit*
7. F, l', *oil*
8. M, les, *United States*
9. M, le, *sugar*
10. F, la, *jewelry*
11. F, la, *aunt*
12. M, les, *butterflies*
13. F, la, *flower*
14. M, le, *market*
15. M, l', *elephant*
16. F, la, *suitcase*
17. M, l', *ocean*
18. M, les, *trains*
19. F, la, *horde*
20. F, les, *lamps*

EXERCISE 1-3:
1. F, *sister*
2. F, *picture*
3. F, *question*
4. F, *house*
5. M, *train*
6. F, *cup*
7. M, *teacher, professor*
8. F, *classroom*
9. F, *girl friend*
10. F, *aunt*
11. M, *uncle*
12. M, *cat*
13. F or M, *pianist*
14. F, *chair*
15. F, *translation*
16. F, *fiancée*
17. F, *typewriter*
18. F, *fork*
19. F, *promise*
20. F, *pension, board and room*
21. M, *cardboard, box*
22. F, *sheet (of paper), leaf*
23. F, *napkin, towel, briefcase*
24. F, *mother tongue*
25. M, *fire*
26. M, *billfold*
27. F, *family*
28. F, *property*
29. F, *chance*
30. M, *cocktail*

EXERCISE 1-4:
1. les croix — *crosses*
2. les bureaux — *desks, offices*
3. les chandails — *sweaters*
4. les pardessus — *overcoats*
5. les bicyclettes — *bicycles*
6. les gâteaux — *cakes*
7. les tours de force — *feats*
8. les parapluies — *umbrellas*
9. les chapeaux — *hats*
10. les chevaux — *horses*
11. les matelas — *mattresses*
12. les festivals — *festivals*
13. les plateaux — *plateaus, trays*
14. les fils — *sons*
15. les arcs-en-ciel — *rainbows*
16. les cheminées — *chimneys*
17. les tire-bouchons — *corkscrews*
18. les vitraux — *stained glass windows*
19. les journaux — *newspapers*
20. les hors-d'oeuvre — *appetizers*

EXERCISE 1-5:
1. La, la — *The girl is buying the green dress.*
2. Le, le — *Milk costs five francs a liter.*
3. Les, le — *The bottles are in the refrigerator.*
4. _____, le, _____ — *Mrs. Rhéault, do you like coffee with or without sugar?*
5. les — *Where are the women?*
6. Le, la — *The president lives in the White House.*
7. L', les — *The man is eating the apples.*
8. les — *I work every Friday.*
9. la, l' — *I went to the mountain last year.*
10. La, la — *The soup is in the kitchen.*
11. les — *Where are the new books?*
12. L', la — *Water is better than beer.*
13. le — *My brother lives in New Orleans.*
14. le — *I like sports a lot.*
15. Le, les — *The boy is having his hair cut.*
16. le, _____ — *We are going to visit the gallery next Tuesday.*
17. L', la — *Oil costs 200 francs a barrel.*
18. le, la — *Lille is a large town in the north of France.*

EXERCISE 1-6:
1. J'aime le pain.
2. Il travaille le lundi.
3. Elle parle bien l'italien.
4. Les enfants vont en Chine.
5. Mademoiselle Delmotte n'est pas là.
6. Les enfants se sont lavé les mains.
7. Les maisons sont chères.
8. Les tomates coûtent quarante francs la livre.
9. J'aime le base-ball.
10. Il écrit bien l'anglais.
11. Les étudiants aiment les vacances.
12. Voulez-vous le journal, Monsieur Favre?
13. Il a la barbe blonde.
14. Aujourd'hui, c'est mardi.
15. La vérité est relative.

EXERCISE 1-7:
1. à l' — *Anne-Marie goes to school often.*
2. au — *I advised the boy to finish his studies.*
3. l' — *The salesman suggests a new model to the buyer.*
4. au — *Little Simone wants to go to the park.*
5. aux — *The Lamants forbid their guests to smoke in the house.*

6. au   *My mother gave the money to the clerk.*
7. au   *Claudine and Régis ask the chauffeur to go faster.*
8. aux   *Paul told the students to shut up.*
9. à   *We are going to London.*
10. aux   *Françoise is going to invite the Duponts but she is not sending an invitation to Mitterand.*

EXERCISE 1-8:

1. des   *I have the students' homework.*
2. du   *The passengers get off the ship.*
3. de la   *I am coming from the station.*
4. de l'   *Mr. Duval arrives from the hotel.*
5. des   *The senator is unaware of the events.*
6. de la   *All people talk about is pollution.*
7. des   *The student needs his textbooks.*
8. des   *The banker deals with finances.*
9. de la   *I am talking about France.*
10. de l'   *She is busy with the apartment.*

EXERCISE 1-9:

1. Oui, nous allons en Russie en été. *Yes, we're going to Russia in the summer.*
2. Oui, nous allons au Danemark au printemps. *Yes, we're going to Denmark in the spring.*
3. Oui, nous allons en Arizona en automne. *Yes, we're going to Arizona in the autumn.*
4. Oui, nous allons au Mexique en hiver. *Yes, we're going to Mexico in the winter.*
5. Oui, nous allons en Chine au printemps. *Yes, we're going to China in the spring.*
6. Oui, nous allons en Israël en hiver. *Yes, we're going to Israel in the winter.*
7. Oui, nous allons au Pérou en automne. *Yes, we're going to Peru in the autumn.*
8. Oui, nous allons aux Etats-Unis en été. *Yes, we're going to the United States in the summer.*
9. Oui, nous allons au Canada en automne. *Yes, we're going to Canada in the autumn.*
10. Oui, nous allons en Angleterre au printemps. *Yes, we're going to England in the spring.*

EXERCISE 1-10:

1. the man   un   *a man*
2. Je voudrais une petite salade, s'il vous plaît.
3. the painting   un   *a painting*
4. the town   une   *a town*
5. the ideas   des   *some ideas*
6. the vase   un   *a vase*
7. the mothers   des   *some mothers*
8. the tree   un   *a tree*
9. the stars   des   *some stars*
10. the station   une   *a station*
11. the translator   un   *a translator*
12. the meals   des   *some meals*

EXERCISE 1-11:

1. Je suis marin.
2. Je voudrais une petite salade, s'il vous plaît.
3. Elle est anglaise.
4. Quel dommage!
5. Il a un couteau et des pommes.
6. Je voudrais une bière, s'il vous plaît.
7. J'ai besoin d'une nouvelle voiture.
8. J'ai un dollar américain et des francs français.
9. Elle est avocate.
10. J'ai cent dollars.
11. Je voudrais de nouvelles chaussures.
12. J'ai une maison.
13. Elle achète du pain, un kilo de viande et une bouteille de lait.
14. Il mange un sandwich et des carottes.
15. C'est un long exercice.

EXERCISE 1-12:

1. du   *There is (some) paper in the drawer.*
2. du   *Every afternoon I drink (some) coffee.*
3. de la   *Do you have (any) change?*
4. des   *Does he want (some) tickets to the theater?*
5. de la   *Do you see (some) smoke on the roof?*
6. des   *I bought (some) flowers for my mother.*
7. des   *You eat (some) french fries with hamburgers.*
8. du   *I want (some) butter for breakfast.*
9. du   *There is (some) honey on the table.*
10. de la   *She really has (a lot of) patience.*

EXERCISE 1-13:

1. des   *He is buying some rolls.*
2. de   *They don't eat bread.*
3. le   *They don't like the bread that I gave them.*
4. des   *They are not university professors.*
5. d', de l'   *He doesn't have any ambition, but he has (some) enthusiasm.*
6. un   *We don't have one package, but two.*
7. de   *They make (some) good cakes.*
8. d'   *You don't have any friends.*
9. de la   *He didn't eat the jam that you made.*
10. des   *Corrected mistakes do not become habits.*
11. de   *I don't see any smoke.*
12. de   *Grandparents don't smoke cigarettes.*

EXERCISE 1-14:

C   1.   *You offer me a few good suggestions.*
E   2.   d'   *This is a study hall.*
D   3.   d'   *He didn't want a glass of water.*
F   4.   des   *The majority of voters are ignorant.*
E   5.   de   *Here is a good piece of meat.*
C   6.   *I see several football players.*
G   7.   d'   *She needs a bicycle.*
G   8.   des   *The garden is surrounded by flowers.*
F   9.   des   *Most of the onions were ruined.*
E   10.   de   *This is a silk dress.*
D   11.   de   *You make too much noise.*
G   12.   de   *He is taking care of the luggage.*

RAISE YOUR GRADES

Gender of nouns

K 1. (F) *Cigarettes are expensive in France.*
K 2. (F) *A lot of things interest me here.*
K 3. (F) *The address is not on the list.*
H 4. (M) *Where has he put the other calendar?*
K 5. (F) *The churches date (back) to the 12th century.*
J 6. (F) *What is the date of the test?*
A 7. (M) *Some of the boys must stay outside.*
B 8. (M) *The office is on the second floor.*
K 9. (F) *Please take the other chair.*
A 10. (M) *Men adore liberty.*
J 11. (F) *Study the lesson before the next class.*
J 12. (F) *I wrote a card to him from Paris.*
A 13. (M) *Children adore her!*
A 14. (M) *Everyone finds him amusing.*
J 15. (F) *That is a private school.*
H 16. (M) *The other wall is covered with paintings.*
J 17. (F) *The beautiful flower has a bizarre name.*
B 18. (M) *Take a pen and write!*
J 19. (F) *What do you see from the window?*
A 20. (M) *Some students are waiting for you at the door.*
B 21. (M) *Write this on the blackboard.*
K 22. (F) *What time is your next class?*
B 23. (M) *The exercise is too easy.*
K 24. (F) *The pages explain the problem.*

B 25. (M) *The best students go to the high school.*
K 26. (F) *Our pronunciation is authentic.*
N 27. (F) *Your studies will help you in the future.*
B 28. (M) *The violin is the instrument he prefers.*
H 29. (M) *His book is full of sarcasm.*
K 30. (F) *We learn by studying other cultures.*
K 31. (F) *The unbelievable beauty of this child fascinates me.*
G 32. (M) *These paintings are masterworks.*
E 33. (M) *As a doctor, he is formidable.*
A. 34. (M) *My grandparents live in Philadelphia.*
K 35. (F) *Vacations come at the end of the year.*
A 36. (M) *Who are the members of these committees?*
K 37. (F) *The heart has its reasons.*
A 38. (M) *Cats are more amusing than dogs.*
C 39. (M) *I keep my bicycle in our garage.*
K 40. (F) *Who has studied anthropology?*
H 41. (M) *I wish you well always.*
D 42. (M) *Where did you spend the other weekend?*
A 43. (M) *He works as a nurse in that hospital.*
G 44. (M) *Summaries are often useful.*
B 45. (M) *You must bring something to eat if you go there.*

Definite articles

46. Les parents vont venir au lycée. *Parents are going to come to the high school.*
47. L'hôtel ne plaît pas à la mère. *The mother is not pleased with the hotel.*
48. Les employés de l'homme sont à ses ordres. *The man's employees are at his command.*
49. Au printemps il pleut beaucoup. *It rains a lot in the spring.*
50. Aux Etats-Unis nous avons les élections en novembre. *In the United States we have our elections in November.*
51. Les élèves du professeur assistent à l'autre classe. *The professor's students help in the other class.*

52. Quelle proportion des femmes participe aux activités? *What proportion of the women participate in the activities?*
53. L'oncle, la tante et les cousins habitent la ville. *The uncle, the aunt, and the cousins live in town.*
54. L'auto ne marche pas, mais vous avez la bicyclette dans le garage. *The car isn't working but you have the bicycle in the garage.*
55. Tu vas avoir quelques lettres des amis et le cadeau du grand-père au prochain anniversaire. *You are going to get some letters from friends and the present from grandfather on your next birthday.*

Indefinite and partitive articles

56. Jacques n'a pas de skis. *Jacques doesn't have any skis.*
57. Cette fille a des admirateurs. *This girl has (some) admirers.*
58. Pourquoi ne prends-tu pas de soupe? *Why don't you have some soup?*
59. Je suis contente de voir tant de gens. *I am happy to see so many people.*

60. Les explorateurs ont du courage. *Explorers have courage.*
61. Ce tableau-là n'est pas un original. *This painting is not an original.*
62. L'italien a des articles partitifs. *Italian has partitive articles.*
63. Nos vendeurs ne font jamais de promesses. *Our salesmen never make promises.*

64. Quand leurs enfants ont-ils du travail? *When do their children work?*
65. Qui n'a plus d'illusions? *Who no longer has illusions?*
66. J'ai très envie de bonbons. *I really want some candy.*
67. Dans ce dessert il y a beaucoup d'oeufs. *There are a lot of eggs in this dessert.*
68. Cet acteur joue dans des tragédies. *This actor does tragedies.*
69. Elle s'occupe d'enfants. *She takes care of children.*
70. Je ne prends que de l'eau. *I take only water.*
71. Au printemps il fait souvent du soleil. *It is often sunny in the spring.*
72. Ce n'est pas de la porcelaine. *This is not china.*
73. Pour faire une omelette il faut des oeufs. *It takes (some) eggs to make an omelette.*
74. Quand j'ai soif, je bois un verre de jus de fruit. *I drink a glass of fruit juice when I am thirsty.*
75. Est-ce que tu manges de la viande? *Do you eat meat?*
76. Votre essai est plein de fautes. *Your essay is full of mistakes.*
77. Il a plus d'idées que moi. *He has more ideas than I.*
78. Elle n'a plus d'amis. *She has no more friends.*
79. Il prend toujours trop de risques. *He always takes too many risks.*
80. Nous ne connaissons pas la majorité de la classe. *We don't know the majority of the class.*

2 ADJECTIVES AND ADVERBS

THIS CHAPTER IS ABOUT

- ☑ **Descriptive Adjectives**
- ☑ **Comparative and Superlative Adjectives**
- ☑ **Adverbs**
- ☑ **Comparative and Superlative Adverbs**
- ☑ **Adverbs of Quantity**
- ☑ **Même and Tout As Adverbs**

An adjective modifies a noun to denote a quality of the thing named, to indicate its quantity or extent, or to specify one thing as distinct from another.

2-1. Descriptive Adjectives

A. Forms of descriptive adjectives

A descriptive adjective *agrees* in *gender* and *number* with the noun it modifies—so, adjectives have four forms: *masculine singular, feminine singular, masculine plural,* and *feminine plural.*

1. The singular forms

- The feminine singular of all adjectives ends in **-e**—to form the regular feminine adjective, add an **-e** to the masculine singular.

M–sing	F–sing	
noir	noir**e**	*black*
élégant	élégant**e**	*elegant*
vert	vert**e**	*green*
grand	grand**e**	*big, great*

- If the masculine singular form of an adjective ends in **-e**, the adjective is *invariable*—that is, *it stays the same in both masculine and feminine forms.*

M–sing	F–sing	
moderne	moderne	*modern*
rouge	rouge	*red*
sobre	sobre	*sober*
utile	utile	*useful*

- For masculine adjectives ending in **-el, -eil, -en, -on, -et, -os,** and **-as,** double the last consonant before adding **-e** to form the feminine.

M–sing	F–sing	
itali**en**	itali**enne**	*Italian*
form**el**	form**elle**	*formal*
gro**s**	gro**sse**	*big*
b**on**	b**onne**	*good*
par**eil**	par**eille**	*like, similar*
gra**s**	gra**sse**	*fat*
mu**et**	mu**ette**	*silent*

24

- A few adjectives have two masculine forms—use the first form before nouns beginning with a consonant, and the second form before nouns beginning with a vowel or a mute h. To form the feminine of these adjectives, double the last consonant and add a final **-e** to the second masculine form.

M–sing—first form	M–sing—second form	F–sing
le **nouveau** roman	le **nouvel an**	la nouve**lle** cuisine
the new novel	*the new year*	*the new cuisine*
ce **beau** gosse	ce **bel h**omme	cette be**lle** fille
that good-looking kid	*that handsome man*	*that beautiful girl*
un **vieux** conte	un **vieil a**nimal	une vieille amie
an old tale	*an old animal*	*an old friend*
un **fou** rire	un **fol a**mour	une fo**lle** aventure
a crazy laugh	*a mad love*	*a wild adventure*

Le **vieux** château est en ruines.	*The old castle is in ruins.*
Le **vieil** artiste est mort.	*The old artist is dead.*
La **vieille** barque est abandonnée.	*The old rowboat is abandoned.*
La France est un **beau** pays.	*France is a beautiful country.*
Le chêne est un **bel** arbre.	*The oak is a beautiful tree.*
La Loire est une **belle** rivière.	*The Loire is a beautiful river.*

> **REMEMBER:** Use the second masculine form only before a noun that begins with a vowel or a mute h.

- Change masculine singular adjectives ending in **-f** to **-ve** to form the feminine.

M–sing	F–sing	
passi**f**	passi**ve**	*passive*
neu**f**	neu**ve**	*new*
sporti**f**	sporti**ve**	*athletic*
acti**f**	acti**ve**	*active*

- When an adjective whose masculine singular form ends in **-eur** is derived from a present participle, the feminine ends in **-euse**. If the adjective is derived from a noun ending in **-tion**, the feminine ends in **-trice**.

	M–sing	F–sing	
moquant	moqu**eur**	moqu**euse**	*mocking*
mentant	ment**eur**	ment**euse**	*lying*
conservation	conserva**teur**	conserva**trice**	*conservative*
révélation	révéla**teur**	révéla**trice**	*revealing*
tentation	tenta**teur**	tenta**trice**	*tempting*

- Certain adjectives that imply comparison simply add **-e** in the feminine.

M–sing	F–sing	
meill**eur**	meilleure	*better*
antéri**eur**	antérieure	*previous*
inféri**eur**	inférieure	*inferior*
extéri**eur**	extérieure	*outer*

- There are some adjectives that follow no definite rules when forming the feminine. Study the following list of some of these adjectives.

M–sing	F–sing	
blanc	blanche	*white*
franc	franche	*frank*
frais	fraîche	*fresh, cool*
sec	sèche	*dry*
épais	épaisse	*thick*
faux	fausse	*false*
doux	douce	*sweet, soft, gentle*
jaloux	jalouse	*jealous*

M–sing	F–sing	
gentil	gentille	*nice*
nul	nulle	*null*
complet	complète	*complete*
discret	discrète	*discreet*
inquiet	inquiète	*worried, anxious*
secret	secrète	*secretive*
public	publique	*public*
turc	turque	*Turk*
grec	grecque	*Greek*
favori	favorite	*favorite*
long	longue	*long*
sot	sotte	*silly*
malin	maligne	*wicked, cunning, clever*

2. The plural forms

- You usually form the plural of an adjective by adding an unpronounced final **-s** to its singular form.

M–sing	M–pl	
le fils impudent	les fils impudents	*the impudent son(s)*
le chapeau bleu	les chapeaux bleus	*the blue hat(s)*

F–sing	F–pl	
la fille impudente	les filles impudentes	*the impudent girl(s)*
la chemise bleue	les chemises bleues	*the blue shirt(s)*

- If the masculine singular adjective ends in **-s** or **-x**, there is no change in the masculine plural form.

M–sing	M–pl	
le fils heureux	les fils heureux	*the happy son(s)*
le manteau gris	les manteaux gris	*the gray coat(s)*

- Most masculine singular adjectives ending in **-al** have masculine plurals ending in **-aux**.

M–sing	M–pl	
roy**al**	roy**aux**	*royal*
or**al**	or**aux**	*oral*
lég**al**	lég**aux**	*legal*

> *NOTE:* The common adjectives, **fatal**, **final**, and **naval**, which end in **-l**, form their plurals regularly—fatal**s**, final**s**, and naval**s**.

- Add an **-x** to masculine singular adjectives ending in **-eau** or **-eu** to form the plural.

M–sing	M–pl	
jum**eau**	jumeau**x**	*twin*
b**eau**	beau**x**	*beautiful*
nouv**eau**	nouveau**x**	*new*

EXERCISE 2-1:   Replace the noun in the following phrases with the noun in the parentheses. Be sure to make any other necessary changes. Then change the new phrase from singular to plural. Use the example as a guide. Answers and translations are at the end of the chapter.

Example: mon tableau favori   **ma peinture**   **mes peintures**
                  (peinture)   **favorite**   **favorites**

1. ce costume bleu (cravate)   _____   _____
2. la phrase complète (exercice)   _____   _____
3. une organisation active (club)   _____   _____
4. notre premier message (lettre)   _____   _____

 5. cette comédie amusante (film) _____ _____
 6. un silence mortel (blessure) _____ _____
 7. l'accent canadien (prononciation) _____ _____
 8. la belle femme (homme) _____ _____
 9. le gentil compliment (carte) _____ _____
10. la nouvelle bicyclette (vélo) _____ _____
11. un air sérieux (position) _____ _____
12. votre meilleur ami (amie) _____ _____
13. cet acteur célèbre (actrice) _____ _____
14. un mot discret (lettre) _____ _____
15. une photo flatteuse (portrait) _____ _____
16. un homme calculateur (personne) _____ _____
17. une vieille histoire (argument) _____ _____
18. la première visite (voyage) _____ _____
19. l'exercice difficile (leçon) _____ _____
20. sa soeur aînée (frère) _____ _____
21. une idée générale (plan) _____ _____
22. cette légende médiévale (conte) _____ _____
23. le beau tableau ancien (peinture) _____ _____
24. le jus frais (fruit) _____ _____
25. ce dessert délicieux (gâteau) _____ _____

B. Position of descriptive adjectives

1. In French, adjectives usually follow the nouns they modify.

Il y a une **collection importante** de **bijoux anciens**. *There is a large collection of ancient jewelry.*
Vos **chaussettes noires** sont dans le **tiroir ouvert**. *Your black socks are in the open drawer.*

2. Some adjectives precede the nouns they modify.

- You may say the adjective before a noun to add emphasis or to indicate your—the speaker's—feelings.

C'est un **adorable enfant**! *He's a lovely child.*
On compte faire une **magnifique promenade** demain. *We're planning to take a wonderful walk tomorrow.*

EXERCISE 2-2: Combine the sentences by using the adjective in an emphatic manner. Answers and translations are at the end of the chapter.

Example: Je vois leur automobile. *I see their car.*
Elle est énorme! *It's enormous.*
Je vois leur énorme automobile! *I see their enormous automobile!*

1. Ce sont mes tapis. Ils sont superbes!_____
2. Voilà le dessert? Il est sensationnel!_____
3. Prenons ce vin-là. Il est magnifique!_____
4. Vous connaissez ces chansons. Elles sont tristes!_____
5. C'est un menteur. Il est formidable!_____

- Some descriptive adjectives normally precede the nouns they modify—such as those on the following list.

M–sing	F–sing	
beau	belle	*handsome, beautiful*
bon	bonne	*good*
gentil	gentille	*nice*
gros	grosse	*big, fat*
jeune	jeune	*young*
joli	jolie	*pretty*

M–sing	F–sing	
long	longue	*long*
mauvais	mauvaise	*bad*
petit	petite	*small*
vieux	vieille	*old*
vilain	vilaine	*ugly*

Tu es un **bon petit garçon**.   *You are a good little boy.*
Une **jolie jeune fille** vous attend.   *A pretty young girl is waiting for you.*

BUT say these adjectives **after** a noun if you want to stress the adjective's meaning.

Ce n'est pas une **peinture belle**.   *That's not what you'd call a beautiful painting.*

Elle cherche un **bureau long**.   *She's looking for a long desk.*

- An indefinite adjective—an adjective that does not specify distinct limits—usually precedes the noun it modifies. Following is a list of indefinite adjectives that precede a noun.

aucun(e)*	*no one, none*
autre*	*other*
chaque	*each, every*
divers(e)	*various*
maint(e)*	*many a*
nul(le)*	*no, no one*
plusieurs*	*several*
quelque	*some*
quelques-uns/unes	*a few*
tel(le)*	*such a*
tout(e)*	*all, whole, everything, every*
tous, (toutes)*	*all, whole, everything, every*
un/une*	*one*

* You can also use these indefinite adjectives as indefinite pronouns (see Sec. 6-10).

Elle n'a **aucune raison** de partir.   *She has no reason to leave.*
J'aimerais vous inviter une **autre fois**.   *I would like to invite you another time.*
Chaque année je voyage en Europe.   *I travel in Europe every year.*
Il y a **divers moyens** de construire une maison.   *There are various ways of building a house.*
Cet été je ne suis allé **nulle part**.   *This summer I didn't go anywhere.*
J'ai **plusieurs choses** à vous dire.   *I have several things to tell you.*
Depuis **quelques temps**, je suis un peu fatigué.   *I have been feeling tired for some time.*
Connaissez-vous une **telle histoire**?   *Do you know such a story?*
Tout le **pays** est en guerre.   *The whole country is at war.*
Tout les **matins** je vais travailler.   *Every morning I go to work.*

- In order to intensify a noun, you may use a form of the adjective **tout** before the article or possessive adjective or pronoun that introduces the noun.

Toute la famille parle français.   *The whole family (all the family) speaks French.*

Tous mes amis disent que je devrais arrêter de fumer.   *All my friends say that I should stop smoking.*

Il a passé **tout un** été en Grèce.   *He spent a whole summer in Greece.*

- Say the adjective qualifying a proper noun before the noun.

le **cruel docteur Favre**   *the cruel doctor Favre*
l'**intelligent Einstein**   *the intelligent Einstein*
mon **meilleur** ami **Gérard**   *my best friend Gérard*

EXERCISE 2-3: Rewrite the following sentences, inserting the correct form of the adjective given in parentheses in its correct position. Answers and translations are at the end of the chapter.

Example: Voilà mon amie. (gentil)   *Here is my friend. (nice)*
                    Voilà ma gentille amie.   *Here is my nice friend.*

1. C'est un meuble. (beau) _____
2. Personne n'est venu. (aucun) _____
3. Je vois les feuilles de papier. (tout) _____
4. J'ai acheté un bureau. (vieux) _____
5. Il mangeait des gâteaux. (trois) _____
6. C'était une femme. (furieux) _____
7. Je regarde un film. (mauvais) _____
8. Les jeunes gens dansent. (tout) _____
9. Ce député a été arrêté. (libéral) _____
10. Elle a choisi une chanson. (long) _____

3. There are a number of common descriptive and indefinite adjectives whose English translation changes according to whether they come before or after a noun. Study the following list of such adjectives.

	Before a Noun	After a Noun
ancien	*former*	*old, ancient*
brave	*worthy, good*	*brave*
certain	*certain, distinct*	*sure, unquestionable*
cher	*dear*	*expensive*
dernier	*past, final*	*last*
différent	*various, sundry*	*not alike, not the same*
grand	*famous*	*tall*
maigre	*scanty, meager*	*lean, thin*
méchant	*naughty*	*wicked*
même	*same*	*very*
pauvre	*pitiable*	*penniless, poor*
propre	*own*	*clean*
sale	*grimy*	*nasty*
seule	*only one*	*alone*
simple	*mere*	*not complicated*
vrai	*real, genuine*	*true*

EXERCISE 2-4: Translate the following sentences into English. Be sure to note the position of the adjective. Answers are at the end of the chapter.

1. Je vois une seule personne. _____
2. Je vois une personne seule. _____
3. Elle est arrivée la semaine dernière. _____
4. Elle est arrivée la dernière semaine. _____
5. C'est un grand homme. _____
6. C'est un homme grand. _____
7. Le musée est dans une ancienne église. _____
8. Le musée est dans une église ancienne. _____
9. Ces enfants sales jouent dans la cour. _____
10. Ces sales enfants jouent dans la cour. _____
11. J'ai de braves voisins. _____
12. J'ai des voisins braves. _____
13. Il écrit avec un certain style. _____
14. Il écrit avec un style certain. _____
15. J'ai de chers souvenirs de la France. _____
16. J'ai des souvenirs chers de la France. _____
17. Le pauvre acteur est devenu célèbre. _____

18. L'acteur pauvre est devenu célèbre. _____
19. Voilà ma propre chambre. _____
20. Voilà ma chambre propre. _____

EXERCISE 2-5: Answer the following questions negatively, using the adjective given in parentheses. Answers and translations are at the end of the chapter.

Example: Y-a-t-il un exercice court à faire?   *Is there a short exercise to do?*
             (long)   *(long)*

          Non, il y a un long exercice à faire. *No, there is a long exercise to do.*

1. Est-ce que c'est un devoir énorme? (petit)
2. Est-ce que c'est un édifice moderne? (ancien)
3. Ont-ils un chien méchant? (gentil)
4. Est-ce que Noël tombe toujours à une date différente? (même)
5. Lit-elle le même livre? (autre)
6. Est-ce que son père est un bel homme? (laid)
7. Ta soeur est-elle une vieille personne? (jeune)
8. Ce magasin a-t-il des choses bon marché? (chères)
9. Monsieur Lévêque est-il notre professeur actuel? (ancien)
10. Les Français font-ils de la mauvaise cuisine? (bonne)
11. Est-ce le temps de voir les anciens amis? (nouveaux)
12. Est-ce que c'est un cousin détesté? (cher)
13. Sort-elle avec un garçon laid? (beau)
14. Marianne a-t-elle l'autre modèle de caméra? (même)
15. Prend-on nouvel autobus tous les jours? (même)

C. Use of descriptive adjectives

1. When you have two or more adjectives of the same category following a noun, connect the adjectives with **et**.

   C'est une **oeuvre intelligente et**   *This is an intelligent and artistic*
       artistique.   *work.*

   BUT with two or more adjectives describing different aspects of a noun, do not use the conjunction.

   C'est un excellent **disque classique**   *This is an excellent French classical*
       français.   *record.*

   NOTE: In general, the adjective describing the most basic characteristic goes closest to the noun.

   Ils regardaient un **programme**   *They were watching an insipid*
       américain insipide.   *American program.*

2. An adjective modifying more than one noun is plural.

   Le nom et le verbe sont **pluriels**.   *The noun and the verb are plural.*

   BUT a series of adjectives collectively modifying a plural noun may be singular.

   Il a invité les **ambassadeurs grec**   *He invited the Greek and Swedish*
       et **suédois**.   *ambassadors.*

EXERCISE 2-6: Combine the sentences by inserting the second adjective into the appropriate position in the first sentence. Answers and translations are at the end of the chapter.

Example: Nous jouons de la musique moderne   *We play modern music. It's*
          Elle est française.   *French.*

          Nous jouons de la musique moderne   *We play modern French music.*
              française.

1. Je fréquente des amis étrangers. Ils sont intéressants.
2. Il a des leçons difficiles. Elles sont compliquées.

3. Alice connaît des chansons gaies. Elles sont amusantes.
4. Nous aurions une opinion sûre. Elle serait certaine.
5. Il achète une voiture japonaise. Elle est bleue.
6. Prenez de ces pommes vertes. Elles sont délicieuses.
7. Qui va écouter cette musique moderne? Elle est ennuyeuse.
8. Nous nous asseyons à une table solide. Elle est lourde.
9. Vous offrez votre aide financière. Elle est considérable.
10. Elles préfèrent les magasins chic. Ils sont chers.

EXERCISE 2-7: Answer the questions affirmatively, placing the adjectives in the appropriate places. Answers and translations are at the end of the chapter.

Example: Est-ce que la leçon est longue et difficile?   *Is the lesson long and difficult?*

Oui, c'est une longue leçon difficile.   *Yes, it is a long, difficult lesson.*

1. Est-ce que la voiture est petite et économique?
2. La petite fille est blonde et jolie, n'est-ce pas?
3. Est-ce que le patron est bête et méchant?
4. Le professeur est gentil et patient, n'est-ce pas?
5. La robe est-elle belle et élégante?
6. Ce garçon est-il jeune et sportif?
7. Est-ce que c'est une date sûre et certaine?
8. Est-ce que cet étudiant est pauvre et malheureux?
9. Le chien est gros et gras, n'est-ce pas?
10. Est-ce que cet acteur est beau et riche?

3. As a general rule, you should express the partitive by **de** alone before a plural adjective. (See Sec. 1-5C.)

Elle porte **de gros cartons**.   *She is carrying big boxes.*
Ils ont fait **de petits gestes**.   *They made small gestures.*

BUT if you want to emphasize the *quantity* of a noun, use the partitive **des**.

Elle porte **des gros cartons**.   *She is carrying a lot of heavy boxes.*
Ils ont fait **des petits gestes**.   *They made a lot of small gestures.*

REMEMBER: **Des autres** means *of the others* or *belonging to the others*—it is not the plural of **un autre/une autre**, *another*. The plural form is always **d'autres**, *other, some other*.

Ils ont **d'autres** chats à fouetter.   *They have other matters to attend to.* (Literally: They have other cats to whip.)

Ne t'occupe pas des affaires **des autres**.   *Don't get involved in other people's business* (the business of others).

EXERCISE 2-8: Respond to the following questions and include the plural adjective in your answer. Answers and translations are at the end of the chapter.

Example: Paul et Marie sont des voisins. Sont-ils gentils?   *Paul and Marie are neighbors. Are they nice?*

Oui, Paul et Marie sont de gentils voisins.   *Yes, Paul and Marie are nice neighbors.*

1. Il y a des châteaux en Touraine. Sont-ils vieux?
2. Nous faisons des promenades à la plage. Sont-elles longues?
3. Voilà des dessins intéressants. Sont-ils jolis?
4. Cet homme a des théories. Sont-elles nouvelles?
5. Il a des idées. Sont-elles bonnes?

6. Elle a fait des erreurs à son examen. Sont-elles petites?
7. Nous avons des voisines italiennes. Sont-elles jeunes?
8. Notre musée a des tableaux modernes. Sont-ils beaux?
9. Il y a des vagues dans l'océan. Sont-elles grandes?
10. Louise a des photos de famille. Sont-elles vieilles?

2-2. Comparative and Superlative Adjectives

Use the comparative and superlative of an adjective to indicate degrees in quality or quantity. There are three degrees—positive, comparative, and superlative.

Positive		Comparative		Superlative	
noir	*black*	**plus** noir	*blacker*	**le plus** noir	*blackest*
moderne	*moderne*	**moins** moderne	*less modern*	**le moins** moderne	*least modern*
haut	*high*	**aussi** haut	*equally as high*	(no superlative of equality)	

A. Formation and use of comparative adjectives

1. To form a comparative adjective, simply add one of the adverbs **plus**, **moins**, or **aussi** before an adjective in the positive. The comparative adjective must agree in gender and number with the first noun in the comparison. The conjunction **que** follows directly after the adjective and before the second noun in the comparison—which is called the *complement of the comparison*.

- You can make comparisons on the basis of superiority—**plus**, *more*:

  Il est **plus aimable que** toi. | *He is more likeable than you.*

- or of inferiority—**moins**, *less*:

  Il est **moins aimable que** toi. | *He is less likeable than you.*

  OR   OR

  He is not as likeable as you.

- or of equality—**aussi**, *as*:

  Il est **aussi aimable que** toi. | *He is as likeable as you.*

  Ses rêves sont **plus agréables que** la réalité. | *His dreams are nicer than reality (is nice).*

  Sa soeur est **moins belle que** sa mère. | *His sister is less beautiful than his mother.*

  Leur français est **aussi correct que** leur anglais. | *Their French is as correct as their English (is correct).*

  > *NOTE:*   You can imply, but not mention, the second noun in a comparison—just as you can in English.

  Ce lac est plus profond. | *This lake is deeper.*
  Le prix est moins important. | *The price is less important.*
  Le ciel est aussi bleu. | *The sky is as blue.*

2. It will help if you remember these two rules about comparative adjectives.

- Shorten **aussi** to **si** after a negative.

  Notre usine est **aussi** moderne **que** la vôtre. | *Our factory is as modern as yours.*

  Notre usine **n'**est **pas si** moderne **que** la vôtre. | *Our factory is not as modern as yours.*

- The preposition **de** must follow **plus** or **moins** before a numerical adjective (see Sec. 3-5).

  Paris a **plus de cinq** millions d'habitants. | *Paris has more than five million inhabitants.*

  Elles ont **moins de deux** mille dollars. | *They have less than two thousand dollars.*

EXERCISE 2-9: Make a logical comparison of superiority, inferiority, or equality by placing the noun given in parentheses at the beginning of your new sentence. Be sure to watch for the agreement of the adjective with the first noun in the comparison; the placement of **que** after the adjective; the use of **si** after a negative; and the use of **plus** or **moins** + **de** before a numerical adjective. Answers and translations are at the end of the chapter.

Example:	Les oranges sont rondes. (les citrons)	*Oranges are round. (lemons)*
	Les citrons sont moins ronds que les oranges.	*Lemons aren't as round as oranges.*

1. Le Brésil est grand. (la Suisse)
2. Le train est rapide. (l'avion)
3. Les hommes sont intelligents. (les femmes)
4. Une semaine est courte. (un mois)
5. Les nuages sont blancs. (la neige)
6. La neige est froide. (la pluie)
7. Le café est chaud. (le thé)
8. Le soleil est brillant. (la lune)
9. Le lait est nourrissant. (la crème)
10. Une plume n'est pas légère. (un livre)
11. Mai a plus de vingt neuf jours. (février)
12. Les fleurs sont chères. (les bijoux)
13. Un tableau est réaliste. (une photo)
14. L'algèbre est difficile. (l'arithmétique)
15. La glace n'est pas solide. (l'eau)

B. Formation and use of superlative adjectives

Use the superlative adjective to denote the utmost degree of quality or quantity.

1. To form a superlative adjective, the definite article **le**, **la**, or **les** precedes a comparative adjective. The definite article must agree in number and gender with the noun it modifies.

Positive		Comparative		Superlative	
actif	*active*	**plus** actif	*more active*	**le plus** actif	*most active*
polie	*polite*	**plus** polie	*more polite*	**la plus** polie	*most polite*
simple	*simple*	**plus** simple	*simpler*	**les plus** simples	*most simple*
vieille	*old*	**plus** vieille	*older*	**les plus** vieilles	*oldest*

2. Always use the preposition **de** before the complement of the superlative—the word or words you use to complete the sense of the superlative.

C'est le garçon **le plus actif du lycée**.	*He is the most active boy in the school.*
Françoise a l'enfant **la plus polie de cette rue**.	*Françoise has the most polite child on this street.*
Le savant a les solutions **les plus simples du monde**.	*The scholar has the simplest solutions in the world.*
Les plus vieilles maisons de la ville sont là.	*The oldest houses in town are here.*

> *NOTE:* When you use an adjective in the superlative form, it goes in its usual position—before or after the noun. (See Sec. 2-1B for adjectives that regularly precede nouns.)

Personne ne connaît mes **pensées les plus intimes**.	*No one knows my most intimate thoughts.*
C'est **le moins intéressant des hommes**.	*He is the least interesting of men.*

3. The following adjectives have irregular comparative and superlative forms.

Positive		Comparative		Superlative	
bon	*good*	meilleur	*better*	le (la) meilleur(e)	*best*
mauvais	*bad*	plus mauvais	*worse*	le (la) plus mauvais(e)	*worst*
		moins mauvais	*worse*	le (la) moins mauvais(e)	*worst*
		pire	*worse*	le (la) pire	*worst*
petit	*small*	plus petit	*smaller*	le (1a) plus petit(e)	*smallest*
		moins petit	*smaller*	le (la) moins petit(e)	*smallest*
		moindre	*lesser*	le (la) moindre	*the least*

La pièce est **bonne**.	*The play is good.*
La pièce est **meilleure**.	*The play is better.*
La pièce est **la meilleure**.	*The play is the best.*
Votre idée est **mauvaise**.	*Your idea is bad.*
Votre idée est **plus mauvaise** que la mienne.	*Your idea is worse than mine.*
Votre idée est **la plus mauvaise** de l'année.	*Your idea is the worst of the year.*
Cette fleur est **petite**.	*This flower is small.*
Cette fleur est **plus petite**.	*This flower is smaller.*
Cette fleur est **la plus petite**.	*This flower is the smallest.*

- Use **plus (moins) mauvais** and **le (la) plus (moins) mauvais(e)** with concrete nouns.

Le **sucre** est **plus mauvais** pour les dents que les fruits.	*Sugar is worse for teeth than fruit (is).*

- Use **pire** and **le (la) pire** with abstract nouns.

La **paresse** est **le pire** des vices.	*Sloth is the worst vice.*

- Use **plus (moins) petit** and **le (la) plus (moins) petit(e)** to compare size.

Mon **appartement** est **plus petit** que le vôtre.	*My apartment is smaller than yours.*
Mon **appartement** est **le plus petit** du bâtiment.	*My apartment is the smallest in the building.*

- Use **moindre** and **le (la) moindre** to compare quantity or importance.

Les **faits** ont **moindre** importance que les circonstances.	*The facts have less importance than the circumstances.*
Je n'ai pas **la moindre** envie de danser.	*I don't have the slightest desire to dance.*

4. You won't have any difficulty identifying the comparative or superlative forms for adjectives that normally follow a noun.

	élégant	*The elegant hat costs 100 francs.*
Le chapeau	**plus élégant** coûte 100 francs.	*The more elegant hat costs 100 francs.*
	le plus élégant	*The most elegant hat costs 100 francs.*

BUT the comparative and superlative forms are the same for adjectives that normally precede a noun—only the context will tell you the difference. You can translate the following sentence in two ways:

Les plus jolies fleurs ne durent qu'un jour.	*The prettiest flowers last only a day.*

OR

The prettier flowers last only a day.

REMEMBER: In English we often use the preposition *in* to introduce the complement of the superlative. Perhaps it will help you to remember to use **de**, *of*, if you think of the superlative as meaning *the most, best,* or *least of all.*

EXERCISE 2-10: Use the elements provided to form sentences containing a superlative. Answers and translations are at the end of the chapter.

| Example: | ma grand'mère/vieille personne/famille | *my grandmother/old person/family* |
| | Ma grand'mère est la plus vieille personne de la famille. | *My grandmother is the oldest person in the family.* |

1. le Brésil/grand pays/Amérique du Sud
2. Rhode Island/grand état/Etats-Unis
3. la Rolls-Royce/voiture élégante/monde
4. l'eau/boisson chère/monde
5. les oeufs/ingrédients importants/omelette

EXERCISE 2-11: Rewrite the following sentences so that the adjective is in the superlative form. Make all the necessary changes. Answers and translations are at the end of the chapter.

| Example: | Connaissez-vous un élève très intelligent dans votre classe? | *Do you know a very intelligent student in your class?* |
| | Connaissez-vous l'élève le plus intelligent de votre classe? | *Do you know the most intelligent student in your class?* |

1. Je pense que le mariage est une bonne institution.
2. C'est une des églises anciennes de la ville.
3. Il dit quelque fois des choses moins profondes.
4. Vous avez une bonne idée.
5. L'hiver est une saison froide.
6. Je vous ai donné une mauvaise raison.
7. Il a mis son vieil imperméable.
8. Je crois que le professeur est très instruit.

2-3. Adverbs

An adverb is an invariable word that usually modifies a verb—but we also use an adverb to modify other adverbs or adjectives.

Marie **écrit souvent** à sa mère.	*Marie often writes to her mother.*
Il a couru **plus lentement**.	*He ran more slowly.*
C'est **très mauvais**.	*It's very bad.*

A. Types of adverbs

There are four types of adverbs.

1. Adverbs of *manner* answer the question *how.*

   bien *good* **mal** *bad* **completèment** *completely* **profondèment** *profoundly*
   Il a **complétément** réussi. *He completely succeeded.*

2. Adverbs of *quantity* answer the question *how much.*

   assez *enough* **très** *very* **trop** *too much* **peu** *little*
   Vous avez **trop** parlé. *You talked too much.*

3. Adverbs of *place* answer the question *where.*

   ici *here* **dehors** *outside* **partout** *everywhere* **loin** *far*
   Voulez-vous aller **dehors**? *Do you want to go outside?*

4. Adverbs of *time* answer the question *when.*

   demain *tomorrow* **toujours** *always* **tôt** *early* **quelquefois** *sometimes*
   Je vais **quelquefois** au cinéma. *I go to the movies sometimes.*

B. Formation of adverbs of manner

1. You form most adverbs of manner by adding the suffix **-ment** to the feminine singular form of a corresponding adjective.

M–sing	F–sing	Adverb	
actif	active	active**ment**	*actively*
discret	discrète	discrète**ment**	*discreetly*
doux	douce	douce**ment**	*sweetly*
formel	formelle	formelle**ment**	*formally*
léger	légère	légère**ment**	*lightly*
seul	seule	seule**ment**	*only*
silencieux	silencieuse	silencieuse**ment**	*silently*

2. Usually when a masculine singular adjective ends in a vowel, you simply add **–ment** to form the adverb.

M–sing	Adverb	
absol**u**	absolu**ment**	*absolutely*
pol**i**	poli**ment**	*politely*
simpl**e**	simple**ment**	*simply*
trist**e**	triste**ment**	*sadly*

3. When a masculine singular adjective ends in **-ant** or **-ent**, the corresponding adverb ends in **-amment** or **-emment**.

M–sing	Adverb	
évid**ent**	évid**emment**	*evidently*
prud**ent**	prud**emment**	*prudently*
suffis**ant**	suffis**amment**	*sufficiently*

There are some exceptions:

M–sing	Adverb	
lent	lent**ement**	*slowly*
présent	présent**ement**	*presently*

4. To form adverbs from a few adjectives, you'll have to change the final **-e** to **-é** before you add **-ment**.

Adjective	Adverb	
aveugl**e**	aveugl**ément**	*blindly*
commod**e**	commod**ément**	*conveniently*
confus**e**	confus**ément**	*confusedly*
énorm**e**	énorm**ément**	*enormously*

5. Many common adverbs of manner do not end in **-ment**.

ainsi	*like this, thus*	**ensemble**	*together*	**mieux**	*better*
bien	*well*	**exprès**	*on purpose*	**pis**	*worse*
comme	*how*	**gratis**	*without charge*	**plutôt**	*rather*
debout	*up, standing*	**mal**	*badly*	**vite**	*quickly*
				volontiers	*gladly*

Comme c'est gentil!	*How nice!*
Mets-toi **debout**.	*Stand up.*
Il est **vite** venu.	*He came quickly.*
Je l'ai fait **volontiers**.	*I did it gladly.*

6. Certain adjectives—like those on the following list—do not have an adverbial form.

âgé	*old, aged*	**inférieur**	*inferior*
célèbre	*famous, celebrated*	**rouge**	*red*
content	*content, glad, satisfied*	**zélé**	*zealous*
fâché	*angry*		

You can express them adverbially by using one of these phrases:

d'un air	*with a _____ air*
d'un ton	*with (in) a _____ tone*
d'une manière	*with (in) a _____ manner*
d'une façon	*in a _____ way (fashion)*
avec	*with _____*
comme	*as _____*
en	*in _____*

d'une manière fâchée	*in an angry way*
d'un air célèbre	*with a celebrated air*
d'un air content	*with a satisfied look*
d'un ton fâché	*in an angry tone*
d'une façon inférieure	*in a condescending way*
en rouge	*in red*
avec zèle	*with zeal, in a zealous way, zealously*

7. Many common adjectives—such as the following—do not change in form when you use them as adverbs.

	Adjective	Adverb
bas	Au **bas** mot, ça coûtera deux mille francs. *At the lowest estimate, it will cost two thousand francs.*	Parlez plus **bas**! *Speak more softly!*
cher	Mes **chers** amis sont arrivés. *My dear friends arrived.*	Les maisons coûtent **cher**. *Houses are expensive.*
droit	L'artiste dessine une ligne **droite**. *The artist is drawing a straight line.*	Va **droit** au but! *Get to the point!*
dur	C'est un travail **dur**. *It's a hard job.*	Travaillez **dur**! *Work hard!*
exprès	Il a reçu un ordre **exprès**. *He received an official order.*	Tu l'a fait **exprès**! *You did it on purpose!*
faux	L'imposteur employait un **faux** nom. *The imposter was using a false name.*	Vous comptez **faux**. *You are counting wrong.*
fort	C'est un homme **fort**. *He is a strong man.*	Il a frappé **fort** à la porte. *He knocked loudly on the door.*
gros	Le chien est gris et **gros**. *The dog is gray and fat.*	L'enfant écrit **gros**. *The child writes big.*
haut	L'alpiniste nous montre une **haute** montagne. *The mountain climber showed us a high mountain.*	Elle portait **haut** la tête. *She held her head high.*
juste	L'épicier a une balance **juste**. *The grocer has accurate scales.*	Il s'est arrêté tout **juste**. *He stopped just in time.*
lourd	Ce carton **lourd** est difficile à porter. *This heavy box is difficult to carry.*	Ce poisson pèse **lourd**. *This fish weighs a lot.*
net	Il nous a donné une explication **nette**. *He gave us a clear explanation.*	Le politicien parle **net**. *The politician speaks candidly.*

REMEMBER:　Adjectives must agree in number and gender with the nouns they modify, but adverbs are invariable.

EXERCISE 2-12: Write the adverbs of manner that correspond to the following adjectives— then translate them. Answers and translations are at the end of the chapter.

Example: necéssaire *necessary*

necéssairement *necessarily*

1. facile	_____	10. autre	_____	
2. fausse	_____	11. heureuse	_____	
3. douce	_____	12. longue	_____	
4. libre	_____	13. prochaine	_____	
5. parfaite	_____	14. seule	_____	
6. froide	_____	15. dernière	_____	
7. deuxième	_____	16. joli	_____	
8. récente	_____	17. sûre	_____	
9. bonne	_____	18. actuelle	_____	

EXERCISE 2-13: Combine the two sentences into a single sentence by changing the adjective in the second sentence into an adverb. Then translate the sentence. Answers and translations are at the end of the chapter.

Example: Les roses sont très belles. *The roses are beautiful.*

C'est vrai. *It's true.*

Les roses sont vraiment très belles. *The roses are truly beautiful.*

1. Notre professeur est canadien. C'est sûr. _____
2. Son accent semble différent. C'est perceptible. _____
3. Ces chocolats sont délicieux. C'est certain. _____
4. Votre frère a l'air malade. C'est sérieux. _____
5. La banque reste fermée. C'est officiel. _____
6. Ce billet est faux. C'est décidé. _____
7. Leurs enfants sont mal élevés. C'est évident. _____
8. Le théâtre devient incompréhensible. C'est indubitable. _____
9. Mes classes sont intéressantes. C'est drôle. _____
10. Cet exercice est terminé. C'est malheureux. _____
11. Ce tableau est beau. C'est suffisant. _____
12. Les fleurs sentent. C'est bon. _____
13. La machine est en panne. C'est incommode. _____
14. La plage devient encombrée. C'est lent. _____
15. Maman est invitée. C'est definitif. _____

C. Position of adverbs

Unfortunately, there are no absolute rules that govern where an adverb should go in a sentence. There are, however, some general rules that will help you use adverbs properly.

1. An adverb usually follows the verb it modifies.

Je **travaille bien**.	*I work well.*
Nous **jouons dehors**.	*We are playing outside.*
Elles **refusent poliment**.	*They refuse politely.*
Ils **partent aujourd'hui**.	*They leave today.*

2. In compound verb tenses, the position of the adverb varies.

- The adverb usually comes between the auxiliary verb and the past participle.

J'**ai bien travaillé**!	*I worked well.*
Elles **ont poliment refusé**!	*They politely refused.*

- BUT most adverbs of time and place come after the past participle.

Nous avons **joué dehors**.	*We played outside.*
Ils sont **partis aujourd'hui**.	*They left today.*

NOTE: Generally the adverbs of time—**toujours, souvent,** and **déjà**—precede the past participle.

Je suis **toujours arrivé** à l'heure.   *I always arrive on time.*
Je suis **souvent arrivé** à l'heure.   *I often arrive on time.*
J'ai **déjà vu** ce film.   *I have already seen this movie.*

- You usually say the adverb of time **puis**, *then*, before the subject of the verb.

Puis elles sont allées au théâtre.   *Then they went to the theather.*

3. The adverbs **assez**, **beaucoup**, **bien**, **mal**, **mieux**, **peu**, **trop**, and **vite** come before the past participle.

Nous avons **peu dormi**.   *We slept little.*
J'ai **assez mangé**.   *I ate enough.*
Elle a **vite répondu**.   *She responded quickly.*

4. Generally say an adverb before the adjective or other adverb it modifies.

Je n'ai jamais mangé un gâteau **aussi bon**,   *I have never eaten a cake so*
  aussi nourrissant.   *good and rich.*
Il est **complétement fou**.   *He is completely crazy.*
Je l'ai fait **trop vite**.   *I did it too quickly.*

5. For emphasis, you may use an adverb at either the beginning or the end of a sentence.

Généralement, j'arrive à l'heure.   *Generally, I arrive on time.*
J'arrive à l'heure, **généralement**.   *I arrive on time generally.*

6. There is one rule about adverbs that you can count on—never put an adverb between a subject and its verb—as we often do in English.

Il va **rarement** au cinéma.   *He rarely goes to the movies.*

7. You may use some adverbs before an adjective or another adverb to intensify its meaning. Study carefully this list of common intensifying adverbs.

à peine	*scarcely*	**fort**	*very*	**plus**	*more*
assez	*rather, enough*	**moins**	*less*	**si**	*so, such*
aussi	*as*	**pas**	*not, un-*	**tout**	*very, completely*
bien	*very*	**peu**	*little, un-*	**très**	*very*

Elle avait de **si** grandes espérances!   *She had such great hopes!*
C'est un détail **moins** important.   *It's a less important detail.*

EXERCISE 2-14: Rewrite the following sentences, placing the adverb given in parentheses in its proper place in the sentence. Answers and translations are at the end of the chapter.
    Example: C'est ce qu'il me faut. (exactement)   *That's what I need. (exactly)*

             C'est exactement ce qu'il me faut.   *That's exactly what I need.*

1. Nous l'avons vu. (souvent)
2. J'ai dormi la nuit dernière. (mal)
3. Elle s'est levée. (rapidement)
4. Il a mangé. (trop)
5. J'ai habité en France. (longtemps)
6. Je n'ai pas fini de travailler. (encore)
7. Il arrive à l'heure. (généralement)
8. Il a téléphoné. (certainement)
9. Elle me l'apporte à signer. (immédiatement)
10. Il part pour l'étranger. (malheureusement)
11. C'est une charmante maison. (vraiment)
12. Ils ont parlé. (lentement)
13. J'ai oublié de le faire. (complètement)
14. Nous avons fini. (justement)

EXERCISE 2-15: Place the intensifying adverb given in parentheses in the appropriate position in the sentence. The key to this exercise is to identify correctly the word that the adverb modifies, then to follow the rules for the position of adverbs. Answers and translations are at the end of the chapter.

Example:	C'est une grande occasion. (très)		*It's a grand occasion. (very)*
	C'est une très grande occasion.		*It's a very grand occasion.*

1. Il a fait une erreur évidente. (si)
2. Une annonce importante arrivera par la poste. (assez)
3. Il répond aux questions difficiles. (moins)
4. Les jolies fleurs ne durent pas longtemps. (plus)
5. C'est un détail insignifiant. (trop)
6. Cette excuse satisfaisante ne trompe personne. (peu)
7. Qui sont ces dames habillées en blanc? (tout)
8. Il a mangé des légumes cuits. (à peine)
9. Elle écrit vite en classe. (aussi)
10. Une coiffure élégante fait de l'effet. (bien)

2-4. Comparative and Superlative Adverbs

Comparative and superlative adverbs indicate degrees in quality, quantity, or manner. There are three degrees—positive, comparative, and superlative.

Positive		Comparative		Superlative	
facilement	*easily*	**plus** facilement	*more easily*	**le plus** facilement	*most easily*
tôt	*early*	**moins** tôt	*less (not as) early*	**le moins** tôt	*least early*
souvent	*often*	**aussi** souvent	*as often*	(no superlative of equality)	

A. Formation and use of comparative adverbs

You form the comparative of an adverb exactly as you form the comparative adjective (see Sec. 2-2A)—use one of the adverbs **plus**, **moins**, or **aussi** (si after a negative verb) before the adverb in a comparison. The conjunction **que** follows directly after the adverb and precedes the second noun in the comparison—the complement of the comparison. Since adverbs are invariable, you don't have to worry about agreement.

Elle court **plus vite que** toi.	*She runs more quickly than you.*
Elle court **moins vite que** toi.	*She runs less quickly than you.*
Elle court **aussi vite que** toi.	*She runs as quickly as you.*
Il court **plus vite que** tous les autres.	*He runs faster than all the others.*
Robert parle **moins sincèrement que** son frère.	*Robert speaks less sincerely than his brother.*
Je dois répondre **aussi correctement que** possible.	*I must answer as correctly as possible.*
Elle ne s'habille pas **si bien que** les **autres**.	*She does not dress as well as the others.*

NOTE: You can imply, but not mention, the second term in a comparison—just as you can in English.

Il chante plus doucement.	*He sings more sweetly.*
Ils se sont plus vaillamment battus.	*They fought more valiantly.*

EXERCISE 2-16: Answer the question with one comparative sentence. Answers and translations are at the end of the chapter.

Example:	Les avions vont vite. Et les trains?		*Planes go fast. And trains?*
	Les trains vont moins vite que les avions.		*Trains go slower than planes.*

1. Un enfant parle lentement. Et un adulte?
2. Un télégramme arrive promptement. Et une lettre?
3. Le cristal se casse facilement. Et le plastique?

4. La neige disparaît rapidement. Et la pluie?
5. Les femmes travaillent diligemment. Et les hommes?
6. L'alouette chante mélodieusement. Et le rossignol?
7. La lune brille intensément. Et le soleil?
8. Un oiseau chante bien. Et un chat?
9. Une tortue nage bien. Et un rhinocéros?
10. Les diamants coûtent cher. Et les perles?

B. Formation and use of superlative adverbs

The superlative adverb denotes the utmost degree of quality, quantity, or manner.

1. To form the superlative adverb, say the definite article **le** before the comparative adverb. Because an adverb is invariable, you always use the masculine singular form of the definite article.

Positive		Comparative		Superlative	
brèvement	*briefly*	**plus** brèvement	*more briefly*	**le plus** brèvement	*most briefly*
souvent	*often*	**moins** souvent	*less often*	**le moins** souvent	*least often*
gentiment	*nicely*	**plus** gentiment	*more nicely*	**le plus** gentiment	*most nicely*
heureusement	*happily*	**plus** heureusement	*less happily*	**le moins** heureusement	*least happily*

2. Always use the preposition **de** before the complement of the superlative.

A l'hôtel, c'est Monsieur X qui reste **le plus brièvement de** tous les touristes.	*It's Mr. X who stays at the hotel the shortest time of all the tourists.*
C'est l'autobus qui passe **le moins souvent de** tous le autobus.	*That's the bus that comes by the least often of all the buses.*
C'est elle qui m'a parlé **le plus gentiment de** tous.	*She is the one who spoke to me the nicest of all.*
De toutes les femmes mariées, c'est Susan qui vit **le moins heureusement**.	*Of all the married women, it's Susan who is the least happy.*

3. The following adverbs form their comparatives and superlatives irregularly.

Positive		Comparative		Superlative	
bien	*well*	mieux	*better*	le mieux	*best*
beaucoup	*much*	plus	*more*	le plus	*most*
mal	*bad*	plus mal	*worse*	le plus mal	*worst*
		pis	*worse*	le pis	*worst*
peu	*little*	moins	*less*	le moins	*least*

C'est elle qui travaille **le mieux**.	*She is the one who works the best.*
Vous êtes l'étudiant qui travaille **le moins**.	*You are the student who works the least.*
Qui est-ce qui gagne **le plus** ici?	*Who earns the most here?*
James ne s'en trouve **pas plus mal**.	*James is none the worse for it.*

> **NOTE:** The adverbs **pis** and **le pis** are archaic—you will rarely find them except in idiomatic expressions.

aller de mal en pis	*to go from bad to worse*
les pis est . . .	*the worst is* . . .
il y a pis	*there is worse, what is worse*
Les choses **vont de mal en pis**.	*Things are going from bad to worse.*

4. English-speakers tend to confuse the adjective **bon** with the adverb **bien**, and the adjective **mauvais** with the adverb **mal**. Study the following chart and you'll see why.

	Positive		Comparative		Superlative	
adj.	bon	*bad*	meilleur	*better*	le(la) meilleur(e)	*best*
adv.	bien	*well*	mieux	*better*	le(la) mieux	*best*
adj.	mauvais	*bad*	plus mauvais	*worse*	le(la) plus mauvais(e)	*worst*
adv.	mal	*badly*	pire	*worse*	le(la) pire	*worst*

The problem is that in English the comparative and superlative forms are the same for both pairs of adjectives and adverbs—*better*, *best* and *worse*, *worst*. Just be sure to use the adjective form to modify a noun and the adverb form to modify a verb, an adjective, or another adverb, and you'll be all right.

Je lis **le meilleur** livre écrit par Daudet.
    adj.

I am reading the best book Daudet wrote.

C'est **la meilleure** méthode de travail.
    adj.

It's the best method of work.

Scott est l'étudiant qui travaille **le mieux**.

Scott is the student who works best.

Thérèse a écrit **le plus mauvais** exam.
       adj.

Thérèse wrote the worst test.

Les plus mauvais exemples attirent
    adj.
toujours l'attention.

The worst examples always attract attention.

La misère est **le pire** des maux.
     adv.

Misery is the worst of all evils.

EXERCISE 2-17: Complete the following sentences by choosing the appropriate comparative or superlative adverb from those given in the parentheses. Answers and translations are at the end of the chapter.

Example: C'est Jean que je connais
        (bien, mieux, le mieux).

It is Jean whom I know (well, better, best).

    C'est Jean que je connais le mieux.

It is Jean whom I know the best.

OR

    C'est Jean que je connais bien.

OR

It is Jean whom I know well.

1. Marie est celle qui chante (mal, pire, le pire).
2. Vous avez manqué le train. (Tant pis! Tant mieux!)
3. Je fais cela (bien, mieux, le mieux) que vous.
4. Elle a réussi à son examen. (Tant mieux! Tant pis!)
5. Elle parle (mal, pire, le pire) que son frère.

2-5. Adverbs of Quantity

A. Some common adverbs of quantity

The best way to learn these common adverbs of quantity is to memorize them!

assez	*enough*	**guère**	*hardly*
aussi	*so*	**moins**	*fewer, less*
autant	*as many, as much*	**peu/un peu**	*little, few/a little*
autrement	*otherwise*	**plus**	*more*
beaucoup	*many, a lot of*	**presque**	*almost*
bien	*very, a lot of*	**si**	*so, such*
combien	*how many, how much*	**tant**	*so many, so much*
comme	*as, like, how*	**tellement**	*so many, so much*
davantage	*more*	**très**	*very*
encore	*still, yet, beside, too*	**trop**	*too much too many*
environ	*about, nearly*		

J'en ai **assez** de lui.

I've had enough of him. (I'm fed up with him.)

L'avion décollera **comme** prévu.	*The plane will take off as anticipated.*
Charles est **encore** amoureux de sa femme.	*Charles is still in love with his wife.*
Après **bien** des questions, j'ai découvert la vérité.	*After asking a lot of questions, I discovered the truth.*

B. Use of adverbs of quantity

1. You must use the preposition **de** after adverbs of quantity and nouns of quantity when they introduce a noun.

Il y a **assez d'eau**.	*There is enough water.*
Nous avons **autant de patience** que vous.	*We have as much patience as you.*
Il a fait **plus d'erreurs**.	*He made more mistakes.*
Vous achetez **trop de chemises**.	*You buy too many shirts.*
J'ai compté une **douzaine de voitures**.	*I counted a dozen cars.*
J'ai vu **une foule d'étudiants**.	*I saw a crowd of students.*

2. Translate **peu de** used as an adverb of quantity as *few* or *little*.

J'ai **peu de** temps.	*I have little time.*
Il a **peu de** problèmes.	*He has few problems.*

BUT translate *little* used as an adverb modifying a verb simply as **peu**.

J'apprends **peu** dans cette classe.	*I learn little in this class.*
Il comprend **peu**.	*He understands little.*

Un peu means a *little* before **de** preceding a noun.

Donnez-moi **un peu de crème**.	*Give me a little cream.*
Avez-vous **un peu de monnaie**?	*Do you have a little change?*

> *NOTE:* Don't confuse **peu** with **petit**, *little*, *small*.
>
> | | |
> |---|---|
> | Une **petite** fille qui parle **peu**. | *A little (small) girl who says little.* |

3. Use **si** to modify an adjective. **Un**, **une**, or **de** comes before **si** if the adjective precedes the noun (see Sec. 2-1B).

La comtesse a **de si beaux** bijoux.	*The countess has such beautiful jewels.*
Votre amie a **de si jolis** yeux.	*Your friend has such pretty eyes.*

BUT if **si** modifies an adjective that follows the noun, leave **un**, **une**, or **de** in its normal position—before the noun.

Elle a **une voix si faible** qu'on ne l'entend pas.	*She has such a weak voice that you don't hear her.*

4. Translate the expression **de plus en plus** as *more and more*, and the expression **de moins en moins** as *less and less*.

Je le vois **de plus en plus** maintenant.	*I see him more and more now.*
Il me plaît **de moins en moins**.	*I like him less and less.*

Also use **de plus en plus** before an adverb or adjective to translate expressions such as *faster and faster*, *blacker and blacker*, *nicer and nicer*, etc.

Elle va **de plus en plus vite** en voiture.	*She drives faster and faster.*
La nuit devient **de plus en plus noire**.	*The night becomes blacker and blacker.*
Ma vie sera **de plus en plus agréable**.	*My life will be nicer and nicer.*

Use **plus de** followed by a noun to express *more*. You don't need an article.

Il veut **plus d'argent**.	*He wants more money.*

Plus and **davantage** both mean *more*. BUT use **davantage** as the last word of a statement or clause—that is, when you do not express the second term of a comparison.

Je gagne **plus** que lui.	*I earn more than he (earns).*
Je gagne **davantage**.	*I earn more.*

5. Never modify **beaucoup** by another adverb of quantity.

Il parle **beaucoup**.	*He talks a lot.*
Il a **beaucoup** de choses à dire.	*He has a lot of things to say.*

6. You can use **bien** instead of **très** to modify an adjective or adverb.

Il fait **bien** froid en hiver.	*It is very cold in winter.*
Il a **bien** mal au dos.	*He has a very bad backache.*

You can also use **bien de** followed by **le**, **la**, or **les** instead of **beaucoup de**.

Paul avait **bien de la** peine.	*Paul had a lot of grief.*
Marie a **bien des** ennuis.	*Marie has a lot of worries.*

> *REMEMBER:* Contract **de** with **le** or **les** to form **du** or **des**.

7. French does not distinguish between *much* and *many*. Translate **autant, beaucoup, combien, moins, peu, tant, tellement,** or **trop** as *much* with a singular noun, and as *many* with a plural noun. plural noun.

autant de billets	*as many tickets*
beaucoup de compliments	*many compliments*
combien de pages	*how many pages*
trop de règles	*too many rules*
pas **autant** de fierté	*not so much pride*
beaucoup d'attention	*much attention*
combien d'argent	*how much money*
trop d'énergie	*too much energy*

EXERCISE 2-18: Answer the following questions, using the cues given in parentheses. Answers and translations are at the end of the chapter.

Example:	Comment travaille-t-il? (peu)	*How does he work? (little)*
	Il travaille peu.	*He works little.*

1. Ecrivez-vous beaucoup? (non, peu)
2. Avez-vous des devoirs à l'école? (peu de)
3. Le directeur fait-il des cadeaux aux employés? (si beaux)
4. A-t-elle une jolie robe qu'on admire? (si jolie)
5. Le travail est-il difficile? (de plus en plus)
6. Le climat devient-il moins agréable? (de moins en moins)
7. Cet employé est-il aussi intelligent que son collègue? (plus que)
8. Le professeur parle-t-il autant que les étudiants? (davantage)
9. Dépense-t-elle dans les grands magasins? (beaucoup)
10. Ce déjeuner est-il bon? (oui, bien)

2-6.   Même and Tout As Adverbs

A. Même

You can use **même** as an adverb—usually following the preposition **à** or **de**.

Je suis **à même** de le faire.	*I am in a position to do it.*
Elle parle fort, et il parle **de même**.	*She speaks loudly and so does he.*
Nous irons tout **de même**.	*We'll go anyway.*

B. Tout

You can also use **tout** as an adverb—in the sense of *quite*, *very*. **Tout** is invariable before an adjective or another adverb.

Il a un costume **tout** neuf.   *He has a brand new suit.*

Tout does not change form before a feminine adjective beginning with a vowel or mute h.

La fille était **tout** hardie.   *The girl was quite daring.*

BUT **tout** does change form before a feminine adjective beginning with a consonant.

Sa robe est **toute** bleue.   *Her dress is solid blue.*

EXERCISE 2-19:   Answer the following question affirmatively, using **même** or **tout** as an adverb. Answers and translations are at the end of the chapter.

1. Etes-vous à même de le faire tout de suite?
2. Elle s'habille bien; et lui, s'habille-t-il de même?
3. Après votre accident, pourrez-vous marcher tout de même?
4. Sera-t-il à même de financer son voyage?
5. Le prendrez-vous tout de même?
6. L'air est-il tout léger après la pluie?
7. Le jardin est-il tout vert?
8. Les enfants s'amusent-ils tout gentiment?
9. L'artiste a-t-il fini tout rapidement?
10. Le travail se fait-il tout facilement?

SUMMARY

1. A descriptive adjective must agree in gender and number with the noun it modifies.
2. Most plurals of adjectives add an unpronounced final **-s** to the singular form.
3. Adjectives *usually follow* the nouns they modify, although some adjectives *normally precede* the nouns they modify. Other adjectives may precede the noun in order to add emphasis or to express the speaker's feelings.
4. A number of common descriptive adjectives have meanings that change according to whether they precede or follow a noun.
5. Generally the partitive is expressed by **de alone** before a plural adjective that precedes a plural noun.
6. Adverbs are invariable, and may modify verbs, adjectives, or other adverbs.
7. Most adverbs of manner are formed by adding **-ment** to the feminine singular of a corresponding adjective.
8. Adverbs usually follow the verbs they modify; in compound tenses, the position of the adverb varies.
9. Adverbs usually precede the adjectives or other adverbs they modify.
10. Never put an adverb between a subject and its verb.

RAISE YOUR GRADES

Adjectives

Incorporate the adjectives given in parentheses into each sentence. Answers and translations are at the end of the chapter.

Example:	Leur commande arrivera demain. (nouvelle/mensuelle)	*Their order will arrive tomorrow.* *(new/monthly)*
	Leur nouvelle commande mensuelle arrivera demain.	*Their new monthly order will* *arrive tomorrow.*

1. Il a son ordinateur. (japonais/petit)
2. C'est un médecin. (intelligent/compétent)
3. Je vous enverrai une lettre. (longue/intéressante)
4. Nous assistons à des matchs. (professionels/bons)
5. Son frère est un commerçant. (petit/entreprenant)
6. Monique n'a pas vu cet accident. (aérien/horrible)
7. Ma mère fait des desserts. (délicieux/grands)

8. J'habite ce quartier. (parisien/ancien)
9. Il y a des poissons. (gros/rouges)
10. Regardez ses cheveux! (blonds/longs)
11. Attention aux chiens! (féroces/méchants)
12. Je connais cet acteur. (bel/comique)
13. N'achetez pas ces verres! (chers/fragiles)
14. Robert conduit une auto. (vieille/anglaise)
15. C'est un garçon. (petit/gentil)
16. Mon père connaît un acteur. (célèbre/ancien)
17. Il arrive seul dans sa voiture. (sale/propre)
18. Il est riche mais c'est un artiste. (pauvre/amateur)
19. Solange élève des chevaux. (beaux/arabes)

Adverbs

In each of the following sentences, include an adverb of manner corresponding to the adjective given in parentheses. Answers and translations are at the end of the chapter.

Example:	Qui répondra à la question? (correct)	*Who will answer the question? (correct)*	
	Qui répondra correctement à la question?	*Who will answer the question correctly*	

20. Paul court dans la rue. (joyeux)
21. Diane écoute son professeur. (attentif)
22. Elles parlent au téléphone. (distinct)
23. Nous verrons ce film. (probable)
24. Il faut répondre. (poli)
25. Les enfants apprennent les langues. (facile)
26. Elle danse après quelques leçons. (meilleur)
27. Ces nouveaux avions traversent l'océan. (vite)
28. Ce critique attaque les acteurs. (cruel)
29. Je pense à votre suggestion. (sérieux)
30. Monique parle quatre langues. (courant)
31. Les ouvriers confrontent leurs employeurs. (franc)
32. Nous ouvrirons la discussion. (présent)
33. Je le ferais. (différent)
34. Nous partons pour l'école. (immédiat)
35. Ils répondent sans réflection. (fou)
36. Il ne faut pas signer ce contrat. (aveugle)
37. Les diplomates discutent la situation. (intelligent)
38. Il leur demande de s'asseoir. (gentil)
39. Mes parents travaillent en ce moment. (énorme)

CHAPTER ANSWERS

EXERCISE 2-1:

1. cette cravate bleue	ces cravates bleues	*this blue tie/these blue ties*
2. l'exercice complet	les exercices complets	*the complete exercise(s)*
3. un club actif	des clubs actifs	*a sports club/some sports clubs*
4. notre première lettre	nos premières lettres	*our first letter(s)*
5. ce film amusant	ces films amusants	*this amusing film/these amusing films*
6. une blessure mortelle	des blessures mortelles	*a mortal wound/some mortal wounds*
7. la prononciation canadienne	les prononciations canadiennes	*the Canadian pronunciation(s)*
8. le bel homme	les beaux hommes	*the handsome man/the handsome men*

9. la gentille carte	les gentilles cartes	*the nice note(s)*
10. le nouveau vélo	les nouveaux vélos	*the new bike(s)*
11. une position sérieuse	des positions sérieuses	*a serious position/some serious positions*
12. votre meilleure amie	vos meilleures amies	*your best friend(s)*
13. cette actrice célèbre	ces actrices célèbres	*this famous actress/these famous actresses*
14. une lettre discrète	des lettres discrètes	*a discreet letter/some discreet letters*
15. un portrait flatteur	des portraits flatteurs	*a flattering portrait/some flattering portraits*
16. une personne calculatrice	des personnes calculatrices	*a scheming person/some scheming people*
17. un vieil argument	de vieux arguments	*an old argument/some old arguments*
18. le premier voyage	les premiers voyages	*the first trip(s)*
19. la leçon difficile	les leçons difficiles	*the difficult lesson(s)*
20. son frère aîné	ses frères aînés	*his oldest brother(s)*
21. un plan général	des plans généraux	*a general plan/some general plans*
22. ce conte médiéval	ces contes médiévaux	*this medieval story/these medieval stories*
23. la belle peinture ancienne	les belles peintures anciennes	*the beautiful old painting(s)*
24. le fruit frais	les fruits frais	*the fresh fruit(s)*
25. ce gâteau délicieux	ces gâteaux délicieux	*this delicious cake/these delicious cakes*

EXERCISE 2-2:

1. Ce sont mes superbes tapis. *These are my gorgeous rugs.*
2. Voilà le sensationnel dessert. *Here is the sensational dessert.*
3. Prenons ce magnifique vin-là. *Have (some of) this magnificent wine.*
4. Vous connaissez ces tristes chansons. *You know these sad songs.*
5. C'est un formidable menteur. *He is a formidable liar.*

EXERCISE 2-3:

1. C'est un beau meuble. *It is a beautiful piece of furniture.*
2. Aucune personne n'est venue. *Not one person came.*
3. Je vois toutes les feuilles de papier. *I see all the sheets of paper.*
4. J'ai acheté un vieux bureau. *I bought an old desk.*
5. Il mangeait trois gâteaux. *He ate three cakes.*
6. C'était une femme furieuse. *She was a furious woman.*
7. Je regarde un mauvais film. *I am watching a bad movie.*
8. Tous les jeunes gens dansent. *All the young people are dancing.*
9. Ce député libéral a été arrêté. *That liberal deputy has been arrested.*
10. Elle a choisi une longue chanson *She chose a long song.*

EXERCISE 2-4:

1. *I see only one person.*
2. *I see a person alone.*
3. *She arrived last week.*
4. *She arrived the final week.*
5. *He is a great man.*
6. *He is a tall man.*
7. *The museum is situated in a former church.*
8. *The museum is situated in an ancient church.*
9. *These dirty children are playing in the courtyard.*
10. *Those nasty kids are playing in the courtyard.*
11. *I have some nice neighbors.*
12. *I have (some) courageous neighbors.*
13. *He writes with a certain style.*
14. *He writes in an unquestionable style.*
15. *I have some dear memories of France.*
16. *I have some expensive souvenirs from France.*
17. *The poor (pitiful) actor became famous.*
18. *The penniless actor became famous.*
19. *Here is my own room.*
20. *Here is my clean room.*

EXERCISE 2-5:

1. Non, c'est un petit devoir. *No, it is a small task.*
2. Non, c'est un édifice ancien. *No, it is an old building.*
3. Non, ils ont un gentil chien. *No, they have a nice dog.*
4. Non, Noël tombe toujours à le même date. *No, Christmas always falls on the same date.*
5. Non, elle lit l'autre livre. *No, she reads the other book.*
6. Non, son père est un homme laid. *No, his father is an ugly man.*
7. Non, ma soeur est une jeune personne. *No, my sister is a young person.*

8. Non, ce magasin a des choses chères. *No, this store has (some) expensive things.*
9. Non, Monsieur Lévèque est notre ancien professeur. *No, Mr. Leveque is our former professor.*
10. Non, les Français font de la bonne cuisine. *No, the French cook well.*
11. Non, c'est le moment de voir les nouveaux amis. *No, it is time to see new friends.*
12. Non, c'est un cher cousin. *No, he is a dear cousin.*
13. Non, elle sort avec un beau garçon. *No, she goes out with (dates) a handsome boy.*
14. Non, Marianne a le même modèle de caméra. *No, Marianne has the same model movie camera.*
15. Non, on prend le même autobus tous les jours. *No, we take the same bus every day.*

EXERCISE 2-6:

1. Je fréquente des amis étrangers intéressants. *I have some strange and interesting friends.*
2. Il a des leçons difficiles et compliquées. *He has some difficult and complicated lessons.*
3. Alice connaît des chansons gaies et amusantes. *Alice knows some gay and amusing songs.*
4. Nous aurions une opinion sûre et certaine. *We shall have a sure and certain opinion.*
5. Il achète une voiture japonaise bleue. *He is buying a blue Japanese car.*
6. Prenez de ces pommes vertes délicieuses. *Take some of these delicious green apples.*
7. Qui va écouter cette musique moderne et ennuyeuse? *Who is going to listen to this boring modern music?*
8. Nous nous asseyons à une table solide et lourde. *We sat down at a heavy, solid table.*
9. Vous offrez votre aide financiére considerable. *You offer your considerable financial aid.*
10. Elles préfèrent les magasins chic et chers. *They prefer chic, expensive stores.*

EXERCISE 2-7:

1. Oui, c'est une petite voiture économique. *Yes, it is an economical small car.*
2. Oui, c'est une jolie petite fille blonde. *Yes, she's a pretty, small blonde (girl).*
3. Oui, c'est un patron bête et méchant. *Yes, he is a stupid, mean boss.*
4. Oui, c'est un gentil professeur patient. *Yes, he is a kind, patient professor.*
5. Oui, c'est une belle robe élégante. *Yes, that is a beautiful, elegant robe.*
6. Oui, c'est un jeune garçon sportif. *Yes, he is an active young boy.*
7. Oui, c'est une date sûre et certaine. *Yes, it's a date for sure.*
8. Oui, c'est un étudiant pauvre et malheureux. *Yes, he is a poor, bad student.*

9. Oui, c'est un gros chien gras. *Yes, he is a big, fat dog.*
10. Oui, c'est un bel acteur riche. *Yes, he is a rich, handsome actor.*

EXERCISE 2-8:

1. Il y a de vieux châteaux en Touraine. *There are some old chateaus in Touraine.*
2. Nous faisons de longues promenades à la plage. *We take long walks on the beach.*
3. Voilà de jolis dessins intéressants. *Here are some pretty and interesting drawings.*
4. Cet homme a de nouvelles théories. *This man has some new theories.*
5. Il a de bonnes idées. *He has some good ideas.*
6. Elle a fait de petites erreurs à son examen. *She has made a few little mistakes on her exam.*
7. Nous avons de jeunes voisines italiennes. *We have some young Italian neighbors.*
8. Notre musée a de beaux tableaux modernes. *Our museum has some beautiful modern paintings.*
9. Il y a de grandes vagues dans l'océan. *There are some large waves in the ocean.*
10. Louise a de vieilles photos de famille. *Louise has some old family photos.*

EXERCISE 2-9:

1. La Suisse est moins grande que le Brésil. *Switzerland is smaller than Brazil.*
2. L'avion est plus rapide que le train. *The plane is faster than the train.*
3. Les femmes sont aussi intelligentes que les hommes. *Women are as intelligent as men.*
4. Un mois est moins court qu'une semaine. *A month is not as short as a week.*
5. La neige est aussi blanche que les nuages. *The snow is as white as the clouds.*
6. La pluie est moins froide que la neige. *Rain is not as cold as snow.*
7. Le thé est aussi chaud que le café. *The tea is as hot as the coffee.*
8. La lune est moins brillante que le soleil. *The moon is not as bright as the sun.*
9. La crème est plus nourrissante que le lait. *Cream is more nourishing than milk.*
10. Un livre est plus lourd qu'une plume. *A book is heavier than a pen.*
11. Février a moins de jours que mai. *February has fewer days than May.*
12. Les bijoux sont plus chers que les fleurs. *Jewelry is more expensive than flowers.*
13. Une photo est plus réaliste qu'un tableau. *A photo is more realistic than a painting.*
14. L'arithmétique est moins difficile que l'algèbre. *Arithmetic is not as difficult as algebra.*
15. La glace est plus solide que l'eau. *Ice is more solid than water.*

EXERCISE 2-10:

1. Le Brésil est le plus grand pays de l'Amérique du Sud. *Brazil is the largest country in South America.*
2. Rhode Island est le moins grand état des Etats-Unis. *Rhode Island is the smallest state in the United States.*
3. La Rolls Royce est la voiture la plus élégante du monde. *The Rolls Royce is the most elegant car in the world.*
4. L'eau est la boisson la moins chère du monde. *Water is the least expensive drink in the world.*
5. Les oeufs sont les ingrédients les plus importants d'une omelette. *Eggs are the most important ingredients in an omelet.*

EXERCISE 2-11:

1. Je pense que le mariage est la meilleure institution. *I think that marriage is the best institution.*
2. C'est une des églises les plus anciennes de la ville. *It is one of the oldest churches in town.*
3. Il dit quelquefois les choses les plus profondes. *He sometimes says the most profound things.*
4. Vous avez la meilleure idée. *You have the best idea.*
5. L'hiver est la saison plus froide. *Winter is the coldest season.*
6. Je vous ai donné la pire raison. *I gave you the worst reason.*
7. Il a mis son plus vieil imperméable. *He put on his oldest raincoat.*
8. Je crois que le professeur est le plus instruit. *I think the professor is the most educated.*

EXERCISE 2-12:

1. facilement	*easily*
2. faussement	*falsely*
3. doucement	*softly*
4. librement	*freely*
5. parfaitement	*perfectly*
6. froidement	*coldly*
7. deuxièmement	*secondly*
8. récemment	*recently*
9. bonnement	*simply*
10. autrement	*otherwise*
11. heureusement	*fortunately*
12. longuement	*at length*
13. prochainement	*soon*
14. seulement	*only*
15. dernièrement	*lately*
16. joliment	*very*
17. sûrement	*definitely*
18. actuellement	*now*

EXERCISE 2-13:

1. Notre professeur est sûrement canadien. *Our professor is definitely Canadian.*
2. Son accent semble perceptiblement différent. *His accent seems perceptibly different.*

3. Ces chocolats sont certainement délicieux. *These chocolates are certainly delicious.*
4. Votre frère a l'air sérieusement malade. *Your brother looks seriously ill.*
5. La banque reste officiellement fermée. *The bank remains officially closed.*
6. Ce billet est décidément faux. *This bill is decidedly counterfeit.*
7. Leurs enfants sont évidemment mal élevés. *Their children are evidently badly brought up.*
8. Le théâtre devient indubitablement incompréhensible. *The theater is becoming undeniably incomprehensible.*
9. Mes classes sont drôlement intéressantes. *My classes are really interesting.*
10. Cet exercice est malheureusement terminé. *This exercise is unfortunately finished.*
11. Ce tableau est suffisamment beau. *This painting is beautiful enough.*
12. Les fleurs sentent bon. *The flowers smell good.*
13. La machine est incommodément en panne. *The machine is inconveniently out-of-order.*
14. La plage devient lentement encombrée. *The beach is slowly becoming crowded.*
15. Maman est definitivement invitée. *Mama was definitely invited.*

EXERCISE 2-14:

1. Nous l'avons souvent vu. *We have often seen him.*
2. J'ai mal dormi la nuit dernière. *I slept badly last night.*
3. Elle s'est levée rapidement. *She got up fast (rapidly).*
4. Il a trop mangé. *He ate too much.*
5. J'ai longtemps habité en France. *I have lived in France a long time.*
6. Je n'ai pas encore fini de travailler. *I have not finished working yet.*
7. Il arrive généralement à l'heure. *He generally arrives on time.*
8. Il a certainement téléphoné. *He certainly did telephone.*
9. Elle me l'apporte à signer immédiatement. *She is bringing it to me to sign immediately.*
10. Malheureusement, il part pour l'étranger. *Unfortunately, he is leaving to go abroad.*
11. C'est vraiment une charmante maison. *It is really a charming house.*
12. Ils ont parlé lentement. *They spoke slowly.*
13. J'ai complètement oublié de le faire. *I completely forgot to do it.*
14. Nous avons justement fini. *We have just now finished.*

EXERCISE 2-15:

1. Il a fait une erreur si évidente. *He made such an obvious mistake.*
2. Une annonce assez importante arrivera par la poste. *A rather important announcement will arrive by mail.*

3. Il répond aux questions les moins difficiles. *He answers the less difficult questions.*

4. Les plus jolies fleurs ne durent pas longtemps. *The prettiest flowers don't last a long time.*

5. C'est un détail trop insignifiant. *It is too insignificant a detail.*

6. Cette excuse peu satisfaisante ne trompe personne. *This unsatisfactory excuse fools no one.*

7. Qui sont ces dames tout habillées en blanc? *Who are these women all dressed in white?*

8. Il a mangé des légumes à peine cuits. *He ate some barely cooked vegetables.*

9. Elle écrit aussi vite en classe. *She writes just as fast in class.*

10. Une coiffure élégante fait bien de l'effet. *An elegant hairdo really makes an impression.*

EXERCISE 2-16:

1. Un adulte parle moins lentement qu'un enfant. *An adult speaks less slowly than a child.*

2. Une lettre arrive moins promptement qu'un télégramme. *A letter doesn't arrive as promptly as a telegram.*

3. Le plastique se casse moins facilement que le cristal. *Plastic breaks less easily than crystal.*

4. La pluie disparaît plus rapidement que la neige. *Rain disappears more rapidly than snow.*

5. Les hommes travaillent aussi diligemment que les femmes. *Men work as diligently as women.*

6. Le rossignol chante aussi mélodieusement que l'alouette. *The nightingale sings as sweetly as the lark.*

7. Le soleil brille plus intensément que la lune. *The sun shines more brightly than the moon.*

8. Un chat chante moins bien qu'un oiseau. *A cat doesn't sing as well as a bird.*

9. Une tortue nage mieux qu'un rhinocéros. *A turtle swims better than a rhinoceros.*

10. Les perles coûtent moins cher que les diamants. *Pearls cost less than diamonds.*

EXERCISE 2-17:

1. Marie est celle qui chante le pire. *Marie is the one who sings the worst.*

2. Vous avez manqué le train. Tant pis! *You have missed the train. Too bad!*

3. Je fais cela mieux que vous. *I do this better than you.*

4. Elle a reussi à son examen. Tant mieux! *She passed her test. Great!*

5. Elle parle pire que son frère. *She speaks worse than her brother.*

EXERCISE 2-18:

1. J'écris peu. *I write little. I don't write much.*

2. J'ai peu de devoirs à l'école. *I have a little homework at school.*

3. Le directeur fait de si beaux cadeaux aux employés. *The manager gives such beautiful gifts to the employees.*

4. Elle a une robe si jolie qu'on l'admire. *She has a dress so pretty that everyone admires it.*

5. Le travail est de plus en plus difficile. *Work is more and more difficult.*

6. Le climat devient de moins en moins agréable. *The climate is becoming less and less agreeable.*

7. Cet employé est plus intelligent que son collègue. *That employee is more intelligent than his colleague.*

8. Le professeur parle davantage. *The professor speaks more.*

9. Elle dèpense beaucoup dans les grands magasins. *She spends a lot in the big stores.*

10. Oui, ce déjeuner est bien bon. *Yes, this lunch is very good.*

EXERCISE 2-19:

1. Oui, je suis à même de le faire tout de suite. *Yes, I am in a position to do it right away.*

2. Oui, il s'habille de même. *Yes, he dresses the same.*

3. Oui, après mon accident, je pourrai marcher tout de même. *Yes, after my accident I'll be able to walk anyway.*

4. Oui, il sera à même de financer son voyage. *Yes, he'll be in a position to pay for his trip.*

5. Oui, nous le prendrons tout de même. *Yes, we'll take it anyway.*

6. Oui, l'air est tout léger après la pluie. *Yes, the air is quite light after the rain.*

7. Oui, le jardin est tout vert. *Yes, the garden is quite green.*

8. Oui, les enfants s'amusent tout gentiment. *Yes, the children are playing very nicely.*

9. Oui, l'artiste a tout fini. *Yes, the artist has finished everything.*

10. Oui, le travail se fait tout facilement. *Yes, the work is done very easily.*

RAISE YOUR GRADES

Adjectives

1. Il a son petit ordinateur japonais. *He has his small Japanese computer.*

2. C'est un médecin intelligent et compétent. *He is an intelligent and competent doctor.*

3. Je vous enverrai une longue lettre intéressante. *I will send you a long, interesting letter.*

4. Nous assistons à de bons matchs professionels. *We attend some good professional matches.*

5. Son frère est un petit commerçant entreprenant. *His (her) brother is a small, enterprising merchant.*
6. Monique n'a pas vu cet horrible accident aérien. *Monique did not see that horrible aerial accident.*
7. Ma mère fait de grands desserts délicieux. *My mother makes some great delicious desserts.*
8. J'habite cet ancien quartier parisien. *I live in this old Paris neighborhood.*
9. Il y a de gros poissons rouges. *There are some big, red fish.*
10. Regardez ses longs cheveux blonds! *Look at his (her) long, blond hair!*
11. Attention aux chiens féroces et méchants! *Beware of evil, ferocious dogs!*
12. Je connais ce bel acteur comique. *I know this handsome comic actor.*

13. N'achetez pas ces verres chers et fragiles. *Don't buy those expensive, fragile glasses.*
14. Robert conduit une vieille auto anglaise. *Robert drives an old English car.*
15. C'est un gentil petit garçon. *He is a nice little boy.*
16. Mon père connaît un ancien acteur célèbre. *My father knows a former well-known actor.*
17. Il arrive seul dans sa propre voiture sale. *He arrives alone in his own dirty car.*
18. Il est riche, mais c'est un pauvre artiste amateur. *He is rich, but he's a lousy amateur artist.*
19. Solange élève de beaux chevaux arabes. *Solange raises beautiful Arabian horses.*

Adverbs

20. Paul court joyeusement dans la rue. *Paul runs happily in the street.*
21. Diane écoute attentivement son professeur. *Diane listens attentively to her professor.*
22. Elles parlent distinctement au téléphone. *They speak distinctly on the telephone.*
23. Nous verrons probablement ce film. *We will probably see this movie.*
24. Il faut répondre poliment. *You must answer politely.*
25. Les enfants apprennent facilement les langues. *Children learn languages easily.*
26. Elle danse mieux après quelques leçons. *She dances well after several lessons.*
27. Ces nouveaux avions traversent vite l'océan. *These new airplanes cross the ocean fast.*
28. Ce critique attaque cruellement les acteurs. *The critic cruelly attacks the actors.*
29. Je pense sérieusement à votre suggestion. *I am thinking seriously about your suggestion.*
30. Monique parle couramment quatre langues. *Monique speaks four languages fluently.*

31. Les ouvriers confrontent franchement leurs employeurs. *The workers confronted their employers frankly.*
32. Nous ouvrirons présentement la discussion. *We will open the discussion presently.*
33. Je le ferais différemment. *I would do it differently.*
34. Nous partons immédiatement pour l'école. *We immediately left for school.*
35. Ils répondent follement sans réflection. *They answered foolishly without thinking.*
36. Il ne faut pas signer aveuglément ce contrat. *You must not sign this contract blindly.*
37. Les diplomates discutent intelligemment la situation. *The diplomats are discussing the situation intelligently.*
38. Il leur demande gentiment de s'asseoir. *He asks them nicely to be seated.*
39. Mes parents travaillent énormement en ce moment. *My parents are working outrageously at this moment.*

3 POSSESSIVES, DEMONSTRATIVES, AND NUMBERS

3-1. Possessive Adjectives

In French the possessive adjective must agree in number and gender with the thing possessed—not with the possessor.

son père	may be either *his father* or *her father*
sa soeur	may be either *his sister* or *her sister*
ses livres	may be either *his books* or *her books*

BUT a possessive adjective agrees in person with the possessor, even though it does not show the possessor's gender.

A. Forms of the possessive adjective

Study the following chart of possessive adjectives.

	Number			
	Singular		Plural	
Person	Masc.	Fem.	Masc. and Fem.	
1st–s	**mon**	**ma**	**mes**	*my*
2nd–s	**ton**	**ta**	**tes**	*your* (familiar)
3rd–s	**son**	**sa**	**ses**	*his, her, its*
1st–pl	**notre**	**notre**	**nos**	*our*
2nd–pl	**votre**	**votre**	**vos**	*your* (formal)
3rd–pl	**leur**	**leur**	**leurs**	*their*

> **REMEMBER:** The masculine and feminine plural possessive adjectives are the same.

Jeanne est **ma** soeur.	*Jeanne is my sister.*
Voilà **ton** sac.	*Here is your purse.*
Où sont **vos** livres?	*Where are your books?*
J'habite dans **leur** maison.	*I live in their house.*
Elle joue avec **leurs** enfants.	*She plays with their children.*

B. Use of the possessive adjective

1. You must use a possessive adjective that agrees in gender and number with the object possessed and in person with the possessor.

C'est **le chien de Marie**.	*It is Marie's dog.*
C'est **son** chien.	*It is her dog.*

C'est **la maison de Paul.**	*It is Paul's house.*
C'est **sa** maison.	*It is his house.*
Jeanne et Marc son **tes amis de Michael.**	*Jeanne and Marc are Michael's friends.*
Ce sont **ses amis.**	*They are his friends.*

2. Use **mon, ton,** or **son** before a noun or an adjective that begins with a vowel or a mute h, regardless of the gender of the noun. Use **ma, ta, sa** before a feminine noun beginning with a pronounced consonant.

Joan est **mon** amie.	*Joan is my friend.*
J'approuve **ton** admirable décision.	*I approve of your admirable decision.*
As-tu entendu **sa** chanson?	*Did you hear his song?*
Allons voir **ma** soeur.	*Let's go see my sister.*

3. Translate **son, sa,** and **ses** according to *who* or *what* is mentioned earlier in the sentence or paragraph—not according to the grammatical gender of the noun.

| Je pense que **nous** savons **notre** français. | *I think that we know our French.* |

The subject of the sentence (**nous**) is in the first person, so you must use a possessive adjective in the first person. And the noun modified by the possessive adjective (**français**) is masculine and singular, so you must use a possessive adjective that agrees in gender and number with the noun. The proper choice is **notre.**

| Chaque **système** a **ses** avantages. | *Each system has its advantages.* |

The subject (**système**) is in the third person, and the modified noun (**avantages**) is masculine plural—so the choice of a possessive adjective should be pretty easy—**ses.** To make it even easier, remember that there is no special feminine form before a noun that begins with a vowel.

| Je connais **Pierre et Gérald.** | *I know Pierre and Gerald.* |
| **Leur** mère est française. | *Their mother is French.* |

The possessive adjective refers back to **Pierre et Gérald** (third person), so it must be in the third person. The modified noun (**mère**) is third-person singular, so you must use a possessive adjective in the third-person singular (**leur**—not leurs).

> *REMEMBER:* The plural form **ses** does *not* mean *their*—it is the form of *his, her,* or *its* that you use before a plural noun. It may help if you remember that the French word for *their*— **leur**—alo ends in **r.**

4. You must use a possessive adjective before each noun in a compound subject or in a series.

| **Mes** frères et **mes** soeurs habitent à Chicago. | *My bothers and sisters live in Chicago.* |
| Donnez-moi **mon** livre, **mon** crayon et **mes** cahiers. | *Give me my books, pencil, and notebooks.* |

5. Always use a singular noun and a singular possessive adjective if each person in a group has just one of something—even though in the correct English translation, you'll use a plural noun.

| Ils lèvent **leur verre.** | *They raise their glasses.* |
| Ils ont **leur livre** sous **le bras.** | *They have their books under their arms.* |

BUT use the plural form of both the noun and the possessive adjective if each person has more than one of something.

| Ils prennent **leurs** repas au restaurant. | *They have their meals at the restaurant.* |
| Vous prêtez **vos** skis à **vos** amies. | *You lend your skis to your friends.* |

EXERCISE 3-1: Fill in the blank with the correct form of the possessive adjective. First you will have to decide if the noun is masculine or feminine, and if it is singular or plural. Then you

can choose the possessive adjective from the column in the chart that agrees in person with the possessor. Answers and translations are at the end of the chapter.

1. Il a _____ instructions dans l'enveloppe.
2. Ils ont _____ stéréo dans l'appartement.
3. Elle porte _____ bracelet au bras gauche.
4. Elles ont _____ photos dans l'album.
5. Nous avons l'examen avant _____ vacances.
6. Tu as un rendez-vous après _____ classe.
7. J'ai _____ machine à écrire au bureau.
8. Il a _____ clé dans le tiroir.
9. Vous avez _____ garage derrière la maison.
10. Georges a _____ raquette et _____ balles.

3-2. Possessive Pronouns

A possessive pronoun refers to a previously mentioned noun and must agree in gender and number with that noun. Like the possessive adjective, the possessive pronoun must agree in person with the possessor—even though, also like the possessive adjective, it does not show the gender of the possessor.

A. Forms of the possessive pronoun

A possessive pronoun is made up of a definite article—**le**, **la**, or **les**—and a derivative form of a possessive adjective. Study the following chart and examples of the use of the possessive pronoun.

Person of the Possessor		POSSESSIVE PRONOUNS				
		Masc–s	Fem–s	Masc–pl	Fem–pl	
1st–s	je	le mien	la mienne	les miens	les miennes	*mine*
2nd–s	tu	le tien	la tienne	les tiens	les tiennes	*yours*
3rd–s	il, elle	le sien	la sienne	les siens	les siennes	*his, hers*
1st–pl	nous	le nôtre	la nôtre	les nôtres	les nôtres	*ours*
2nd–pl	vous	le vôtre	la vôtre	les vôtres	les vôtres	*yours*
3rd–pl	ils, elles	le leur	la leur	les leurs	les leurs	*theirs*

NOTE: Unlike the possessive adjectives—notre(s) and votre(s)—the possessive pronouns in the third person have a circumflex over the ô—le nôtre, les nôtres, le vôtre, les vôtres.

1. Il a son billet et j'espère que tu as **le tien**.
He has his ticket and I hope that you have yours.

2. Ils vont de leur maison à **la nôtre**.
They are going from their house to ours.

3. Ma veste? Je n'en changerais pas la mienne contre **la vôtre**.
My jacket? I wouldn't change mine for yours.

4. Tes notes sont moins bonnes que **les miennes**.
Your grades aren't as good as mine.

5. Ils pourront garder **les leurs** la prochaine fois.
They can keep theirs the next time.

6. Leur porte? J'aime **la leur**.
Their door? I like theirs.

7. Voici ma place. Voilà **la vôtre**.
Here is my seat. There is yours.

8. Votre pays est grand. **Le nôtre** est petit.
Your country is big. Ours is small.

9. Lequel préférez-vous? **Le mien** ou **le sien**?
Which do you prefer? Mine or his?

REMEMBER: The possessive adjective part of the possessive pronoun must agree in person with the possessor and in gender and number with the object possessed. The following chart will help you keep this straight!

		one possessor only			several possessors	
		masc	**fem**		**masc + fem**	
only one object possessed	1st	**mien**	**mienne**	*mine*	**nôtre**	*ours*
	2nd	**tien**	**tienne**	*yours* (fam)		
		vôtre	**vôtre**	*yours* (form)	**vôtre**	*yours*
	3rd	**sien**	**sienne**	*his, hers*	**leur**	*his, hers*
several objects possessed	1st	**miens**	**miennes**	*mine*	**nôtres**	*ours*
	2nd	**tiens**	**tiennes**	*yours* (fam)		
		vôtres	**vôtres**	*yours* (form)	**vôtres**	*yours*
	3rd	**siens**	**siennes**	*his, hers*	**leurs**	*theirs*

Now let's refer to the preceding numbered examples and examine more closely the agreement between both parts of the possessive pronoun and the previously mentioned noun. To choose the correct possessive pronoun, you must know the number and gender of the noun possessed and the person of the possessor. Notice that the possessor is not always the subject of the sentence.

						possessive pronoun	
sentence	possessor	person	object possessed	number	gender	definite article	possessive adjective
1	tu	2nd–s	billet	s	masc	le	tien
2	(nous)	1st–pl	maison	s	fem	la	nôtre
3	je	1st–s	veste	s	fem	la	mienne
	(vous)	2nd–pl	veste	s	fem	la	vôtre
4	(je)	1st–s	notes	pl	fem	les	miennes
5	ils	3rd–pl	?	pl	?	les	leurs
6	(ils)	3rd–pl	porte	s	fem	la	leur
7	(vous)	3rd–s	place	s	fem	la	vôtre
8	(nous)	1st–pl	pays	s	masc	le	mien
9	(je)	1st–s	lequel	s	masc	le	mien
	(il)	3rd–s	lequel	s	masc	le	sien

REMEMBER: The definite article part of the possessive pronoun must agree in number and gender with the object possessed. The possessive adjective part must also agree in gender and number with the object possessed—but also in person with the possessor.

Voici **mon** livre.

livre is the object possessed
mon is the possessive adjective
agrees in number and gender with the object possessed
agrees in person with the possessor—**je**

Voilà **le tien**.

le tien is the possessive pronoun
le is the definite article part
agrees in number and gender with the object possessed

> **tien** is the possessive adjective part
> > agrees in number and
> > > gender with the object
> > > possessed
> > agrees in person with the
> > > possessor—**tu**

B. Contractions of the possessive pronoun with à or de

When the articles **le** and **les** of the possessive pronoun immediately follow the preposition **à**, form the contractions **au** and **aux**. The articles **le** and **les** immediately after **de** form **du** and **des**.

Occupez-vous de vos affaires et je m'occuperai **des miennes**.	*Take care of your business and I'll take care of mine.*
Ils obéissent à leurs parents et nous obéissons **aux nôtres**.	*They obey their parents and we obey ours.*

EXERCISE 3-2: Indicate the number and gender of the noun phrase given in parentheses and the person of the possessor in the blanks following the sentences. Then substitute the correct possessive pronoun for the phrase in parentheses. Remember that the possessor is not always the subject of the sentence. Be sure to form contractions if the preposition **à** or **de** precedes a definite article. Answers and translations are at the end of the chapter.

Example: Tu préfères venir à (mon appartement).   ___s___ ___m___ ___1st s___
Tu préfères venir *au mien*.

	number	gender	person of possessor
1. Il a (mon portefeuille) aussi. Il a _____ aussi.	_____	_____	_____
2. Ce sont (tes gants). Ce sont _____.	_____	_____	_____
3. Ils proposeront (ma candidature). Ils proposeront _____.	_____	_____	_____
4. (Nos lois) sont justes. _____ sont justes.	_____	_____	_____
5. Vous aimez conduire (leur voiture). Vous aimez conduire _____.	_____	_____	_____
6. Paul prépare (son examen). Paul prépare _____.	_____	_____	_____
7. Marie a reçu (son diplôme). Marie a reçu _____.	_____	_____	_____
8. Chaque pays a (son charme). Chaque pays a _____	_____	_____	_____
9. Tu aimerais que je te parle de (mes projets). Tu aimerais que je te parle de _____.	_____	_____	_____
10. Chacun a (ses propres raisons). Chacun a _____.	_____	_____	_____

3-3. Demonstrative Adjectives

A demonstrative adjective introduces a noun and functions much as a definite article does. But the demonstrative adjective points out definitely which noun is being referred to—almost as if the speaker were using a finger to point at the noun. The demonstrative adjective must always modify a noun—it can never stand alone.

You can translate a demonstrative adjective as either *this* or *that* in the singular, and either *these* or *those* in the plural.

A. Forms of the demonstrative adjective

There are four forms of the demonstrative adjective—**ce**, **cet**, **cette**, and **ces**.

	singular		plural	
masc	**ce** garçon	*this, that boy*		
	cet avion	*this, that plane*	**ces** étudiantes	*these, those students*
fem	**cette** fille	*this, that girl*		
	cette étudiante	*this, that student*		

> **REMEMBER:** There is only one form of the demonstrative adjective in the plural—**ces**.

Ce sénateur a des aspirations à la Présidence.	*This (that) senator has presidential aspirations.*
Je passe toujours devant **cette** même maison.	*I always pass by this (that) same house.*
Ces exemples constituent une liste complète.	*These (those) examples constitute a complete list.*

> **NOTE:** Use **cet** before a singular masculine noun that begins with a vowel or mute h, and before an adjective that begins with a vowel that precedes a singular masculine noun.

Cet homme est mon père.	*This (that) man is my father.*
Cet autre homme est mon oncle.	*This (that) other man is my uncle.*

EXERCISE 3-3: Fill in the blank with the correct form of the demonstrative adjective. Answers and translations are at the end of the chapter.

1. _____ exercise est très facile.
2. _____ garçon arrive toujours en retard.
3. Sur _____ page on explique les démonstratifs.
4. _____ homme défend son honneur.
5. _____ autre chemin est plus court.
6. _____ faits sont importants.
7. _____ qualités sont essentielles.
8. _____ autres étudiants sont présents.
9. _____ automobile est dans le garage.
10. _____ amies arrivent ce soir.

B. Addition of -ci and -là

1. Add the adverb **-ci**, *here*, to a noun modified by a demonstrative adjective if you want to indicate that the person or object is *close to you* (the speaker).

2. Add the adverb **-là**, *there*, to a noun modified by a demonstrative adjective if you want to indicate that the person or object is *at a distance from you* (the speaker).

cet officier-**ci**	*this officer*	cette année-**ci**	*this year*	ces exemples-**ci**	*these examples*
cet officier-**là**	*that officer*	cette année-**là**	*that year*	ces exemples-**là**	*those examples*

EXERCISE 3-4: Replace the possessive adjectives in the sentences with demonstrative adjectives, using the adverbs **-ci** and **-là** as appropriate. Answers and translations are at the end of the chapter.

Example:	Ma photo est belle, mais votre photo est laide.	*My picture is pretty but your picture is ugly.*
	Cette photo-ci est belle, mais cette photo-là est laide.	*This picture is pretty but that picture is ugly.*

1. Mon exercice est facile, mais votre exercice est difficile.

2. Notre champagne est bon, mais leur champagne est mauvais.
3. Vos idées sont justes, mais mes idées sont fausses.
4. Sa phrase est longue, mais ma phrase est courte.
5. Votre hôtel est loin d'ici, mais mon hôtel est à côté.

3-4. Demonstrative Pronouns

A demonstrative pronoun takes the place of a noun and functions as a noun. There are two types of demonstrative pronouns—variable demonstrative pronouns which show gender and number; and neuter demonstrative pronouns which do not show gender and number.

A. Forms of the variable demonstrative pronoun

A variable demonstrative pronoun must agree in number and gender with the noun it replaces. Study carefully the following table of variable demonstrative pronouns:

M–sing	**celui**	*the one* *this one* *that one*	M–pl	**ceux**	*the ones* *these* *those*
F–sing	**celle**	*the one* *this one* *that one*	F–pl	**celles**	*the ones* *these* *those*

B. Use of the variable demonstrative pronoun

A variable demonstrative pronoun never stands alone—it is always followed by a prepositional phrase, or a relative clause beginning with **que** or **qui**, or the adverb **-ci** or **-là**.

1. A variable demonstrative pronoun followed by a prepositional phrase:

Ces photos et **celle de ma fille** ont été vendues.
These pictures and the one (picture) of my daughter were sold.

Celui à droite est crochu.
The one on the right is crooked.

Ceux de mes vêtements que j'ai apportés sont nouveaux.
(Those of) my clothes that I brought are new.

2. A variable demonstrative pronoun followed by a relative clause beginning with **que** or **qui**:

Je donnerai deux mille francs à **celui qui aura la solution.**
I'll give two thousand francs to the one who has the answer.

Nos disques sont **ceux que le voleur a pris.**
Our records are the ones that the thief took.

Ceux que tu voulais remercier sont déjà partis.
Those whom you wanted to thank have already gone.

3. You may add **-ci** or **-là** to a variable demonstrative pronoun:

- Add **-ci** to a demonstrative pronoun to indicate that the person or object is *close to the speaker*. Translate the **demonstrative pronoun** plus **-ci** as *this one* or *these*.
- Add **-là** to a demonstrative pronoun to indicate that the person or object is *at a distance from the speaker*. Translate the **demonstrative pronoun** plus **-là** as *that one* or *those*.

J'aime mieux **celui-ci.**
I like this one better.

Celles-ci sont des violettes.
These are violets.

Je préfère **ceux-ci** à **celles-là.**
I prefer these to those.

Nous te donnons **celle-là.**
We're giving you that one.

> *NOTE:* A variable demonstrative pronoun sometimes means *the former* or *the latter*. When two nouns are mentioned, *the former* is the first noun—translate it as **celui-là, celles-là,** etc. *The latter* is the second noun mentioned—translate it as **celle-ci, ceux-ci,** etc.

Il écrit des romans d'amour et de la poésie; **ceux-là** ont plus succès que **celle-ci.**
He writes romances and poetry; the former are more successful than the latter.

EXERCISE 3-5: Replace the noun phrase given in parentheses with the appropriate form of the variable demonstrative pronoun. Then translate the sentence with the variable demonstrative pronoun. Answers and translations are at the end of the chapter.

Example:	Rendez-moi (la clé) que vous avez empruntée.	*Give me back the key that you borrowed.*
	Rendez-moi celle que vous avez empruntée.	*Give me back the one that you borrowed.*

1. Qui t'a suggéré (cette coiffure)?

2. Regarde (ce beau costume) que j'ai.

3. (Ces erreurs-ci) sont impardonnables.

4. (Ce train) part à 6 heures et (l'autre) part à minuit.

5. Apportez-moi (cet article) que vous m'avez promis.

6. Qui aurait pensé qu'elle se serait mariée avec (cet homme)?

7. (Ces montagnes) sont les plus hautes de l'Europe.

8. (Ce pain) pour les oiseaux n'est plus bon à manger.

9. Françoise lira (cette phrase) et elle pensera à moi.

10. (Cet exercice-ci) illustrent le même point grammatical.

C. Forms of the neuter demonstrative pronoun

A neuter demonstrative pronoun does not have gender or number, so it cannot show agreement in gender or number with the noun it replaces. Study the following neuter demonstrative pronouns.

ceci	*this, it*
cela (ça)	*that, it*
ce	*he, she, it, this, that, these, those*

> *NOTE:* Use **ça**—a contraction of **cela**—informally in spoken French, or to emphasize an exclamation.

Je n'ai jamais vu **ça**.	*I've never seen anything like that.*
Comment **ça** va, toi?	*How's it going?*
Ça, c'est formidable!	*That's wonderful!*

D. Use of the neuter demonstrative pronoun

Neuter demonstrative pronouns usually refer to events, ideas, or indefinite concepts. The neuter demonstrative pronoun always stands alone—that is, it doesn't need another noun or phrase to complete it.

> *REMEMBER:* Variable demonstrative pronouns—**celui, ceux, celle(s)**—never stand alone. Neuter demonstrative pronouns—**ceci, cela (ça), ce**—always stand alone.

1. Use **ceci** or **cela** as the subject or object of any verb but **être**, *to be*. Also use **ceci** or **cela** if you want to point out something that has not been previously mentioned.

> *NOTE:* **Ceci** usually refers to something near, and **cela** to something far away; but this is not always so—you may use **cela** in either case, unless you are drawing a contrast.

Ceci me rend fou.	*This is driving me crazy.*
Cela n'a aucune espèce d'importance.	*That has no importance whatsoever.*
As-tu vraiment fait **cela**?	*Did you really do that?*
Probablement, à cause de **ceci**, vous gagnerez.	*Because of this, you will probably win.*

2. You must use **ce** to mean *he*, *she*, or *it* when the subject noun phrase follows the verb **être**. **Ce** does not replace the noun phrase, but merely occupies the empty subject position—so, **ce** has no gender or number.

Ce sont Paul et Louise.	*It's Paul and Louise.*
	(They are Paul and Louise.)
C'est mon meilleur ami.	*He's my best friend.*
C'étaient des arbres énormes.	*They were enormous trees.*

> **REMEMBER:** When a word referring to nationality, religion, or profession follows **être**, that word functions as an adjective and you must use an appropriate subject pronoun—**il**, **ils**, **elle**, or **elles**.

Elle est médecin.	*She's a doctor.*
Il est juif.	*He is Jewish.*
Ils sont péruviens.	*They are Peruvian.*

> BUT when such a word is modified and forms a noun phrase which functions as the subject of the sentence, you must use **ce**.

Ce sont **des mécaniciens experts**.	*They are expert mechanics.*
C'est mon avocate.	*She's my lawyer.*

EXERCISE 3-6: Replace the phrase given in parentheses with the appropriate neuter demonstrative pronoun. Then translate the sentence. Answers and translations are at the end of the chapter.

Example:	Il déteste (manger en plein air).	*He hates eating outdoors.*
	Il déteste *cela*.	*He hates that.*

1. Je sais (que ce sera ta dernière visite).

2. (Le fait qu'il a 98 ans) est très impressionant.

3. (Ce que tu viens de dire) est vrai.

4. Elle lui donne (tout ce qu'elle a).

5. (Leur devoir) est dû demain.

6. (Voir quelqu'un souffrir) me rend triste.

7. (Qu'elle habite si loin de la ville) était inimaginable.

8. (Laurent et Simon) sont des Français typiques.

9. (Cet homme) est un grand ministre.

10. J'attends (ton retour en France).

11. (La Russie) est le plus grand pays du monde.

12. Il n'avait pas compris (le fait que c'était trop tard).

13. (Passer une nuit paisible) était mon seul espoir.

14. (Le capitalisme) est un système économique.

15. (Cette déclaration récente) a choqué beaucoup de gens.

EXERCISE 3-7: Answer the following questions incorporating the suggestions given in parentheses and using either **ceci** or **cela**. Answers and translations are at the end of the chapter.

1. Qu'est-ce qui vous arrive en courant trop vite? (je tombe)
2. Est-ce que ceci vous plaît? (non)
3. Tout va bien? (très bien)

4. Que pensez-vous de cela? (c'est ridicule)

5. Est-ce que ça vous rappelle quelque chose? (oui, beaucoup)

EXERCISE 3-8: Translate the following sentences into French using either **il, elle est** or **c'est**. Answers are at the end of the chapter.

1. It's a book.

2. He is French.

3. She is a tall American.

4. She is a doctor.

5. He is a secretary.

6. He is an excellent professor.

7. It's a beautiful city.

8. She is a good friend.

9. They are young.

10. They are old citizens.

EXERCISE 3-9: Translate the following sentences into French using a neuter demonstrative pronoun. Answers are at the end of the chapter.

1. It is too heavy.

2. It must be interesting.

3. It will be expensive.

4. Is it for me that you said that?

5. It will be up to him to come.

3-5. Numbers

There are two types of numbers—*cardinal numbers*, which you can also use as nouns or pronouns, and *ordinal numbers*.

A. Cardinal numbers

1. Cardinal numbers are the numbers you use for counting. They have no gender—except for **une/une**, *one*, which must agree in gender with the noun it modifies. Study the following list of cardinal numbers.

1	un/une	17	dix-sept	61	soixante et un
2	deux	18	dix-huit	62	soixante-deux
3	trois	19	dix-neuf	70	soixante-dix
4	quatre	20	vingt	71	soixante et onze
5	cinq	21	vingt et un	72	soixante-douze
6	six	22	vingt-deux	80	quatre-vingts
7	sept	30	trente	81	quatre-vingt-un
8	huit	31	trente et un	90	quatre-vingt-dix
9	neuf	32	trente-deux	91	quatre-vingt-onze
10	dix	40	quarante	92	quatre-vingt-douze
11	onze	41	quarante et un	100	cent
12	douze	42	quarante-deux	101	cent un
13	treize	50	cinquante	200	deux cents
14	quatorze	51	cinquante et un	1.000	mille
15	quinze	52	cinquante-deux	2.000	deux mille
16	seize	61	soixante		

2. You'll need to remember these special uses and spellings of cardinal numbers.

- Replace the hyphen with **et**, *and*, in **vingt et un**, **trente et un**, **quarante et un**, **cinquante et un**, **soixante et un**, and **soixante et onze**.
- Drop the final -s of both **quatre vingts** and **cents** when they precede another number.

  quatre-vingt-dix   *90*   **deux cents**   *200*   **deux cent quatre**   *204*
- Spell **mille** the same in both the plural and the singular.

  | 1.000 | **mille** | *1,000* | *one thousand* |
  | 2.000 | **deux mille** | *2,000* | *two thousand* |

- In French, use a period to separate numbers by thousands—where we use a comma.

French	American
2.358	*2,358*
3.250	*3,250*
98.734	*98,734*

- In French, use a comma to separate a full integer from a decimal—where we use a decimal point.

French		American	
7,8	**sept virgule huit**	7.8	*three point eight*
5,9	**cinq virgule neuf**	5.9	*five point nine*

- **Million** is a noun which can be preceded by **un** and followed by **de**.

  Un million de francs n'est pas une fortune.   *A (one) million francs is not a fortune.*

  BUT never put **un** in front of **cent** or **mille**.

  Elle a **cent** ans et **mille** souvenirs.   *She's a (one) hundred years old and has a thousand memories.*

EXERCISE 3-10:   Complete each sentence with the correct French number, completely spelled out. **Font** means *make*—as in **six et six font douze**, *six and six make twelve*. **Fois** means *times*, so you should multiply. Answers and translations are at the end of the chapter.

1. Quarante et vingt font _____.
2. Il y a _____ jours dans une année.
3. Trois fois quatre font _____.
4. Sept et dix font _____.
5. Il y a _____ ou _____ jours dans un mois.
6. Il y a _____ états aux Etats-Unis.
7. Soixante et onze moins trois font _____.
8. Il y a _____ lettres dans l'alphabet.
9. Cent moins un font _____.
10. Cet exercice a _____ phrases.

B. Ordinal numbers

1. To form French ordinal numbers, you simply add **-ième** to the cardinal numbers—except for **premier** and **second**. If a cardinal number ends in **-e**, drop the **-e**. Study the following list of ordinal numbers.

1ᵉ	**premier, première**	*1st*	*first*
2ᵉ	**second(e)** OR **deuxième**	*2nd*	*second*
3ᵉ	**troisième**	*3rd*	*third*
4ᵉ	**quatrième**	*4th*	*fourth*
5ᵉ	**cinquième**	*5th*	*fifth*
6ᵉ	**sixième**	*6th*	*sixth*
	le dernier, la dernière		*the last*

2. An ordinal number is an adjective that must agree in gender and number—singular or plural—with the noun it modifies.

Mes **premières impressions** sont
   bonnes.
                My first impressions are good
                (ones).

Mon **sixième enfant** est **le dernier**!
       My sixth child is the last (one)!

3. **Le premier** means *the first of the month*. Indicate all other dates with cardinal numbers plus the definite article **le**—**le deux**, **le trente et un**. You don't need a preposition before the date.

Je suis né **le premier octobre**.
      I was born (on) the first of October.

Ma soeur est née **le cinq mai**.
      My sister was born (on) the fifth of May.

> *NOTE:* **Premier** also means *the first* in a succession,
> such as **Napoléon Premier**, *Napoléon I*. His successors
> would be **Napoléon Deux**, **Napoléon Trois**, and so on.

4. When you use an ordinal number as a fraction, the ordinal number becomes a noun that requires a modifying adjective. There are a few special forms.

un/une demi(e) OR **la moitié**   *one-half*

un tiers   *one-third*

un quart   *one-fourth*

BUT most follow the pattern:

un cinquième   *one-fifth*

cinq sixièmes   *five-sixths*

Le franc a perdu **un huitième** de sa
   valeur.
      The franc has lost an eighth of
      its value.

La moitié de la classe parle espagnol.
      Half of the class speak Spanish.

EXERCISE 3-11: Complete each sentence with the correct ordinal number. Answers and translations are at the end of the chapter.

1. C'est la _____ phrase de cet exercise.
2. Elle est dans le _____ chapitre.
3. Juin est le _____ mois de l'année.
4. La lettre *z* est la _____ lettre de l'alphabet.
5. Voici la _____ phrase de cet exercise.
6. Cinquante pour-cent représente la _____ du total.
7. Le premier étage français est le _____ étage américain.
8. La nouvelle année commence le _____ janvier.
9. Quinze minutes représentent un _____ d'heure.
10. Et voilà la _____ phrase de cet exercise.

C. Time

1. French uses a form of the verb **être**—**il est**—in expressions of time.

Quelle heure **est-il**?
      What time is it?

Il est trois heures quarante-cinq.
      It's three forty-five.

Il est une heure cinq.
      It's five minutes past one.

2. There are also some idiomatic expressions you can use in telling time.

- To tell time by *quarter-hour intervals*, add **et** and the interval.

Il est cinq heures **et quart (demie)**.
      It's a quarter past five (half-past).

- To tell the number of *minutes before the hour*, add **moins** and the number of minutes or the quarter-hour interval.

Il est onze heures **moins vingt-cinq**
   (dix, le quart).
      It's twenty-five (ten, a quarter) to
      eleven.

- Use **midi** for *noon* and **minuit** for *midnight*.

Il est **midi** et demi.
      It's twelve-thirty P.M.
      OR *It's half-past noon.*

Il est **minuit** et quart.   *It's a quarter after midnight.*
                              OR *It's twelve-fifteen* A.M.

- The French often use the twenty-four hour clock to avoid confusion between morning and afternoon hours.

La pièce commence à **20 heures**.   *The play begins at 8:00* P.M.

EXERCISE 3-12: Rewrite the following sentences, replacing the numbers by completely spelled–out words. Use an idiomatic expression wherever possible. Answers and translations are at the end of the chapter.

1. Je me réveille à 5 h 45.
2. Je me lève à 6 h 00.
3. Je déjeune à 6 h 30.
4. Mon bureau ouvre à 7 h 15.
5. Je vois le premier client à 7 h 20.
6. A 11 h 00, je commence à avoir faim.
7. Je sors du bureau à 12 h 00.
8. Je reviens à 12 h 55.
9. Mon dernier client a rendez-vous à 14 h 20. .
10. Je suis prêt à partir à 15 h 05.

SUMMARY

1. The possessive adjective must agree in number with the thing possessed and in person with the possessor.
2. **Ma, ta,** and **sa** introduce feminine nouns beginning with a pronounced consonant.
3. **Son, sa,** and **ses** are used according to who or what is mentioned earlier in the sentence or paragraph.
4. A possessive pronoun consists of a definite article and a derivative form of a possessive adjective.
5. A demonstrative adjective points out definitely which noun is being referred to. The demonstrative adjective never stands alone.
6. A variable demonstrative pronoun must agree in number and gender with the noun it replaces; and it must be followed by a prepositional phrase, a relative clause beginning with **que** or **qui,** or the adverb **-ci** or **-là**—it never stands alone.
7. The neuter demonstrative pronoun usually refers to events, ideas, or indefinite concepts. It does not need another noun or phrase to complete it—it always stands alone.
8. **C'est** and **ce sont** must be used instead of **il, elle est** or **ils, elles sont** when the sentence subject comes after the verb.

RAISE YOUR GRADES

Possessive and demonstrative adjectives

Change the object noun phrases given in parentheses from plural to singular. Answers and translations are at the end of the chapter.

Example: Personne ne choisirait   *Nobody would choose those*
            (ces couleurs voyantes).   *(these) loud colors.*

            Personne ne choisirait   *Nobody would chose this*
            cette couleur voyante.   *(that) loud color.*

1. Nous comptions voir (nos autres amis) en Italie.
2. Combien coûtent (ces belles nappes) en lin?
3. Elle a montré (ses diplômes) à tout le monde.
4. Mes parents garent (leurs voitures) derrière la maison.
5. J'aimerais visiter (ces villes).

6. Penses-tu inviter (ces autres étudiants)?
7. Ne lui raconte pas (tes rêves)!
8. Il faut vous occuper de (vos clients).
9. Je n'ai pas oublié (mes anciens camarades).
10. Arrêtez (ces hommes-là)!

Possessive and demonstrative pronouns

Replace the noun phrases given in parentheses with the appropriate possessive or demonstrative pronouns. Answers and translations are at the end of the chapter.

Example:	Il voudrait assister à (cette conférence-là).	*He would like to attend that lecture.*
	Il voudrait assister à celle-là.	*He would like to attend that one.*

11. Moi aussi, j'aime (ma petite soeur).
12. (Ton idée) était meilleure.
13. (Ce grand morceau) à droite me convient tout à fait.
14. Nous irons à (leur mariage).
15. Qui est (ce bel homme-là)?
16. Marie ferait n'importe quoi pour (ses parents).
17. Je crois que je prendrai (cette robe-ci) et (cette autre robe).
18. Ils sont entrés par (la porte) du milieu.
19. Il a les (deux jambes) cassées.
20. (Ce portrait) que tu admirais a été vendu.
21. Qu'est-ce que tu penses de (mon projet)?
22. (Ce garage) à côté et (ce garage) au coin de la rue sont chers.
23. (Le premier) est faux et (le second) est exagéré.
24. Si vous nous aidez avec (nos valises) nous vous aiderons avec (vos valises) la prochaine fois.
25. (Les gens) qui pensent aux autres sont prévenants.

CHAPTER ANSWERS

EXERCISE 3-1:

1. Il a ses instructions dans l'enveloppe. *He has his instructions in the envelope.*
2. Ils ont leur stéréo dans l'appartement. *They have their stereo in the apartment.*
3. Elle porte son bracelet au bras gauche. *She has her bracelet on her left arm.*
4. Elles ont leurs photos dans l'album. *They have their photos in the album.*
5. Nous avons l'examen avant nos vacances. *We have the test before our vacation.*
6. Tu as un rendez-vous après ta classe. *You have a meeting after your class.*
7. J'ai ma machine à écrire au bureau. *I have my typewriter at the office.*
8. Il a sa clé dans le tiroir. *He has his key in the drawer.*
9. Vous avez votre garage derrière la maison. *You have your garage behind the house.*
10. Georges a sa raquette et ses balles. *Georges has his racquets and his balls.*

EXERCISE 3-2:

1. s, masc, 1st	Il a le mien aussi.	*He has mine too.*
2. pl, masc, 2nd	Ce sont les tiens.	*These are yours.*
3. s, fem, 1st	Ils proposeront la mienne.	*They will propose mine.*
4. pl, fem, 1st	Les nôtres sont justes.	*Ours are fair.*
5. s, fem, 3rd	Vous aimez conduire la leur.	*You like to drive theirs.*
6. s, masc, 3rd	Paul prépare le sien.	*Paul prepares his.*
7. s, masc, 3rd	Marie a reçu le sien.	*Marie received hers.*
8. s, masc, 3rd	Chaque pays a le sien.	*Each country has its (own).*
9. pl, masc, 1st	Tu aimerais que je te parle des miens.	*You would like me to tell you about mine.*
10. pl, fem, 3rd	Chacun a les siennes.	*Everyone has his (own), her (own).*

EXERCISE 3-3:

1. Cet exercice est très facile. *This exercise is very easy.*
2. Ce garçon arrive toujours en retard. *That boy always arrives late.*
3. Sur cette page on explique les démonstratifs. *On this page the demonstratives are explained.*
4. Cet homme défend son honneur. *This man defends his honor.*
5. Cet autre chemin est plus court. *That other road is shorter.*
6. Ces faits sont importants. *These facts are important.*
7. Ces qualités sont essentielles. *These qualities are essential.*
8. Ces autres étudiants sont présents. *Those other students are present.*
9. Cette automobile est dans le garage. *That automobile is in the garage.*
10. Ces amies arrivent ce soir. *Those friends arrive tonight.*

EXERCISE 3-4:

1. Cet exercice-ci est facile, mais cet exercice-là est difficile. *This exercise is easy, but that exercise is hard.*
2. Ce champagne-ci est bon, mais ce champagne-là est mauvais. *This champagne is good, but that champagne is bad.*
3. Ces idées-là sont justes, mais ces idées-ci sont fausses. *Those ideas are correct, but these ideas are false.*
4. Cette phrase-là est longue, mais cette phrase-ci est courte. *That sentence is long, but this sentence is short.*
5. Cet hôtel-là est loin d'ici, mais cet hôtel-ci est à côté. *That hotel is far from here, but this hotel is next door.*

EXERCISE 3-5:

1. Qui t'a suggéré celle-là? *Who suggested that (one) to you?* (fem)
2. Regarde celui-ci. *Look at this one.* (masc)
3. Celles-ci sont impardonnables. *These are unforgivable.*
4. Celui-ci part à 6 heures et celui-là part à minuit. *This one leaves at six o'clock and that one leaves at midnight.*
5. Apportez-moi celui que vous m'avez promis. *Bring me the one that you promised me.*
6. Qui aurait pensé qu'elle se serait mariée avec celui-là? *Who would have thought that she would have married that one?*
7. Celles-ci sont les plus hautes de l'Europe. *These are the highest in Europe.*
8. Celui pour les oiseaux n'est plus bon à manger. *That one for the birds is no longer good to eat.*
9. Françoise lira celle-ci et elle pensera à moi. *Françoise will read this one and think of me.*
10. Celui-ci et le dernier illustrent la même structure grammaticale. *This one and the last (one) illustrate the same grammatical structure.*

EXERCISE 3-6:

1. Je sais cela. *I know that.*
2. C'est très impressionant. *That's very impressive.*
3. C'est vrai. *It's true.*
4. Elle lui donne cela. *She gives him that.*
5. C'est dû demain. *It's due tomorrow.*
6. Ceci (cela) me rend triste. *This (that) makes me sad.*
7. C'était inimaginable. *It was unthinkable.*
8. Ce sont des Français typiques. *They are typical Frenchmen.*
9. C'est un grand ministre. *He is a famous minister.*
10. J'attends cela. *I'm waiting for that.*
11. C'est le plus grand pays du monde. *It's the largest country in the world.*
12. Il n'avait pas compris cela. *He didn't understand that.*
13. C'était mon seul espoir. *That was my only hope.*
14. C'est un système économique. *It's an economic system.*
15. Ceci (cela) a choqué beaucoup de gens. *This (that) shocked a lot of people.*

EXERCISE 3-7:

1. Ça m'arrive de tomber en courant vite. *It happens that I fall down when I run fast.*
2. Non, cela ne me plaît pas. *No, I do not like that.*
3. Oui, ça va très bien. *Yes, things are going very well.*
4. Je pense que c'est ridicule. *I think that this is ridiculous.*
5. Oui, ça me rappelle beaucoup de choses. *Yes, that reminds me of a lot of things.*

EXERCISE 3-8:

1. C'est un livre.
2. Il est français.
3. C'est une grande Américaine.
4. Elle est docteur.
5. Il est secrétaire.
6. C'est un excellent professeur.
7. C'est une belle ville.
8. C'est une bonne amie.
9. Ils sont jeunes.
10. Ce sont de vieux citoyens.

EXERCISE 3-9:

1. C'est trop lourd.
2. Ce doit être intéressant.
3. Ce sera cher.
4. Est-ce pour moi que vous dites cela?
5. Ce sera à lui de venir.

EXERCISE 3-10:

1. Quarante et vingt font soixante. *Forty and twenty is sixty.*
2. Il y a trois cent soixante-cinq jours dans une année. *There are 365 days in a year.*
3. Trois fois quatre font douze. *Three times four is twelve.*
4. Sept et dix font dix-sept. *Seven and ten is seventeen.*
5. Il y a trente ou trente et un jours dans un mois. *There are thirty or thirty-one days in a month.*
6. Il y a cinquante états aux Etats-Unis. *There are fifty states in the United States.*
7. Soixante et onze moins trois font soixante-huit. *Seventy-one minus three is sixty-eight.*
8. Il y a vingt-six lettres dans l'alphabet. *There are twenty-six letters in the alphabet.*
9. Cent moins un font quatre-vingt-dix-neuf. *One hundred minus one is ninety-nine.*
10. Cet exercice a dix phrases. *This exercise has ten sentences.*

EXERCISE 3-11:

1. C'est la première phrase de cet exercice. *This is the first sentence of this exercise.*
2. Elle est dans le troisième chapitre. *It is in the third chapter.*
3. Juin est le sixième mois de l'année. *June is the sixth month of the year.*
4. La lettre z est la vingt-sixième (dernière) lettre de l'alphabet. *The letter z is the twenty-sixth (last) letter of the alphabet.*
5. Voici la cinquième phrase de cet exercice. *Here is the fifth sentence of this exercise.*
6. Cinquante pour-cent représente la moitié du total. *Fifty percent represents half of the total.*

7. Le premier étage français est le deuxième étage américain. *The first French floor is the second American floor.* OR *The first floor in France is the second floor in America.*
8. La nouvelle année commence le premier janvier. *The new year begins January first.*
9. Quinze minutes représentent un quart d'heure. *Fifteen minutes represent a quarter of an hour.*
10. Et voilà la dixième phrase de cet exercice. *And here is the tenth sentence of this exercise.*

EXERCISE 3-12:

1. Je me réveille à six heures moins le quart (or cinq heures quarante-cinq). *I wake up at 5:45 A.M.*
2. Je me lève à six heures. *I get up at six o'clock.*
3. Je déjeune à six heures et demie. *I have breakfast at 6:30 A.M.*
4. Mon bureau ouvre à sept heures et quart. *My office opens at 7:15 A.M.*
5. Je vois mon premier client à sept heures vingt. *I see my first client at 7:20 A.M.*
6. A onze heures, je commence à avoir faim. *At eleven o'clock I start to get hungry.*
7. Je sors du bureau à midi. *I leave the office at noon.*
8. Je reviens à une heure moins cinq. *I return at five to one.*
9. Mon dernier client a rendez-vous à quatorze heures vingt. *My last client has an appointment at 2:20 P.M.*
10. Je suis prêt à partir à quinze heures cinq. *I am ready to leave at 3:05 P.M.*

RAISE YOUR GRADES

Possessive and demonstrative adjectives

1. Nous comptions voir notre autre ami en Italie. *We counted on seeing our other friend in Italy.*
2. Combien coûte cette belle nappe en lin? *How much does this pretty linen tablecloth cost?*
3. Elle a montré son diplôme à tout le monde. *She showed her diploma to everyone.*
4. Mes parents garent leur voiture derrière la maison. *My parents park their car behind the house.*
5. J'aimerais visiter cette ville. *I would like to visit that town.*
6. Penses-tu inviter cet autre étudiant? *Do you think you'll invite that other student?*
7. Ne lui raconte pas ton rêve! *Don't tell him your dream!*
8. Il faut vous occuper de votre client. *You have to take care of your customer.*
9. Je n'ai pas oublié mon ancien camarade. *I have not forgotten my old friend.*
10. Arrêtez cet homme-là! *Stop that man there!*

Possessive and demonstrative pronouns

11. Moi aussi, j'aime la mienne. *Me too, I like mine.*
12. La tienne était meilleure. *Yours was better.*
13. Celui à droite me convient tout à fait. *That one on the right suits me fine.*
14. Nous irons au leur. *We will go to theirs.*
15. Qui est celui-là? *Who is that?*
16. Marie ferait n'importe quoi pour les siens. *Marie will do anything for hers.*
17. Je crois que je prendrai celle-ci et celle-là. *I think that I'll take this one and that one.*
18. Ils sont entrés par celle du milieu. *They entered by that one in the middle.*
19. Il a cassé les siennes. *He broke his.*
20. Celui que tu admirais a été vendu. *The one that you admired were sold.*

21. Qu'est-ce que tu penses du mien? *What do you think of mine?*
22. Celui à côté et celui au coin de la rue sont chers. *The one next door and the one at the end of the street are expensive.*
23. Celui-là est faux et celui-ci est exagéré. *That one is false and this one is exaggerated.*
24. Si vous nous aidez avec les nôtres nous vous aiderons avec les vôtres la prochaine fois. *If you help us with ours, we will help you with yours next time.*
25. Ceux qui pensent aux autres sont prévenants. *Those who think of others are considerate.*

UNIT EXAM I

NOUNS AND DEFINITE ARTICLES

Change the nouns given in the parentheses to the singular. Pay careful attention to the correct form of the definite article or its contraction.

1. (Les machines à écrire) sont (aux bureaux).

2. On vérifie (les noms) dans (les annonces).

3. Henriette laisse (les clefs) sur (les portes).

4. Ils apprécient (les lettres) (des étudiants).

5. Patricia accompagne (les enfants) (aux leçons).

6. Le public applaudit (les discours) (des sénateurs).

7. (Les samedis) il n'y a pas d'étudiants (aux écoles).

8. Il y a un beau panorama (des toits) (des maisons).

9. Guillaume prépare (les autres exercices) et (les autres questions).

10. Il est difficile de téléphoner (aux médecins) (aux hôpitaux).

ADJECTIVES AND INDEFINITE ARTICLES

Answer the following questions negatively, referring to a person of the opposite sex.

Example:	C'est **un immigrant suédois**?	*Is that a Swedish immigrant?*
	Non, c'est **une immigrante suédoise**.	*No, it's a Swedish immigrant woman.*

11. C'est une bonne musicienne?

12. C'est un jeune Arabe?

13. C'est une Canadienne Française?

14. Il a une cousine américaine?

15. Elle appelle l'autre infirmier?

16. Il habite avec un gentil oncle?

17. On choisit une étudiante consciencieuse?

18. Il cherche un vieil ami?

19. On présente un acteur célèbre?

20. On invite une belle étrangère?

INDEFINITE AND PARTITIVE ARTICLES

Answer the following questions using the cues given in parentheses and the appropriate form of the indefinite or partitive article.

21. Qu'est-ce qu'il mange au déjeuner? (soupe/fromage/fruits)

22. Qu'est-ce qu'il désire pour commencer? (hors d'oeuvre)

23. Qu'est-ce qu'elle voudrait pour écrire une lettre? (papier)

24. Qu'est-ce qu'elle n'a pas dans son stylo? (encre)

25. Qu'est-ce qu'il y a au zoo? (animaux féroces)

26. Qu'est-ce qu'il y a sur la table? (beaucoup/pain)

27. Combien coûte une Rolls-Royce? (trop/argent)

28. Qu'est-ce qu'il n'y a pas dans le désert? (plantes luxuriantes)

29. Qu'est-ce qu'il a comme famille? (mère/père/frères/soeurs)

POSSESSIVE ADJECTIVES

Answer the following questions in the affirmative, using the appropriate form of the possessive adjective. Pay careful attention to the shifts in person—*my/your, our/your*.

Example: C'est mon verre?   *Is that my glass?*

                 Oui, c'est **ton** (**votre**) verre.   *Yes, it's your glass.*

30. C'est votre père?

31. C'est le frère de Sylvie?

32. C'est la famille de Louis?

33. C'est votre chaise?

34. Ce sont nos verres?

35. Ce sont les soeurs de Paul et de Louise?

36. C'est la maison des Pinot?

37. Ce sont les camarades d'Henri?

POSSESSIVE PRONOUNS

Answer questions 30-37 using possessive pronouns in place of the possessive adjective and noun.

Example: C'est mon verre?   *Is that my glass?*

                 Oui, c'est **le tien** (**le vôtre**).   *Yes, it's yours.*

DEMONSTRATIVE ADJECTIVES

Answer the following questions in the affirmative, replacing the articles and possessives given in parentheses with demonstrative adjectives.

Example: (Les) magasins sont fermés,   *The stores are closed, aren't*
              n'est-ce pas?   *they?*

                 Oui, **ces** magasins sont fermés.   *Yes, these stores are closed.*

46. (Son) article est intéressant, n'est-ce pas?

47. (Leur) auto est blanche, n'est-ce pas?

48. (Les) jeunes filles sont élégantes, n'est-ce pas?

49. (Le) livre est amusant, n'est-ce pas?

50. (Mes) exercices sont corrects, n'est-ce pas?

DEMONSTRATIVE PRONOUNS

Answer the following questions affirmatively, using demonstrative pronouns in place of the words given in parentheses.

Example: Cette page est plus longue   *Is this page longer than the*
              que (l'autre)?   *other?*

> Oui, cette page est plus longue que **celle-là**. *Yes, this page is longer than that one.*

51. Cet exercice-ci est plus facile que le précédent?

52. Son accent est comme (l'accent) du professeur?

53. Les questions en français sont plus difficiles que (les autres questions)?

54. La musique classique est (la musique) que Gérard préfère?

55. Les étudiants qui sont présents sont plus nombreux que (les étudiants) qui sont absents?

NUMBERS

Complete the following sentences with the correct number—completely spelled out.

56. Le mois de décembre a _____ jours mais le mois de février a seulement _____ ou _____ jours.

57. Une année a _____ mois, _____ semaines, et _____ jours.

58. La lettre **A** est la _____ lettre de l'alphabet; **D** est la _____ lettre de l'alphabet.

59. En Amérique une jeune personne est adulte à _____ ans et vote dans les élections à _____ ans.

60. Il y a _____ états aux Etats-Unis et chaque état a deux sénateurs pour un total de _____ sénateurs.

61. La Déclaration de l'Indépendance Américaine date de l'année _____.

ADVERBS

Combine the following pairs of sentences into a single sentence containing an adverb.

62. Mon train arrive à la station. Le train est lent.

63. Les spectateurs observent le match. Les spectateurs sont attentifs.

64. L'auto accélère. L'auto est vite.

65. Les enfants sont très contents. C'est probable.

66. Mes parents sont en vacances. J'en suis malheureux!

EXAM ANSWERS

Nouns and definite articles

1. La machine à écrire est au bureau. *The typewriter is on the desk.*
2. On vérifie le nom dans l'annonce. *They verify the name on the announcement.*
3. Henriette laisse la clef sur la porte. *Henriette leaves the key in the door.*
4. Ils apprécient la lettre de l'étudiant. *They appreciate the letter from the student.*
5. Patricia accompagne l'enfant à la leçon. *Patricia goes with the child to the lesson.*
6. Le public applaudit le discours du sénateur. *The public applauds the senator's speech.*
7. Le samedi il n'y a pas d'étudiants à l'école. *On Saturday there aren't any students at school.*
8. Il y a un beau panorama du toit de la maison. *There is a beautiful view from the roof of the house.*
9. Guillaume prépare l'autre exercice et l'autre question. *Guillaume prepares the other exercise and the other question.*
10. Il est difficile de téléphoner au médecin à l'hôpital. *It's hard to call the doctor at the hospital.*

Adjectives and indefinite articles

11. Non, c'est un bon musicien. *No, it's a good male musician.*

12. Non, c'est une jeune Arabe. *No, it's a young Arab girl.*
13. Non, c'est un Canadien Français. *No, it's a French-Canadian man.*
14. Non, il a un cousin américain. *No, he has a male American cousin.*
15. Non, elle appelle l'autre infirmière. *No, she calls the other female nurse.*
16. Non, il habite avec une gentille tante. *No, he lives with a nice aunt.*
17. Non, on choisit un étudiant consciencieux. *No, they choose a conscientious male student.*
18. Non, il cherche une vieille amie. *No, he is looking for an old female friend.*
19. Non, on présente une actrice célèbre. *No, they introduce a famous actress.*
20. Non, on invite un bel étranger. *No, we invite a handsome stranger.*

Indefinite and partitive articles

21. Il mange de la soupe, du fromage, et des fruits au déjeuner. *He eats soup, cheese, and fruit for lunch.*
22. Il désire un hors d'oeuvre (des hors d'oeuvre) pour commencer. *He wants an appetizer (some appetizers) to begin.*
23. Elle voudrait du papier pour écrire une letter. *She would like paper to write a letter.*
24. Elle n'a pas d'encre dans son stylo. *She has no ink in her pen.*
25. Il y a des animaux féroces au zoo. *There are fierce animals in the zoo.*
26. Il y a beaucoup de pain sur la table. *There is a lot of bread on the table.*
27. Une Rolls-Royce coûte trop d'argent. *A Rolls-Royce costs too much money.*
28. Il n'y a pas de plantes luxuriantes dans le désert. *There are not luxurious plants in the desert.*
29. Il a une mère, un père, des frères, et des soeurs. *He has a mother, a father, brothers, and sisters.*

Possessive adjectives

30. Oui, c'est mon père. *Yes, he's my father.*
31. Oui, c'est son frère. *Yes, he's her brother.*
32. Oui, c'est sa famille. *Yes, that's his family.*
33. Oui, c'est ma chaise. *Yes, that's my chair.*
34. Oui, ce sont nos (vos) verres. *Yes, those are our (your) glasses.*
35. Oui, ce sont leurs soeurs. *Yes, those are their sisters.*
36. Oui, c'est leur maison. *Yes, it's their house.*
37. Oui, ce sont ses camarades. *Yes, those are his friends.*

Possessive pronouns

38. Oui, c'est le mien. *Yes, it's mine.*
39. Oui, c'est le sien. *Yes, it's hers.*
40. Oui, c'est la sienne. *Yes, it's his.*

41. Oui, c'est la mienne. *Yes, it's mine.*
42. Oui, ce sont les nôtres (les vôtres.) *Yes, they're ours (yours.)*
43. Oui, ce sont les leurs. *Yes, those are theirs.*
44. Oui, c'est la leur. *Yes, it's theirs.*
45. Oui, ce sont les siens. *Yes, they're his.*

Demonstrative adjectives

46. Oui, cet article est intéressant. *Yes, this article is interesting.*
47. Oui, cette auto est blanche. *Yes, that car is white.*
48. Oui, ces jeunes filles sont élégantes. *Yes, those girls are elegant.*
49. Oui, ce livre est amusant. *Yes, this book is amusing.*
50. Oui, ces exercices sont corrects. *Yes, those exercises are correct.*

Demonstrative pronouns

51. Oui, cet exercice-ci est plus facile que celui-là. *Yes, this exercise is easier than that one.*
52. Oui, son accent est comme celui du professeur. *Yes, his accent is like the teacher's.*
53. Oui, les questions en français sont plus difficiles que celles-là. *Yes, the questions in French are harder than those.*
54. Oui, la musique classique est celle que Gérard préfère. *Yes, classical music is the kind Gérard prefers.*
55. Oui, les étudiants qui sont présents sont plus nombreux que ceux qui sont absents. *Yes, the students who are present outnumber those who are absent.*

Numbers

56. Le mois de décembre a trente et un jours mais le mois de février a seulement vingt-huit ou vingt-neuf jours. *December has 31 days but February has only 28 or 29 days.*
57. Une année a douze mois, cinquante-deux semaines, et trois cent soixante-cinq jours. *A year has 12 months, 52 weeks, and 365 days.*
58. La lettre **A** est la première lettre de l'alphabet; **D** est la quatrième lettre de l'alphabet. *The letter **A** is the first letter of the alphabet; **D** is the fourth letter of the alphabet.*
59. En Amérique une jeune personne est adulte à vingt et un ans et vote à dix-huit ans. *In America a young person is an adult at 21 and votes at 18.*
60. Il y a cinquante états aux Etats-Unis et chaque état a deux sénateurs pour un total de cent sénateurs. *There are fifty states in the United States and each state has two senators for a total of one hundred senators.*
61. La Déclaration de l'Indépendance américaine date de l'année dix-sept cent soixante-seize. *The American Declaration of Independence dates from 1776.*

Adverbs

62. Mon train arrive lentement à la station. *My train pulls into the station slowly.*

63. Les spectateurs observent attentivement le match. *The spectators watch the game attentively.*

64. L'auto accélère vite. *The car accelerates quickly.*

65. Les enfants sont probablement très contents. *The children are probably very happy.*

66. Malheureusement, mes parents sont en vacances. (Mes parents sont malheureusement en vacances.) (Mes parents sont en vacances, malheureusement.) *Unfortunately, my parents are on vacation. (My parents are unfortunately on vacation). (My parents are on vacation, unfortunately.)*

4 THE PRESENT TENSE

THIS CHAPTER IS ABOUT

☑ **Subject Pronouns**
☑ **The Present Indicative of Regular –er Verbs**
☑ **The Present Indicative of Regular –ir Verbs**
☑ **The Present Indicative of Regular –re Verbs**
☑ **Spelling Changes in -er Verbs**
☑ **Infinitives**
☑ **Present Participles**
☑ **Negatives**

4-1. Subject Pronouns

A subject pronoun functions as the subject of a sentence.

1st person	*the speaker*	OR	*speakers*
	je		**nous**
2nd person	*the one spoken to*	OR	*ones spoken to*
	tu		**vous**
3rd person	*the one or thing spoken of*	OR	*the ones or things spoken of*
	il, elle, on		**ils, elles**

A. Forms of the subject pronoun

Study the following table and examples of sentences with subject pronouns.

Person	Singular		Plural		
1st	je	*I*	nous	*we*	
2nd	tu	*you (fam)*	vous	*you*	*(formal singular, informal and formal plural)*
3rd-masc	il	*he, it*	ils	*they*	
3rd-fem	elle	*she, it*	elle	*they*	
	on	*one, they, we, people*			

Je suis américain.	*I am American.*
Tu es français.	*You are French.*
Il est intelligent.	*He is intelligent.*
Nous sommes américains.	*We are Americans.*
Vous êtes très impressionés.	*You are very impressed.*
Elles sont anglaises.	*They are English.*
On est content.	*We are happy.*

B. Some comments about the subject pronoun

1. Both **tu** and **vous** mean *you.* Use **tu** when you are speaking to a relative, friend, classmate, child, or to an animal—**vous** when you are speaking to an adult, a stranger, or to more than one person.

Mon chéri, **tu** veux venir avec moi au cinéma?	*My dear, do you want to come to the movies with me?*
Philippe, **tu** dois manger tes épinards!	*Philippe, you must eat your spinach!*

Monsieur Duval, **vous** êtes bien aimable.	*Mr. Duval, you are very nice.*
Monsieur et Madame Durand, **vous** êtes les bienvenus.	*Mr. and Mrs. Durand, you are welcome.*

2. When the subject of a sentence is someone indefinite, use **on** with a verb in the third person singular. You can use **on** to mean *we, they, you,* or *people.*

On ne **sait** jamais ce qu'il pense.	*You never know what he is thinking.*
On dit que les bons comptes font les bons amis.	*They say that good accounts make for good friends.*
On reste dîner chez nos parents.	*We are staying at our parents' place for dinner.*
On dit toujours cela!	*People always say that!*

3. The third person subject pronouns **il(s)** and **elle(s)** are the only subject pronouns that show gender—as well as person and number.

J'aime **le caviar**, mais **il** est très cher.	*I like caviar, but it's very expensive.*
Elles (mes clès) sont dans mon sac et **il (mon sac)** est dans ma voiture.	*They (my keys) are in my purse and it (my purse) is in my car.*
Nous connaissons ces **jeunes gens; ils** sont très sympathiques.	*We know some young people; they are very pleasant.*
Anne-Marie est ingénieur et **elle** habite rue Brey.	*Anne-Marie is an engineer and she lives on Brey Street.*

EXERCISE 4-1: Answer the following questions in the affirmative. Replace the subject of the sentence with a subject pronoun. Answers and translations are at the end of the chapter.

Example:	Est-ce que notre professeur est absent aujourd'hui?	*Is our professor absent today?*
	Oui, il est absent aujourd'hui.	*Yes, he is absent today.*

1. Est-ce que les feuilles sont rouges en automne?

2. Est-ce que votre tante est en Normandie cet été?

3. Est-ce que leur devoir est dû demain?

4. Est-ce que Sophie est anglaise?

5. Est-ce que les enfants sont malades?

6. Est-ce que vos parents sont catholiques?

7. Est-ce que sa cousine est en Europe?

8. Est-ce que vos rêves sont toujours en couleurs?

9. Est-ce que le docteur Martin est à l'hôpital aujourd'hui?

10. Est-ce que les questions sont compliquées?

4-2. The Present Indicative of Regular –er Verbs

To conjugate a verb, you add the appropriate endings to denote *person, number, tense,* and *mood* to a verb stem or, in some cases, directly to an infinitive. Most French verbs are **regular**—that is, they follow a predictable pattern. Other verbs, like **être** and **avoir**, are **irregular**—they vary from the pattern. Even irregular verbs, however, follow some general patterns which will help you learn them (see Sec. 5-3).

Find the stem of regular **-er** verbs by dropping the **-er**. Then add the following personal endings to form the present indicative.

person	singular	plural
1st	-e	-ons
2nd	-es	-ez
3rd	-e	-ent

A. The model -er verb—parler

parler, *to speak*   stem: **parl**

je parl**e**	*I speak, am speaking*
tu parl**es**	*you speak, are speaking*
il, elle parl**e**	*he, she speaks, is speaking*
on parl**e**	*one speaks, we, they, people speak*
nous parl**ons**	*we speak, are speaking*
vous parl**ez**	*you speak, are speaking*
ils, elles parl**ent**	*they speak, are speaking*

Je parle anglais.	*I speak English.*
Tu parles bien le français.	*You speak French well.*
Elle parle trop.	*She talks too much.*
Nous parlons beaucoup de langues.	*We speak a lot of languages.*
Vous parlez très doucement.	*You speak very softly.*
Ils parlent souvent à leurs parents.	*They speak to their parents often.*

> *NOTE:* When the subject of a sentence is a noun rather than a subject pronoun, you must use the third-person form of the verb—singular or plural.

L'anglais est ma langue maternelle.	*English is my mother tongue.*
Ses parents sont en vacances.	*His parents are on vacation.*

EXERCISE 4-2: Fill in the blank in each sentence with the correct form of the present indicative tense of **parler**. Answers and translations are at the end of the chapter.

1. Vous _____ trop.
2. Il ne _____ pas à son père.
3. Je _____ un peu le français.
4. Elles _____ anglais et français.
5. Tu _____ bien.
6. Nous _____ souvent à ma mère.
7. Je _____ des vacances.
8. Elle lui _____ d'amour.
9. Quelle surprise! Vous _____ français.
10. _____ -tu anglais?

B. Other regular -er verbs

All verbs whose infinitives end in **-er** are regular—except **aller**, *to go*. Here is a list of some commonly used regular **-er** verbs.

aimer	*to love, like*	étudier	*to study*	passer	*to pass*
apporter	*to bring*	fermer	*to close*	penser	*to think*
arriver	*to arrive*	habiter	*to inhabit, live in*	porter	*to carry, wear*
chanter	*to sing*	jouer	*to play*	préparer	*to prepare*
commencer	*to begin*	monter	*to go up, climb*	regarder	*to look at*
demander	*to ask*	montrer	*to show*	rester	*to stay*
donner	*to give*	oublier	*to forget*	travailler	*to work*
				trouver	*to find*

J'aime la campagne.	*I love the country.*
Ils arrivent toujours à l'heure.	*They always arrive on time.*
Le film commence aujourd'hui.	*The movie begins today.*
Les enfants jouent tout le temps.	*Children play all the time.*
Il regarde la télévision.	*He is looking at television.*
Elle lui **donne** un crayon.	*She gives him a pencil.*
Vous restez ici jusqu'à l'aube.	*You stay here until dawn.*
Nous montons au premier.	*We are going up to the first floor.*
Je travaille trop dur.	*I work too hard.*

EXERCISE 4-3: Replace the subject in the following sentences with the one given in parentheses. Answers and translations are at the end of the chapter.

Example: Nous apportons toujours le vin.   *We always bring the wine.*
(vous)   *(you)*
Vous apportez toujours le vin.   *You always bring the wine.*

1. Elle porte une jolie robe. (je)

2. Vous n'étudiez pas assez. (ils)

3. Je prépare un repas pour la famille. (elle)

4. Les mères regardent leurs enfants. (elles)

5. Ils chantent ensemble le jeudi. (nous)

6. Est-ce que tu aimes ma robe? (Charles)

7. Les agents de police arrêtent les voleurs. (vous)

8. Tu fermes la porte. (nous)

9. Elle donne un cadeau au concierge. (je)

10. Denise montre le chien aux enfants. (Anne et Matthieu)

4-3. The Present Indicative of Regular –ir Verbs

Find the stem of regular -ir verbs by dropping the -ir. Then add the following personal endings to form the present indicative.

person	singular	plural
1st	-is	-issons
2nd	-is	-issez
3rd	-it	-issent

A. The model -ir verb—finir

finir, *to finish*   stem: **fini**

je fin**is**	*I finish, am finishing*
tu fin**is**	*you finish, are finishing*
il, elle fin**it**	*he, she finishes, is finishing*
on fin**it**	*one finishes, we, they, people finish*
nous fin**issons**	*we finish, are finishing*
vous fin**issez**	*you finish, are finishing*
ils, elles fin**issent**	*they finish, are finishing*

Je finis mon travail à quatre heures et demie.	*I finish my work at 4:30 P.M.*
Tu finis à six heures.	*You finish at six o'clock.*
On finit à dix heures moins dix.	*We finish at ten minutes to ten.*
Nous finissons nos vacances aux Etats-Unis.	*We are finishing our vacation in the United States.*
Vous finissez toujours à l'heure.	*You always finish on time.*
Les Montand finissent leur repas.	*The Montands are finishing their dinner.*

EXERCISE 4-4: Fill in the blank in each sentence with the correct form of the present indicative tense of **finir**. Answers and translations are at the end of the chapter.

1. Si vous _____ à l'heure, vous pouvez partir.
2. Quand il _____ son travail, il est très heureux.
3. Le spectacle _____ à trois heures de l'après-midi.
4. Les cours _____ au mois de juin.
5. Est-ce que vous _____ la première?
6. Tout est bien qui _____ bien.

7. Les couturières _____ les robes à la maison.
8. _____ -tu tes exercices aujourd'hui?
9. Nous _____ notre dessert quand nous avons faim.
10. Rachel _____ son petit déjeuner avant sa soeur.

B. Other regular -ir verbs

Although there are many irregular verbs whose infinitives end in **-ir**, these commonly used verbs follow the pattern of **finir**—in all tenses.

agir	*to act*	maigrir	*to get thin*	réunir	*to gather*
bâtir	*to build*	nourrir	*to nourish, feed*	réussir	*to succeed*
choisir	*to choose*	obéir (a)	*to obey*	rougir	*to blush*
fleurir	*to bloom, flower*	punir	*to punish*	subir	*to undergo*
grandir	*to grow (larger)*	réfléchir	*to reflect*	trahir	*to betray*
guérir	*to recover, heal*	remplir	*to fill*		

Il maigrit parce qu'il ne mange pas. — *He is getting thin because he doesn't eat.*

Nous choisissons un président trop fréquemment. — *We choose a president too often.*

Tu obéis à tes parents. — *You obey your parents.*

Elles réfléchissent avant de répondre. — *They reflect before answering.*

Je ne **punis** pas les enfants pour leurs bêtises. — *I do not punish the children for their mistakes.*

Les enfants guérissent rapidement. — *Children heal rapidly.*

Ruth remplit les tasses. — *Ruth fills the cups.*

Jay réussit dans sa profession. — *Jay is succeeding in his career.*

Ils agissent ensemble. — *They act together.*

EXERCISE 4-5: Complete the following sentences using the correct form of the verb given in parentheses. Answers and translations are at the end of the chapter.

1. Le charpentier (bâtir) _____ une maison.
2. Elle (choisir) _____ le parfum le plus cher.
3. Certains enfants (grandir) _____ vite.
4. Les médecins (guérir) _____ les malades avec des médicaments.
5. Les parents sévères (punir) _____ leurs enfants.
6. Il (réfléchir) _____ avant de répondre aux questions.
7. Avec son régime, elle (maigrir) _____.
8. Pourquoi (subir) _____ -tu sa mauvaise humeur?
9. Les fermiers (nourrir) _____ les animaux de la ferme.
10. (Obéir) _____ vous à la loi?

4-4. The Present Indicative of Regular –re Verbs

Find the stem of regular **-re** verbs by dropping the **-re**. Then add the following personal endings to form the present indicative.

person	singular	plural
1st	-s	-ons
2nd	-s	-ez
3rd	-(t)	-ent

NOTE: The verb **rompre**, *to break*, and all its compounds— **interrompre**, *to interrupt*, **corrompre**, *to corrupt*—are spelled with a final **-t** in the third person singular.

Il rompt le pain avant le déjeuner. — *He breaks the bread into pieces before lunch.*

NOTE: The plural endings are the same as those of the first conjugation **-er** verbs.

A. The model -re verb—vendre

vendre, *to sell*   stem: **vend**

je vend**s**	*I sell, am selling*
tu vend**s**	*you sell, are selling*
il, elle vend	*he, she sells, is selling*
on vend	*one sells, we, they, people sell*
nous vend**ons**	*we sell, are selling*
vous vend**ez**	*you sell, are selling*
ils, elles vend**ent**	*they sell, are selling*

Je vends mes fleurs.	*I sell my flowers.*
Vends-tu tes peintures?	*Are you selling your paintings?*
Brigitte ne **vend** pas ses oeuvres.	*Brigitte isn't selling her works.*
Nous vendons des assurances.	*We sell insurance.*
Vous vendez des oeufs frais?	*Do you sell fresh eggs?*
Les Ricoeur vendent leur maison.	*The Ricoeurs are selling their house.*

EXERCISE 4-6: Replace the subject in the following sentences with the one given in parentheses. Answers and translations are at the end of the chapter.

1. Le marchand de meubles vend des tables. (ils)

2. Je ne vends pas à crédit. (nous)

3. Madame Duval vend des chapeaux. (vous)

4. Si vous vendez trop cher, personne n'achète. (je)

5. Les joailliers vendent de beaux bijoux. (elle)

6. Nous vendons des livres d'occasion. (ils)

7. Est-ce qu'on vend des objets d'art dans cette boutique? (vous)

8. Combien vendez-vous ces tapis? (tu)

9. Pierre vend sa bicyclette bon marché. (Yvonne)

10. Les bons commerçants vendent bien les marchandises. (nous)

B. Other regular -re verbs

Although there are many irregular verbs whose infinitives end in **-re**, these commonly used verbs follow the pattern of **vendre** in all tenses.

attendre	*to wait*		mordre	*to bite*
confondre	*to confuse*		pendre	*to hang*
défendre	*to defend, forbid*		perdre	*to lose*
dépendre	*to depend*		rendre	*to give back*
descendre	*to descend, get off*		répondre	*to answer*
entendre	*to hear*		rompre	*to break*
étendre	*to spread out*			

J'attends l'autobus.	*I am waiting for the bus.*
Le général défend son pays.	*The general defends his country.*
Ça dépend!	*That depends!*
Descendez-vous à la prochaine station?	*Do you get off at the next station?*
Nous entendons chanter les oiseaux.	*We are listening to the birds sing.*
Elle étend une nappe sur la table.	*She spreads the cloth on the table.*
Ne **confondez** pas les deux choses.	*Don't get the two things confused.*
Marie mord dans la pomme.	*Marie takes a bite out of the apple.*
Le téléphone interrompt notre conversation.	*The telephone interrupts our conversation..*
Je ne **perds** jamais mes gants.	*I never lose my gloves.*

EXERCISE 4-7: Complete the following sentences using the correct form of the verb given in parentheses. Answers and translations are at the end of the chapter.

1. Je (rendre) _____ les livres à la bibliothèque.
2. Ce garçon (dépendre) _____ trop de ses parents.
3. Il (confondre) _____ les paroles du discours.
4. Les présidents (rompre) _____ les relations entre pays.
5. L'argent (corrompre) _____ parfois les hommes.
6. Vous (interrompre) _____ trop souvent.
7. Mon père (perdre) _____ ses cheveux.
8. Nous (rendre) _____ nos livres à la bibliothèque.
9. Les chiens méchants (mordre) _____ quand il fait chaud.
10. Les costumes (pendre) _____ dans le placard.

4-5. Spelling Changes in –er Verbs

Some regular **-er** verbs change the spelling of their stems—usually to preserve a particular sound.

A. For verbs whose infinitives end in -cer, change the c to ç before an *a* or an *o*.

commencer, *to begin*   present participle: **commençant,** *beginning*

je commence	nous commen**ç**ons
tu commences	vous commencez
il commence	ils commencent

Some other verbs whose spelling changes in this way are

annoncer	*to announce, declare*	menacer	*to threaten*
avancer	*to advance, promote*	placer	*to place, put*
effacer	*to efface, erase*	prononcer	*to pronounce*
exercer	*to exercise, practice*	remplacer	*to replace*
lancer	*to throw*	renoncer	*to give up*

B. For verbs whose infinitives end in -ger, add an e after the g before an *a* or an *o*.

manger, *to eat*   present participle: **mangeant,** *eating*

je mange	nous man**ge**ons
tu manges	vous mangez
elle mange	elles mangent

Some other verbs whose spelling changes in this way are

arranger	*to arrange*	infliger	*to inflict*	protéger	*to protect*
bouger	*to move*	nager	*to swim*	songer	*to imagine*
changer	*to change*	neiger	*to snow*	soulager	*to ease (pain)*
corriger	*to correct*	obliger	*to oblige*	voyager	*to travel*
déranger	*to bother, disturb*	partager	*to share*		
exiger	*to require*	plonger	*to dive, plunge*		

C. For verbs whose infinitives end in -yer, change the y to i before an unpronounced e.

employer, *to employ, use*

j'emplo**i**e	nous employons
tu emplo**i**es	vous employez
on emplo**i**e	ils emplo**i**ent

Some other verbs whose spelling changes in this way are

ennuyer	*to bore*	essuyer	*to wipe*	nettoyer	*to clean*
noyer	*to drown, flood*				

Les pluies **nettoient** les rues.	*The rains clean the streets.*
Tu **essuies** les verres.	*You wipe the glasses.*

> **NOTE:** For verbs whose infinitives end in **-ayer**, you may keep the **y** or change it to **i**.

balayer, *to sweep*	Le vent **balaye** (**balaie**) les nuages.	*The wind sweeps away the clouds.*
payer, *to pay*	Il **paye** (**paie**) pour entrer.	*He pays in order to get in.*

D. If there is an unpronounced e in the syllable before an infinitive ending, change the e to è if the next syllable also contains an unpronounced e.

acheter, *to buy*

j'achète	nous achetons
tu achètes	vous achetez
elle achète	elles achètent

Some other verbs whose spelling changes in this way are

achever	*to achieve*	lever	*to raise*
élever	*to raise, bring up*	mener	*to lead*
emmener	*to take (someone) away*	peser	*to weight*

E. For some verbs whose infinitives end in -eler or -eter, double the l or the t if there is an unpronounced e in the next syllable.

jeter, *to throw*   **appeler**, *to call, name*

je jette	nous jetons	j'appelle	nous appelons
tu jettes	vous jetez	tu appelles	vous appelez
on jette	ils jettent	il appelle	ils appellent

BUT

geler, *to freeze*

je gèle	nous gelons
tu gèles	vous gelez
elle gèle	elles gèlent

F. If there is an é in the syllable before the infinitive ending, change the é to è if the next syllable contains an unpronounced e.

céder, *to yield*

je cède	nous cédons
tu cèdes	vous cédez
on cède	ils cèdent

Other verbs whose spelling changes in this way are

célébrer	*to celebrate*	préférer	*to prefer*
compléter	*to complete*	posséder	*to possess*
espérer	*to hope*	protéger	*to protect*
exagérer	*to exaggerate*	répéter	*to repeat*
interpréter	*to interpret*	révéler	*to reveal*

> *REMEMBER:* Protéger also adds an **e** after the **g** before an *a* or an *o*.

> *NOTE:* The verb **créer**, *to create*, keeps the **é** in all its forms.

EXERCISE 4-8: Replace the subject of each of the following sentences with the subject pronoun given in parentheses. Answers and translations are at the end of the chapter.

    1. Il annonce les nouvelles à la radio. (nous)

    2. Je mange trois fois par jour. (nous)

    3. Vous partagez le gâteau. (nous)

    4. J'emploie de l'encre bleue. (vous)

    5. Elle s'ennuie ici. (vous)

    6. Tu achètes des chaussures. (nous)

7. Vous emmenez les enfants. (ils)

8. Vous levez le drapeau. (je)

9. Vous jetez de vieux livres. (votre mère)

10. Je préfère le café. (nous)

4-6. Infinitives

An infinitive is a verb form that has neither tense nor person—it is the form you find listed in the dictionary. When there is more than one verb in a simple sentence, all but the first verb are infinitives.

Je refuse de **mentir**.   *I refuse to lie.*

The infinitive phrase **de mentir** completes the meaning of the verb **refuse**. The preposition **de** connects the two verbs.

A. Infinitives introduced by de

1. When the first verb of a sentence describes an activity that is independent of the activity of the following verb, use the preposition **de** to introduce the infinitive.

Nous **décidons de rentrer** chez nous.   *We decide to go back home.*
J'oublie toujours **d'éteindre** la radio.   *I always forget to turn off the radio.*

(For a list of common verbs that require **de** before an infinitive, see the Appendix.)

EXERCISE 4-9: Combine the following pairs of sentences into a single sentence containing a verb in infinitive form. Answers and translations are at the end of the chapter.

Example: Le propriétaire nettoie-t-il le   *Will the landlord clean up the*
          jardin? Oui, il promet de le faire.   *garden? Yes, he promises to.*

          Le propriétaire promet de nettoyer   *The landlord promises to clean up*
          le jardin.   *the garden.*

1. Accompagnez-vous les enfants? Oui, nous acceptons de le faire.

2. Le pilote annonce-t-il le départ? Non, il oublie de le faire.

3. Mangez-vous à midi? Oui, nous finissons de le faire.

4. Manque-t-il son autobus? Oui, il risque de le faire.

5. Est-ce que vous votez pour notre parti? Oui, je décide de le faire.

6. Est-ce qu'elle travaille des heures supplémentaires? Non, elle refuse de le faire.

7. Est-ce que tu emploies la voiture de ton père? Oui, je promets de le faire.

8. Assistent-ils aux cours le samedi? Non, ils évitent de le faire.

9. Aidez-vous vos parents? Oui, je jure de le faire.

10. Complète-t-il ses devoirs? Oui, il tâche de le faire.

2. Use **de** to introduce an infinitive following a performative verb—a verb that in being said performs the act it describes, such as *"I'm telling you to leave that alone!"* In French the performative verbs are

commander	*to command, order someone*
demander	*to ask of someone*
dire	*to tell someone*
ordonner	*to order someone*
permettre	*to permit someone*
promettre	*to promise someone*

and sometimes **écrire**, *to write (someone)*, and **téléphoner**, *to telephone (someone)*.

Le juge **dit** à Michel **de payer** ses dettes.

The judge tells Michel to pay his debts.

Il faut **demander** aux voisins **de venir**.

We ask the neighbors to come.

Est-ce qu'ils **permettent** à tout le monde **de voir** le portrait?

Do they let everyone see the portrait?

EXERCISE 4-10: Answer each of the following questions using the cue in the response in an infinitive form. Answers and translations are at the end of the chapter.

Example: Qu'est-ce que le capitaine commande aux soldats. (Qu'ils attaquent!)

What does the captain command the soldiers? (That they attack!)

Le capitaine commande aux soldats d'attaquer.

The captain commands the soldiers to attack!

1. Qu'est-ce que nous écrivons à nos amis? Qu'ils viennent par le prochain avion.
2. Qu'est-ce qu'elle dit à Pierre? Qu'il regarde la première page du journal.
3. Qu'est-ce que le médecin ordonne à la malade? Qu'elle reste une semaine au lit.
4. Qu'est-ce que ses parents ne permettent pas à Louise? Qu'elle passe la nuit dehors.
5. Qu'est-ce que le client commande au serveur? Qu'il apporte une bouteille de champagne.

3. When an infinitive follows an adjective or a noun that is not its direct object, you must use **de** to introduce the infinitive.

Cet instructeur n'a pas **le temps de** te **parler**.

That instructor doesn't have time to talk to you.

Il est **difficile de trouver** le mot juste.

It's hard to find the right word.

EXERCISE 4-11: Combine the following pairs of sentences into a single sentence containing a verb in infinitive form. Answers and translations are at the end of the chapter.

Example: Il est facile. On répond aux questions.

It's easy. You answer the questions.

Il est facile de répondre aux questions.

It's easy to answer the questions.

1. Mon médecin a l'habitude. Il soigne les malades.
2. Il est impossible. On arrive à l'heure.
3. Je n'ai vraiment pas envie. Je ne prépare pas le dîner.
4. Henri-Roger n'as pas le temps. Il ne déjeune pas.
5. Nous sommes bien obligés. Nous remercions nos clients.
6. Il est nécessaire. On paie ses taxes.
7. Elles sont vraiment contentes. Elles finissent leurs études.
8. J'ai le plaisir. Je présente mes amis à mes parents.
9. Elle est enchantée. Elle voyage en première classe.
10. Il est surprenant. On remarque toutes ces erreurs.

B. Infinitives introduced by à

1. Use the preposition **à** to introduce an infinitive
   • when an intervening noun is the object of both the main verb and the infinitive:

Apportez-moi **quelque chose à manger**!

Bring me something to eat!

Votre voisin a des **livres à vendre**.

Your neighbor has some books to sell.

- when the actions of the two verbs begin at the same time:

Ils **commencent à comprendre** le concept.	*They are beginning to understand the concept.*
Les provocateurs les **incitent à désobéir**.	*The provocateurs incite them into disobeying.*
Je **cherche à trouver** de l'argent.	*I'm making an effort to come up with the money.*

2. The following is a list of some of the more common verbs which require **à** before an infinitive.

s'amuser à	*to have a good time _____ ing*
apprendre à	*to learn to*
continuer à	*to continue _____ ing*
se décider à	*to get around to*
s'habituer à	*to get used to*
s'intéresser à	*to be involved in _____ ing*
inviter (quelqu'un) à	*to invite (someone) to*
se mettre à	*to start to*
se préparer à	*to get ready to*
réussir à	*to succeed in _____ ing*
tarder à	*to be late in _____ ing*

EXERCISE 4-12: Answer each question in complete form by incorporating the question into the suggested response. Answers and translations are at the end of the chapter.

Example: Faites-vous du ski? Oui, j'apprends.   *Do you ski? Yes, I'm learning.*
J'apprends à faire du ski.   *I'm learning to ski.*

1. Critique-t-il ses enfants? Oui, mais il hésite.

2. Profitons-nous du beau temps? Oui, nous commençons.

3. Etudie-t-elle le russe? Oui, elle continue.

4. Demandez-vous votre passeport? Oui, mais je tarde.

5. Finissons-nous cet exercice? Oui, nous réussissons.

C. Infinitives introduced by other prepositions

In French, if the object of a preposition is a verb, that object will be an infinitive—not a participle as in English. The only exception to this is the preposition **en**—which does require a participle (see Sec. 4-7). Before an infinitive which follows a verb, use the preposition **pour** to mean *in order to*, and the preposition **sans** to mean *without _____ ing*.

Je prends ces notes **pour** ne pas oublier.	*I'm taking notes (in order) not to forget.*
Ils étudient **pour** avoir de bonnes notes.	*They study (in order) to get good grades.*
Il s'en va **sans** me **parler**.	*He goes away without speaking to me.*
Les enfants écoutent **sans comprendre**.	*Children listen without understanding.*

NOTE: The use of **pour** is optional with verbs indicating a change of place.

Il **est venu** (**pour**) vous chercher.	*He came (in order) to pick you up.*

EXERCISE 4-13: Combine each pair of sentences into a single sentence with an infinitive introduced by **pour** or **sans**—depending upon the meaning of the sentence. Answers and translations are at the end of the chapter.

1. Vous achetez des provisions. Vous préparez les repas.

2. Les enfants traversent la rue. Ils ne regardent pas.

3. Catherine quitte la maison. Elle ne ferme pas les fenêtres.

4. Son marie travaille 50 heures par semaine. Il avance dans sa carrière.

5. Le corbeau ouvre son grand bec. Il montre sa belle voix.

D. Infinitives directly following a verb

1. Use an infinitive without an intervening preposition after a verb that denotes *wanting*, *hoping*, or *intending* to do something—but not actually doing it.

Ils **doivent faire** leurs valises.	*They must pack their bags.*
J'aime prendre une douche froide le matin.	*I like to take a cold shower in the morning.*
Nous ne **pouvons** pas vous **guarantir** une chambre.	*We can't guarantee a room for you.*

2. Use an infinitive without a preposition after verbs of perception such as **voir**, *to see*, **regarder**, *to look at*, **observer**, *to observe*, **entendre**, *to hear*, **écouter**, *to listen*, and **sentir**, *to feel*. In these cases, the subject of the infinitive becomes the direct object of the entire verb phrase.

Elle **entend sonner la sonnette**.	*She hears the bell ring.*

3. Use an infinitive without a preposition after intransitive verbs—verbs that do not take an object—denoting a change of place.

Nous **montons chercher** nos raquettes.	*We're going upstairs to get our rackets.*
Les jardiniers **reviennent travailler** demain.	*The gardeners are coming back to work tomorrow.*

EXERCISE 4-14: Combine the following pairs of sentences into a single sentence containing a verb in infinitive form. Answers and translations are at the end of the chapter.

1. Est-ce qu'on étudie la grammaire? Il faut le faire!

2. Est-ce vous voyagez en Europe? Je désire le faire.

3. Annoncent-ils la bonne nouvelle? Ils viennent le faire.

4. Est-ce que quelqu'un sonne à la porte? Je l'entends.

5. Parlent-elles au téléphone? Elles aiment le faire.

6. Est-ce que Paul dîne seul au restaurant? Il préfère le faire.

7. Le train arrive-t-il? On l'entend.

8. Travaillez-vous dans le jardin? Je déteste le faire.

9. Prépare-t-elle des plats chinois? Elle préfère le faire.

10. Echangeons-nous les cadeaux de nos amis? Nous pouvons le faire.

11. Rentrent-ils de bonne heure? Ils doivent le faire.

12. Partez-vous tout de suite après la cérémonie? Je vais le faire.

13. Achetez-vous une nouvelle voiture? Nous pensons le faire.

14. Joue-t-elle au tennis? Tout le monde la regarde.

15. Manges-tu maintenant? Je descends tout de suite!

4-7. Present Participles

A. Form of the present participles

Form the present participle of all verbs—except **être**, **avoir**, and **savoir**—by dropping **-ons** from the first person plural (**nous**) form of the present indicative, and adding **-ant**.

infinitive	**nous** form	present participle	
regarder	nous regard**ons**	regard**ant**	*regarding*
grandir	nous grandiss**ons**	grandiss**ant**	*growing*
prendre	nous pren**ons**	pren**ant**	*taking*
vouloir	nous voul**ons**	voul**ant**	*voulant*

NOTE: You'll simply have to memorize the present participles of **être**, **avoir**, and **savoir**.

infinitive	present participle	
être	**étant**	*being*
avoir	**ayant**	*having*
savoir	**sachant**	*knowing*

B. Use of the present participle

1. You may use the present participle as an adjective which must agree in gender and number with the noun it modifies.

une soiré**e** dansant**e**	*an evening of dancing*
des cri**s** perçant**s**	*piercing cries*

2. Use a present participle as the verb in an abbreviated clause to describe a secondary event or action—in this case, the present participle is invariable.

On a vu des voleurs **courant** dans la rue.	*We saw some thieves (who were) running down the street.*
Ils ont passé des moments agréables, **parlant** et **discutant**.	*They spent some pleasant moments, (as they were) talking and discussing.*

3. The preposition **en** is the only preposition you can use to introduce a present participle. In this case, **en** functions adverbially and means *in*, *while*, or *by doing something*.

Elle s'est fait mal **en descendant** la pente.	*She hurt herself (while) coming down the slope.*

> *NOTE:* When a present participle follows the preposition **en**, it always refers to the subject of the sentence, but remains invariable.

Nous les avons remarqués **en traversant** le boulevard.	*We saw them while (we were) crossing the boulevard.*
En disant cela, il m'a embrassée.	*Upon saying that, he kissed me.*
En étudiant, on arrive à avoir de bonnes notes.	*By studying you can succeed in getting good grades.*

EXERCISE 4-15: Replace the phrases given in parentheses with the appropriate form of the present participle. Answers and translations are at the end of the chapter.

1. Vous apprenez bien une langue (si vous la pratiquez beaucoup).

2. Les valises arrivent sur des tapis (qui roulent).

3. (A force de chercher) je trouve une bonne réponse.

4. Il s'en va sur la montagne (pendant qu'il chante et siffle).

5. Je n'ai jamais vu une soucoupe (qui vole).

6. J'écoute (en même temps que pense à autre chose).

7. Elle n'est pas contente d'être une femme (qui obéit)!

8. Ne parle pas (pendant que tu manges).

9. Tu deviens bronzé (si tu restes au soleil).

10. Ils arrivent (en train de crier) parce qu'ils ont gagné.

4-8. Negatives

A. Simple negation

1. Make an affirmative sentence negative by saying **ne** before the verb and **pas** after it.

   Je **ne** comprends **pas** son point de vue.   *I don't understand his point of view.*

2. **Ne** is a negative particle which alerts the listener to the eventual negative meaning of the sentence. **Pas**, *not*, is the negative completer—use it when there is no other negative word in the sentence. **Pas** follows a verb that has a person and tense ending or a present participle, but precedes an infinitive.

   Je vous prie de **ne pas fumer** ici.   *I beg you not to smoke here.*
   Vous faites une erreur en   *You're making a mistake by*
      n'écoutant pas.   *not listening.*

   > *NOTE:* **Ne** alone does not make a sentence negative—it sometimes indicates a degree of negative feeling which is not completely expressed. In these cases, the **ne**—called *expletive* or *pleonastic ne*—is optional.

   Elle a peur que je (**ne**) la voie.   *She's afraid I will see her.*
                                          (Heaven forbid!)

   Allez, vite, avant qu'il (**ne**) vienne!   *Come on, quick, before he comes!*
                                            (That's all we need!)

   Ne before the verb in the adverbial expression **ne . . . que** suggests a negative idea, but the sentence itself remains affirmative.

   Nous **n'avons qu'**à recommencer   *All we have to do is start at the*
   au début.   *beginning again.*

EXERCISE 4-16: Answer the following questions in the negative. Answers and translations are at the end of the chapter.

1. Est-ce que 4 précède 3?
2. Est-ce qu'il neige en été?
3. Mangeons-nous le dessert avant la salade?
4. Etudiez-vous le chinois ce semestre?
5. Fermons-nous les fenêtres en juillet?
6. Est-ce que nous déjeunons à 4 heures?
7. Fume-t-on en atterrissant en avion?
8. Préférez-vous échouer aux examens?
9. Arrivez-vous en retard à toutes vos classes?
10. Les professeurs apprécient-ils les erreurs des étudiants?

B. Negative adverbs

Use the particle **ne** before the verb in a sentence containing a negative adverb. Negative adverbs follow a conjugated verb, but may precede infinitives. The negative adverbs are

point	*not at all*
plus	*no (not any) more*
jamais	*not ever, never*
guère	*hardly*
nulle part	*nowhere (follows an infinitive)*

Cela **ne** m'**intéresse point.**   *That doesn't interest me at all.*
Nous **ne voyons plus** ces gens-là.   *We don't see those people anymore.*
Ne parlez jamais sans penser!   *Never speak without thinking!*
Il est préférable de **ne plus**   *It's better not to think about those*
   penser à ces choses.   *things any more.*

> *REMEMBER:* Never use **pas** in a sentence containing a negative adverb.

EXERCISE 4-17: Answer the following questions in the negative by replacing the positive adverbs given in parentheses with their negative opposites. Answers and translations are at the end of the chapter.

1. Répondez-vous (toujours) en anglais?
2. Est-ce que vous descendez (encore une fois) à cette station?
3. Regrette-il (beaucoup) ses actions?
4. Est-ce que Guy téléphone (quelquefois) à Yvette?
5. Vos camarades travaillent-ils (continuellement)?

C. Negative nouns and pronouns

A negative noun or pronoun may be the subject or object of the verb, or the object of a preposition. Use the particle **ne** before the verb if a sentence contains one of the following negative nouns or pronouns.

rien	*not anything, nothing*
personne	*not anyone, no one*
aucun (-une)	*not one (of them)*

Son amitié **ne** m'**apporte rien**.	*Her friendship doesn't add anything to my life.*
Rien ne fait mal comme une migraine.	*Nothing hurts like a migraine.*
Je **n'accuse personne**!	*I'm not pointing my finger at anyone!*
Personne ne sympathise avec lui.	*No one understands his problems.*
Nous **n'**en **avons pris aucun**.	*We didn't take a single one of them.*
Aucun n'est valable.	*Not one of them is valid.*

> *NOTE:* **Aucun(e)** also functions as a negative adjective meaning *no* or *not one* (*of something*). When you introduce a noun phrase with **aucun**, the sentence becomes negative and you must use **ne** before the verb.

Jean-Pierre **n'a aucun** talent pour la musique.	*Jean-Pierre has no talent for music.*
Aucune manifestation **n'a** lieu en hiver.	*No demonstration takes place in winter.*

EXERCISE 4-18: Answer the following questions negatively, using **rien**, **personne**, or **aucun(e)** in place of the words given in parentheses. Answers and translations are at the end of the chapter.

1. (Qui) parle cinq langues dans votre famille?
2. (Qu'est-ce qui) précède la lettre **A** dans l'alphabet?
3. (Qui) regardez-vous en ce moment?
4. (Quel) pays est plus grand que la Russie?
5. (Que) mange-t-on en parlant?
6. (Quelle) lettre précède la lettre **A** dans l'alphabet?
7. (Que) refusez-vous dans un restaurant de luxe?
8. (Qui) proteste quand vous sortez le soir?
9. (Qui est-ce que) vous détestez?
10. (Qui) ressemble à Astérix?

D. Negative conjunctions

1. **Ni . . . ni**—used in a pair or a series—is a negative conjunction meaning *neither . . . nor*. Use the particle **ne** before the verb in a sentence containing **ni . . . ni**.

Ni ma mère **ni** mon père **ne** me **comprennent**.	*Neither my mother nor my father understands me.*
Cela **ne** me **fait ni** froid **ni** chaud.	*That doesn't affect me in the least.*

Je **ne** le ferais **ni** par amour
ni par haine.

*I wouldn't do it for love
or spite.*

2. Do not use a quantifier—**du**, **de la**, **des**, **un**, **une**—after the negative conjunction **ni**.

Je n'ai **ni voiture ni bicyclette**.
Mes amis ne mangent **ni viande ni
poisson**.

*I have neither a car nor a bicycle.
My friends eat neither (any) meat
nor (any) fish.*

> ***REMEMBER:*** Always use the particle **ne** before a verb in a sentence containing one or more negative adverbs, conjunctions, or noun phrases.

Yves **ne** prend **plus jamais rien**.
Personne ne va **nulle part**.

*Yves never drinks anything anymore.
Nobody goes anywhere.*

EXERCISE 4-19: Make the following sentences negative by replacing the conjunctions **(ou) . . . ou**, *(either) . . . or*, and **(et) . . . et**, *(both) . . . and*, with **ni . . . ni**. Answers and translations are at the end of the chapter.

1. Il abandonne et famille et foyer.
2. La mer et le soleil me suffisent.
3. On offre du thé ou du café.
4. Vous écoutez avec intérêt et avec attention.
5. Les Américains prennent un apéritif et un digestif.

SUMMARY

1. The subject pronouns are **je**, **tu**, **il**, **elle**, **on**, **nous**, **vous**, **ils**, and **elles**. The subject pronoun and its verb must agree in number and person.
2. **On** is an indefinite pronoun used as a subject pronoun with a third person singular verb.
3. The present indicative of regular **-er** verbs adds the endings **-e**, **-es**, **-e**, **-ons**, **-ez**, and **-ent** to the infinitive stem.
4. The present indicative of regular **–ir** verbs adds the endings **–is**, **–is**, **–it**, **–issons**, **–issez**, and **–issent** to the infinitive stem.
5. The present indicative of regular **-re** verbs adds the endings **-s**, **-s**, **-(t)**, **-ons**, **-ez**, and **-ent** to the infinitive stem.
6. When there is more than one verb in a simple sentence, all but the first verb are infinitives. Some infinitives follow the main verb without an intervening preposition, others require **à**, **de**, or another preposition.
7. Form the present participle of all verbs—except **être** and **avoir** and **savoir**—by dropping **-ons** from the **nous** form of the present indicative, and adding **-ant**.
8. An affirmative sentence becomes negative when **ne** precedes the verb and **pas** follows it.

RAISE YOUR GRADES

Regular verbs

Identify the conjugation to which the verb in each sentence belongs by writing **A** (regular **-er**), **B** (regular **-ir**), or **C** (regular **-re**) in the space provided before the number. Then rewrite the sentence, substituting the subject given in parentheses and making any necessary changes in the form of the verb. Answers and translations are at the end of the chapter.

_____ 1. Nous choisissons les meilleurs plats. (ils)
_____ 2. L'agent attend toujours votre réponse. (je)
_____ 3. Pourquoi hésites-tu à parler? (vous)
_____ 4. Nicole et Guy décident de partir en France. (nous)
_____ 5. Les camions transportent des marchandises. (le train)

_____ **6.** Un ambassadeur établit des rapports diplomatiques. (vous)
_____ **7.** Quand est-ce que tu finis ce semestre? (nous)
_____ **8.** Jean-Pierre et Richard descendent à l'Hôtel du Louvre. (Anne)
_____ **9.** Pourquoi interrompez-vous tout le temps? (il)
_____ **10.** A quelle heure mangent-ils? (nous)
_____ **11.** Où préférez-vous déjeuner aujourd'hui? (elles)
_____ **12.** Pourquoi punit-elle ces enfants? (tu)
_____ **13.** Les meilleurs étudiants répondent en français. (un bon élève)
_____ **14.** Les gens achètent les provisions au marché. (nous)
_____ **15.** Ecoutez-vous les informations à la radio? (il)
_____ **16.** Un bon citoyen obéit à la loi. (nous)
_____ **17.** Nous ne jetons pas l'argent par les fenêtres. (on)
_____ **18.** Quand commencez-vous à travailler? (nous)
_____ **19.** Elle saisit l'occasion pour annoncer léur départ. (je)
_____ **20.** Vendez-vous cette vieille auto? (tu)

Infinitives

Combine the following pairs of sentences into a single sentence containing an infinitive in the verb phrase. Be sure to use the appropriate preposition, where necessary. Answers and translations are at the end of the chapter.

Example:	Paul est content. Il a de bonnes notes.	*Paul is happy. He has good grades.*
	Paul est content d'avoir de bonnes notes.	*Paul is happy to have good grades.*

21. J'hésite. Je déclare mes intentions.
22. Nous refusons. Nous n'allons pas à l'opéra.
23. Vous achetez des fruits. Vous mangez des fruits.
24. Elle n'a pas besoin. Elle ne va pas à la banque.
25. Le professeur commence. Il explique la leçon.
26. J'ai très peur. Je ne voyage pas en avion.
27. Robert apporte un livre. Il lit un livre.
28. Tu invites tes amis. Ils viennent chez toi.
29. Les enfants apprennent. Ils comptent de un à dix.
30. Vous décidez. Vous partez dans trois jours.
31. Nous sommes bien obligés. Nous payons nos taxes.
32. Il est impossible. On ne trouve pas de taxi.
33. Je promets. Je viens à votre soirée.
34. Elles veulent bien. Elles font sa connaissance.
35. Tu as la mauvaise idée. Tu conduis toute la nuit.
36. Je pense cela. Je passe les vacances à la plage.
37. Le poète écoute la pluie. La pluie tombe.
38. Les sénateurs continuent. Ils discutent la guerre.
39. Jacques et Claire aiment cela. Ils sont ensemble.
40. Mon père ne nous permet pas. Nous ne rentrons pas à minuit.
41. Je travaille nuit et jour. Je gagne bien ma vie.
42. On ne fait pas d'omelettes. On ne casse pas d'oeufs.
43. Nous ne pouvons pas. Nous n'allons pas en France à bicyclette.
44. Le chef cherche une secrétaire. Elle remplace l'autre.
45. A 18 ans, les enfants arrêtent. Il ne grandissent plus.

Negatives

Answer the following questions in the negative, using negative adverbs or negative noun phrases when possible. Answers and translations are at the end of the chapter.

Example:	A-t-il quelque chose de sérieux?	*Does he have something serious?*
	Non, il n'a rien de sérieux.	*No, he has nothing serious.*

46. Y a-t-il quelqu'un à la porte?
47. Qui fait du tourisme au pôle nord?

48. Avez-vous quelque chose à dire?
49. Est-ce que tu aimes la mousse au chocolat?
50. Qui accompagnez-vous à l'aéroport?
51. A-t-il des frères et des soeurs?
52. Qu'est-ce qui est bon marché chez Tiffany?
53. Où allez-vous pour les vacances de Pâques?
54. Voyez-vous toujours vos amis de l'école élementaire?
55. Parlez-vous quelquefois anglais dans la classe de français?
56. Y-a-t-il enormément de pétrole en France?
57. Parle-t-on espagnol au Brésil?
58. Reste-t-il encore des Indiens en Argentine?
59. Est-ce que Paul et Jean êtes américains?
60. Laisse-t-elle ses cléfs quelque part?

CHAPTER ANSWERS

EXERCISE 4-1:

1. Oui, elles sont rouges en automne. *Yes, they are red in autumn.*
2. Oui, elle est en Normandie cet été. *Yes, she is in Normandy this summer.*
3. Oui, il est dû demain. *Yes, it will be due tomorrow.*
4. Oui, elle est anglaise. *Yes, she is English.*
5. Oui, ils sont malades. *Yes, they are sick.*
6. Oui, ils sont catholiques. *Yes, they are Catholic.*
7. Oui, elle est en Europe. *Yes, she is in Europe.*
8. Oui, ils sont toujours en couleurs. *Yes, they are always in color.*
9. Oui, il est à l'hôpital aujourd'hui. *Yes, he is at the hospital today.*
10. Oui, elles sont compliquées. *Yes, they are complicated.*

EXERCISE 4-2:

1. Vous parlez trop. *You talk too much.*
2. Il ne parle pas à son père. *He doesn't speak to his father.*
3. Je parle un peu français. *I speak a little French.*
4. Elles parlent anglais et français. *They speak English and French.*
5. Tu parles bien. *You speak well.*
6. Nous parlons souvent à ma mère. *We speak to my mother often.*
7. Je parle des vacances. *I talk about my vacation.*
8. Elle lui parle d'amour. *She speaks to him of love.*
9. Quelle surprise! Vous parlez français. *What a surprise! You speak French.*
10. Parles-tu anglais? *Do you speak English?*

EXERCISE 4-3:

1. Je porte une jolie robe. *I am wearing a pretty dress.*

2. Ils n'étudient pas assez. *They don't study enough.*
3. Elle prépare un repas pour la famille. *She is making a meal for the family.*
4. Elles regardent leurs enfants. *They watch their children.*
5. Nous chantons ensemble le jeudi. *We sing together on Thursdays.*
6. Est-ce que Charles aime ma robe? *Does Charles like my dress?*
7. Vous arrêtez les voleurs. *You stop the thieves.*
8. Nous fermons la porte. *We are closing the door.*
9. Je donne un cadeau au concierge. *I am giving a gift to the building manager.*
10. Anne et Matthieu montrent le chien aux enfants. *Anne and Matthew show the dog to the children.*

EXERCISE 4-4:

1. Si vous finissez à l'heure, vous pouvez partir. *If you finish on time, you can go.*
2. Quand il finit son travail, il est très heureux. *When he finishes his work, he is very happy.*
3. Le spectacle finit à trois heures de l'après-midi. *The performance finishes at three o'clock in the afternoon.*
4. Les cours finissent au mois de juin. *Classes finish in June.*
5. Est-ce que vous finissez la première? *Are you finishing on the first?*
6. Tout est bien qui finit bien. *All's well that ends well.*
7. Les couturières finissent les robes à la maison. *The dressmakers finish the dresses at home.*
8. Finis-tu tes exercices aujourd'hui? *Are you finishing your exercises today?*
9. Nous finissons notre dessert quand nous avons faim. *We finish our dessert when we are hungry.*
10. Rachel finit son petit déjeuner avant sa soeur. *Rachel finishes her breakfast before her sister.*

EXERCISE 4-5:

1. Le charpentier bâtit une maison. *The carpenter builds a house.*
2. Elle choisit le parfum le plus cher. *She chooses the most expensive perfume.*
3. Certains enfants grandissent vite. *Some children grow up fast.*
4. Les médecins guérissent les malades avec des médicaments. *Doctors cure the sick with medicines.*
5. Les parents sévères punissent leurs enfants. *Strict parents punish their children.*
6. Il réfléchit avant de répondre aux questions. *He thinks before answering questions.*
7. Avec son régime, elle maigrit. *She is losing weight on her diet.*
8. Pourquoi subis-tu sa mauvaise humeur? *Why do you put up with his bad mood?*
9. Les fermiers nourrissent les animaux de la ferme. *Farmers feed the farm animals.*
10. Obéissez-vous à la loi? *Do you obey the law?*

EXERCISE 4-6:

1. Ils vendent des tables. *They sell tables.*
2. Nous ne vendons pas à crédit. *We do not sell on credit.*
3. Vous vendez des chapeaux. *You sell hats.*
4. Si je vends trop cher, personne n'achète. *If I sell too expensively, no one buys.*
5. Elle vend de beaux bijoux. *She sells beautiful jewels.*
6. Ils vendent des livres d'occasion. *They sell second-hand books.*
7. Est-ce que vous vendez des objets d'art dans cette boutique? *Do you sell art objects in this store?*
8. Combien vends-tu ces tapis? *How much are these rugs?*
9. Yvonne vend sa bicyclette bon marché. *Yvonne is selling her bicycle cheap.*
10. Nous vendons bien les marchandises. *We sell our merchandise easily.*

EXERCISE 4-7:

1. Je rends les livres à la bibliothèque. *I return the books to the library.*
2. Ce garçon dépend trop de ses parents. *That boy depends too much on his parents.*
3. Il confond les paroles du discours. *He confuses the words of the speech.*
4. Les présidents rompent les relations entre pays. *The presidents are breaking off relations between the countries.*
5. L'argent corrompt parfois les hommes. *Money often corrupts men.*
6. Vous interrompez trop souvent. *You interrupt too often.*
7. Mon père perd ses cheveux. *My father is losing his hair.*
8. Nous rendons nos livres à la bibliothèque. *We return our books to the library.*
9. Les chiens méchants mordent quand il fait chaud. *Mean dogs bite when the weather is hot.*
10. Les costumes pendent dans le placard. *The suits hang in the closet.*

EXERCISE 4-8:

1. Nous annonçons les nouvelles à la radio. *We announce the news on the radio.*
2. Nous mangeons trois fois par jour. *We eat three times a day.*
3. Nous partageons le gâteau. *We share the cake.*
4. Vous employez de l'encre bleue. *You use blue ink.*
5. Vous vous ennuyez ici. *You are bored here.*
6. Nous achetons des chaussures. *We are buying shoes.*
7. Ils emmènent les enfants. *They are taking the children.*
8. Je lève le drapeau. *I raise the flag.*
9. Votre mère jette de vieux livres. *Your mother throws away old books.*
10. Nous préférons le café. *We prefer coffee.*

EXERCISE 4-9:

1. Nous acceptons d'accompagner les enfants. *We agree to go with the children.*
2. Le pilote oublie d'annoncer le départ. *The pilot forgets to announce the departure.*
3. Nous finissons de manger à midi. *We finish eating at noon.*
4. Il risque de manquer son autobus. *He takes a chance on missing the bus.*
5. Je décide de voter pour votre parti. *I decide to vote for your party.*
6. Elle refuse de travailler des heures supplémentaires. *She refuses to work any additional hours.*
7. Je promets d'employer la voiture de mon père. *I promise to use my father's car.*
8. Ils évitent d'assister aux cours le samedi. *They avoid attending classes on Saturday.*
9. Je jure d'aider mes parents. *I vow to help my parents.*
10. Il tâche de compléter ses devoirs. *He tries to complete his homework.*

EXERCISE 4-10:

1. Nous écrivons à nos amis de venir par le prochain avion. *We write our friends to come on the next plane.*
2. Elle dit à Pierre de regarder la première page du journal. *She tells Pierre to look at the first page of the newpaper.*
3. Le médecin ordonne à la malade de rester une semaine au lit. *The doctor orders the patient to stay in bed a week.*
4. Ses parents ne permettent pas à Louise de passer la nuit dehors. *Her parents don't allow Louise to stay out overnight.*
5. Le client commande au serveur d'apporter une bouteille de champagne. *The customer asks the waiter to bring a bottle of champagne.*

EXERCISE 4-11:

1. Mon médecin a l'habitude de soigner les malades. *My doctor usually cares for patients.*
2. Il est impossible d'arriver à l'heure. *It is impossible to arrive on time.*
3. Je n'ai vraiment pas envie de préparer le dîner. *I truly don't feel like cooking dinner.*
4. Henri-Roger n'a pas le temps de déjeuner. *Henri-Roger doesn't have time to lunch.*
5. Nous sommes bien obligés de remercier nos clients. *We'd like to thank our customers.*
6. Il est nécessaire de payer ses taxes. *He must pay his taxes.*
7. Elles sont vraiment contentes de finir leurs études. *They are really happy to finish their studies.*
8. J'ai le plaisir de présenter mes amis à mes parents. *It gives me pleasure to introduce my friends to my parents.*
9. Elle est enchantée de voyager en première classe. *She is delighted to travel first class.*
10. Il est surprenant de remarquer toutes ces erreurs. *It is surprising to find all these errors.*

EXERCISE 4-12:

1. Il hésite à critiquer ses enfants. *He hesitates to criticize his children.*
2. Nous commençons à profiter du beau temps. *We are beginning to take advantage of the good weather.*
3. Elle continue à étudier le russe. *She continues to study Russian.*
4. Je tarde à demander mon passeport. *It's time for me to get my passport.*
5. Nous réussissons à finir cet exercice. *We succeed in finishing this exercise.*

EXERCISE 4-13:

1. Vous achetez des provisions pour préparer les repas. *You buy groceries in order to make meals.*
2. Les enfants traversent la rue sans regarder. *Children cross the street without looking.*
3. Catherine quitte la maison sans fermer les fenêtres. *Catherine left the house without closing the windows.*
4. Son mari travaille 50 heures par semaine pour avancer dans sa carrière. *Her husband works 50 hours a week in order to get ahead.*
5. Le corbeau ouvre son grand bec pour montrer sa belle voix. *The crow opens his big beak in order to show off his beautiful voice.*

EXERCISE 4-14:

1. Il faut étudier la grammaire. *It is necessary to study grammar.*
2. Je désire voyager en Europe. *I want to travel to Europe.*
3. Ils viennent annoncer la bonne nouvelle. *They are coming to announce the good news.*
4. J'entends quelqu'un sonner à la porte. *I hear someone ringing at the door.*
5. Elles aiment parler au téléphone. *They like to talk on the telephone.*
6. Il préfère dîner seul au restaurant. *He prefers to dine alone at a restaurant.*
7. On entend le train arriver. *They see the train arrive.*
8. Je déteste travailler dans le jardin. *I detest working in the garden.*
9. Elle préfère préparer des plats chinois. *She prefers to prepare Chinese dishes.*
10. Nous pouvons échanger les cadeaux de nos amis. *We can exchange our friends' presents.*
11. Ils doivent rentrer de bonne heure. *They must come back early.*
12. Je vais partir tout de suite après la cérémonie. *I am going to leave right after the ceremony.*
13. Nous pensons acheter une nouvelle voiture. *We are thinking of buying a new car.*
14. Tout le monde la regarde jouer au tennis. *Everyone watches her play tennis.*
15. Je descends manger tout de suite! *I'm coming down to eat right away!*

EXERCISE 4-15:

1. Vous apprenez bien une langue en la pratiquant beaucoup. *You learn a language well by speaking it.*
2. Les valises arrivent sur des tapis roulants. *The suitcases arrive on a conveyor belt.*
3. En cherchant, je trouve une bonne réponse. *While searching, I found a good answer.*
4. Il s'en va sur la montagne chantant et sifflant. *He goes to the mountain, singing and whistling.*
5. Je n'ai jamais vu une soucoupe volante. *I have never seen a flying saucer.*
6. J'écoute en pensant à autre chose. *I listen while thinking of other things.*
7. Elle n'est pas contente d'être une femme obéissante! *She is not content to be an obedient woman!*
8. Ne parle pas en mangeant. *Don't talk while you're eating.*
9. Tu deviens bronzé en restant au soleil. *You become tan from staying in the sun.*
10. Ils arrivent en criant parce qu'ils ont gagné. *They arrived shouting because they had won.*

EXERCISE 4-16:

1. Non, 4 ne précède pas 3. *No. 4 does not come before 3.*
2. Non, il ne neige pas en été. *No, it doesn't snow in summer.*
3. Non, nous ne mangeons pas le dessert avant la salade. *No, we don't eat the dessert before the salad.*
4. Non, je n'étudie pas le chinois ce semestre. *No, I'm not studying Chinese this semester.*
5. Non, nous ne fermons pas les fenêtres en juillet. *No, we don't close the windows in July.*
6. Non, nous ne déjeunons pas à 4 heures. *No, we don't have lunch at 4 o'clock.*

7. Non, on ne fume pas en atterrissant en avion. *No, you don't smoke while landing in an airplane.*

8. Non, je préfère ne pas échouer aux examens. *No, I prefer not to fail tests.*

9. Non, je n'arrive pas en retard à toutes mes classes. *No, I don't come late to all my classes.*

10. Non, les professeurs n'apprécient pas les erreurs des étudiants. *No, the professors don't appreciate the students' mistakes.*

EXERCISE 4-17:

1. Non, je ne réponds jamais en anglais. *No, I never answer in English.*

2. Non, je ne descends plus à cette station. *No, I don't get off at this station anymore.*

3. Non, il ne regrette point ses actions. *No, he doesn't regret his actions at all.*

4. Non, Guy ne téléphone jamais à Yvette. *No, Guy never calls Yvette.*

5. Non, mes camarades ne travaillent jamais. *No, my friends never work.*

EXERCISE 4-18:

1. Personne ne parle cinq langues dans ma famille. *No one in my family speaks five languages.*

2. Rien ne précède le lettre **A** dans l'alphabet. *Nothing precedes the letter A in the alphabet.*

3. Je ne regarde personne en ce moment. *I'm not recommending anyone at this moment.*

4. Aucun pays n'est plus grand que la Russie. *No country is larger than Russia.*

5. On ne mange rien en parlant. *One shouldn't eat anything while speaking.*

6. Aucune lettre ne précède la lettre **A** dans l'alphabet. *No letter precedes the letter A in the alphabet.*

7. Je ne refuse rien dans un restaurant de luxe. *I'm not refused anything in a deluxe restaurant.*

8. Personne ne proteste quand je sors le soir. *Nobody objects when I go out at night.*

9. Je ne déteste personne. *I don't detest anyone.*

10. Personne ne ressemble à Astérix. *No one resembles Asterisk.*

EXERCISE 4-19:

1. Il n'abandonne ni famille ni foyer. *He abandons neither family nor home.*

2. Ni la mer ni le soleil ne me suffisent. *Neither the sea nor the sun is enough for me.*

3. On n'offre ni thé ni café. *They offer neither tea nor coffee.*

4. Vous n'écoutez ni avec intérêt ni avec attention. *You listen with neither interest nor attention.*

5. Les Américains ne prennent ni apéritif ni digestif. *Americans take neither an appetizer nor an after dinner drink.*

RAISE YOUR GRADES

Regular verbs

B 1. Ils choisissent les meilleurs plats. *They choose the best dishes.*

C 2. J'attends toujours votre réponse. *I'm always waiting for your answer.*

A 3. Pourquoi hésitez-vous à parler? *Why do you hesitate to speak?*

A 4. Nous décidons de partir en France. *We decide to leave for France.*

A 5. Le train transporte des marchandises. *The train carries merchandise.*

B 6. Vous établissez des rapports diplomatiques. *You establish diplomatic relations.*

B 7. Quand est-ce que nous finissons ce semestre? *When do we finish this semester?*

C 8. Anne descend à l'Hôtel du Louvre. *Anne stays at the Hotel du Louvre.*

C 9. Pourquoi interrompt-il tout le temps? *Why does he interrupt all the time?*

A 10. A quelle heure mangeons-nous? *What time do we eat?*

A 11. Où préfèrent-elles déjeuner aujourd'hui? *Where do they want to have lunch today?*

B 12. Pourquoi punis-tu ces enfants? *Why are you punishing these children?*

C 13. Un bon élève répond en français. *A good student answers in French.*

A 14. Nous achetons les provisions au marché. *We buy groceries cheap.*

A 15. Écoute-t-il les informations à la radio? *Does he listen to the news on the radio?*

B 16. Nous obéissons à la loi. *We obey the law.*

A 17. On ne jette pas l'argent par les fenêtres. *One doesn't throw money out the window.*

A 18. Quand commençons-nous à travailler? *When do we begin to work?*

B 19. Je saisis l'occasion pour annoncer leur départ. *I take this opportunity to announce their departure.*

C 20. Vends-tu cette vieille auto? *Are you selling this old car?*

Infinitives

21. J'hésite à déclarer mes intentions. *I hesitate to declare my intentions.*

22. Nous refusons d'aller à l'opéra. *We refuse to go to the opera.*

23. Vous achetez des fruits à manger. *You buy fruit to eat.*

24. Elle n'a pas besoin d'aller à la banque. *She doesn't need to go to the bank.*
25. Le professeur commence à expliquer la leçon. *The professor begins to explain the lesson.*
26. J'ai très peur de voyager en avion. *I'm very frightened of traveling by plane.*
27. Robert apporte un livre à lire. *Robert brings a book to read.*
28. Tu invites tes amis à venir chez toi. *You invite your friends to come to your house.*
29. Les enfants apprennent à compter de un à dix. *Children learn to count from one to ten.*
30. Vous décidez de partir dans trois jours. *You decide to leave in three days.*
31. Nous sommes bien obligés de payer nos taxes. *We must pay our taxes.*
32. Il est impossible de trouver un taxi. *It is impossible to find a taxi.*
33. Je promets de venir à votre soirée. *I promise to come to your party.*
34. Elles veulent bien faire sa connaissance. *They very much want to meet him.*
35. Tu as la mauvaise idée de conduire toute la nuit. *You have the bad idea of driving all night.*
36. Je pense passer les vacances à la plage. *I am thinking of spending my vacation at the beach.*
37. Le poète écoute tomber la pluie. *The poet listens to the rain fall.*
38. Les sénateurs continuent à discuter la guerre. *The senators continue discussing the war.*
39. Jacques et Claire aiment être ensemble. *Jacques and Claire love to be together.*
40. Mon père ne nous permet pas de rentrer à minuit. *My father does not allow us to come home at midnight.*
41. Je travaille nuit et jour pour bien gagner ma vie. *I work night and day in order to make a good living.*
42. On ne fait pas d'omelettes sans casser d'oeufs. *You can't make an omelet without breaking some eggs.*
43. Nous ne pouvons pas aller en France à bicyclette. *We cannot go to France on a bicycle.*
44. Le chef cherche un secrétaire pour remplacer l'autre. *The boss is looking for a secretary to replace the other one.*
45. A 18 ans, les enfants arrêtent de grandir. *At 18 years children stop growing.*

Negatives

46. Non, il n'y a personne à la porte. *No, there is no one at the door.*
47. Personne de fait du tourisme au pôle nord. *No one takes a trip to the north pole.*
48. Non, je n'ai rien à dire. *No, I have nothing to say.*
49. Non, je n'aime pas la mousse au chocolat. *No, I don't like chocolate mousse.*
50. Je n'accompagne personne à l'aéroport. *I'm not going with anyone to the airport.*
51. Non, il n'a ni frères ni soeurs. *No, he has neither brothers nor sisters.*
52. Rien n'est bon marché chez Tiffany. *Nothing is cheap at Tiffany's.*
53. Je ne vais nulle part pour les vacances de Pâques. *I'm not going anywhere for Easter vacation.*
54. Non, je ne vois plus mes amis de l'école élémentaire. *No, I no longer see my friends from school.*
55. Non, je ne parle jamais anglais dans la classe de français. *No, I never speak English in French class.*
56. Non, il n'y a point de pétrole en France. *No, there is no oil in France.*
57. Non, on ne parle pas espagnol au Brésil. *No, they don't speak Spanish in Brazil.*
58. Non, il ne reste plus d'Indiens en Argentine. *No, there are no longer Indians in Argentina.*
59. Non, ni Paul ni Jean ne sommes américains. *No, neither Paul nor Jean is American.*
60. Non, elle ne laisse ses clefs nulle part. *No, she didn't leave her keys anywhere.*

5 PRESENT TENSE OF IRREGULAR VERBS

THIS CHAPTER IS ABOUT

☑ **The Verb Etre,** *To Be*
☑ **The Verb Avoir,** *To Have*
☑ **Patterns of Irregular Verbs in the Present Tense**

5-1. The Verb Etre, *To Be*

Etre, *to be*, is the most frequently used French verb. It is an irregular verb which has a different present tense form for each of the six persons. Since **être** does not follow a predictable pattern, you must simply memorize its different forms.

A. Present tense of être

être, *to be*

je **suis**	*I am*	nous **sommes**	*we are*
tu **es**	*you are*	vous **êtes**	*you are*
il, elle **est**	*he, she is*	ils, elles **sont**	*they are*
on **est**	*one is, we, you, people are*		

B. Use of être as a main verb

Use **être** as the main verb in a sentence to identify or describe the subject.

Paris **est la capitale de la France.**	*Paris is the capital of France.*
Ses idées **sont brillantes.**	*Her ideas are brilliant.*
Leur maison **est à côté de la banque.**	*Their house is next to the bank.*

> *REMEMBER:* When the subject of a sentence is a noun rather than a subject pronoun, always use the third-person form of the verb—singular or plural.

EXERCISE 5-1: Answer the following questions using the cues given in parentheses. Answers and translations are at the end of the chapter.

Example:	Qui est le meilleur étudiant de la classe? (vous)	*Who is the best student in the class? (you)*
	Vous êtes le meilleur étudiant de la classe.	*You are the best student in the class.*

1. Qu'est-ce qui est à la première page? (les photos)
2. Qui sont les plus jolies filles? (mes soeurs)
3. Qui est cet homme sur la photo? (tu)
4. Qui est le plus grand garçon? (Paul)
5. Qui est notre assistant au laboratoire? (Claude)
6. Qui est libre demain matin? (je)
7. Qui est mexicain? (nous)
8. Qui est le prochain candidat? (vous)
9. Qu'est-ce qui est dans ce carnet? (les adresses)
10. Qui est spécialiste en histoire? (Monsieur Duguay)

5-2. The Verb Avoir, *To Have*

Avoir is the second most frequently used verb in French. **Avoir** is also an irregular verb, so you will have to memorize its present tense forms.

A. Present tense of avoir

avoir, *to have*

j'**ai**	*I have*	nous **avons**	*we have*
tu **as**	*you have*	vous **avez**	*you have*
il, elle **a**	*he, she has*	ils, elles **ont**	*they have*
on **a**	*one has, we, you, people have*		

EXERCISE 5-2: Answer the questions according to the cues given in parentheses and using the appropriate form of **avoir**. Answers and translations are at the end of the chapter.

1. Qui a un chapeau ridicule? (Robert)
2. Qui a une classe cet après-midi? (nous)
3. Qui a les plus jolis yeux? (mes soeurs)
4. Qu'est-ce qui a un bec et des ailes? (les oiseaux)
5. Qui a le temps de prendre un café? (je)
6. Qui a de la chance? (tu)
7. Qui a la voiture la plus rapide? (vous)
8. Qui a une répétition ce soir? (les acteurs)
9. Qui a l'air féroce? (ces chiens-là)
10. Qui a le temps d'étudier? (nous)

B. Uses of avoir as a main verb

1. Use **avoir** as a main verb to indicate the relationship between a noun or noun phrase and the sentence subject.

Chaque danseur **a** un rôle difficile.	*Each dancer has a difficult part.*
Nous **avons** des cours le matin.	*We have courses in the morning.*
Ils **ont** quelque chose à faire.	*They have things to do.*

2. Use **avoir and a noun** to form many idiomatic expressions in French, which use a form of the verb *to be and an adjective* in English. These expressions are idiomatic because no article introduces the noun, and the entire phrase forms a single unit of meaning. The following is a list of the most common of these expressions.

avoir . . . ans	*to be . . . years old*
avoir besoin de	*to need*
avoir chaud	*to be warm*
avoir de la chance	*to be lucky*
avoir envie de	*to feel like (doing or having something)*
avoir faim	*to be hungry*
avoir froid	*to be cold*
avoir honte	*to be ashamed*
avoir mal (à la tête)	*to hurt (to have a headache)*
avoir peur	*to be afraid*
avoir raison	*to be right*
avoir soif	*to be thirsty*
avoir sommeil	*to be sleepy*
avoir tort	*to be wrong*

Après le travail j'**ai faim** et j'**ai sommeil**.	*After work I'm hungry and sleepy.*
Le cycliste **a mal** à la jambe.	*The cyclist's leg hurts.*
J'ai soif; j'**ai besoin d'**eau.	*I'm thirsty; I need (some) water.*
Brigitte **a envie de** courir.	*Brigitte feels like running.*

> *NOTE:* Use the personal expressions **avoir chaud**, *to be warm*, and **avoir froid**, *to be cold*, when you refer to how you or someone else *feels*. BUT use the impersonal expression **il fait** to refer to the *weather*.

Nous **avons** très **chaud** parce qu'il **fait chaud**.   *We are very warm because it's hot out.*

> You may also use these impersonal expressions to talk about the weather:

il fait beau (temps)	*it's nice out*
il fait mauvais (temps)	*it's bad out*
il fait du vent	*it's windy*
il fait de la pluie OU **il pleut**	*it's raining*
il fait de la neige OU **il neige**	*it's snowing*

3. Use the third person singular of **avoir** in the invariable expression **il y a**, *there is, there are*, simply to say that something exists.

Il y a un examen demain.   *There is an exam tomorrow.*
Il y a des mouches dans ma soupe!   *There are flies in my soup!*

4. You may also use **il y a** to mean *ago, for,* or *since.*

Je suis partie **il y a** un mois.   *I left a month ago.*
Il y a deux heures que Martine l'attend.   *Martine has been waiting for him for two hours.*

5. **Il y a** also has some idiomatic uses.

Qu'est-ce qu'il y a?   *What's the matter?*
Il n'y a pas de quoi.   *Don't mention it.*

EXERCISE 5-3: Answer the following questions using an *idiomatic expression* with **avoir**. Answers and translations are at the end of the chapter.

1. Qu'avez-vous avant de manger?
2. Qu'avons-nous avant de boire?
3. Qu'est-ce qu'on a quand on est malade?
4. Qu'est-ce que tu as en face du danger?
5. Qu'est-ce que j'ai avant de dormir?
6. Qu'est-ce que vous avez si vous donnez la bonne réponse?
7. Qu'est-ce que vous avez si vous donnez la mauvaise réponse?
8. Qu'est-ce que tu as si tu gagnes à la loterie?
9. Qu'est-ce que nous avons en hiver?
10. Qu'est-ce que les gens ont en été?

5-3. Patterns of Irregular Verbs in the Present Tense

All irregular verbs—except **aller**, *to go*—have infinitives that end in **-(o)ir** or **-re**. Although many common verbs besides **être** and **avoir** are irregular, most of them follow some general patterns.

A. Present tense singular forms of irregular verbs

Most irregular verbs end in **-s, -s, -t** in the three singular forms.

1. For some verbs, add these endings directly to the infinitive stem.

conduire, *to drive*	**croire**, *to believe*	**courir**, *to run*
je conduis	je crois	je cours
tu conduis	tu crois	tu cours
il conduit	il croit	il court

dire, *to tell, say*	**écrire**, *to write*	**faire**, *to do, make*
je dis	j'écris	je fais
tu dis	tu écris	tu fais
il dit	elle écrit	elle fait

lire, *to read*	**produire**, *to produce*	**voir**, *to see*
je lis	je produis	je vois
tu lis	tu produis	tu vois
elle lit	elle produit	on voit

> *NOTE:* Verbs whose stem ends in **-d** or **-t**, and those verbs based on **vaincre**, *to conquer*, do not add the final **-t** in the third person singular.

admettre, *to admit*	**battre**, *to hit*	**comprendre**, *to understand*
j'admets	je bats	je comprends
tu admets	tu bats	tu comprends
il admet	elle bat	on comprend

convaincre, *to convince*	**coudre**, *to sew*	**mettre**, *to put*
je convaincs	je couds	je mets
tu convaincs	tu couds	tu mets
on convainc	il coud	elle met

2. The following verbs drop their final stem consonant before adding **-s, -s, -t**.

battre, *to beat*	**dormir**, *to sleep*	**mettre**, *to put*	**partir**, *to leave*
je bats	je dors	je mets	je pars
tu bats	tu dors	tu mets	tu pars
il bat	elle dort	on met	il part

savoir, *to know*	**servir**, *to serve*
je sais	je sers
tu sais	tu sers
elle sait	on sert

> *NOTE:* All verbs ending in **-indre** also drop their final stem consonant before adding **-s, -s, -t**.

craindre, *to fear*	**joindre**, *to put together*
je crains	je joins
tu crains	tu joins
il craint	elle joint

3. Some verbs undergo a vowel change when the last vowel of the stem is stressed.

acquérir, *to acquire*	**mourir**, *to die*	**venir**, *to come*	**tenir**, *to hold*
j'acquiers	je meurs	je viens	je tiens
tu acquiers	tu meurs	tu viens	tu tiens
il acquiert	elle meurt	on vient	il tient

> *NOTE:* The verbs **devoir** and **savoir** change vowels as well as drop the final stem consonants in the singular.

devoir, *must*	**savoir**, *to know*
je **dois**	je **sais**
tu **dois**	tu **sais**
il **doit**	elle **sait**

The verbs **pouvoir** and **vouloir** also change vowels and drop the final stem consonants—in addition, they use an old spelling for the final **-us**—**-ux**.

pouvoir, *to be able*	vouloir, *to want*
je **peux**	je **veux**
tu **peux**	tu **veux**
on **peut**	il **veut**

4. The verb **cueillir**, *to pick*, and its compounds, and verbs whose infinitives end in **-vrir** or **-frir** follow the pattern of regular **-er** verbs.

ouvrir, *to open*	offrir, *to offer*	accueillir, *to welcome*
j'ouvre	j'offre	j'accueille
tu ouvres	tu offres	tu accueilles
elle ouvre	on offre	il accueille

  REMEMBER: Only the verbs **être**, **avoir**, and **aller** follow no predictable pattern in the present singular.

être, *to be*	avoir, *to have*	aller, *to go*
je **suis**	j'**ai**	je **vais**
tu **es**	tu **as**	tu **vas**
elle **est**	on **a**	il **va**

EXERCISE 5-4: Substitute the subject given in parentheses into each of the following sentences, making any necessary changes in the form of the verb. Answers and translations are at the end of the chapter.

1. On boit souvent du thé glacé en été. (je)
2. Est-ce que j'obtiens ta permission? (il)
3. Va-t-on au laboratoire pour apprendre la prononciation? (elle)
4. Souffres-tu en pensant aux autres? (on)
5. Je fais la cuisine tous les soirs. (ma femme)
6. Est-ce que j'écris de longs exercices? (tu)
7. Tu conduis bien, mais un peu trop vite. (je)
8. Prends-tu tes cours au sérieux? (il)
9. Est-ce que je viens à toutes tes fêtes? (Robert)
10. Tu lis cette phrase en ce moment. (je)
11. Bernard éteint-il la lampe avant de sortir? (Marie)
12. Je convaincs les clients acheter les livres. (tu)
13. Il résoud tous les problèmes. (tu)
14. Qu'en dis-tu? (on)
15. Anne-Marie ne sait pas mon adresse. (tu)
16. On ne peut pas continuer comme cela. (je)
17. Tu dois venir plus souvent. (Rodolphe)
18. Où met-on les parapluies? (tu)
19. Je crains le mauvais temps. (l'agriculteur)
20. Pourquoi ne cueilles-tu pas ces roses? (elle)

B. Present tense plural forms of irregular verbs

The most common endings for the plural of the present tense are **-ons**, **-ez**, and **-ent**. Only **être**, **avoir**, **aller**, **dire**, and **faire** are irregular in the present plural.

1. The following verbs add the plural endings directly to the infinitive stem.

battre, *to beat*	courir, *to run*	couvrir, *to cover*
nous batt**ons**	nous cour**ons**	nous couvr**ons**
vous batt**ez**	vous cour**ez**	vous couvr**ez**
ils batt**ent**	elles cour**ent**	ils couvr**ent**

croire, *to believe*	découvrir, *to discover*	dormir, *to sleep*
nous croy**ons**	nous découvr**ons**	nous dorm**ons**
vous croy**ez**	vous découvr**ez**	vous dorm**ez**
elles croi**ent**	ils découvr**ent**	elles dorm**ent**

mettre, *to put*	**offrir**, *to offer*	**partir**, *to leave*
nous mett**ons**	nous off**rons**	nous part**ons**
vous mett**ez**	vous off**rez**	vous part**ez**
ils mett**ent**	elles off**rent**	ils part**ent**
savoir, *to know*	**sentir**, *to feel*	**souffrir**, *to suffer*
nous sav**ons**	nous sent**ons**	nous souff**rons**
vous sav**ez**	vous sent**ez**	vous souff**rez**
elles sav**ent**	ils sent**ent**	elles souff**rent**
vaincre, *to conquer*	**voir**, *to see*	**sortir**, *to go out*
nous vainqu**ons**	nous voy**ons**	nous sort**ons**
vous vainqu**ez**	vous voy**ez**	vous sort**ez**
ils vainqu**ent**	elles voy**ent**	ils sort**ent**

> *NOTE:* In verbs like **voir** and **croire**, the **-y-** in the **nous** and **vous** forms is simply an alternate spelling for **-i-** in nonfinal syllables. The **-qu-** in the plural forms of **vaincre** maintains the *hard c* pronunciation of the infinitive.

2. Some verbs add a consonant (or consonants) to the stem before the plural endings.

coudre, *to sew*	**craindre**, *to fear*
nous cou**sons**	nous crai**gnons**
vous cou**sez**	vous crai**gnez**
elles cou**sent**	ils crai**gnent**
connaître, *to be familiar with*	**écrire**, *to write*
nous connai**ssons**	nous écri**vons**
vous connai**ssez**	vous écri**vez**
elles connai**ssent**	ils écri**vent**
lire, *to read*	**produire**, *to produce*
nous li**sons**	nous produi**sons**
vous li**sez**	vous produi**sez**
elles li**sent**	ils produi**sent**

> *NOTE:* All verbs ending in **-uire** add an **-s**—following the pattern of **produire**. All verbs ending in **-indre** add **-gn-**—following the pattern of **craindre**.

3. Some verbs drop a consonant before the plural endings are added.

prendre, *to take*	**résoudre**, *to resolve*
nous pre**nons**	nous réso**lvons**
vous pre**nez**	vous réso**lvez**
elles pren**nent**	ils réso**lvent**

> *NOTE:* All compounds of **prendre** follow the same pattern. All verbs ending in **-oudre** follow the pattern of **résoudre**.

4. When there is a vowel change in the singular, the vowel in the third person plural (**ils, elles**) corresponds to that of the singular forms. **Savoir** is the only exception—its plural is regular.

acquérir, *to acquire*	**mourir**, *to die*	**devoir**, *must*
(j'acqu**ie**rs)	(tu m**eu**rs)	(je d**oi**s)
nous acqu**é**rons	nous mourons	nous devons
vous acqu**é**rez	vous mourez	vous devez
elles acqu**iè**rent	ils m**eu**rent	elles d**oi**vent

boire, *to drink*	**venir**, *to come*
(il **b**o**it**)	(on **v**ient)
nous buvons	nous venons
vous buvez	vous venez
ils **b**oivent	elles **v**iennent

NOTE:　**Boire** is the only verb whose **nous** and **vous** forms have a vowel which does not occur in the infinitive or in the singular forms.

NOTE:　Use the double **-nn-** spelling in the third personal plural of all verbs based on **venir**, **tenir**, and **prendre**—**ils comprennent**, *they understand*; **elles obtiennent**, *they obtain*; **ils reviennent**, *they come back*.

REMEMBER:

* **être** is the only verb whose first person plural does not end in **-ons**—**nous sommes**.
* **être**, **faire**, and **dire** are the only verbs whose second person plural forms do not end in **-ez**—**vous êtes, vous faites, vous dites**.
* **être**, **faire**, **avoir**, and **aller** are the only verbs whose third person plural forms do not end in **-ent**—**ils sont, ils font, ils ont, ils vont**.

(See the Appendix for the complete conjugation of common irregular verbs.)

EXERCISE 5-5:　Rewrite the following sentences by replacing the subjects with those given in parentheses. Answers and translations are at the end of the chapter.

Example:　　Nous découvrons la vérité. (les juges)　　*We discover the truth. (the judges)*

　　　　　　Les juges découvrent la vérité.　　*Judges discover the truth.*

1. Je crains les tremblements de terre. (ils)
2. Leur voiture démarre sans hésitation. (nos vélos)
3. Cette administration offre des emplois. (nous)
4. Ils éteignent toutes les lampes. (nous)
5. Je crois à cette histoire. (elles)
6. Les étudiants sortent tous les soirs. (vous)
7. Nous écrivons de longues lettres. (elles)
8. Le policier écrit son rapport. (nous)
9. Le théâtre ouvre à minuit. (les cinémas)
10. On écrit des cartes postales de France. (nous)
11. Les enfants dorment tranquillement par terre. (vous)
12. Les sciences conquièrent les obstacles. (nous)
13. Elles font toujours des erreurs. (vous)
14. Pauline sert dans un restaurant. (ses amies)
15. Nous courons trois kilomètres chaque matin. (Elle)
16. J'obtiens les meilleurs fruits. (nous)
17. Elle ne peut pas refuser de venir. (ils)
18. Nous voulons être à l'heure. (Jean et Sylvie)
19. J'attends depuis ce matin. (Les clients)
20. Tu mets la table pour six personnes. (Les serveurs)
21. On ne lit pas les journaux étrangers. (ils)
22. Vous peignez les murs de votre chambre. (nous)

23. Je ne sais pas quoi faire. (Les pilotes)
24. Votre avenir prend un tournant intéressant. (vos destinées)
25. Nous offrons notre opinion. (vous)

SUMMARY

1. The present tense of the irregular verb **être** is je **suis**, tu **es**, il **est**, nous **sommes**, vous **êtes**, ils **sont**.
2. The present tense of the irregular verb avoir is j'**ai**, tu **as**, il **a**, nous **avons**, vous **avez**, ils **ont**.
3. The singular forms of most irregular verbs end in **-s**, **-s**, **-t**, except after final **-t** and **-d**.
4. Verbs ending in **-vrir**, **-ffrir**, and those based on **cueillir**, have the **-e**, **-es**, **-e** endings.
5. The plural endings for all verbs except **être**, **aller**, **avoir**, **faire**, and **dire** are **-ons**, **-ez**, and **-ent**.
6. Most irregular verbs follow a fairly consistent pattern. Verbs following unusual patterns may add consonants and/or change vowels in the final syllable.

RAISE YOUR GRADES

Present indicative

Decide whether the present tense forms of the verb in each of the following sentences is regular or irregular. Then write the letter from the following list that corresponds with its conjugation. Answers and translations are at the end of the chapter.

A   **-er** verb
B   **-ir** verb
C   **-re** verb
D   irregular verb

_____ 1. Je réussis où les autres ne réussissent pas.
_____ 2. Croyez-vous qu'elle croit cette histoire?
_____ 3. Ma mère boit du thé pendant que nous buvons du café.
_____ 4. Nous répondons à la question s'il n'y répond pas.
_____ 5. Partez-vous quand il part ou quand je pars?
_____ 6. Si vous ne conduisez pas, je conduis moi-même.
_____ 7. Elle vit près de la maison où vivent les Lévèque.
_____ 8. Si vous écrivez, ils vont écrire aussi.
_____ 9. Personne ne peint comme vous peignez.
_____ 10. Jean choisit le dessin, mais vous choisissez la couleur.
_____ 11. Nous appelons le numéro qu'il appelle.
_____ 12. Je complète cet exercice sans compléter mon travail.
_____ 13. Ils applaudissent quand il ne faut pas applaudir.
_____ 14. Vous recevez tout ce que les autres reçoivent.
_____ 15. Je sais que vous ne savez pas son adresse.
_____ 16. Quand elle entre, nous entrons avec elle.
_____ 17. Si tu peux le faire nous pouvons t'aider.
_____ 18. Ma radio produit un son que les autres ne produisent pas.
_____ 19. Je sens pour vous ce que vous ne sentez pas pour moi.
_____ 20. Quand nous ouvrons nos cadeaux, elle ouvre les siens.
_____ 21. N'entendez-vous pas ce que j'entends?
_____ 22. Tu mens, elle ment . . .vous mentez tous!
_____ 23. Elle admet son erreur sans admettre sa culpabilité.
_____ 24. Nous ne suivons pas les mêmes cours que tu suis.
_____ 25. Un adulte comprend ce que les enfants ne comprennent pas.

On the basis of your classification of the verbs in the preceding sentences, write the six present indicative forms of the verbs numbered as follows. Answers and translations are at the end of the chapter.

7.	12.	15.
je _____	je _____	je _____
tu _____	tu _____	tu _____
on _____	il _____	elle _____
nous _____	nous _____	nous _____
vous _____	vous _____	vous _____
ils _____	elles _____	ils _____

18.	19.	23.
je _____	je _____	je _____
tu _____	tu _____	tu _____
Paul _____	Brigitte _____	elle _____
nous _____	elle et moi _____	toi et moi _____
elle et toi _____	vous et lui _____	Paul et toi _____
ils _____	lui et elle _____	les autres _____

CHAPTER ANSWERS

EXERCISE 5-1:

1. Les photos sont à la première page. *The pictures are on the first page.*
2. Mes soeurs sont les plus jolies filles. *My sisters are the prettiest girls.*
3. Tu es cet homme sur la photo. *You are that man in the photo.*
4. Paul est le plus grand garçon. *Paul is the biggest boy.*
5. Claude est notre assistant au laboratoire. *Claude is our laboratory assistant.*
6. Je suis libre demain matin. *I am free tomorrow morning.*
7. Nous sommes mexicains. *We are Mexican.*
8. Vous êtes le prochain candidat. *You are the next candidate.*
9. Les adresses sont dans ce carnet. *The addresses are in the notebook.*
10. Monsieur Duguay est spécialiste en histoire. *Mr. Duguay is a specialist in history.*

EXERCISE 5-2:

1. Robert a un chapeau ridicule. *Robert has a ridiculous hat.*
2. Nous avons une classe cet après-midi. *We have a class this afternoon.*
3. Mes soeurs ont les plus jolis yeux. *My sisters have the prettiest eyes.*
4. Les oiseaux ont un bec et des ailes. *Birds have beaks and wings.*
5. J'ai le temps de prendre un café. *I have time for coffee.*
6. Tu as de la chance. *You are lucky.*
7. Vous avez la voiture la plus rapide. *You have the fastest car.*

8. Les acteurs ont une répétition ce soir. *The actors have a rehearsal this evening.*
9. Ces chiens-là ont l'air féroce. *Those dogs look ferocious.*
10. Nous avons le temps d'étudier. *We have time to study.*

EXERCISE 5-3:

1. J'ai faim avant de manger. *I'm hungry before I eat.*
2. Nous avons soif avant de boire. *We're thirsty before drinking.*
3. On a mal quand on est malade. *We feel bad when we are sick.*
4. J'ai peur en face du danger. *I'm afraid in the face of danger.*
5. Vous avez sommeil avant de dormir. *You are sleepy before sleeping.*
6. J'ai raison si je donne la bonne réponse. *I'm right if I give the right answer.*
7. J'ai tort si je donne la mauvaise réponse. *I'm wrong if I give the wrong answer.*
8. J'ai de la chance si je gagne à la loterie. *I'm lucky if I win the lottery.*
9. Nous avons froid en hiver. *We are cold in winter.*
10. Les gens ont chaud en été. *People are hot in summer.*

EXERCISE 5-4:

1. Je bois souvent du thé glacé en été. *I often drink ice tea in the summer.*
2. Est-ce qu'il obtient ta permission? *Does he get your permission?*

3. Va-t-elle au laboratoire pour apprendre la prononciation? *Does she go to the laboratory in order to learn pronunciation?*

4. Souffre-t-on en pensant aux autres? *Does one suffer in thinking of others?*

5. Ma femme fait la cuisine tous les soirs. *My wife cooks every evening.*

6. Est-ce que tu écris de longs exercices? *Do you write the long exercises?*

7. Je conduis bien, mais un peu trop vite. *I drive well, but a little too fast.*

8. Prend-il ses cours au sérieux? *Does he take his courses seriously?*

9. Est-ce que Robert vient à toutes tes fêtes? *Does Robert come to all your parties?*

10. Je lis cette phrase en ce moment. *I am reading this sentence at this moment.*

11. Marie éteint-elle la lampe avant de sortir? *Does Marie put out the lights before going out?*

12. Tu convaincs les clients de les acheter. *You convince the customers to buy them.*

13. Tu résouds tous les problèmes. *You solve all the problems.*

14. Qu'en dit-on? *What does one say about it?*

15. Tu ne sais pas mon adresse. *You don't know my address.*

16. Je ne peux pas continuer comme cela. *I can't go on like that.*

17. Rodolphe doit venir plus souvent. *Rudolphe must come more often.*

18. Où mets-tu les parapluies? *Where do you put the umbrellas?*

19. L'agriculteur craint le mauvais temps. *The farmer is afraid of bad weather.*

20. Pourquoi ne cueille-t-elle pas ces roses? *Why doesn't she pick these roses?*

EXERCISE 5-5:

1. Ils craignent les tremblements de terre. *They are afraid of earthquakes.*

2. Nos vélos démarrent sans hésitation. *Our bikes take off without trouble.*

3. Nous offrons des emplois. *We offer jobs.*

4. Nous éteignons toutes les lampes. *We turn off all the lamps.*

5. Elles croient à cette histoire. *They believe in this story.*

6. Vous sortez tous les soirs. *You go out every evening.*

7. Elles écrivent de longues lettres. *They write long letters.*

8. Nous écrivons notre rapport. *We write our report.*

9. Les cinémas ouvrent à minuit. *The movie theaters open up at midnight.*

10. Nous écrivons des cartes postales de France. *We write some postcards from France.*

11. Vous dormez tranquillement par terre. *You sleep comfortably on the floor.*

12. Nous conquérons les obstacles. *We overcome the obstacles.*

13. Vous faites toujours des erreurs. *You always make mistakes.*

14. Ses amies servent dans un restaurant. *His friends are waitresses in a restaurant.*

15. Elle court trois kilomètres chaque matin. *She runs three kilometers every morning.*

16. Nous obtenons les meilleurs fruits. *We get the best fruit.*

17. Ils ne peuvent pas refuser de venir. *They cannot refuse to come.*

18. Jean et Sylvie veulent être à l'heure. *Jean and Sylvie want to be on time.*

19. Les clients attendent depuis ce matin. *The customers have been waiting since this morning.*

20. Les serveurs mettent la table pour six personnes. *The waiters set the table for six people.*

21. Ils ne lisent pas les journaux étrangers. *They don't read the foreign newspapers.*

22. Nous peignons les murs de notre chambre. *We paint the walls of our room.*

23. Les pilotes ne savent pas quoi faire. *The pilots don't know what to do.*

24. Vos destinées prennent un tournant intéressant. *Your luck is taking an interesting turn.*

25. Vous offrez votre opinion. *You give your opinion.*

RAISE YOUR GRADES

Present indicative

B 1. I succeed where others don't succeed.

D 2. Do you believe that she believes that story?

D 3. My mother drinks tea while we drink coffee.

C 4. We answer the question if he doesn't answer it.

D 5. Are you leaving when he leaves or when I leave?

D 6. If you don't drive, I'll drive myself.

D 7. She lives near the house where the Lévèques live.

D 8. If you write, they also are going to write.

D 9. No one paints like you paint.

B 10. Jean chooses the design but you choose the color.

A 11. We call the same number that he calls.

A 12. I complete this exercise without completing my work.

B 13. They applaud when you don't have to applaud.

D 14. You receive everything the others receive.

D 15. I know that you don't know my address.

A 16. When she enters, we enter with her.

D 17. If you can do it, we can help you.

D 18. My radio makes sounds that others don't make.

D 19. I feel for you what you don't feel for me.

D 20. When we open our presents, she opens hers.

C 21. Don't you hear what I hear?

D 22. You lie, she lies . . .you all lie!

D 23. She admits her mistake without admitting her guilt.

D 24. We take the same courses that you take.

D 25. An adult understands what children don't understand.

7. vivre
je vis
tu vis
on vit
nous vivons
vous vivez
ils vivent

12. compléter
je complète
tu complètes
il complète
nous complétons
vous complétez
elles complètent

15. savoir
je sais
tu sais
elle sait
nous savons
vous savez
ils savent

18. produire
je produis
tu produis
Paul produit
nous produisons
elle et toi produisez
ils produisent

19. sentir
je sens
tu sens
Brigitte sent
elle et moi sentons
vous et lui sentez
lui et elle sentent

23. admettre
j'admets
tu admets
on admet
toi et moi admettons
Paul et toi admettez
les autres admettent

6 OBJECT PRONOUNS

THIS CHAPTER IS ABOUT

- ☑ **Disjunctive Pronouns**
- ☑ **Direct Object Pronouns**
- ☑ **The Pronoun En**
- ☑ **Indirect Object Pronouns**
- ☑ **The Pronoun Y**
- ☑ **Reflexive Pronouns**
- ☑ **Order of Object Pronouns**

Like nouns, pronouns may be sentence subjects or object of verbs and prepositions. The pronoun for each person takes different forms according to its function—except for **nous** and **vous**, which are invariable.

6-1. Disjunctive Pronouns

A disjunctive pronoun always refers to a person, unlike the direct and indirect object pronouns which may refer either to persons or to things. Also, unlike the other object pronouns, a disjunctive pronoun does not have to come immediately before or after the verb.

A. Forms of the disjunctive pronoun

Person	Singular		Plural	
1st	**moi**	*me*	**nous**	*us*
2nd	**toi**	*you*	**vous**	*you*
3rd–masc	**lui**	*him*	**eux**	*them*
3rd–fem	**elle**	*her*	**elles**	*them*

NOTE: Make it a point to learn the forms **lui/eux**—**pour lui, pour eux**—and you'll find the other forms come naturally.

B. Use of the disjunctive pronoun

1. Use a disjunctive pronoun to repeat and emphasize the subject of a sentence.

   Moi, je ne vois pas du tout cela. — *Me, I can't imagine it.*
   Laurent n'a aucune considération, **lui**. — *Laurent is completely inconsiderate, that guy.*
   Vous trouvez cela amusant, **vous**? — *You think that's funny?*

2. Use disjunctive pronouns for a compound subject. When a compound subject consists of different persons, use the appropriate plural subject pronoun immediately after the disjunctive pronouns.

   Toi et lui, vous faites un beau couple. — *You and he make a good couple.*
   Eux et moi, nous sommes au courant. — *They and I know what's going on.*

3. Use a disjunctive pronoun alone—without a verb—in answer to a question or before a relative clause.

Qui a fait cela? **Pas moi!**	*Who did that? Not I!*
Qui est là? **Eux.**	*Who's there? They (are).*
Moi, qui aime la musique, je n'aime pas écouter la radio.	*I, who love music, do not like to listen to the radio.*

4. Use a disjunctive pronoun after a preposition.

Avec lui ou **sans lui,** nous partons à 21 heures.	*With him or without him, we're leaving at 9 p.m.*
Entre nous, elle ne va pas sortir avec toi.	*Between us, she's not going out with you.*
Nous pensons souvent **à toi.**	*We think of you often.*
Elle a peur **de nous.**	*She is afraid of us.*

BUT do not use a disjunctive pronoun if the prepositional phrase beginning with **à** signifies an indirect object—use the pronoun **y.**

Je pense **à ce problème.**	*I am thinking about this problem.*
J'y pense.	*I am thinking about it.*

OR if a prepositional phrase beginning with **de** refers to *a thing* or *a concept*—use the pronoun **en.**

Je parle **de ce roman.**	*I am talking about this novel.*
J'en parle.	*I am talking about it.*

5. Use a disjunctive pronoun after **ne . . . que** constructions.

Elle **ne** voit **que lui.**	*She sees only him.*

- also after **que** in a comparison:

Elle est plus jeune **que moi,** et plus âgée **qu'eux.**	*She is younger than I, and older than they.*

- and with the conjunction **ni . . . ni,** *neither . . . nor:*

Elles ne verront **ni toi ni moi.**	*They will see neither you nor I.*

6. Use disjunctive pronouns when you have a compound object. Sum up the compound object with the appropriate plural object pronoun before the verb.

Ils **vous** l'a dit, **à toi et à eux.**	*He told it to you, to you and to them.*

7. Use **à** with a disjunctive pronoun in place of an indirect object pronoun if the direct object is **me, te, se, nous,** and **vous.**

Nous **vous** présentons **à elles.**	*We introduce you to them.*

8. Use a disjunctive pronoun after **être à** to indicate possession—or that it's someone's turn.

Cette voiture **est à moi.**	*That car is mine.*
C'est à moi à jouer.	*It's my turn to play.*

9. Use a disjunctive pronoun after **ce** plus **être.**

C'est moi!	*It is I! (It's me!)*

EXERCISE 6-1: Answer the questions affirmatively using at least one disjunctive pronoun in each answer. Answers and translations are at the end of the chapter.

Example:	Paul et Anne partent-ils pour Paris mercredi?	*Are Paul and Anne leaving for Paris Wednesday?*
	Oui, elle et lui, ils partent pour Paris mercredi.	*Yes, they leave for Paris Wednesday.*

1. Est-ce que ce sont vos soeurs qui parlent italien?
2. C'est vous qui avez faim?
3. Les étudiants arrivent-ils avant le professeur?
4. Est-ce que c'est Paul qui aime le film?
5. Ce sont les autres les coupables?
6. Savez-vous la vérité, elle et toi?

7. Partez-vous sans Anne-Marie et Guillaume?
8. Connaît-il son métier mieux que son assistant?
9. Tu préfères les romans, toi?
10. Est-ce que je suis plus intelligent que vous?

6-2. Direct Object Pronouns

In French a direct object noun is one that follows the verb directly without an intervening preposition. Articles and adjectives may be part of the direct object.

Elle lit **le paragraphe** à haute voix.	*She reads the paragraph out loud.*
Il explique **la proposition** aux locataires.	*He explains the proposition to the tenants.*

A. Forms of the direct object pronoun

Study the following table and examples of direct object pronouns.

Person	Singular		Plural	
1st	**me (m')/moi**	*me*	**nous**	*us*
2nd	**te (t')/toi**	*you*	**vous**	*you*
3rd–masc	**le**	*him, it*	**les**	*them*
3rd–fem	**la**	*her, it*	**les**	*them*

> *NOTE:* When **me** and **te** are the final pronouns in an affirmative command, they become **moi** and **toi.**

B. Position and use of the direct object pronoun

1. Unlike direct object nouns, direct object pronouns come before the verb—except in affirmative commands.

Paul **m'invite** à prendre un café.	*Paul invites me for a cup of coffee.*
Je **les emballe** dans du papier.	*I wrap them up in paper.*
Vous ne **nous sortez** jamais.	*You never take us out.*
Je tiens à **le** voir.	*I am anxious to see him.*

BUT

Arrêtez-la!	*Stop her!*

> *NOTE:* The direct object pronouns **le** and **la** elide with a following verb beginning with a vowel or mute h—BUT do not contract with a preceding preposition.

Nous sommes très contents **de l'**entendre.	*We are very glad to hear it.*
Je n'ai pas le courage **de le** confronter.	*I don't have the courage to confront him.*

> *REMEMBER:* The verb must agree in person and number with the subject of the sentence—even though the direct object may be closer to the verb.

Nous vous **proposons** une soirée amusante.	*We are planning an interesting evening for you.*

EXERCISE 6-2: Answer the questions, replacing all nouns with the appropriate subject pronouns and/or direct object pronouns. Answers and translations are at the end of the chapter.

Example:	Les enfants regardent-ils beaucoup la télévision?	*Do children watch television a lot?*
	Oui, ils la regardent beaucoup.	*Yes, they watch it a lot.*

1. Comprenez-vous cet exercice?
2. Les Français admirent-ils Jeanne d'Arc?

3. Les parents grondent-ils leurs enfants?
4. Est-ce que les astronautes explorent les étoiles?
5. Ecrivez-vous cette phrase en anglais?
6. Les artistes visitent-ils les galeries?
7. Les étudiantes apprennent-elles les sciences?
8. La secrétaire tape-t-elle les lettres à la machine?
9. François écoute-t-il la radio le soir?
10. Les ménagères font-elles le marché le matin?

EXERCISE 6-3: Answer the following questions affirmatively, paying careful attention to the shifts from subject to object pronoun. Translate your answers into English. Answers and translations are at the end of the chapter.

> Example: Me comprenez-vous? *Do you understand me?*
> Oui, je vous comprends. *Yes, I understand you.*

1. Le vend-il?

2. Nous sers-tu?

3. Me prend-il au sérieux?

4. Vous aime-t-il?

5. L'admirez-vous?

6. Est-ce que je les oublie?

7. Est-ce qu'on m'attend?

8. Est-ce que je t'ennuie?

9. Robert les connaît-il?

10. Nous corrigez-vous?

2. When there is more than one verb in a verb phrase, the direct object pronoun comes before the verb whose object it is.

Je **le vois** venir.	*I know what he's getting at.* *(I see him coming.)*
Elle vient de dire de ne pas **les mettre** au four.	*She just said not to put them in the oven.*
Il va **vous demander** votre opinion.	*He is going to ask you your opinion.*

EXERCISE 6-4: Answer the following questions by including the response given in parentheses. Answers and translations are at the end of the chapter.

> Example: Qu'est-ce que Michel voit? *What does Michel see?*
> (Vous arrivez à bicyclette.) *(You arrive on a bicycle.)*
> Michel vous voit arriver à bicyclette. *Michel sees you arriving on a bicycle.*

1. Que proposez-vous de faire? (Je vous accompagne en voiture.)
2. Qu'est-ce qu'ils apprennent à faire? (Ils le finissent rapidement.)
3. Qu'est-ce que Paul dit de faire? (Apportez-les à la prochaine réunion.)
4. Qu'est-ce que les gendarmes sont obligés de faire? (Il les arrêtent.)
5. Pourquoi est-on surpris? (On me voit à la télévision.)
6. Pourquoi ne venez-vous pas me chercher? (Je n'ai pas le temps.)
7. Qu'est-ce que les voisins entendent? (Nous jouons de la guitare.)
8. Qu'est-ce que tes professeurs commencent à faire? (Ils me comprennent mieux.)
9. Pourquoi a-t-il besoin de courage? (Il les confronte.)
10. De quoi avez-vous peur? (Je les regarde en face.)

3. Use the neuter direct object pronoun **le** when the complement is

- a clause:

Je sais **que Harold va venir à bicyclette**.	*I know that Harold is going to come on a bicycle.*
Je **le** sais.	*I know it.*
Il dit **quand il va venir**.	*He says when he is going to come.*
Il **l'**a dit.	*He said it.*

- an infinitive:

Elle peut **rester**.	*She can stay.*
Elle **le** peut.	*She can do it.*
Je veux **aller au magasin**.	*I want to go to the store.*
Je **le** veux.	*I want (to do) it.*

- an adjective—whether it is masculine or feminine:

Jack est **grand** et Hélène **l'**est aussi.	*Jack is tall and so is Hélène.*
Tes phrases sont **correctes** et les miennes **le** sont aussi.	*Your sentences are correct and so are mine.*

EXERCISE 6-5: Answer the following questions affirmatively, replacing the complement clause, infinitive phrase, or adjective with the neuter direct object pronoun **le**. Answers and translations are at the end of the chapter.

1. Savez-vous quand vos amis viennent dîner?
2. Préfère-t-il que son nom reste secret?
3. Est-ce qu'elle désire habiter en France?
4. Voulez-vous visiter le musée?
5. Marie doit-elle préparer ses examens?
6. Est-ce que ses employés sont compétents?
7. Elles sont françaises, n'est-ce pas?
8. Est-ce que vos frères pensent devenir politiciens?
9. Est-ce que Monsieur Dupont est catholique?
10. Les hommes et les femmes sont égaux, n'est-ce pas?

6-3. The Pronoun En

A. The partitive pronoun en

The partitive pronoun **en** replaces a direct object used in a partitive sense (see Sec. 1-5).

1. Like other object pronouns, **en** comes before the verb—except in affirmative commands.

Il y a du gâteau.	*There is some cake.*
Il **en** mange.	*He eats some of it.*
Nous **en** mangeons.	*We are eating some of it.*
N'**en** prenez pas!	*Don't take any (of it)!*
Prenez-**en**!	*Take some (of it)!*

> **NOTE:** We often omit the words *of it* or *of them* in English— never omit the pronoun **en** in French!

2. Use the partitive pronoun **en** to refer both to people and to things.

Je vois **des enfants**.	*I see some children.*
J'**en** vois.	*I see some (of them).*
Je veux connaître **des Français**.	*I want to know some French people.*
Je veux **en** connaître.	*I want to know some (of them).*

> **REMEMBER:** When there is more than one verb in the same clause, the pronoun goes before the verb whose object it is (see Sec. 6-1).

Ne traversez pas les rails!	*Don't cross the tracks!*
Un train peut **en cacher** un autre..	*One train may be hiding another.*
BUT	
Nous **en voyons** échouer chaque mois.	*We see some of them fail every month.*

3. When a direct object is a number or an expression of quantity, use the partitive pronoun **en** before the verb to replace the noun—but not the number.

Ont-ils **deux enfants**?	*Do they have two children?*
Oui, ils **en** ont **deux**.	*Yes, they have two (of them).*
Achetez-vous **un kilo d'oranges**?	*Are you buying a kilo of oranges?*
Oui, j'**en** achète **un kilo**.	*Yes, I'm buying a kilo (of them).*

EXERCISE 6-6:   Answer the following questions by replacing the number in the question with the correct number. Answers and translations are at the end of the chapter.

Example:	La Renault coûte-t-elle cinq mille dollars? (huit mille)	*Does the Renault cost five thousand dollars? (8 thousand)*
	Non, elle en coûte huit mille.	*No, it costs eight thousand.*

1. Y a-t-il 40 états aux Etats-Unis?
2. Avez-vous trois mains?
3. Est-ce qu'il y a 80 sénateurs à Washington?
4. L'alphabet a-t-il 35 lettres?
5. Est-ce qu'une bicyclette a quatre roues?
6. Est-ce que ce livre contient 500 pages?
7. Avez-vous un nez?
8. Combien de personnes y a-t-il dans un couple?
9. Y a-t-il 10 jours dans une semaine?
10. Combien d'oeufs achète-t-on à la fois?

4. You must always use the partitive pronoun **en** with the indefinite pronouns **plusieurs**, *several*, and **quelques-uns/unes**, *a few*—even though we don't have to translate it in English.

Avez-vous **un crayon**?	*Do you have a pencil?*
J'**en** ai **plusieurs**.	*I have several (of them).*
Elle **en** a **quelques-uns**.	*She has a few (of them).*
Est-ce qu'elle a **des tableaux** à vendre?	*Does she have some paintings for sale?*
Oui, elle **en** a **quelques-uns** à vendre.	*Yes, she has a few (of them) for sale.*

EXERCISE 6-7:   Answer the questions using the pronoun **en** in place of the partitive noun phrases. Answers and translations are at the end of the chapter.

Example:	Les soldats ont-ils du courage?	*Do soldiers have courage?*
	Oui, ils en ont.	*Yes, they have (some).*

1. Faites-vous souvent des bêtises?
2. Est-ce que ta voiture consomme trop d'essence?
3. A-t-on jamais trop d'argent?
4. Prend-on du thé dans un bar?
5. Y a-t-il de la neige en été?
6. Buvez-vous du champagne au petit déjeuner?
7. Fait-on de l'exercice pour rester en forme?
8. Trouve-t-on des livres à la bibliothèque?
9. Y a-t-il beaucoup d'eau dans le désert?
10. Faut-il de la patience pour élever des enfants?

B. The adverbial pronoun en

1. The adverbial pronoun **en** refers to a place *from which* someone leaves or something is taken.

A quelle heure sortez-vous **du bureau**?	*What time do you leave the office?*
J'**en** sors à cinq heures.	*I leave (from there) at five o'clock.*

Vient-elle **de Rome**?   *Is she from Rome?*
Non, elle n'**en** vient pas.   *No, she isn't (from there).*

Je prends **l'enveloppe** et j'**en** retire   *I take the envelope and pull out*
la lettre.   *the letter.*

2. The adverbial pronoun **en** refers to a prepositional phrase beginning with **de**—whose object is *usually* not a person.

Elles parlent **de leur vêtements**.   *They are talking about their clothes.*
Elles **en** parlent.   *They are talking about them.*

As-tu honte **de cela**?   *Are you ashamed of that?*
Oui, j'**en** ai honte.   *Yes, I am ashamed (of that).*

Nous doutons **de leurs intentions**.   *We are not sure of their intentions.*
Nous **en** doutons.   *We are not sure (of them).*

EXERCISE 6-8: Answer the following questions in both the affirmative and the negative, using the pronoun **en**. Answers and translations are at the end of the chapter.

Example: Est-ce qu'il a le courage de ses   Does he have the courage of his
convictions?   convictions?

Oui, il en a le courage.   Yes, he has the courage (of them).

Non, il n'en a pas le courage.   No, he doesn't have the courage
(of them).

1. Avez-vous le temps de jouer aux cartes?
2. Leurs parents ont-ils envie de visiter la Russie?
3. Sortez-vous de la maison ce soir?
4. Vos grand-parents viennent-ils d'Europe?
5. A-t-on besoin de gagner beaucoup d'argent?
6. Est-ce que vous avez envie de voir la France?
7. Retire-t-il tout son argent de la banque?
8. Avez-vous peur des serpents?
9. Les hommes politiques parlent-ils d'éviter la guerre?
10. Est-ce que votre table est couverte de papiers?

6-4. Indirect Object Pronouns

The indirect object is usually the person or persons *to whom* or *for whom* something is done. In French an indirect object noun is always preceded by the preposition **à** (or one of its contractions—**au, aux**)—BUT not all nouns preceded by **à** are indirect objects.

Il lance la balle **à son frère**.   *He throws the ball to his brother.*
Elle lit le livre **à ses enfants**.   *She reads the book to her children.*
Nous décidons à la dernière minute.   *We decide at the last minute.*

A. Forms of the indirect object pronoun

The forms of the indirect object pronoun are the same as those of the direct object pronoun—except in the third person, singular and plural. Indirect object pronouns do not show gender.

Person	Singular		Plural	
1st	**me (m')/moi**	*(to) me*	**nous**	*(to) us*
2nd	**te (t')/toi**	*(to) you*	**vous**	*(to) you*
3rd	**lui**	*(to) him, her, it*	**leur**	*(to) them*

NOTE: When **me** and **te** are the final pronouns in a command, they become **moi** and **toi**. Also note that, unlike the *possessive adjective* **leur(s)**, the *pronoun* **leur** never has a final **-s**.

B. Position of the indirect object pronoun

Like the direct object pronoun, the indirect object pronoun comes before the verb—except in affirmative commands.

Le vendeur **leur** donne un rabais.	*The salesman gives them a discount.*
Nous ne **lui** parlons jamais.	*We never speak to him.*
Mon éditeur **me** téléphone du bureau.	*My editor calls me at the office.*
Pourquoi ne **nous** obéit-il pas?	*Why don't you obey him?*

BUT

Répondez-moi!	*Answer me!*

> *NOTE:*　The indirect object pronouns include **à**, *to* or *for*, as part of their meaning. Never use a preposition before a direct object pronoun.

Il **lui** lance la balle.	*He throws him the ball.*

EXERCISE 6-9:　Answer the following questions affirmatively using an indirect object pronoun. Answers and translations are at the end of the chapter.

Example:　Ressemblent-elle à son père?　*Does she look like her father?*
　　　　　Oui, elle lui ressemble.　　*Yes, she looks like him.*

1. Parlent-ils aux spectateurs?
2. Offrez-vous un verre de vin à vos invités?
3. Dis-tu la vérité à tes parents?
4. Répondent-ils aux professeurs?
5. Donne-t-il sa place à la vieille dame?
6. Les soldats obéissent-ils à leur commandant?
7. Ressemblez-vous à votre mère?
8. Obéissons-nous à toutes les lois?
9. Les reporters posent-ils des questions aux gens célèbres?
10. Est-ce que tu montres tes tableaux à ce client?

EXERCISE 6-10:　Answer the following questions affirmatively, paying special attention to the shift of indirect object pronouns. Then translate your answers into English. Answers and translations are at the end of the chapter.

Example:　Me réponds-tu?　*Will you answer me?*
　　　　　Oui, je te réponds!　*Yes, I'm answering you!*

1. Te répond-il?
2. Leur ressemblent-elles?
3. Lui obéit-on?
4. Nous promets-tu?
5. Me demandez-vous?
6. Vous parlent-ils?
7. Leur téléphonez-vous?
8. Lui écrit-elle?
9. T'offre-t-il quelque chose?
10. M'envoyez-vous des nouvelles?

6-5.　The Pronoun Y

A.　The adverbial pronoun y refers to a previously mentioned location which is the object of a preposition of place such as à, chez, dans, en, sous, or sur. In these cases, translate y as *there*.

Il est **dans son bureau**.	*He is in his office.*
Il **y** est.	*He is there.*

Je vais **au bureau de poste**.   *I am going to the post office.*
   Y allez-vous tout de suite?   *Are you going there right away?*

> *NOTE:* When no specific location is intended, use **là** instead of **y**.

>   Est-il **là**?   *Is he there?* OR *Is he here?*

B. **Y often refers to a prepositional phrase whose object is something other than a place or person. In these cases, y has the sense of** *concerning it* **or** *about it.*

Je crois **au progrès**.   *I believe in progress.*
   Y croyez-vous?   *Do you believe in it?*

Elle répond **à la question**, mais elle y   *She answers the question, but she*
   répond mal.   *answers it incorrectly.*

> *NOTE:* Do not use **y** to mean about or to a person. Use **à** with a disjunctive pronoun (see Sec. 6-1) or the appropriate indirect object pronoun (see Sec. 6-4).

>   Elle répond mal **à la directrice**.   *She talks back to the principal.*
>   Elle **lui** répond mal.   *She talks back to her.*

EXERCISE 6-11: Answer the following questions using the information given in the parentheses. Replace the underlined prepositional phrase with the pronoun **y**. Answers and translations are at the end of the chapter.

   Example: Que prenez-vous dans votre café?   *What do you take in your coffee?*
                  (du lait et du sucre)   *(milk and sugar)*
              J'y prends du lait et du sucre.   *I take milk and sugar in it.*

1. Allez-vous souvent <u>au théâtre</u>? (non, jamais)
2. Répondez-vous <u>à toutes ces lettres</u>? (oui, immédiatement)
3. Quand voyagent-ils <u>en Chine</u>? (le mois prochain)
4. Est-ce que ces mots sont <u>dans votre dictionnaire</u>? (non, pas tous)
5. Voyez-vous quelque chose <u>sur mon bureau</u>. (non, rien)
6. Vont-elles téléphoner <u>à l'université</u> demain? (oui, à 9 heures)
7. Faut-il obéir <u>à ces ordres</u>? (oui, sans question)
8. Contribuez-vous <u>à la confusion générale</u>? (non, pas du tout!)
9. Est-ce que ces vieux films passent <u>à la télévision</u>? (oui, toujours)
10. Gare-t-il sa voiture <u>derrière la maison</u>? (non, son vélo)

6-6. Reflexive Pronouns

A reflexive pronoun repeats the subject noun or pronoun in the form of a second pronoun. The reflexive pronoun is the direct object or the indirect object of the verb, and refers to the same person or thing as the subject of the verb.

A. Forms of the reflexive pronoun

Person	Singular	Plural
1st	me (m')/moi	nous
2nd	te (t')/toi	vous
3rd	se (s')	se

Je me lève at **je me regarde** dans   *I get (myself) up and I look at myself*
   le miroir.   *in the mirror.*
Elles s'ennuient ou **elles s'amusent**,   *They are bored (bore themselves) or*
   selon le cas.   *have a good time (amuse themselves)*
                                           depending on the circumstances.

B. Use of the reflexive pronoun

1. The reflexive pronoun must agree in person and number with the subject of the sentence.

Nous nous servons à table.	*We help ourselves to the food.*
Je m'occupe des enfants, mais **je** n'aime pas **m'occuper** des animaux.	*I take care of children, but I don't like to take care of animals.*

2. The reflexive pronoun comes before the verb—except in affirmative commands.

Ils **se l'approprient**.	*They take it for themselves.*
Je **me lève** à six heures du matin.	*I get up at six o'clock in the morning.*

BUT

Assieds-toi immédiatement!	*Sit down immediately!*

> *NOTE:* Even though we sometimes understand the reflexive pronoun without expressing it in English, you must always express it in French.

La **voiture s'arrête**.	*The car stops (itself).*

3. Elide **me**, **te**, and **se** before a verb beginning with a vowel or a mute h.

Je **m'impatiente** si vous ne me téléphonez pas.	*I am impatient if you don't call me.*

> *NOTE:* You can sometimes translate a verb that has no reflexive equivalent in English with the help of the word get.

Ils **se marient** au mois de septembre.	*They are getting married in September.*
Nous **nous lavons** et nous **nous rasons** avant de sortir.	*We get washed and we get shaved before going out.*

EXERCISE 6-12: Answer the following questions in the negative, indicating that the person involved does the action to himself or herself. Answers and translations are at the end of the chapter.

Example:	Est-ce que sa mère l'habille?	*Does his mother dress him?*
	Non, il s'habille.	*No, he dresses himself.*

1. Est-ce qu'il vous corrige?
2. M'aides-tu?
3. Est-ce que quelqu'un nous sert à table?
4. Est-ce que quelqu'un invite ces gens-là?
5. Est-ce que quelqu'un te coupe les cheveux?
6. Arrête-t-on le moteur?
7. Allez-vous me conduire au marché?
8. Présentez-vous ces jeunes filles?
9. Est-ce que quelqu'un la réveille?
10. L' amuses-tu?

4. When the action of a verb is performed by the subject on its own body, use a reflexive pronoun and the definite article—instead of the possessive adjective.

Elle **se** brosse **les** cheveux.	*She brushes her hair.*

> *REMEMBER:* Use the definite article instead of a possessive adjective before parts of the body (see Sec. 1-3). BUT if an adjective modifies the part of the body—except for **droit**, *right*, or **gauche**, *left*—do *not* use a reflexive pronoun, and *do* use a possessive adjective.

Elle brosse **ses beaux cheveux blonds**.	*She brushes her beautiful blond hair.*

BUT

Il **se** casse le bras **droit**.	*He breaks his right arm.*

5. Although the infinitives of reflexive verbs are listed in the dictionary with **se**, the pronoun you use in any given sentence depends upon the person referred to.

Nous **vous** disons de **vous reposer**.	*We tell you to relax.*
Je **lui** dis de **se reposer**.	*I tell him to relax.*
Il **me** dit de **me reposer**.	*He tells me to relax.*
Elles **nous** disent de **nous reposer**.	*They tell us to relax.*

6. You can make many verbs reflexive verbs with only a slight change in meaning. The reflexive pronoun may be direct or indirect.

Je **regarde** Janet.	*I look at Janet.*
Je me regarde dans le miroir.	*I look at myself in the mirror.*
Il **achète** un livre.	*He buys a book.*
Il s'achète un livre.	*He buys himself a book.*

BUT the meaning of some verbs—**idiomatically reflexive verbs**—changes when they become reflexive.

amuser	*to amuse*	s'amuser	*to have a good time*
appeler	*to call*	s'appeler	*to be named*
attendre	*to wait for*	s'attendre (à)	*to expect*
demander	*to ask (for)*	se demander	*to wonder*
douter (de)	*to doubt*	se douter (de)	*to suspect*
élever	*to raise*	s'élever	*to rise*
lever	*to raise up*	se lever	*to get up*
mettre	*to put*	se mettre (à)	*to begin*
passer	*to pass*	se passer (de)	*to do without*
plaindre	*to pity*	se plaindre	*to complain*
rappeler	*to call back*	se rappeler	*to remember*
rendre compte (de)	*to give an account (of)*	se rendre compte (de)	*to realize, be aware of*
sauver	*to save*	se sauver	*to run away*
servir	*to serve*	se servir (de)	*to use*
tromper	*to deceive*	se tromper	*to be mistaken*
trouver	*to find*	se trouver	*to be situated*

Je **mets** le couvert pour dîner	*I set the table for dinner.*
Je me mets à travailler.	*I begin to work.*
Il doit **rendre compte** de son temps libre.	*He has to account for his free time.*
Il doit **se rendre compte** de l'heure.	*He must realize what time it is.*

EXERCISE 6-13: Replace the verb in parentheses with an idiomatically reflexive verb having the same meaning. Answers and translations are at the end of the chapter.

Example: Quand (commencez)-vous à faire les valises?	*When do you begin to pack?*
Quand vous mettez-vous à faire les valises?	*When do you begin to pack?*

1. Nous (utilisons) souvent notre machine à écrire.
2. Les enfants (vont au lit) avant minuit.
3. Le détective (soupçonne) qu'un crime a été commis.
4. Je prends le sac et je (pars en courant).
5. Les étudiants (protestent) que les examens sont longs.

7. Some verbs—**essentially** or **exclusively reflexive verbs**—must always have a pronoun. Following is a list of some of the more common of these verbs.

s'abstenir (de)	*to abstain (from)*	s'évader	*to escape*
s'écrier	*to exclaim*	s'évanouir	*to faint, vanish*
s'écrouler	*to tumble down*	se fier à	*to trust*
s'effondrer	*to cave in*	se méfier de	*to mistrust*
s'efforcer de	*to strive to*	se moquer de	*to make fun of*
s'emparer de	*to grab*	se repentir	*to repent*
s'en aller	*to leave, go away*	se soucier de	*to care about*
s'enfuir	*to flee*	se suicider	*to commit suicide*
s'envoler	*to fly off*	se taire	*to keep silent, be quiet*

Elle s'écrie: "Au feu!"	*She cries out: "Fire!"*
Je m'en vais parce que je suis pressée.	*I'm leaving because I'm in a hurry.*
Les étudiants s'efforcent d'apprendre leurs leçons.	*The students strive to learn their lessons.*
Vous vous souciez trop de votre travail.	*You take your work too seriously.*
Elle se moque toujours de lui.	*She always makes fun of him.*
Nous nous taisons quand quelqu'un parle.	*We keep silent when someone speaks.*

EXERCISE 6-14:   Replace the verb in parentheses with an essentially reflexive verb having the same meaning. Answers and translations are at the end of the chapter.

Example:	Tu (perds conscience) quand tu vois du sang.	*You lose consciousness when you see blood.*
	Tu t'évanouis quand tu vois du sang.	*You faint when you see blood.*

1. Il faut (faire attention aux) chemins dangereux.
2. Les diplomates (partent) par le Concorde cet après-midi.
3. Juliette (choisit la mort) quand elle voit Roméo mort.
4. Je (n'oublie pas) ma promesse.
5. Les animaux (font un effort pour) survivre dans le désert.
6. Il est facile de (ridiculiser) les personnages célèbres.

C. Reciprocal verbs

A reflexive verb has a reciprocal meaning when two or more subjects act upon one another—not upon themselves.

Ils **se blâment**.	reflexive:	*They blame themselves.*
	reciprocal:	*They blame each other.*

1. If the verb does not show clearly whether the action is reciprocal or reflexive, add **l'un l'autre**, *each other*, or **les uns les autres**, *one another*, to avoid ambiguity.

Ils se blâment **l'un l'autre**.	*They blame each other.*
Mes parents s'aiment beaucoup **les uns les autres**.	*My relatives love one another very much.*

2. With a verb that requires a prepositional complement—that is, a verb that must be followed by **à** or **de**—insert the preposition between **l'un** and **l'autre** or between **les uns** and **les autres**. Contract **à** and **de** with the article **l'** or **les**.

Ils se moquent **les uns des autres**.	*They make fun of one another.*
Mon amie et moi, nous nous fions **l'une à l'autre**.	*My friend and I trust each other.*

EXERCISE 6-15:   Rewrite the sentences using a reciprocal verb. Answers and translations are at the end of the chapter.

Example:	Elle l'adore et il l'adore aussi.	*She loves him and he loves her too.*
	Ils s'adorent.	*They love each other.*

1. Je vous comprends et vous me comprenez.
2. Vous la traitez bien et elle vous traite bien aussi.
3. Mon oncle aide ma tante et elle l'aide à son tour.
4. Je lui parle et il me parle en même temps.
5. Vous détestez vos voisins et ils vous détestent.

6-7. Order of Object Pronouns

The basic order of object pronouns is direct before indirect for pronouns like **le**, **la**, **les**, **lui**, **leur**, which have a separate form for direct and indirect objects. BUT the pronouns **me**, **te**, **se**, **nous**, **vous**, which may be direct, indirect, or reflexive, are always said first—no matter what their function is.

A. Priority of reflexive pronouns

A reflexive pronoun or any pronoun that can function as a reflexive pronoun—**me**, **te**, **se**, **nous**, **vous**—comes first.

Les clients **se** les arrachent.	*The customers tear them out of one another's hands.*
Nous ne **t**'en empêchons pas.	*We're not stopping you from doing it.*
Les voisins **nous** la présentent.	*The neighbors introduce her to us.*
Les voisins **me** les présentent.	*The neighbors introduce them to me.*

> *REMEMBER:* Use **à** with a disjunctive pronoun in place of an indirect object pronoun after **me**, **te**, **se**, **nous** and **vous** (see Sec. 6-1).

EXERCISE 6-16: Answer the following questions affirmatively, using pronouns whenever possible. Pay special attention to the place of **me**, **te**, **se**, **nous**, and **vous**. Answers and translations are at the end of the chapter.

1. Est-ce que je vous explique les conséquences?
2. Te rappelles-tu cet incident?
3. Nous prépare-t-il les passeports?
4. Me donnes-tu cette occasion?
5. Est-ce qu'on se prête la voiture facilement?
6. Nous présentez-vous à votre femme?
7. Nous présentez-vous votre femme?
8. Se coupent-ils les cheveux?
9. Est-ce que tu vas me montrer l'appartement?
10. Se donne-t-elle la peine d'écouter?

B. Direct object pronouns before indirect

When there is not a pronoun that can be reflexive or the pronoun **y** or **en**, the direct object pronoun precedes the indirect object pronoun.

Il faut **les leur** pardonner.	*You have to forgive them (for) them.*

EXERCISE 6-17: Replace the indirect object noun in the following sentences with the appropriate indirect object pronoun. Answers and translations are at the end of the chapter.

Example:	Le garçon apporte le café aux clients.	*The waiter brings coffee to the customers.*
	Il leur apporte le café.	*He brings them coffee.*

1. Il donne le cadeau à sa mère.
2. Mon père écrit la lettre à l'éditeur du journal.
3. Chantal parle doucement au chien.
4. René envoie les poèmes à Catherine.
5. Les étudiantes apprennent bien la leçon.
6. Jacques dit toujours la vérité à ses parents.
7. Dominique parle à Marie avant le cours.

8. Ma soeur donne ses vieux vêtements aux pauvres.
9. Le professeur pose la question à ses étudiants.
10. Henri donne les fleurs à sa petite amie.

EXERCISE 6-18:   Now replace any direct object nouns in the preceding sentences with the appropriate direct object pronouns. Answers and translations are at the end of the chapter.

| Example: | Le garçon apporte le café aux clients. | *The waiter brings coffee to the customers.* |
| | Il l'apporte aux clients. | *He brings it to them.* |

EXERCISE 6-19:   Finally, replace both the direct and indirect object nouns in the preceding sentences with the appropriate object pronouns. Answers and translations are at the end of the chapter.

| Example: | Le garçon apporte le café aux clients. | *The waiter brings coffee to the customers.* |
| | Il le leur apporte. | *He brings it to them.* |

C. Order of y and en

The pronouns **y** and **en**—but not both together—are always in last position before the verb.

| Il s'**y** rend à contre-coeur. | *He reports there unwillingly.* |
| Il ne faut pas lui **en** donner. | *You mustn't give him any.* |

> *NOTE:* You can use the partitive pronoun **en** with the expression **il y a**.
>
> | Je ne sais pas s'**il y en a** ou s'**il n'y en a pas**. | *I don't know if there are any or there aren't any.* |

EXERCISE 6-20:   Answer the following questions, using pronouns whenever possible. Answers and translations are at the end of the chapter.

| Example: | Parles-tu à tes camarades de mon affaire? | *Do you talk to your friends about my situation?* |
| | Oui, je leur en parle. | *Yes, I talk to them about it.* |

1. Vois-tu ma valise sur l'armoire?
2. Est-ce qu'on donne des médicaments aux malades?
3. Mettent-ils le plan de la ville dans la voiture?
4. Ecris-tu mon numéro de téléphone dans ton carnet?
5. Vos parents et vous, parlez-vous de la politique au maire?

D. Briefly, the order of object pronouns follows these priorities:

1) pronouns that can be either direct or indirect objects
2) all other object pronouns—direct before indirect
3) y or en—but not together

which produces this order:

$$\begin{pmatrix} me \\ te \\ se \\ nous \\ vous \end{pmatrix} \quad \begin{pmatrix} le & \\ la & lui \\ les & leur \end{pmatrix} \quad \begin{pmatrix} y \\ en \end{pmatrix}$$

EXERCISE 6-21:   Answer the following questions affirmatively, using two object pronouns. Answers and translations are at the end of the chapter.

| Example: | Recommande-t-il de l'aspirine à ses malades? | *Does he recommend aspirin to his patients?* |
| | Oui, il leur en recommande. | *Yes, he recommends (some of) it to them.* |

1. Offre-t-il le spectacle au public?
2. Regardez-vous les nouvelles à la télévision?
3. Est-ce que nous prenons le déjeuner en plein air?
4. Me recommandez-vous ce film?
5. Donne-t-elle des photos à ses admirateurs?
6. Est-ce que les négociants promettent des rabais à leurs clients?
7. Me permettez-vous une cigarette?
8. Se rend-il compte du danger?
9. Est-ce que je dois m'asseoir dans le fauteuil?
10. Rendez-vous tous ces cadeaux aux amis?

E. Pronouns in affirmative commands

Object pronouns follow the verb in an affirmative command in the same order as they do in English.

Donnez-**le-lui**!	*Give it to him!*
Apportez-**m'en**!	*Bring me some!*
Prêtez-**la-lui**!	*Lend it to her!*
Achète-**le-nous**!	*Buy it for us!*

NOTE: If the direct object in an affirmative command is **moi**, **toi**, **nous**, or **vous**, express the indirect object by **à plus a disjunctive pronoun** (see Sec. 6-1).

Présentez-**vous à eux**.	*Introduce yourself to them.*
Présentez-**moi à eux**.	*Introduce me to them.*
Présentez-**nous à elles**.	*Introduce us to them.*

NOTE: The object pronouns in a negative command precede the verb and follow the normal order.

Ne me la donnez pas!	*Don't give it to me!*
Ne te dépêche pas!	*Don't hurry!*
Ne m'en donnez pas!	*Don't give me any!*
N'y allez pas!	*Don't go there!*

EXERCISE 6-22: Respond to each of the following questions with an affirmative command containing two pronouns. Answers and translations are at the end of the chapter.

Example: Préférez-vous que je présente ma carte au secrétaire?   *Do you prefer me to present my card to the secretary?*

Oui, présentez-la-lui!   *Yes, present it to him!*

1. Veux-tu que je pose la question au directeur?
2. Désirez-vous que je montre les photos aux visiteurs?
3. Préfères-tu que je laisse le choix au patron?
4. Exigez-vous que je demande une réponse à la dame?
5. Demandes-tu que je t'apporte ton déjeuner?

EXERCISE 6-23: Now respond to the preceding questions with a negative command containing two pronouns. Answers and translations are at the end of the chapter.

SUMMARY

1. The disjunctive pronoun—**moi, toi, lui, elle, nous, vous, eux, elles**—emphasizes the subject of a sentence, follows a preposition, responds to a question, introduces a relative clause, or indicates possession.
2. The direct object pronoun—**me, te, le, la, nous, vous, les**—comes before the verb except in an affirmative command.

3. The partitive pronoun **en** replaces a direct object used in a partitive sense. The adverbial pronoun **en** refers to a prepositional phrase beginning with the preposition **de** whose object is usually not a person.

4. The indirect object pronoun—**me, te, lui, nous, vous, leur**—comes before the verb, except in an affirmative command.

5. The adverbial pronoun **y** refers to a previously mentioned location, or to a prepositional phrase whose object is something other than a place or person.

6. A reflexive pronoun repeats the subject noun or pronoun in the form of a second noun.

7. The order of object pronouns is 1) pronouns that may be direct or indirect; 2) all other pronouns—direct before indirect; and 3) y or en.

8. In an affirmative command, object pronouns follow the verb in the same order as they do in English.

RAISE YOUR GRADES

Object pronouns

Underline the object pronoun in each of the following sentences. Then find its description in the list below, and write the corresponding letter in the space provided. Answers and translations are at the end of the chapter.

A Direct Object Pronoun
B Indirect Object Pronoun
C Disjunctive Pronoun
D Reflexive Direct Object
E Reflexive Indirect Object

_____ 1. Nous ne le connaissons pas.
_____ 2. Voulez-vous prendre un café avec moi?
_____ 3. Je vous adore.
_____ 4. Attendez-moi!
_____ 5. Qu'est-ce que vous lui dites?
_____ 6. Nous nous demandons pourquoi vous êtes là.
_____ 7. Leur emploi du temps ne leur permet pas de venir.
_____ 8. Moi, je ne comprends rien!
_____ 9. Nous nous rencontrons tous les mardis.
_____ 10. La voyez-vous derrière cet arbre?
_____ 11. Il n'en a certainement pas.
_____ 12. Qui a un message pour lui?
_____ 13. Je vais écrire pour lui demander.
_____ 14. Nous mettons nos lunettes pour les regarder.
_____ 15. Envoyez-moi de vos nouvelles.
_____ 16. Il se lave le visage et les mains.
_____ 17. Qu'est-ce qu'elle va faire sans nous?
_____ 18. Chez eux on mange toujours bien.
_____ 19. Asseyez-vous un instant!
_____ 20. Nous te souhaitons un bon anniversaire.

Commands

Change the following affirmative commands to negative commands with the pronouns in the appropriate order. Then translate your answer into English. Answers and translations are at the end of the chapter.

Example: Expliquez-le-lui! *Explain it to him!*
Ne le lui expliquez pas! *Don't explain it to him!*

21. Offrez-leur-en!

22. Envoyez-les-moi!

23. Adressez-vous-y!

24. Ecrivez-la-nous!

25. Asseyez-vous-y!

26. Servez-vous-en!

27. Prête-m'en!

28. Va-t-en!

29. Donnez-le-leur!

30. Lave-la-moi!

CHAPTER ANSWERS

EXERCISE 6-1:

1. Oui, ce sont elles qui parlent italien. *Yes, it is they who speak Italian.*
2. Oui, c'est moi qui ai faim. *Yes, it's I who am hungry.*
3. Oui, ils arrivent avant lui. *Yes, they arrive before him.*
4. Oui, c'est lui qui aime le film. *Yes, it is he who likes the movie.*
5. Oui, ce sont eux. *Yes, it is they. (They are the ones.)*
6. Oui, elle et moi, nous savons la vérité. *Yes, she and I know the truth.*
7. Oui, nous partons sans eux. *Yes, we leave without them.*
8. Oui, il connaît son métier mieux que lui. *Yes, he knows his business better than he.*
9. Oui, moi, je préfère les romans. *Yes, I prefer novels.*
10. Oui, vous êtes plus intelligent que moi. *Yes, you are more intelligent than I.*

EXERCISE 6-2:

1. *Do you understand this exercise?*
   Oui, je le comprends.
   Yes, I understand it.
2. *Do the French admire Joan of Arc?*
   Oui, ils l'admirent.
   Yes, they admire her.
3. *Do parents scold their children?*
   Oui, ils les grondent.
   Yes, they scold them.
4. *Do astronauts explore the stars?*
   Oui, ils les explorent.
   Yes, they explore them.
5. *Are you writing this sentence in English?*
   Oui, je l'écris en anglais.
   Yes, I am writing it in English.
6. *Do artists visit galleries?*
   Oui, ils les visitent.
   Yes, they visit them.
7. *Do students learn the sciences?*
   Oui, elles les apprennent.
   Yes, they learn them.
8. *Is the secretary writing the letters on the typewriter?*
   Oui, elle les tapent à la machine.
   Yes, she is writing them on the typewriter.
9. *Is François listening to the radio this evening?*
   Oui, il l'écoute le soir.
   Yes, he's listening to it this evening.
10. *Do the housewives do the shopping in the morning?*
    Oui, elles le font le matin.
    Yes, they do it in the morning.

EXERCISE 6-3:

1. Oui, il le vend. *Yes, he's selling it.*
2. Oui, je vous sers. *Yes, I'll serve you.*
3. Oui, il te (vous) prend au sérieux. *Yes, he takes you seriously.*
4. Oui, il m'aime. *Yes, he likes me.*
5. Oui, je l'admire. *Yes, I admire him (her, it).*
6. Oui, vous les oubliez. OR Oui, tu les oublies. *Yes, you forget them.*
7. Oui, on t'attend (vous attend). *Yes, they're waiting for you.*
8. Oui, tu m'ennuies. *Yes, you're bothering me.*
9. Oui, Robert les connaît. *Yes, Robert knows them.*
10. Oui, je vous corrige. *Yes, I'm correcting you.*

EXERCISE 6-4:

1. Je propose de vous accompagner en voiture. *I propose to accompany you by car.*
2. Ils apprennent à le finir rapidement. *They are learning to finish it quickly.*
3. Paul dit de les apporter à la prochaine réunion. *Paul says to take them to the next reunion.*
4. Les gendarmes sont obligés de les arrêter. *The police had to arrest them.*
5. On est surpris de me voir à la télévision. *They were surprised to see me on television.*
6. Je n'ai pas le temps de venir vous chercher. *I don't have time to come to get you.*

7. Les voisins nous entendent jouer de la guitare. *The neighbors hear us play the guitar.*

8. Mes professeurs commencent à me comprendre mieux. *My professors are beginning to understand me better.*

9. Il a besoin de courage pour les confronter. *He needs the courage to confront them.*

10. J'ai peur de les regarder en face. *I am afraid of looking them in the face.*

EXERCISE 6-5:

1. Oui, je le sais. *Yes, I know when (it).*
2. Oui, il le préfère. *Yes, he prefers it.*
3. Oui, elle le désire. *Yes, she wants to.*
4. Oui, je le veux. *Yes, I want to.*
5. Oui, Marie le doit. *Yes, she must do it.*
6. Oui, ses employés le sont. *Yes, his employees are (that).*
7. Oui, elles le sont. *Yes, they are.*
8. Oui, mes frères le pensent. *Yes, my brothers are thinking of it.*
9. Oui, Monsieur Dupont l'est. *Yes, Mr. Dupont is (that).*
10. Oui, les hommes et les femmes le sont. *Yes, men and women are (that).*

EXERCISE 6-6:

1. Non, il y en a 50. *No, there are 50 (of them).*
2. Non, j'en ai deux. *No, I have two (of them).*
3. Non, il y en a 100. *No, there are 100 (of them).*
4. Non, il en a 26. *No, it has 26 (of them).*

5. Non, une bicyclette en a deux. *No, a bicycle has two (of them).*
6. Non, il en contient 200. *No, it has 200 (of them).*
7. Oui, j'en ai un. *Yes, I have one (of them).*
8. Il y en a deux dans un couple. *There are two (of them) in a couple.*
9. Non, il y en a 7 dans une semaine. *No, there are 7 (of them) in a week.*
10. On en achète 12 à la fois. *You buy 12 (of them) at a time.*

EXERCISE 6-7:

1. Oui, j'en fais souvent. *Yes, I often make them.*
2. Oui, ma voiture en consomme trop. *Yes, my car uses too much (of it).*
3. Non, on n'en a jamais trop. *No, one never has too much (of it).*
4. Non, on n'en prend pas dans un bar. *No, one doesn't get it in a bar.*
5. Non, il n'y en a pas en été. *No, there isn't any (of it) in summer.*
6. Non, je n'en bois pas au petit déjeuner. *No, I don't drink it at breakfast.*
7. Oui, on en fait pour rester en forme. *Yes, one does it to stay in shape.*
8. Oui, on en trouve à la bibliothèque. *Yes, you find them at the library.*
9. Non, il n'y en a pas beaucoup dans le désert. *No, there isn't a lot (of it) in the desert.*
10. Oui, il en faut pour en élever. *Yes, it's necessary to have it in order to raise them.*

EXERCISE 6-8:

1. Oui, j'en ai le temps. *Yes, I have the time.* Non, je n'en ai pas le temps. *No, I don't have the time.*
2. Oui, ils en ont envie. *Yes, they want to go there.* Non, ils en ont pas envie. *No, they don't want to go there.*
3. Oui, j'en sors ce soir. *Yes, I'm going out of it tonight.* Non, je n'en sors pas ce soir. *No, I'm not going out of it tonight.*
4. Oui, ils en viennent. *Yes, they come from there.* Non, ils n'en viennent pas. *No they don't come from there.*
5. Oui, on en a besoin. *Yes, one needs to do it.* Non, on n'en a pas besoin. *No, one doesn't need to do it.*
6. Oui, j'en ai envie. *Yes, I want to do that.* Non, je n'en ai pas envie. *No, I don't want to do that.*
7. Oui, il en retire tout son argent. *Yes, he takes all his money out of it.* Non, il n'en retire pas tout son argent. *No, he does not take all his money out of it.*
8. Oui, j'en ai peur. *Yes, I am afraid of them.* Non, je n'en ai pas peur. *No, I'm not afraid of them.*
9. Oui, ils en parlent. *Yes, they're talking of it.* Non, ils n'en parlent pas. *No, they're not talking of it.*
10. Oui, elle en est couverte. *Yes, it is covered with them.* Non, elle n'en est pas couverte. *No, it's not covered with them.*

EXERCISE 6-9:

1. Oui, ils leur parlent. *Yes, they speak to them.*
2. Oui, je leur offre un verre de vin. *Yes, I offer them a glass of wine.*
3. Oui, je leur dis la vérité. *Yes, I tell them the truth.*
4. Oui, ils leur répondent. *Yes, they answer them.*
5. Oui, il lui donne sa place. *Yes, he gives her his seat.*

6. Oui, les soldats lui obéissent. *Yes, the soldiers obey him.*
7. Oui, je lui ressemble. *Yes, I look like her.*
8. Oui, nous y obéissons. *Yes, we obey them.*
9. Oui, les reporters leur posent des questions. *Yes, the reporters ask them questions.*
10. Oui, je lui montre mes tableaux. *Yes, I am showing him my paintings.*

EXERCISE 6-10:

1. Oui, il me répond. *Yes, he answers me.*
2. Oui, elles leur ressemblent. *Yes, they resemble them.*
3. Oui, on lui obéit. *Yes, one obeys him.*
4. Oui, je vous promets. *Yes, I promise you.*
5. Oui, je vous demande. (Oui, je te demande.) *Yes, I ask you.*
6. Oui, ils me parlent. *Yes, they speak to me.*
7. Oui, je leur téléphone. *Yes, I call them.*
8. Oui, elle lui écrit. *Yes, she writes him.*
9. Oui, il m'offre quelque chose. *Yes, he offers me something.*
10. Oui, je vous envoie des nouvelles. (Oui, je t'envoie des nouvelles.) *Yes, I send you some news.*

EXERCISE 6-11:

1. Non, je n'y vais jamais. *No, I never go there.*
2. Oui, j'y réponds immédiatement. *Yes, I answer them immediately.*
3. Ils y voyagent le mois prochain. *They are traveling there next month.*
4. Non, ils n'y sont pas tous. *No, they are not all there.*
5. Non, je n'y vois rien. *No, I don't see anything there.*
6. Oui, elles vont y téléphoner à 9 heures. *Yes, they're going to call there at 9 a.m.*
7. Oui, il faut y obéir sans question. *Yes, you must obey them without question.*
8. Non, je n'y contribue pas du tout! *No, I don't contribute to it at all!*
9. Oui, ils y passent toujours. *Yes, they always go there.*
10. Non, il y gare son vélo. *No, he parks his bike there.*

EXERCISE 6-12:

1. Non, je me corrige. *No, I correct myself.*
2. Non, je m'aide. *No, I help myself.*
3. Non, nous nous servons. *No, we help ourselves.*
4. Non, ils s'invitent. *No, they invite themselves.*
5. Non, je me coupe les cheveux. *No, I cut my own hair.*
6. Non, le moteur s'arrête. *No, the engine stops by itself.*
7. Non, vous allez vous conduire. *No, you are going to drive yourself.*
8. Non, ces jeunes filles se présentent. *No, these girls introduce themselves.*
9. Non, elle se réveille. *No, she wakes up by herself.*
10. Non, il (elle) s'amuse. *No, he (she) amuses himself (herself).*

EXERCISE 6-13:

1. Nous nous servons souvent de notre machine à écrire. *We often use our typewriter.*
2. Les enfants se couchent avant minuit. *Children go to bed before midnight.*
3. Le détective se doute qu'un crime a été commis. *The detective suspects that a crime was committed.*
4. Je prends le sac et je me sauve. *I pack my bag and run away.*
5. Les étudiants se plaignent que les examens sont longs. *The students complain that the tests are too long.*

EXERCISE 6-14:

1. Il faut se méfier des chemins dangereux. *You must be cautious on dangerous roads.*
2. Les diplomates s'en vont par le Concorde cet après-midi. *The diplomats leave this afternoon on the Concorde.*
3. Juliette se suicide quand elle voit Roméo mort. *Juliette kills herself when she sees Romeo dead.*
4. Je me souviens de ma promesse. *I remember my promise.*
5. Les animaux s'efforcent de survivre dans le désert. *Animals strive to survive in the desert.*
6. Il est facile de se moquer des personnages célèbres. *It's easy to make fun of famous people.*

EXERCISE 6-15:

1. Nous nous comprenons. *We understand each other.*
2. Vous vous traitez bien. *You treat one another well.*
3. Mon oncle et ma tante s'aident. *My aunt and uncle help each other.*
4. Nous nous parlons en même temps. *We speak to each other at the same time.*
5. Vous et vos voisins, vous vous détestez. *You and your neighbors detest one another.*

EXERCISE 6-16:

1. Oui, vous me les expliquez. *Yes, you explain them to me.*
2. Oui, je me le rappelle. *Yes, I remember it.*
3. Oui, il nous les prépare. *Yes, he takes care of them for us.*
4. Oui, je te la donne. *Yes, I give it to you.*
5. Oui, on se la prête facilement. *Yes, people lend it to one another readily.*
6. Oui, je vous présente à elle. *Yes, I introduce you to her.*
7. Oui, nous vous la présentons. *Yes we introduce her to you.*
8. Oui, ils se les coupent. *Yes, they cut it themselves (for one another).*
9. Oui, je vais te le montrer. *Yes, I am going to show it to you.*
10. Oui, elle s'en donne la peine (elle se la donne). *Yes, she takes the trouble to do it (she does take it).*

EXERCISE 6-17:

1. Il lui donne un cadeau. *He gives her a present.*
2. Mon père lui écrit la lettre. *He writes him the letter.*

3. Chantal lui parle doucement. *Chantal spoke to it softly.*
4. René lui envoie des poèmes. *René sends poems to her.*
5. Les étudiantes apprennent bien la leçon. *The students learn the lesson well. (No indirect object)*
6. Jacques leur dit toujours la vérité. *Jacques always tells them the truth.*
7. Dominique lui parle avant le cours. *Dominique speaks to her before class.*
8. Ma soeur leur donne ses vieux vêtements. *My sister gives them her old clothes.*
9. Le professeur leur pose une question. *The professor asks them a question.*
10. Henri lui donne des fleurs. *Henri gives her flowers.*

EXERCISE 6-18:
1. Il le donne à sa mère. *He gives it to his mother.*
2. Mon père l'écrit à l'éditeur du journal. *My father writes it to the editor of the paper.*
3. Chantal parle doucement au chien. *Chantal speaks softly to the dog. (No direct object)*
4. René les envoie à Catherine. *René sends them to Catherine.*
5. Les étudiantes l'apprennent bien. *The students learn it well.*
6. Jacques la dit toujours à ses parents. *Jacques always tells it to his parents.*
7. Dominique parle à Marie avant le cours. *Dominique speaks to Marie before class. (No direct object)*
8. Ma soeur les donne aux pauvres. *My sister gives them to the poor.*
9. Le professeur la pose à ses étudiants. *The professor asks it of his students.*
10. Henri les donne à sa petite amie. *Henri gives them to his girlfriend.*

EXERCISE 6-19:
1. Il le lui donne. *He gives it to her.*
2. Mon père la lui écrit. *My father writes it to him.*
3. Chantal lui parle doucement. *Chantal speaks softly to it.*
4. René les lui envoie. *René sends them to her.*
5. Les étudiantes l'apprennent bien. *The students learn it well.*
6. Jacques la leur dit toujours. *Jacques always tells it to them.*
7. Dominique lui parle avant le cours. *Dominique speaks to her before class.*

8. Ma soeur les leur donne. *My sister gives them to them.*
9. Le professeur la leur pose. *The professor asks it of them.*
10. Henri les lui donne. *Henri gives them to her.*

EXERCISE 6-20:
1. Oui, je l'y vois. *Yes, I see it there.*
2. Oui, on leur en donne. *Yes, one gives them to them.*
3. Oui, ils l'y mettent. *Yes, they put it there.*
4. Oui, je l'y écris. *Yes, I wrote it in it.*
5. Oui, nous lui en parlons. *Yes, we talk to him about it.*

EXERCISE 6-21:
1. Oui, il le lui offre. *Yes, he offers it to them.*
2. Oui, je les y regarde. *Yes, I watch it there.*
3. Oui, nous l'y prenons. *Yes, we have it there.*
4. Oui, je vous le recommande. *Yes, I recommend it to you.*
5. Oui, elle leur en donne. *Yes, she gives them some (of them).*
6. Oui, ils leur en promettent. *Yes, they promise it to them.*
7. Oui, je vous en permets une. *Yes, I'll allow you one.*
8. Oui, il s'en rend compte. *Yes, he is aware of it.*
9. Oui, vous devez vous y asseoir. *Yes, you must sit in it.*
10. Oui, je les leur rends. *Yes, I am returning them to them.*

EXERCISE 6-22:
1. Oui, pose-la-lui! *Yes, ask it of him!*
2. Oui, montrez-les-leur! *Yes, show them to them!*
3. Oui, laisse-le-lui! *Yes, leave it to him!*
4. Oui, demandez-lui-en-une! *Yes, ask her for one (of them)!*
5. Oui, apporte-le-moi! *Yes, bring it to me!*

EXERCISE 6-23:
1. Non, ne le lui posez pas! *No, don't ask it of him!*
2. Non, ne les leur montrez pas! *No, don't show them to them!*
3. Non, ne le lui laissez pas! *No, don't leave it to him!*
4. Non, ne lui en demandez pas une! *No, don't ask her for one (of them)!*
5. Non, ne me l'apportez pas! *No, don't bring it to me!*

RAISE YOUR GRADES
Object pronouns
A 1. **le**   *We don't know it.*
C 2. **moi** *Will you have coffee with me?*
A 3. **vous** *I adore you.*

A	4.	**moi**	*Wait for me!*
B	5.	**lui**	*What do you say to him?*
E	6.	**nous**	*We ask ourselves why you are there.*
B	7.	**leur**	*Their schedule does not allow them to come.*
C	8.	**Moi**	*Me, I understand nothing!*
D	9.	**nous**	*We all meet on Tuesdays.*
A	10.	**La**	*Do you see her behind that tree?*
A	11.	**en**	*He certainly doesn't have it (any of it).*
C	12.	**lui**	*Who has a message for him?*
B	13.	**lui**	*I am going to write in order to ask him.*
A	14.	**les**	*We put on our glasses in order to watch them.*
B	15.	**moi**	*Send me your news.*
E	16.	**se**	*He washes his face and his hands.*
C	17.	**nous**	*What is she going to do without us?*
C	18.	**eux**	*We always eat well at their place.*
D	19.	**vous**	*Sit down a minute!*
B	20.	**te**	*We wish you a happy birthday.*

Commands

21. Ne leur en offrez pas! *Don't offer them any!*
22. Ne me les envoyez pas! *Don't send them to me!*
23. Ne vous y adressez pas! *Don't inquire there!*
24. Ne nous l'écrivez pas! *Don't write it to us!*
25. Ne vous y asseyez pas! *Don't sit there!*
26. Ne vous en servez pas! *Don't use it (them)!*
27. Ne m'en prête pas! *Don't lend me any!*
28. Ne t'en va pas! *Don't go there!*
29. Ne le leur donnez pas! *Don't give it to them!*
30. Ne me la lave pas! *Don't wash it for me!*

UNIT EXAM II

SUBJECT PRONOUNS

Replace the underlined subjects with those in parentheses, making any necessary changes in the form of the verb.

1. Les bons étudiants répondent en français. (nous)
2. Pourquoi choisissez-vous toujours la mauvaise forme? (il)
3. Le téléphone interrompt notre conversation. (Elles)
4. Essaies-tu la robe avant de l'acheter? (vous)
5. On mange normalement à six heures et demie. (nous)
6. Il répète distinctement le nom du candidat. (vous)
7. Est-ce que tes amis arrivent ce soir? (tu)
8. Quand finit-elle la présentation? (ils)
9. Nous préférons la salade après la viande. (je)
10. Ils déclarent que tout est en ordre. (elle)
11. Pourquoi attendez-vous si longtemps? (on)
12. Est-ce que tu rougis facilement? (je)
13. Nous commençons à 21:00 heures. (tu)
14. Tu entends le son de la pluie. (vous)
15. On établit de bons rapports avec les clients. (ils)
16. Elle perd la tête facilement. (je)
17. On réussit bien aux examens. (nous)
18. Où descendez-vous de l'autobus? (tu)

INFINITIVES

Combine each of the following pairs of sentences logically into a single sentence containing a conjugated verb and an infinitive. Use a connecting preposition where necessary.

19. Il ne mange pas d'escargots. Il refuse.
20. Nous passons des examens. Nous le détestons.
21. La petite fille danse très bien. Elle commence.
22. Cet étudiant prépare sa dissertation. Il finit.
23. Tous les jeunes gens sont au match. Ils le désirent.
24. Je n'écoute pas les instructions. Je réponds.
25. On part en voyage. On prépare la valise.

IRREGULAR VERBS

Use the appropriate form of the irregular verb in parentheses in place of the regular verb in each of the following sentences.

26. Qui choisit la glace au chocolat? (prendre)

27. Il ne réalise pas les implications. (savoir)

28. Les élèves restent debout devant la classe. (être)

29. Ils partent en Italie en bateau. (aller)

30. Nous possédons un chalet à la montagne. (avoir)

31. Vous vous préparez un sandwich et une salade. (faire)

32. Ces demoiselles arrivent un peu plus tard. (venir)

33. Je compose une lettre sur mes derniers exploits. (écrire)

34. Pourquoi racontez-vous ces histoires aux enfants? (dire)

35. Mes grands-parents fréquentent les Cléry. (connaître)

36. Elle habite au Caire avec son mari. (vivre)

OBJECT PRONOUNS

Answer the following questions affirmatively introducing at least two object pronouns.

37. Vous promenez vous souvent au parc avec vos camarades?

38. Rendez-vous toujours vos livres à la bibliothèque?

39. Rêvez-vous à votre mère dans votre sommeil?

40. Prêtez-vous quelquefois votre bicyclette à un ami?

41. Un yacht coûte-t-il beaucoup d'argent à son propriétaire?

Write the appropriate commands telling the following people to do the following things. Use object pronouns.

42. Dites à votre mère de vous préparer un café.

43. Dites à deux amis de ne pas vous casser la bicyclette.

44. Dites à l'agent de police de vous rendre votre passeport.

45. Dites à quelqu'un de ne pas s'occuper de vous.

EXAM ANSWERS

Subject pronouns

1. Nous répondons en français. *We are answering in French.*
2. Pourquoi choisit-il toujours la mauvaise forme? *Why does he always choose the wrong form?*
3. Elles interrompent notre conversation. *They interrupt our conversation.*
4. Essayez-vous la robe avant de l'acheter? *Do you try on the dress before buying it?*
5. Nous mangeons normalement à six heures et demie. *We usually eat at six thirty.*
6. Vous répétez distinctement le nom du candidat. *You repeat the candidate's name distinctly.*
7. Est-ce que tu arrives ce soir? *Will you be arriving this evening?*
8. Quand finissent-ils la présentation? *When are they going to end the show?*
9. Je préfère la salade après la viande. *I prefer my salad after my entree.*
10. Elle déclare que tout est en ordre. *She declares that everything is in order.*
11. Pourquoi attend-on si longtemps? *Why are we waiting (for) so long?*
12. Est-ce que je rougis facilement? *Do I blush easily?*
13. Tu commences à 21:00 heures. *You start at 9:00 P.M.*
14. Vous entendez le son de la pluie. *You hear the sound of the rain.*
15. Ils établissent de bons rapports avec les clients. *They establish good relations with their customers.*

16. Je perds la tête facilement. *I'm easily confused.*
17. Nous réussissons bien aux examens. *We succeed in our exams.*
18. Ou descend-tu de l'autobus? *Where do you get off the bus?*

Infinitives

19. Il refuse de manger des escargots. *He refuses to eat snails.*
20. Nous détestons passer des examens. *We hate to take exams.*
21. La petite fille commence à très bien danser. *The little girl is beginning to dance very well.*
22. Cet étudiant finit de préparer sa dissertation. *This student is finishing up his thesis.*
23. Tous les jeunes gens veulent aller au match. *All the young people want to go to the game.*
24. Je réponds sans écouter les instructions. *I answer without listening to the instructions.*
25. On prépare sa valise pour partir en voyage. *You pack your bag to leave on a trip.*

Irregular verbs

26. Qui prend la glace au chocolat? *Who is having chocolate ice cream?*
27. Il ne sait pas les implications. *He doesn't know the implications.*
28. Les élèves sont debout devant la classe. *The pupils are standing in front of the class.*
29. Ils vont en Italie par bateau. *They are going to Italy by boat.*

30. Nous avons un chalet à la montagne. *We have a cabin in the mountains.*
31. Vous vous faites un sandwich et une salade. *You are making yourself a sandwich and a salad.*
32. Ces demoiselles viennent un peu plus tard. *The young ladies are coming a little later.*
33. J'écris une lettre sur mes derniers exploits. *I am writing a letter about my latest adventures.*
34. Pourquoi dites-vous ces histoires aux enfants? *Why are you telling those stories to the children?*
35. Mes grands-parents connaissent les Cléry. *My grandparents know the Clerys.*
36. Elle vit au Caire avec son mari. *She lives in Cairo with her husband.*

Object pronouns

37. Je m'y promène souvent avec eux. *I walk there often with them.*
38. Je les y rends toujours. *I always return them there.*
39. Je rêve à elle dans mon sommeil. *I dream of her in my sleep.*
40. Je la lui prête quelquefois. *I lend it to him sometimes.*
41. Il lui en coûte beaucoup. *It costs him a lot of money.*
42. Prépare-m'en un, s'il te plait. *Make me one, please.*
43. Ne me la cassez pas! *Don't break it for me!*
44. Rendez-le moi! *Give it back to me!*
45. Ne vous occupez pas de moi! *Leave me alone?*

7 PAST PARTICIPLE AND PAST VERB FORMS

THIS CHAPTER IS ABOUT

☑ **Past Participles**
☑ **Le Passé Composé,** *The Compound Past Tense*
☑ **L'imparfait,** *The Imperfect Past Tense*
☑ **Contrasting Use of Past Tense Forms**

7-1. Past Participles

A. Formation of past participles

Past participles are derived from verbs, but are not used as verbs since they do not have tense or personal endings.

1. The past participles of all **-er** verbs end in **-é**.

Infinitive		Past Participle	
parl**er**	*to speak*	**parlé**	*spoken*
mang**er**	*to eat*	**mangé**	*eaten*
tomb**er**	*to fall*	**tombé**	*fallen*
all**er**	*to go*	**allé**	*gone*

> *NOTE:* The irregular verbs **être** and **naître** also have past participles ending in **-é**.

Infinitive		Past Participle	
être	*to be*	**été**	*been*
naître	*to be born*	**né**	*(been) born*

2. The past participles of regular **-ir** verbs and many irregular verbs ending in **-ir** end in **-i**.

Infinitive		Past Participle	
chois**ir**	*to choose*	**choisi**	*chosen*
grand**ir**	*to grow*	**grandi**	*grown*
sort**ir**	*to go out*	**sorti**	*gone out*
dorm**ir**	*to sleep*	**dormi**	*slept*
cueill**ir**	*to gather, pick*	**cueilli**	*gathered, picked*
faill**ir**	*to almost _____*	**failli**	*almost _____*

> *NOTE:* The past participles of the verbs **rire** and **suivre** and all their compounds also end in **-i**.

Infinitive		Past Participle	
rire	*to laugh*	**ri**	*laughed*
sourire	*to smile*	**souri**	*smiled*
suivre	*to follow*	**suivi**	*followed*
poursuivre	*to pursue*	**poursuivi**	*pursued*

3. Many verbs have past participles ending in **-u**.

- All regular and many irregular **-re** verbs have past participles ending **-u**.

Infinitive		Past Participle	
mordre	*to bite*	**mordu**	*bitten*
rompre	*to break*	**rompu**	*broken*
rendre	*to give back*	**rendu**	*given back*

- The verb **vivre** and its compounds have an irregular past participle stem and the **-u** ending.

Infinitive		Past Participle	
vivre	*to live*	**vécu**	*lived*
survivre	*to survive*	**survécu**	*survived*

- Irregular verbs ending in **-oire**, **-oir**, **-aire**, and **-aître**—except **faire** and **naître**—have past participles ending in **-u**.

Infinitive		Past Participle	
appar**aître**	*to appear*	**apparu**	*appeared*
av**oir**	*to have*	**eu**	*had*
apercev**oir**	*to notice*	**aperçu**	*noticed*
b**oire**	*to drink*	**bu**	*drunk*
conn**aître**	*to know (about)*	**connu**	*known (about)*
concev**oir**	*to conceive*	**conçu**	*conceived*
décev**oir**	*to disappoint*	**déçu**	*disappointed*
émouv**oir**	*to move, touch*	**ému**	*moved, touched*
dev**oir**	*must, owe*	**dû**	*owed*
fall**oir**	*to be necessary*	**fallu**	*been necessary*
percev**oir**	*to perceive*	**perçu**	*perceived*
pl**aire**	*to please*	**plu**	*pleased*
pouv**oir**	*to be able*	**pu**	*been able*
sav**oir**	*to know (a fact)*	**su**	*known (a fact)*
se t**aire**	*to be silent*	**tu**	*been silent*
val**oir**	*to be worth*	**valu**	*valued*
voul**oir**	*to want, wish*	**voulu**	*wanted, wished*

NOTE: The infinitive stem of these verbs is always shortened.

- Irregular verbs whose infinitives end in **-oudre** have irregular past participle stems and the **-u** ending.

Infinitive		Past Participle	
ré**soudre**	*to resolve*	**résolu**	*resolved*
moudre	*to grind*	**moulu**	*ground*
coudre	*to sew*	**cousu**	*sewn*

- A few irregular verbs ending in **-ir** and **-ire** and their compounds have past participles ending in **-u**.

Infinitive		Past Participle	
cour**ir**	*to run*	**couru**	*run*
deven**ir**	*to become*	**devenu**	*become*
é**lire**	*to elect*	**élu**	*elected*
lire	*to read*	**lu**	*read*
parcour**ir**	*to run through*	**parcouru**	*run through*
reten**ir**	*to retain*	**retenu**	*retained*
ten**ir**	*to hold, grasp*	**tenu**	*held, grasped*
ven**ir**	*to come*	**venu**	*come*

4. Some irregular verbs have past participles ending in consonants.

- The irregular verbs **prendre**, **mettre**, **asseoir**, their compounds, and verbs ending in **-quérir** have past participles ending in **-is**. The infinitive stem is shortened.

Infinitive		Past Participle	
ac**quérir**	*to acquire*	**acquis**	*acquired*
s'**asseoir**	*to sit down*	**assis**	*sat down*
com**mettre**	*to commit*	**commis**	*committed*
com**prendre**	*to understand*	**compris**	*understood*
con**quérir**	*to conquer*	**conquis**	*conquered*
prendre	*to take*	**pris**	*taken*

- Verbs whose infinitives end in **-frir** or **-vrir** have past participles ending in **-ert**.

Infinitive		Past Participle	
cou**vrir**	*to cover*	**couvert**	*covered*
of**frir**	*to offer, give*	**offert**	*offered, given*
ou**vrir**	*to open*	**ouvert**	*opened*
souf**frir**	*to suffer*	**souffert**	*suffered*

- The common irregular verbs **faire**, **dire**, and **écrire**, their compounds, and all verbs ending in **-indre** or **-uire** have past participles which are identical to the third-person singular of the present tense.

Infinitive		3rd Sing Pres	Past Participle	
cond**uire**	*to drive*	il conduit	**conduit**	*driven*
cra**indre**	*to fear*	il craint	**craint**	*feared*
décrire	*to describe*	il décrit	**décrit**	*described*
dire	*to say*	il dit	**dit**	*said*
écrire	*to write*	il écrit	**écrit**	*written*
faire	*to do, make*	il fait	**fait**	*done, made*
jo**indre**	*to join*	il joint	**joint**	*joined*
pe**indre**	*to paint*	il peint	**peint**	*painted*
prod**uire**	*to produce*	il produit	**produit**	*produced*

NOTE: The past participle of **mourir**, *to die,* is **mort**, *died, dead.*

REMEMBER: You cannot use a past participle *alone* as the verb in a sentence. A verb has personal endings and a specific tense—a participle has neither.

B. Past participles as adjectives

1. When a past participle modifies a noun, it follows that noun and agrees with it in gender and number.

le **héro mort**	*the dead hero*
la **personne mentionnée**	*the person mentioned*
les **articles cités**	*the cited articles*

EXERCISE 7-1: Replace the prepositional phrase in parentheses with the appropriate form of the past participle. Answers and translations are at the end of the chapter.

Example: C'est une femme (à respecter). *She is a woman to respect.*

C'est une femme respectée. *She's a respected woman.*

1. J'ai un contrat (à signer).
2. Il y a des compositions (à écrire).
3. Voila une idée (à retenir).
4. C'est une fenêtre (à ouvrir).
5. Quel est le résultat (à obtenir)?

6. Elle a ses valises (à faire).
7. C'est un obstacle (à vaincre).
8. Nous avons des articles (à publier).
9. C'est une leçon (à apprendre).
10. C'est un dessin (à peindre).

C. Passive sentences

1. In a passive sentence, the direct object of a transitive verb (see Sec. 7-2) becomes the subject of the sentence. Only transitive verbs can be used passively.

Les jardiniers **arrosent les plantes**. | *The gardeners water the plants.*
Les plantes sont arrosées par les jardiniers. | *The plants are watered by the gardeners.*

2. To form a passive sentence, use the appropriate person and tense of **être** with the past participle of the main verb. In a passive sentence, the past participle is an adjective and agrees in gender and number with the subject of the sentence.

On **critique** les films violents. | *They criticize violent films.*
Les films violents **sont critiqués**. | *Violent films are criticized.*

> **NOTE:** A passive sentence is *not always* a past-tense sentence. The verb **être** indicates the tense of the sentence.

Les rues **sont** lavées par la pluie. | *The streets are washed by the rain.*

EXERCISE 7-2: Change the verbs in the following sentences to past participles. You'll also have to change the order of the words. Answers and translations are at the end of the chapter.
Example: On élimine les erreurs. | *They eliminate the mistakes.*
Les erreurs sont éliminées. | *The mistakes are eliminated.*

1. On voit ces films à la télévision.
2. On ferme les fenêtres à cause de la pluie.
3. On peint les murs en blanc.
4. On sert les clients comme il faut.
5. On prend ces photos comme souvenir.
6. On écrit souvent ces mots incorrectement.
7. On met cette lettre à la poste.
8. On conduit l'auto pour lui.
9. On vend le journal dans la rue.
10. On offre une cigarette à la dame.

7-2. Le Passé Composé, *The Compound Past Tense*

A. Formation of the passé composé with avoir

Form the passé composé of transitive verbs—verbs that can be followed directly by a noun phrase without an intervening preposition—by combining the present tense of **avoir** with the past participle of the main verb.

Le garçon **prend notre commande**. | *The waiter is taking our order.*
Le garçon **a pris** notre commande. | *The waiter took our order.*

> **NOTE:** The past participle *does not* create the past meaning; the combination of **avoir** and the past participle *does*. This is not clear in English where many verbs have the same form for the past participle and the simple past tense.
>
> *I* slept *for eight hours.* *I* have slept *for eight hours.*
>
> In French, you must combine the auxiliary verb with the past participle to convey a past meaning.

B. Translation of the passé composé

You often translate a verb in the passé composé into English by a simple one-word past tense.

J'ai mis la lettre à la poste hier.	*I mailed the letter yesterday.*
Les sénateurs **ont voté** pour la nouvelle loi.	*The senators voted for the new law.*

BUT you may also translate the passé composé by the English present perfect—a verb formed with *have* or *has*—if the event has taken place quite recently.

Les senateurs **ont voté** pour la nouvelle loi.	*The senators have voted for the new law.*

C. Use of the passé composé

The passé composé always refers to a new situation or turn of events in the past.

Il **a plu** hier.	*It rained yesterday.*

(This sentence implies that it was not raining before yesterday.)

Il **a enlevé** son manteau et puis il **a regardé** la lettre.	*He took off his coat and then looked at the letter.*

(In this sentence there are two new events, one after the other.)

The passé composé also describes a series of repeated, but not continuous, actions in the past.

L'assassin **a tiré quatre fois**.	*The killer fired four shots.*

EXERCISE 7-3:   Answer the following questions in the passé composé, using the cues given in parentheses. Answers and translations are at the end of the chapter.

1. Qui a préparé tous ces hors-d'oeuvre? (nous)
2. Qui a eu cette bonne idée? (les étudiants)
3. Qui a pris le dernier morceau de fromage? (vous)
4. Qu'est-ce qui a ennuyé les promeneurs? (les insectes)
5. Qui a mis cette bouteille par terre? (je)
6. Qui est-ce qui a oublié ses clés? (elle)
7. Qui a reçu la permission de partir? (tu)
8. Qu'est-ce qui a cassé la vitre? (le vent)
9. Qui a compris cette explication? (les autres)
10. Qui a été en France? (on)

EXERCISE 7-4:   Express the following as events in the past by including the expression of past time in parentheses and using the passé composé of the verb. Answers and translations are at the end of the chapter.

1. Le match commence. (il y a vingt minutes)
2. Je dis cela en classe. (la semaine dernière)
3. Il découvre la vérité. (avant cette année)
4. Patricia obtient une bourse. (le trimestre dernier)
5. Mes parents voyagent en Europe. (l'été dernier)
6. Il faut considérer les alternatives. (en 1968)
7. La France produit moins de vin. (l'année dernière)
8. Il pleut à verse. (hier soir)
9. Ma mère fait un grand gâteau. (pour mon dernier anniversaire)
10. Je dors pendant huit heures. (la nuit dernière)
11. L'équipe de notre école gagne le match. (avant-hier)
12. Je rencontre ses parents. (pendant leur visite récente)
13. Jean-Louis a l'air ridicule. (l'autre jour)
14. Nous prenons une décision importante. (la dernière fois)

D. Use of pronouns in the passé composé

- All personal pronouns and **y** and **en** precede **avoir** in the passé composé.

Il **l'a** bien grondé.	*He gave him a good scolding.*
Je **lui en ai** montré trois.	*I showed him three of them.*
Ils n'**y ont** jamais trouvé de poissons.	*They never found any fish there.*
Les soldats **leur ont** obéi.	*The soldiers obeyed them.*
Vous **m'avez** fait grand plaisir.	*You pleased me a great deal.*
Qui **vous a** dit cela?	*Who told you that?*

- A past participle modifies its direct object, and agrees with it in gender and number if the direct object precedes the past participle.

La **réponse** que j'**ai donnée** est correcte.	*The answer I gave is correct.*
Est-ce que tu connais **les endroits** qu'elle **a décrits**?	*Are you familiar with the places she described?*

When the object pronouns precede their verbs in the passé composé, the past participle agrees with them.

Ce vendeur **nous** a **insultés**.	*That salesman insulted us.*
Ma **fille**? Je l'ai **envoyée** à l'université!	*My daughter? I sent her to the university!*

> *NOTE:* A past participle does not agree with an indirect object or with a direct object that follows a verb.

Elle **vous a téléphoné** de la banque.	*She called you from the bank.*

(**vous** is the *indirect object* of the verb—there is no agreement)

Les agents **lui ont demandé** sa **carte d'identité**.	*The police asked her for her identification.*

(**lui** is the *indirect object* of the verb and **carte d'identité** is the direct object *following* the verb—there is no agreement)

EXERCISE 7-5: Answer the following questions affirmatively, using a pronoun to replace the direct or indirect object given in parentheses. Pay careful attention to the agreement or lack of agreement between objects and past participles. Answers and translations are at the end of the chapter.

Example: Marie a-t-elle regardé (les tableaux de l'exposition)?	*Has Mary looked at (the pictures of the exhibit)?*
Oui, elle les a regardés.	*Yes, she looked at them.*

1. Avez-vous rendu (ses disques) à Peter?
2. A-t-il acheté (la maison de la rue Voltaire)?
3. Les enfants ont-ils téléphoné (à leurs parents)?
4. Les pilotes ont-ils bien compris (les instructions de la tour de contrôle)?
5. Avez-vous déjà vu (le dernier film de Werner Herzog)?
6. L'enfant a-t-il cru (l'histoire du *Petit Chaperon-Rouge*)? A-t-il aimé (cette histoire)?
7. M'avez-vous envoyé (les photos de Tahiti)?
8. Vos amis vous ont-ils donné (leur nouvelle adresse)?
9. A-t-elle rencontré (son étudiante) cet été?
10. Avez-vous acheté (ces fleurs magnifiques)?

E. Formation of the passé composé with être

1. To form the passé composé of the following intransitive verbs that indicate a change of place or state, use the present tense of **être** plus the past participle of the main verb.

aller	**allé**	*gone*
venir	**venu**	*come*
arriver	**arrivé**	*arrived*

partir	**parti**	*left*
entrer	**entré**	*entered*
sortir	**sorti**	*gone out*
monter	**monté**	*gone up*
descendre	**descendu**	*gone down*
mourir	**mort**	*died*
naitre	**né**	*(been) born*
retourner	**retourné**	*returned*
tomber	**tombé**	*fallen*
rester	**resté**	*remained*
passer	**passé**	*passed*
demeurer	**demeuré**	*stayed*

NOTE: Compounds of these verbs are also conjugated with **être**.

Le porteur **est monté** chercher les bagages.	*The bellboy went (has gone) up to get the bags.*
Tu **est rentré** tard hier soir.	*You came home late last night.*
Je **suis passé** devant le magasin.	*I passed by the store.*

Since intransitive verbs never have a direct object, the past participle of intransitive verbs conjugated with **être** functions as a complement adjective that agrees with the subject of the sentence.

Ces **fleurs** sont **arrivées** ce matin.	*Those flowers came this morning.*
Sa **mère** est **partie** après la cérémonie.	*His mother left after the ceremony.*

EXERCISE 7-6: Express the following sentences as events in the past by including the expression of past time in parentheses and using the passé composé of the verb. Answers and translations are at the end of the chapter.

1. Vous arrivez à temps. (hier soir)
2. Patricia revient de ses vacances. (mardi dernier)
3. Nous partons à l'aube. (avant-hier)
4. Il sort subitement. (pendant notre dernière visite)
5. Les skieurs tombent. (le premier jour)
6. Mes amis viennent en grand nombre. (vendredi dernier)
7. Son grand-père meurt. (en 1978)
8. Tu entres à l'université. (le semestre dernier)
9. Les prix restent stables. (avant cette année)
10. Je passe te dire bonjour. (il y a dix minutes)
11. Elle demeure silencieuse. (la dernière fois)
12. Tes soeurs montent changer de robe. (tout à l'heure)
13. Qui va à la banque? (ce matin)
14. Pourquoi descendez-vous ici? (l'année dernière)
15. Avec qui revenez-vous? (hier)

2. You may use certain verbs that are ordinarily intransitive—**descendre**, **monter**, **passer**, and **sortir**—to indicate that *something is being moved* down, up, past, or out. In this case, use **avoir** to form the passé composé—since the verb now has a direct object.

La femme **a sorti ses bijoux** du coffre.	*The woman took her jewelry out of the safe.*
Nous **avons descendu le lit** du premier étage.	*We brought the bed down from the second floor.*

REMEMBER: When you conjugate these verbs with **avoir**, the past participle modifies a preceding direct object and agrees with it in gender and number.

La **pièce** qu'ils ont **montée** a eu un grand succès.	*The play they put on was a hit.*
Je **les** ai **passés** à mon voisin.	*I passed them to the person next to me.*

EXERCISE 7-7: Answer the following questions using the cues in parentheses to indicate that the event took place in the past. Form the passé composé with être or avoir, according to the meaning of each question. Answers and translations are at the end of the chapter.

1. Quand sortez-vous? (hier)
2. Sortez-vous votre auto du garage? (Oui, . . . ce matin)
3. Est-ce qu'ils descendent au Grand-Hôtel maintenant? (Non, . . . la dernière fois)
4. Descendent-ils les valises? (Non, . . . avant de dire au revoir)
5. Montent-ils tout en haut de la Tour Eiffel? (Non, . . . à leur première visite)
6. Montez-vous l'escalier? (Oui, . . . quatre à quatre)
7. L'autobus va-t-il passer devant le magasin? (Non, . . . déjà)
8. Passe-t-elle son dernier examen? (Non, . . . en 1984)

3. To form the passé composé of all verbs used reflexively, use **être**.

Je me suis trouvé en face du musée.	*I found myself in front of the museum.*
Ils se sont serré la main.	*They shook hands (with one another).*

The past participle of reflexive verbs agrees in gender and number with a preceding direct object. The reflexive pronoun of an essentially reflexive verb is always its direct object. (See Sec. 6-6.)

Madeleine **s'est efforcée** de sourire.	*Madeleine made an effort to smile.*

BUT the past participle does not agree with a preceding indirect object.

Nous **nous** sommes **enlevé** la chemise. (**la chemise** is the direct object—not **nous**)	*We took off our shirts.*
Je me **le** suis **offert**. (**le** is the direct object—not **me**)	*I treated myself to it.*

NOTE: In sentences where there is no explicit direct object, it may not be clear what the function of the reflexive pronoun is.

Elles se sont parlé.	*They spoke to one another.*

To determine whether or not the reflexive pronoun is the direct object, repeat it in a longer form—**moi-même**, *myself,* **toi-même**, *yourself,* **lui-même**, *himself,* **elle-même**, *herself,* **nous-mêmes**, *ourselves,* **vous-même(s)**, *yourself(selves),* **eux-mêmes**, *themselves*—at the end of the sentence. If the longer form needs the preposition **à** to make sense, the reflexive pronoun is not the direct object. If the longer form does not need **à**, the reflexive pronoun is the direct object—and the past participle must agree with it.

Elles se sont parlé (**à elles-mêmes**).	*They talked to one another.*

BUT

Nous nous sommes battus (**nous-mêmes**).	*We fought (one another).*
Elle s'en est allée (elle-même).	*She went away (herself).*

REMEMBER: A past participle may agree with a) an immediately preceding noun, b) a preceding direct object, or c) the subject of an intransitive verb. The past participle never agrees with an indirect object pronoun or the pronouns **y** and **en**.

EXERCISE 7-8: Answer the questions negatively in the passé composé. Answers and translations are at the end of the chapter.

Example: Se parlent-ils? *Do they speak to one another?*

Non, ils ne se sont jamais parlé. *No, they've never spoken to one another.*

1. Vous moquez-vous de vos professeurs?
2. Se coupe-t-elle les cheveux?
3. Est-ce que vos enfants se battent?
4. Te lèves-tu à l'aube?
5. S'efforcent-ils de parler correctement?
6. Est-ce que vous vous considérez comme supérieur?
7. Se voient-elles souvent?
8. S'habille-t-elle en noir?
9. Est-ce que tu t'en vas sans dire au revoir?
10. Se demandent-ils pourquoi nous sommes toujours en retard?

F. Position of adverbs in the passé composé

1. Common short adverbs like **beaucoup**, **bien**, **mal**, **vite**, **trop**, **assez**, **mieux**, **déjà**, and **encore** follow the auxiliary verb.

   Tu **as beaucoup** mangé. *You ate (have eaten) a lot.*
   Elle **a vite** compris. *She understood right away.*

2. Longer adverbs may follow the past participle or be said at the end of the sentence.

   Nous avons **regardé attentivement** le film.
   OR *We watched the film attentively.*
   Nous avons regardé le film **attentivement**.

EXERCISE 7-9: Answer the following questions in the passé composé, using the adverbials given in parentheses. Answers and translations are at the end of the chapter.

Example: Quand le facteur vient-il? (ce matin) *When is the mailman coming? (this morning)*

Voyons, le facteur est venu ce matin! *Hey, the mailman came this morning!*

1. Quand votre soeur arrive-t-elle? (hier)
2. A quelle heure le train pour Rouen part-il? (déjà)
3. En quel mois les élèves rentrent-ils au lycée? (en septembre)
4. Retournes-tu en Europe? (l'été dernier)
5. Quand devenez-vous citoyens? (l'année dernière)
6. A quelle heure vont-ils à la messe? (à dix heures)
7. Quand les feuilles tombent-elles? (en automne)
8. En quel mois votre bébé va-t-il naître? (le mois dernier)
9. A quelle heure reviennent-elles? (il y a 20 minutes)
10. Quand les satellites descendent-ils? (avant-hier)

G. Interrogatives in the passé composé

Ask a question in the passé composé by saying the verb before the subject pronoun. It is important to remember that **avoir**—not the past participle—is the verb.

Avons-nous reçu notre chèque? *Did we receive (have we received) our check?*

If the subject of the sentence is a noun rather than a pronoun, ask a question by repeating that noun in pronoun form after the auxiliary verb.

Vos amis ont-ils lu vos lettres? *Did your friends read (have your friends read) your letters?*

Cette actrice a-t-elle bien jouè? *Was that actress good in that role?*
Les Roland ont-ils vraiment divorcé? *Did the Rolands really get divorced?*
Le train est-il déjà parti? *Did the train leave already?*

EXERCISE 7-10: Use the inverted question form and the adverb **vraiment** to express surprise concerning the following statements. Answers and translations are at the end of the chapter.

Example:	Les Russes ont envoyé une femme sur la lune.	*The Russians have put a woman on the moon.*
	Les Russes ont-ils vraiment envoyé une femme sur la lune?	*Have the Russians truly put a woman on the moon?*

1. Laurent a décidé d'abandonner sa carrière.
2. Les chercheurs ont développé un vaccin contre la grippe.
3. Nous avons trouvé un lingot d'or sous notre matelas.
4. Ils ont lu tes lettres avec grand plaisir.
5. Les enfants ont laissé leurs affaires partout.
6. Elle a oublié de prendre son billet.
7. Mathilde a réussi à son examen.
8. Les travaux ont commencé en avril.
9. Le gouvernment a proposé des réformes importantes.
10. La France a beaucoup changé depuis la guerre.

H. Negation in the passé composé

In the passé composé, the negative particle **ne** precedes any object pronouns and the auxiliary verb. The negative completers—**pas**, **rien**, **jamais**, **point**, and **plus**—follow the auxiliary verb.

Je **n'ai jamais** vu une telle confusion.	*I never saw such confusion.*
Ils **ne se sont plus** parlé.	*They don't speak to one another any more.*
Tu **n'as rien** vu encore.	*You haven't seen anything yet.*
Les médecins **ne le lui ont point** défendu.	*The doctors did not forbid him (her) to do it.*

EXERCISE 7-11: Answer the questions in the negative, using the negative word given in parentheses. Answers and translations are at the end of the chapter.

1. A-t-il pu voir le directeur? (jamais)
2. Est-ce que l'avion est arrivé à l'heure? (point)
3. Est-ce que vous avez obtenu le résultat voulu? (pas)
4. Se sont-ils réconciliés? (pas encore)
5. A-t-on revu ces gens après leur première visite? (plus)
6. T'es-tu fait mal en tombant? (jamais)
7. Qu'est-ce que les responsables ont expliqué? (rien)
8. Avons-nous réussi à l'examen? (point)

EXERCISE 7-12: Answer the questions negatively in the passé composé, using the cues given in parentheses. Answers and translations are at the end of the chapter.

Example:	La laissez-vous ici? (hier)	*Are you leaving it here?*
	Non, mais je l'ai laissée ici hier.	*No, but I left it here yesterday.*

1. En avez-vous besoin? (une fois)
2. Veut-il y entrer? (à neuf heures)
3. La cuisine lui plaît-elle? (l'autre jour)
4. La vois-tu? (le week-end dernier)
5. La conduit-il à l'université? (avant-hier)
6. Ces lettres, les écrivez-vous? (hier)
7. Devez-vous y rester tard? (la semaine dernière)
8. Le disons-nous? (l'autre fois)
9. Leur écrivent-ils souvent? (pour leur anniversaire)
10. La soutient-elle? (une fois)

EXERCISE 7-13: Answer the questions affirmatively, replacing the words in parentheses with pronouns. Answers and translations are at the end of the chapter.

Example: Avons-nous expliqué   *Have we explained the statements*
          (les phrases aux lecteurs)?   *to the readers?*

          Oui, nous les leur avons   *Yes, we have explained them*
          expliquées.   *to them.*

1. Einstein a-t-il élaboré (la théorie de la relativité)?
2. Les socialistes ont-ils promis (la retraite anticipée aux ouvriers)?
3. Le maire a-t-il accordé (une interview au journaliste)?
4. Christophe Colomb a-t-il découvert (l'Amérique)?
5. Les Américains ont-ils envoyé (une fusée sur Jupiter)?
6. Rockefeller a-t-il acquis (sa fortune) avant la guerre?
7. Shakespeare a-t-il écrit (toutes ses pièces) en anglais?
8. Abélard a-t-il écrit (ses plus belles lettres à Héloise)?
9. Est-ce que les usines ont installé (ces machines) au 19ème siècle?
10. Est-ce que Sartre a publié (ses romans) avant sa mort?

EXERCISE 7-14: Answer the questions negatively, replacing the noun phrases in parentheses with pronouns. Answers and translations are at the end of the chapter.

Example: Ils prennent (leur dessert).   *They're having their dessert.*
          Et hier soir?   *And last night?*

          Heir soir, ils ne l'ont pas pris. *Las night they didn't have it.*

1. Ils font (cette erreur). Et la dernière fois?
2. (Mes enfants) apportent (leur bicyclette). Et l'été dernier?
3. Nous faisons (nos exercises). Et l'autre jour?
4. Tu étudies (tes leçons). Et avant le dernier examen?
5. Il perd (son temps). Et l'autre fois?
6. Je suis (le cours d'espagnol). Et le trimestre dernier?
7. Vous apportez (votre sandwich). Et à l'autre pique-nique?
8. Je prends trop (de risques). Et pendant le match?
9. Nous recevons (une bonne note). Et au dernier examen?
10. Je peux venir à (la réunion). Et hier?

7-3. L'imparfait, *The Imperfect Past Tense*

A. Formation of the imparfait

1. To form the imparfait, drop the **-ons** from the present first-person plural (**nous**) form of all verbs—except **être**—and add the following endings.

Sing	Plural
-ais	-ions
-ais	-iez
-ait	-aient

Infinitive	Plural stem	Imparfait
parler	**parl**ons	je **parlais**, *I spoke*, tu **parlais**, il **parlait**, nous **parlions**, vous parliez, ils **parlaient**
choisir	**choisiss**ons	je **choisissais**, *I chose*, tu **choisissais**, elle **choisissait**, nous **choisissions**, vous **choisissiez**, elles **choisissaient**
attendre	**attend**ons	j'**attendais**, *I waited*, tu **attendais**, on **attendait**, nous **attendions**, vous **attendiez**, ils **attendaient**

NOTE: Verbs whose plural stem ends in -**ç** or -**ge**—**nous commençons, nous mangeons**—retain that spelling except before -**ions** and -**iez**.

je commençais, *I began*   BUT   nous commencions, we began
tu mangeais, *you ate*   vous mangiez, you ate

2. The verb **être** and impersonal verbs use the infinitive stem in the imparfait.

être, *to be*   j'**étais**, *I was*, tu **étais**, il **était**, nous **étions**, vous **étiez**,
                           elles **étaient**
falloir, *to be necessary*   il **fallait**   *it was necessary*
pleuvoir, *to rain*   il **pleuvait**   *it was raining*
neiger, *to snow*   il **neigeait**   *it was snowing*

EXERCISE 7-15:   Answer the following questions in relation to a past state of affairs. Answers and translations are at the end of the chapter.

Example: Elles sont prêtes. Et la dernière   *They are ready. And the last*
           fois?   *time?*

           Elles étaient prêtes la dernière fois *They were ready the last time,*
           aussi.   *too.*

1. Nous sommes fatigués. Et après le dernier match?
2. Mon camarade est devant la télé. Et avant mon arrivée?
3. Tu es chez toi. Et ce matin?
4. Vous êtes un peu inquiet(s). Et hier soir?
5. Mes parents sont contents de mes notes. Et le trimestre dernier?
6. Le Président des Etats-Unis est un homme? Et le dernier?
7. Je suis en très mauvaise forme. Et samedi dernier?
8. Elles sont en vacances. Et la semaine dernière?
9. Il est assez précoce pour son âge. Et comme bébé?
10. C'est une journée splendide! Et hier?

B. Use of the imparfait

1. Use the imparfait to tell about ongoing situations or states of affairs in the past without reference to when they began.

Nous **étions** les seuls Américains à   *We were the only Americans on*
bord.   *board.*
Les nageurs **retournaient** à la   *The swimmers were returning to the*
plage au moment de l'accident.   *beach at the moment of the*
                                             accident.

2. Use the imparfait to make generalizations about former times.

Les Druides **pratiquaient** leur culte   *The Druids practiced their religion*
dans la forêt.   *in the forest.*
Pendant la guerre on ne **trouvait**   *During the war, you couldn't get*
pas de beurre.   *butter.*

3. Use the imparfait to supply background information.

Il **faisait** froid, mais il n'y **avait** pas de   *It was cold, but there wasn't any*
neige.   *snow.*

4. Use the imparfait to describe habitual past actions.

Les gens riches **passaient** l'été à   *Rich people spent the summer in*
Deauville.   *Deauville.*
Le professeur **donnait** des conférences   *The professor gave lectures in*
pour gagner de l'argent.   *order to earn money.*

EXERCISE 7-16:   Rewrite the following sentences which describe situations, habits, and generalizations true in the present to indicate that they were also true in the past. Answers and translations are at the end of the chapter.

1. Les skieurs vont souvent à la montagne.
2. Cet artiste peint surtout des paysages.

3. Les étudiants rient fréquemment en classe.
4. Je regarde la télévision de temps en temps.
5. Vous dites toujours votre opinion.
6. Nous étudions avant chaque examen.
7. Les touristes achètent des glaces en attendant.
8. Tu prends le métro quelquefois.
9. On lit souvent des choses surprenantes.
10. Ils ne peuvent pas se rappeler son nom.
11. Je dors huit heures par nuit.
12. D'habitude, les enfants aiment jouer dehors.
13. Nous courons pour arriver à temps.
14. Qui a le bon numéro?
15. Tu ne sais pas son adresse.
16. Il fait ses exercices régulièrement.
17. Je ne veux pas recommencer cette histoire.
18. Il faut passer un examen d'histoire ancienne.
19. Combien de cours suis-tu normalement?
20. En été, on mange souvent en plein air.

EXERCISE 7-17: Replace the underlined expressions of present time with the past time expressions given in parentheses, changing the verb in each sentence from the present to the imparfait. Answers and translations are at the end of the chapter.

1. Je vais à la plage tous les jours cet été. (l'été dernier)
2. Vous devez compléter ce travail en cinq minutes. (hier)
3. Il est content de vous voir ce soir. (l'autre jour)
4. Elle voit beaucoup ses amis actuellement. (à ce moment-là)
5. Ces jours-ci, ils sortent beaucoup ensemble. (A cette époque-là)
6. A présent, les meilleurs vins viennent de France. (Dans le temps)
7. Sur le champ, je ne peux pas répondre à votre question. (La dernière fois)
8. En ce moment, nous avons énormément de travail. (Le semestre dernier)
9. Au vingtième siècle il y a de graves problèmes politiques. (Au 19ème siècle)
10. La science moderne ne réussit pas à tout expliquer. (ancienne)

7-4. Contrasting Use of Past Tense Forms

Whether you use the passé composé or the imparfait depends upon the way you view a past event or situation.

1. Use the passé composé to describe an event whose entire duration—including its beginning—falls within the past time frame you're talking about.

> Quand il **a ouvert** la cage, l'oiseau **s'est envolé**.   *When he opened the cage, the bird got away.*
> (two events, each beginning during the time under consideration)

Use the imparfait to describe an event which was already under way at the past moment you're talking about.

> Il **chantait** pendant que je **jouais** du piano.   *He sang while I played the piano.*
> (two simultaneous occurrences, neither necessarily beginning at the moment under consideration)

2. Use the passé composé to say that something new took place or that the situation changed—otherwise, use the imparfait.

> Le public **applaudissait** quand l'acteur **est entré**.   *The audience was applauding when the actor entered.*
> (a continuing state of affairs which began at some unspecified time before the moment under consideration, followed by a new event which began at that moment)
> Le public **a applaudi** quand l'acteur **est entré**.   *The audience applauded when the actor entered.*
> (two separate events described from their beginnings)

Il **a plu** hier.	*It rained yesterday.*
(it began raining yesterday)	
Il **pleuvait** hier.	*It was raining yesterday.*
(it was raining yesterday, but you don't know when it began)	
J'**ai eu** cette bague de mon père.	*I got this ring from my father.*
(literally, began to have this ring)	
J'**avais** cette bague avant mon mariage.	*I had this ring before my marriage.*
(no mention of when you received the ring)	
Mes parents **se sont connus** à Nice.	*My parents met in Nice.*
(literally, began to know one another in Nice)	
Mes parents **se connaissaient** depuis longtemps.	*My parents had known each other for a long time.*
(no mention of when this state of affairs began)	
Les invités **ont été choqués** par l'arrivée de la police.	*The guests were shocked by the arrival of the police.*
(a change in the situation)	
Les invités **étaient** contents du dîner.	*The guests were pleased with the dinner.*

(no indication of when this was true; could have been during or after dinner)

3. In French the expressions **venir de + infinitive** and **aller + infinitive** indicate the immediate past or future. Do not use these expressions in the passé composé.

J'**allais** vous **demander** ce que cela **voulait dire**.	*I was going to ask you what that meant.*
Elle **venait d'arriver** quand je l'ai vue.	*She had just arrived when I saw her.*

EXERCISE 7-18: Answer the following questions in the passé composé or the imparfait according to whether or not something happened at the moment under consideration. Answers and translations are at the end of the chapter.

Example:	Le pétrole a une grande importance. Et au 17ème siècle?	*Oil is of great importance. And in the 17th century?*
	Le pétrole n'avait pas une grande importance au 17ème siècle.	*Oil was not of great importance in the 17th century.*

1. On traverse l'Atlantique en avion. Et il y a 100 ans?
2. La France est une république. Et au Moyen-Age?
3. Les journaux paraissent tous les jours. Et ce matin?
4. On fait la cuisine à l'aide de machines. Et autrefois?
5. Les jeunes gens regardent la télévision. Et leurs grands-parents à leur âge?
6. Nous prenons du vin avec les repas. Et à l'âge de sept ans?
7. L'école reprend en automne. Et l'année dernière?
8. Je me lave les dents. Et hier soir?
9. Elle s'habille elle-même. Et à l'âge de deux ans?
10. Ces exercices sont en français. Et au chapitre 3?

EXERCISE 7-19: Answer the following questions affirmatively, indicating that the action took place not just once, but continually. Answers and translations are at the end of the chapter.

Example:	Cet enfant a-t-il jamais menti?	*Did that child ever lie?*
	Bien sûr qu'il a menti; il mentait tout le temps.	*Of course he lied; he lied all the time.*

1. Avez-vous fait du camping?
2. Est-ce qu'elles sont sorties avec leurs amis?
3. A-t-elle assisté aux conférences de chimie?
4. Henriette a-t-elle jamais suivi son instinct?
5. Est-ce que tu as jamais fait de la peinture?

    6. Lui a-t-elle dit la vérité?
    7. Avez-vous déjà récité des vers?
    8. A-t-elle jamais bu du café express?
    9. Tes parents ont-ils passé des vacances à la montagne?
    10. Est-ce que j'ai exagéré?

EXERCISE 7-20: Use the imparfait and the passé composé to indicate that the first action in each sentence was interrupted by the second. Answers and translations are at the end of the chapter.

       Example: Tu es arrivé et puis il est sorti.   *You arrived and then he left.*
                        Tu arrivais et il est sorti.   *You were arriving and he left.*

    1. J'ai dormi et puis le téléphone a sonné.
    2. Madeleine a souri et puis je l'ai embrassée.
    3. Il a regardé par la fenêtre et puis il m'a vu.
    4. Nous avons étudié et puis elle est arrivée.
    5. Les étudiants se sont assis et puis le professeur est entré.
    6. Vous avez servi le repas et puis les invités ont commencé à se parler.
    7. Tu as mangé des escargots et puis les gens t'ont regardé de travers.
    8. Le rideau est tombé et puis le public a commencé à sortir.
    9. Il a plu et puis j'ai cherché mon parapluie.
    10. J'ai lu le journal et puis je me suis endormie.

EXERCISE 7-21: Use **pendant que** and the imparfait to indicate that the actions in the following sentences went on simultaneously, rather than one after the other. Answers and translations are at the end of the chapter.

       Example: Il s'est moqué de moi et je me suis   *He made fun of me and I got*
                        fâché.   *angry.*
                        Il se moquait de moi pendant que   *He made fun of me while I got*
                        je me fâchais.   *angry.*

    1. Tu as appris et tu as lu.
    2. Elle s'est promenée et elle a chanté.
    3. J'ai mangé et j'ai regardé la télévision.
    4. Vous avez pris un bain et vous avez écouté la radio..
    5. Les employés ont travaillé et le patron les a surveillés.
    6. Le porteur a descendu la malle et je me suis occupé des valises.
    7. Nous avons bu et nous nous sommes reposés au soleil.
    8. J'ai admiré les roses et j'ai visité son jardin.
    9. L'eau a bouilli et j'ai remué les pâtes.
    10. Tu es resté à la maison et tes copains sont partis pour la plage.

EXERCISE 7-22: Write the following sentences in the past as if they described:

         a) two simultaneous ongoing events
         b) two separate events, one after the other

Answers and translations are at the end of the chapter.

       Example: Je le critique et il me répond   *I criticize him and he talks back to*
                        mal.   *me.*
                        a) Je le critiquais et il me   *I was criticizing him and he was*
                           repondait mal   *responding badly.*
                        b) Je l'ai critiqué et il m'a   *I criticized him and he responded*
                         mal répondu.   *badly.*

    1. Ces choses arrivent et tout le monde se fâche.
    2. La pluie commence, mais je n'y fais pas attention.
    3. Le facteur arrive quand je sors.
    4. Ils se réunissent et ils choisissent un président.
    5. Les enfants partent, mais leurs parents ne pleurent pas.

6. Nous lisons la lettre et nous sommes contents.
7. Tu t'en vas et je pense à toi.
8. Quand la température descend, tout le monde met un manteau.
9. J'emprunte des disques et je les écoute à la maison.
10. Elle nettoie sa chambre, mais elle ne range pas ses affaires.

SUMMARY

1. The past participle may function as an adjective, following the noun it modifies and agreeing with it in gender and number.
2. Past participles of transitive verbs are used to make passive sentences. The verb **être** indicates the tense of the sentence and the past participle agrees in gender and number with its subject.
3. The passé composé of transitive verbs consists of the present tense of **avoir** and the past participle of the verb.
4. The passé composé of a limited number of intransitive and all reflexive verbs consists of the present tense of **être** and the past participle of the verb.
5. A past participle always agrees in gender and number with a preceding direct object noun or pronoun. A past participle conjugated with **être** agrees in gender and number with its subject unless there is a preceding direct object or indirect object pronoun. There is *never* any agreement with indirect objects, **y**, or **en**.
6. The imparfait is a simple past verb form based on the plural stem of the present tense to which you add the endings -**ais**, -**ais**, -**ait**, -**ions**, -**iez**, -**aient**. **Etre** and impersonal verbs form the imparfait from the infinitive stem.

RAISE YOUR GRADES

Passé composé and imparfait

Decide why the imparfait or the passé composé has been used for each verb in the sentences in the numbered list. Then find the reason in the list below and write its letter before the number of the sentence in the space provided. Answers and translations are at the end of the chapter.

A new event or situation in the past
B continuing action or state of affairs in the past
C habitual past action
D idiomatic expression of time
E simultaneous past actions
F one event after another in the past

_____ _____ 1. Il faisait beau quand je me suis levé.
_____ _____ 2. L'enfant pleurait parce qu'il était perdu.
_____ _____ 3. Où alliez-vous quand je vous ai vu?
_____ _____ 4. Mes cousins venaient de nous rendre visite.
_____ _____ 5. Emma aimait lire des romans d'amour.
_____ _____ 6. A l'âge de 12 ans, je rougissais facilement.
_____ _____ 7. Ils ne pouvaient pas comprendre ce que tu disais.
_____ _____ 8. Les assiettes sont tombées quand j'ai glissé.
_____ _____ 9. Nous le connaissions avant son grand succès.
_____ _____ 10. Ma mère préparait le repas et je travaillais.
_____ _____ 11. Nous allions vous interrompre.
_____ _____ 12. La France avait 50 millions d'habitants en 1832.
_____ _____ 13. Où les avez-vous connus?
_____ _____ 14. A la compagne nous faisions des promenades.
_____ _____ 15. Elle a su la vérité parce qu'il ne pouvait pas mentir.
_____ _____ 16. Je voulais partir mais je n'en ai pas eu le courage.
_____ _____ 17. Elle l'a embrassé et il en a été bien content.

_____ _____ **18.** Georges avait mal à la gorge et il a appelé le médecin.
_____ _____ **19.** Sa mère est morte avant la guerre.
_____ _____ **20.** Le facteur est venu au moment où je sortais.

Past participle agreement

For each sentence in the following numbered list, decide why the past participle agrees or does not agree with a noun or pronoun in the sentence. Then find that reason in the list below and write its letter before the number of the sentence in the space provided. Answers and translations are at the end of the chapter.

A no agreement—no preceding direct object
B no agreement—indirect object intervenes
C modifies and agrees with subject
D modifies and agrees with preceding direct object
E modifies and agrees with immediately preceding noun

_____ **21.** Ils ne se la sont pas achetée.
_____ **22.** Les enfants sont tombés sur la glace.
_____ **23.** Ce sont les seuls livres recommandés.
_____ **24.** Mes cousins se sont envoyé des cadeaux.
_____ **25.** Nous leur avons montré nos photos.
_____ **26.** Les ouvriers ont travaillé dur.
_____ **27.** Aux heures indiquées, les trains arrivent.
_____ **28.** Allons enfants de la patrie, le jour de gloire est arrivé.
_____ **29.** Elle s'est décidée à le faire.
_____ **30.** Les étudiants se sont moqués de leur professeur.
_____ **31.** Les vieillards restent enfermés dans leur chambre.
_____ **32.** Il est reparti sous la pluie.
_____ **33.** Je lui ai demandé s'il voulait m'accompagner.
_____ **34.** Mes amis m'en ont parlé sérieusement.
_____ **35.** Elle espère que ses invités n'ont pas oublié.

Passive sentences

Rewrite the following sentences in the passive form, using the verb **être** to indicate the tense. Answers and translations are at the end of the chapter.

Example: Les touristes ont pris ces photos.   *The tourists took these pictures.*

                Ces photos ont été prises par les touristes.   *These pictures were taken by the tourists.*

36. Mes camarades vont recommander un restaurant.
37. Ce dentiste a arraché deux dents.
38. On sert le dîner.
39. L'orchestre a joué de la musique classique.
40. On a rassuré les passagers.
41. Mon frère et moi allons réparer ce ballon.
42. Le professeur a corrigé tous les examens.
43. Le maire proclame un jour de fête.
44. Le chauffeur va conduire notre voiture.
45. Vous corrigez cet exercice.

CHAPTER ANSWERS

EXERCISE 7-1:

1. J'ai un contrat signé. *I have a signed contract.*
2. Il y a des compositions écrites. *There are some written compositions.*
3. Voilà une idée retenue. *Here is a remembered idea.*
4. C'est une fenêtre ouverte. *It is an open window.*
5. Quel est le résultat obtenu? *What is the result obtained? What result did you obtain?*
6. Elle a ses valises faites. *She has her suitcases packed.*

7. C'est un obstacle vaincu. *It's an obstacle overcome.*

8. Nous avons des articles publiés. *We have some published articles.*

9. C'est une leçon apprise. *It's a lesson learned.*

10. C'est un dessin peint. *It's a painted drawing.*

EXERCISE 7-2:

1. Ces films sont vus à la télévision. *These films are seen on television.*

2. Les fenêtres sont fermées à cause de la pluie. *The windows are closed because of the rain.*

3. Les murs sont peints en blanc. *The walls are painted white.*

4. Les clients sont servis comme il faut. *The customers are served politely.*

5. Ces photos sont prises comme souvenir. *These pictures are taken as mementos.*

6. Ces mots sont souvent écrits incorrectement. *These words are often written incorrectly.*

7. Cette lettre est mise à la poste. *This letter is mailed.*

8. L'auto est conduite pour lui. *The car is driven for him.*

9. Le journal est vendu dans la rue. *The paper is sold on the street.*

10. Une cigarette est offerte à la dame. *A cigarette is offered to the woman.*

EXERCISE 7-3:

1. Nous avons préparé tous ces hors-d'oeuvre. *We prepared all these appetizers.*

2. Les étudiants ont eu cette bonne idée. *The students had this good idea.*

3. Vous avez pris le dernier morceau de fromage. *You took the last piece of cheese.*

4. Les insectes ont ennuyé les promeneurs. *The insects bothered the strollers.*

5. J'ai mis cette bouteille par terre. *I put this bottle on the ground.*

6. Elle a oublié ses clés. *She forgot her keys.*

7. Tu as reçu la permission de partir. *You received permission to leave.*

8. Le vent a cassé la vitre. *The wind broke the window pane.*

9. Les autres ont compris cette explication. *The others understood this explanation.*

10. On a été en France. *We went to France.*

EXERCISE 7-4:

1. Le match a commencé il y a vingt minutes. *The game began twenty minutes ago.*

2. J'ai dit cela en classe la semaine dernière. *I said that in class last week.*

3. Il a découvert la vérité avant cette année. *He discovered the truth before this year.*

4. Patricia a obtenu une bourse le trimestre dernier. *Patricia got a scholarship last trimester.*

5. Mes parents ont voyagé en Europe l'été dernier. *My parents traveled in Europe last summer.*

6. Il a fallu considérer les alternatives in 1968. *It was necessary to consider the alternatives in 1968.*

7. La France a produit moins de vin l'année dernière. *France produced less wine last year.*

8. Il a plu à verse hier soir. *It poured last night.*

9. Ma mère a fait un grand gâteau pour mon dernier anniversaire. *My mother made a big cake for my last birthday.*

10. J'ai dormi pendant huit heures la nuit dernière. *I slept for eight hours last night.*

11. L'équipe de notre école a gagné le match avant-hier. *Our school team won the game the day before yesterday.*

12. J'ai rencontré ses parents pendant leur visite récente. *I met her parents during their recent visit.*

13. Jean-Louis a eu l'air ridicule l'autre jour. *Jean-Louis looked ridiculous the other day.*

14. Nous avons pris une décision importante la dernière fois. *We made an important decision the last time.*

EXERCISE 7-5:

1. Oui, elle les a rendus à Peter. *Yes, she returned them to Peter.*

2. Oui, il l'a achetée. *Yes, he bought it.*

3. Oui, ils leurs ont téléphoné. *Yes, they telephoned them.*

4. Oui, ils les ont bien comprises. *Yes, they understood them well.*

5. Oui, je l'ai déjà vu. *Yes, I already saw it.*

6. Oui, il l'a crue. Il l'a aimée. *Yes, he believed it. He liked it.*

7. Oui, je vous les ai déjà envoyées. *Yes, I sent them to you already.*

8. Oui, ils me l'ont donnee. *Yes, they have given it to me.*

9. Oui, elle l'a rencontrée cet été. *Yes, she met her this summer.*

10. Oui, je les ai achetées. *Yes, I bought them.*

EXERCISE 7-6:

1. Vous êtes arrivé(s) à temps hier soir. *You arrived on time last night.*

2. Patricia est revenue de ses vacances mardi dernier. *Patricia returned from her vacation last Tuesday.*

3. Nous sommes partis à l'aube avant-hier. *We left at dawn the day before yesterday.*

4. Il est sorti subitement pendant notre dernière visite. *He left the room abruptly during his last visit.*

5. Les skieurs sont tombés le premier jour. *The skiers fell down the first day.*

6. Mes amis sont venus en grand nombre vendredi dernier. *My friends came in great number last Friday.*

7. Son grand-père est mort en 1978. *His grand-father passed away in 1978.*

8. Tu es entré à l'université le semestre dernier. *You entered the university last semester.*

9. Les prix sont restés stables avant cette année. *Prices stayed stable before this year.*

10. Je suis passé te dire bonjour il y a dix minutes. *I came to say hello to you five minutes ago.*

11. Elle est demeurée silencieuse la dernière fois. *She remained silent the last time.*

12. Tes soeurs sont montées se changer de robe tout à l'heure. *Your sisters went upstairs to change their dresses a moment ago.*

13. Qui est allé à la banque ce matin? *Who went to the bank this morning?*

14. Pourquoi êtes-vous descendu(s) ici l'année dernière? *Why did you stay here last year?*

15. Avec qui êtes-vous revenu(s) hier? *With whom did you come back yesterday?*

EXERCISE 7-7:

1. Je suis sorti hier. *I went out yesterday.*

2. Oui, j'ai sorti mon auto du garage ce matin. *Yes, I took my car out of the garage this morning.*

3. Non, ils sont descendus au Grand Hôtel la dernière fois. *No, they stayed at the Grand Hotel last time.*

4. Non, ils ont descendu les valises avant de dire au revoir. *No, they took the suitcases down before saying good-bye.*

5. Non, ils sont montés tout en haut de la Tour Eiffel à leur première visite. *No, they went all the way up the Eiffel Tower during their first visit.*

6. Oui, j'ai monté l'escalier quatre à quatre. *Yes, I climbed the stairs two at a time.*

7. Non, l'autobus est déjà passé devant le magasin. *No, the bus has already passed by the store.*

8. Non, elle a passé son dernier examen en 1984. *No, she took her last exam in 1984.*

EXERCISE 7-8:

1. Non, je ne me suis jamais moqué de mes professeurs. *No, I have never made fun of my professors.*

2. Non, elle ne s'est jamais coupé les cheveux. *No, she never cut her hair.*

3. Non, ils ne se sont jamais battus. *No, they never fought.*

4. Non, je ne me suis jamais levé à l'aube. *No, I never got up at dawn.*

5. Non, ils ne se sont jamais efforcés de parler correctement. *No, they never tried to speak correctly.*

6. Non, je ne me suis jamais considéré comme supérieur. *No, I never considered myself superior.*

7. Non, elles ne se sont jamais vues. *No, they never saw one another.*

8. Non, elle ne s'est jamais habillée en noir. *No, she never wore black.*

9. Non, je ne m'en suis jamais allé sans dire au revoir. *No, I never left without saying good-bye.*

10. Non, ils ne se sont jamais demandé pourquoi nous sommes toujours en retard. *No, they never wondered why we were always late.*

EXERCISE 7-9:

1. Voyons, ma soeur est arrivée hier! *Hey, my sister arrived yesterday!*

2. Voyons, le train pour Rouen est déjà parti! *Hey, the train for Rouen already left!*

3. Voyons, les élèves sont rentré(e)s au lycée en septembre! *Hey, the students returned to school in September!*

4. Voyons, je suis déjà retourné(e) en Europe l'été dernier! *Hey, I already went back to Europe last summer!*

5. Voyons, nous sommes devenus citoyens l'année dernière! *Hey, we became citizens last year!*

6. Voyons, ils sont allés à la messe à dix heures! *Hey, they went to mass at ten o'clock!*

7. Voyons, les feuilles sont tombées en automne! *Hey, the leaves fell in autumn.*

8. Voyons, notre (mon) bébé est né le mois dernier! *Hey, our (my) baby was born last month!*

9. Voyons, elles sont revenues il y a 20 minutes! *Hey, she came back 20 minutes ago!*

10. Voyons, les satellites sont descendus avant-hier! *Hey, the satellites came down the day before yesterday!*

EXERCISE 7-10:

1. Laurent a-t-il vraiment décidé d'abandonner sa carrière? *Has Laurent truly decided to abandon his career?*

2. Les chercheurs ont-ils vraiment développé un vaccin contre la grippe? *Have researchers really developed a vaccine for the flu?*

3. Avons-nous vraiment trouvé un lingot d'or sous notre matelas? *Have we really found a gold ingot under our mattress?*

4. Ont-ils vraiment lu tes lettres avec grand plaisir? *Have they really read your letters with great pleasure?*

5. Les enfants ont-ils vraiment laissé leurs affaires partout? *Have the children really left their things all over?*

6. A-t-elle vraiment oublié de prendre son billet? *Did she truly forget to take her ticket?*

7. Mathilde a-t-elle vraiment réussi à son examen? *Did Mathilde really pass her test?*

8. Les travaux ont-ils vraiment commencé en avril? *Did the workers really begin in April?*

9. Le gouvernement a-t-il vraiment proposé des réformes importantes? *Has the government really proposed some important reforms?*

10. La France a-t-elle vraiment beaucoup changé depuis la guerre? *Has France really changed a lot since the war?*

EXERCISE 7-11:

1. Non, il n'a jamais pu voir le directeur. *No, he was never able to see the director.*
2. Non, l'avion n'est point arrivé à l'heure. *No, the plane did not arrive on time.*
3. Non, je n'ai pas obtenu le résultat voulu. *No, I didn't obtain the desired result.*
4. Non, ils ne se sont pas encore réconciliés. *No, they have not reconciled yet.*
5. Non, on n'a jamais revu ces gens après leur première visite. *No, we didn't see them any more after their first visit.*
6. Non, je ne me suis jamais fait mal en tombant. *No, I never hurt myself while falling.*
7. Non, les responsables n'ont rien expliqué. *No, the ones responsible didn't explain anything.*
8. Non, nous n'avons point réussi à l'examen. *No, we didn't succeed in the test.*

EXERCISE 7-12:

1. Non, mais j'en ai eu besoin une fois. *No, but I needed it one time.*
2. Non, mais il a voulu y entrer à neuf heures. *No, but he wanted to go in there at nine o'clock.*
3. Non, mais la cuisine lui a plu l'autre jour. *No, but she liked the cooking the other day.*
4. Non, mais je l'ai vue le week-end dernier. *No, but I saw her last weekend.*
5. Non, mais il l'a conduite à l'université avant-hier. *No, but he drove her to the university the day before yesterday.*
6. Non, mais je les ai écrites hier. *No, but I wrote them yesterday.*
7. Non, mais j'ai dû y rester tard la semaine dernière. *No, but I had to stay late last week.*
8. Non, mais nous l'avons dit l'autre fois. *No, but we said it the other time.*
9. Non, mais ils leur ont écrit pour leur anniversaire. *No, but they wrote them on their anniversary.*
10. Non, mais elle l'a soutenue une fois. *No, but she stood up for her one time.*

EXERCISE 7-13:

1. Oui, Einstein l'a élaborée. *Yes, Einstein elaborated it.*
2. Oui, les socialistes la leur ont promise. *Yes, the socialists promised it to them.*
3. Oui, le maire lui en a accordé une. *Yes, the mayor granted one (of them) to him.*
4. Oui, Christophe Colomb l'a découverte. *Yes, Christopher Columbus discovered it.*
5. Oui, les Américains y en ont envoyé une. *Yes, the Americans sent one there.*
6. Oui, Rockefeller l'a acquise avant la guerre. *Yes, Rockefeller acquired it before the war.*
7. Oui, Shakespeare les a toutes écrites en anglais. *Yes, Shakespeare wrote all of them in English.*
8. Oui, Abélard les lui a écrites. *Yes, Abelard wrote them to her.*
9. Oui, les usines les ont installées au 19ème siècle. *Yes, the factories installed them in the 19th century.*
10. Oui, Sartre les a publiés avant sa mort. *Yes, Sartre published them before his death.*

EXERCISE 7-14:

1. La dernière fois, ils ne l'ont pas faite. *Last time they didn't make it.*
2. L'été dernier, ils ne l'ont pas apportée. *Last summer they didn't bring it.*
3. L'autre jour, nous ne les avons pas faits. *The other day we didn't do them.*
4. Avant le dernier examen, je ne les ai pas étudiées. *Before the last test I didn't study them.*
5. L'autre fois, il ne l'a pas perdu. *The other time he didn't lose it.*
6. Le trimestre dernier, vous ne l'avez pas suivi. *Last trimester you didn't take it.*
7. A l'autre pique-nique, je ne l'ai pas apporté. *At the other picnic I didn't bring it.*
8. Pendant le match, vous n'en avez pas pris trop. *During the game you didn't take too many.*
9. Au dernier examen, nous n'en avons pas reçu une bonne. *On the last test we didn't get a good one (of them).*
10. Hier, vous n'avez pas pu y venir. *Yesterday you weren't able to come (to it).*

EXERCISE 7-15:

1. Nous étions fatigués après le dernier match aussi. *We were tired after the last game, too.*
2. Mon camarade était devant la télé avant mon arrivée aussi. *My friend was in front of the TV before I came, too.*
3. J'étais chez moi ce matin aussi. *I was at home this morning, too.*
4. J'étais un peu inquiet hier soir aussi. *I was a little nervous yesterday evening, too.*
5. Mes parents étaient contents de mes notes le trimestre dernier aussi. *My parents were happy with my grades last trimester, too.*
6. Le dernier Président des Etats-Unis était un homme aussi. *The last president of the United States was a man, too.*
7. Vous étiez en très mauvaise forme samedi dernier aussi. *You were in very bad form last Saturday, too.*
8. Elles étaient en vacances la semaine dernière aussi. *They were on vacation last week, too.*
9. Il était assez précoce comme bébé aussi. *He was very precocious as a baby, too.*

10. C'était une journée splendide hier aussi. *It was a great day yesterday, too.*

EXERCISE 7-16:

1. Les skieurs allaient souvent à la montagne. *The skiers often went to the mountains.*
2. Cet artiste peignait surtout des paysages. *That artist mostly painted landscapes.*
3. Les étudiants riaient fréquemment en classe. *The students often laughed in class.*
4. Je regardais la télévision de temps en temps. *I watched television from time to time.*
5. Vous disiez toujours votre opinion. *You always gave your opinion.*
6. Nous étudiions avant chaque examen. *We studied before each test.*
7. Les touristes achetaient des glaces en attendant. *The tourists bought ice cream while waiting.*
8. Tu prenais le métro quelquefois. *You took the subway sometimes.*
9. On lisait souvent des choses surprenantes. *You often read surprising things.*
10. Ils ne pouvaient pas se rappeler son nom. *They weren't able to remember his name.*
11. Je dormais huit heures par nuit. *I slept eight hours a night.*
12. D'habitude, les enfants aimaient jouer dehors. *The children usually liked to play outdoors.*
13. Nous courions pour arriver à temps. *We ran in order to arrive in time.*
14. Qui avait le bon numéro? *Who had the first number?*
15. Tu ne savais pas son adresse. *You didn't know his address.*
16. Il faisait ses exercices régulièrement. *He did his exercises regularly.*
17. Je ne voulais pas recommencer cette histoire. *I wouldn't repeat this story.*
18. Il fallait passer un examen d'histoire ancienne. *It was necessary to pass an ancient history test.*
19. Combien de cours suivais-tu normalement? *How many classes did you normally take?*
20. En été, on mangeait souvent en plein air. *In summer we often eat outdoors.*

EXERCISE 7-17:

1. J'allais à la plage tous les jours l'été dernier. *I went to the beach every day last summer.*
2. Vous deviez compléter ce travail hier. *You had to finish this work yesterday.*
3. Il était content de vous voir l'autre jour. *He was happy to see you the other day.*
4. Elle voyait beaucoup ses amis à ce moment-là. *She saw a lot of her friends at that moment.*
5. A cette époque-là, ils sortaient beaucoup ensemble. *At that time, they went out a lot together.*

6. Dans le temps, les meilleurs vins venaient de France. *Formerly, the best wines came from France.*
7. La dernière fois, je ne pouvais pas répondre à votre question. *Last time I couldn't answer your question.*
8. Le semestre dernier, nous avions énormément de travail. *Last semester we had an enormous amount of work.*
9. Au 19ème siècle il y avait de graves problèmes politiques. *In the 19th century, there were serious political problems.*
10. La science ancienne ne réussissait pas à tout expliquer. *Ancient science did not succeed in explaining everything.*

EXERCISE 7-18:

1. On ne traversait pas l'Atlantique en avion il y a 100 ans. *They did not cross the Atlantic by plane 100 years ago.*
2. La France n'était pas une république au Moyen-Age. *France was not a republic in the Middle Ages.*
3. Les journaux ont paru ce matin. *The newspapers came out this morning.*
4. On ne faisait pas la cuisine à l'aide de machines autrefois. *Formerly they did not cook with the help of machines.*
5. Leurs grands-parents ne regardaient pas la télévision à leur âge. *Their grandparents didn't watch television when they were their age.*
6. Nous ne prenions pas de vin avec les repas à l'âge de sept ans. *We didn't have wine with meals at the age of seven.*
7. L'école a repris en automne l'année dernière. *School began again last fall.*
8. Je me suis lavé les dents hier soir. *I brushed my teeth last night.*
9. Elle ne s'habillait pas elle-même à l'âge de deux ans. *She didn't dress herself at the age of two.*
10. Les exercices étaient en français au chapitre 3. *The exercises were in French in Chapter 3.*

EXERCISE 7-19:

1. Bien sûr que j'ai fait du camping; je faisais du camping tout le temps! *Of course I went camping; I went camping all the time!*
2. Bien sûr qu'elles sont sorties avec leurs amis; elles sortaient avec leurs amis tout le temps! *Of course they left with their friends; they left with their friends all the time!*
3. Bien sûr qu'elle a assisté aux conférences de chimie; elle assistait aux conférences de chimie tout le temps! *Of course she attended the chemistry conferences; she attended the chemistry conferences all the time!*
4. Bien sûr qu'Henriette a suivi son instinct; Henriette suivait son instinct tout le temps!

Of course Henriette followed her instinct; Henriette followed her instinct all the time!

5. Bien sûr que j'ai fait de la peinture; je faisais de la peinture tout le temps! *Of course I painted; I painted all the time!*

6. Bien sûr qu'elle lui a dit la vérité; elle lui disait la vérité tout le temps! *Of course she told him the truth; she told him the truth all the time!*

7. Bien sûr que j'ai récité des vers; je récitais des vers tout le temps! *Of course I recited (some) verses; I recited (some) verses all the time!*

8. Bien sûr qu'elle a bu du café express; elle buvait du café express tout le temps! *Of course she drank espresso; she drank espresso all the time!*

9. Bien sûr que mes parents ont passé des vacances à la montagne; mes parents passaient des vacances à la montagne tout le temps! *Of course my parents spent their vacation in the mountains; my parents spent their vacation in the mountains all the time!*

10. Bien sûr que vous avez exagéré; vous exagériez tout le temps! *Of course you exaggerated; you exaggerated all the time!*

EXERCISE 7-20:

1. Je dormais quand le téléphone a sonné. *I was sleeping when the telephone rang.*

2. Madeleine souriait quand je l'ai embrassée. *Madeleine was smiling when I hugged her.*

3. Il regardait par la fenêtre quand il m'a vu. *He was looking out the window when he saw me.*

4. Nous étudiions quand elle est arrivée. *We were studying when she arrived.*

5. Les étudiants s'asseyaient quand le professeur est entré. *The students were sitting down when the professor entered.*

6. Vous serviez le repas quand les invités ont commencé à se parler. *You were serving the meal when the guests began talking.*

7. Tu mangeais des escargots quand les gens t'ont regardé de travers. *You were eating snails when the people looked at you oddly.*

8. Le rideau tombait quand le public a commencé à sortir. *The curtain was falling when the audience began to leave.*

9. Il pleuvait quand j'ai cherché mon parapluie. *It was raining when I looked for my umbrella.*

10. Je lisais le journal quand je me suis endormie. *I was reading the paper when I fell asleep.*

EXERCISE 7-21:

1. Tu apprenais pendant que tu lisais. *You learned while you read.*

2. Elle se promenait pendant qu'elle chantait. *She walked while she sang.*

3. Je mangeais pendant que je regardais la télévision. *I ate while I watched television.*

4. Vous preniez un bain pendant que vous écoutiez la radio. *You took a bath while you listened to the radio.*

5. Les employés travaillaient pendant que le patron les surveillait. *The employees worked while the boss supervised them.*

6. Le porteur descendait la malle pendant que je m'occupais des valises. *The porter brought down the trunk while I took care of the suitcases.*

7. Nous buvions pendant que nous nous reposions au soleil. *We drank while we laid in the sun.*

8. J'admirais les roses pendant que je visitais son jardin. *I admired the roses while I visited his garden.*

9. L'eau bouillait pendant que je remuais les pâtes. *The water boiled while I stirred the batter.*

10. Tu restais à la maison pendant que tes copains partaient pour la plage. *You stayed in the house while your buddies went to the beach.*

EXERCISE 7-22:

1. a) Ces choses arrivaient et tout le monde se fâchait. *These things were (always) happening and everyone was angry.* b) Ces choses sont arrivées et tout le monde s'est fâché. *These things happened and everyone got angry.*

2. a) La pluie commençait, mais je n'y faisais pas attention. *The rain was beginning but I wasn't paying attention to it.* b) La pluie a commencé, mais je n'y ai pas fait attention. *The rain began but I paid no attention to it.*

3. a) Le facteur arrivait quand je sortais. *The postman was arriving when I was leaving.* b) Le facteur est arrivé quand je suis sorti. *The postman arrived when I left.*

4. a) Ils se réunissaient et ils choisissaient un président. *They were meeting and choosing a president.* b) Ils se sont réunis et ils ont choisi un président. *They met and chose a president.*

5. a) Les enfants partaient, mais leurs parents ne pleuraient pas. *The children were leaving but their parents weren't crying.* b) Les enfants sont partis, mais leurs parents n'ont pas pleuré. *The children left but their parents didn't cry.*

6. a) Nous lisions la lettre et nous étions contents. *We were reading the letter and we were happy.* b) Nous avons lu la lettre et nous avons été contents. *We read the letter and we were happy.*

7. a) Tu t'en allais et je pensais à toi. *You were leaving and I was thinking of you.* b) Tu t'en es allé et j'ai pensé à toi. *You left and I thought of you.*

8. a) Quand la température descendait, tout le monde mettait un manteau. *When the*

temperature was falling, everyone was putting on a coat. b) Quand la température est descendue, tout le monde a mis un manteau. *When the temperature fell, everyone put on a coat.*

9. a) J'empruntais des disques et je les écoutais à la maison. *I borrowed some records and I was listening to them at home.* b) J'ai emprunté des disques et je les ai écoutés à la maison. *I borrowed some records and I listened to them at home.*

10. a) Elle nettoyait sa chambre, mais elle ne rangeait pas ses affaires. *She was cleaning her room but she was not putting her affairs in order.* b) Elle a nettoyé sa chambre, mais elle n'a pas rangé ses affaires. *She cleaned her room but she didn't put her affairs in order.*

RAISE YOUR GRADES

Passé composé and imparfait

B A 1. *It was beautiful when I left.*
E E 2. *The child cried because he was lost.*
B A 3. *Where were you going when I saw you?*
 D 4. *My cousins just came from visiting us.*
 C 5. *Emma liked to read romance novels.*
 C 6. *When I was twelve, I blushed easily.*
E E 7. *They couldn't understand what you said.*
F F 8. *The plates fell when I slipped.*
 B 9. *We knew him before his big success.*
E E 10. *My mother made the meal and I worked.*
 D 11. *We were going to interrupt you.*

B 12. *France had 50 million inhabitants in 1832.*
A 13. *Where did you know them?*
C 14. *We took walks in the country.*
A B 15. *She knew the truth because he couldn't lie.*
B A 16. *I wanted to leave, but I didn't have the courage.*
F F 17. *She kissed him and he was very happy.*
B A 18. *George had a sore throat and he called the doctor.*
A 19. *His (her) mother died before the war.*
A B 20. *The postman came at the moment I left.*

Past participle agreement

D 21. *They didn't buy it.*
C 22. *The children fell on the ice.*
E 23. *These are the only recommended books.*
A 24. *My cousins sent (some) presents to one another.*
B 25. *We showed them our photos.*
A 26. *The workers worked hard.*
E 27. *At the indicated hours, the trains arrived.*
C 28. *Onward children of the fatherland, the day of glory has arrived.*

C 29. *She decided to do it.*
C 30. *The students made fun of their professor.*
C 31. *The old people stayed shut up in their room.*
C 32. *He went out again in the rain.*
B 33. *I asked him if he wanted to come with me.*
B 34. *My friends spoke to me seriously about it.*
A 35. *She hopes that her guests haven't forgotten (didn't forget).*

Passive sentences

36. Un restaurant va être recommandé par mes camarades. *A restaurant is going to be recommended by my friends.*
37. Deux dents ont été arrachées par ce dentiste. *Two teeth were extracted by that dentist.*
38. Le dîner est servi. *Dinner is served.*
39. De la musique classique a été jouée par l'orchestre. *Some classical music was played by the orchestra.*
40. Les passagers ont été rassurés. *The passengers were reassured.*
41. Ce ballon va être réparé par mon frère et moi. *This ball is going to be repaired by my brother and me.*
42. Tous les examens ont été corrigés par le professeur. *All the tests are to be corrected by the professor.*
43. Un jour de fête est proclamé par le maire. *A holiday is proclaimed by the mayor.*
44. Notre voiture va être conduite par le chauffeur. *Our car is going to be driven by the chauffeur.*
45. Cet exercice est corrigé par vous. *This exercise is corrected by you.*

8 FUTURE, CONDITIONAL, AND PERFECT TENSES

THIS CHAPTER IS ABOUT

☑ **The Future Tense**
☑ **The Conditional**
☑ **The Perfect Tenses**
☑ **Conditional Sentences**

8-1. The Future Tense

The time at which an event occurs does not always correspond to the tense you use to describe it. In informal spoken French, you usually use a present tense verb with an adverb like **demain**, *tomorrow*, or a double verb construction to refer to the future. In more formal French, you indicate the future by adding future tense endings to the infinitive or future stem of a main verb.

A. Formation of the future tense

1. To form the future tense of all but a few irregular verbs, add the following endings to the complete infinitive—without the final **-e**.

Singular	Plural
-ai	-ons
-as	-ez
-a	-ont

> *NOTE:* The future endings are the last syllable of the appropriate form of the verb **avoir**.

commencer, *to begin*

je commence**rai**	nous commence**rons**	
tu commence**ras**	vous commence**rez**	*I, you, he, we, they will begin*
il commence**ra**	ils commence**ront**	

prendre, *to take*

je prend**rai**	nous prend**rons**	
tu prend**ras**	vous prend**rez**	*I, you, she, we, they will take*
elle prend**ra**	elles prend**ront**	

2. Regular verbs that have minor spelling changes in the present tense (see Sec. 4-5) have similar spellings in the future tense—BUT **-é-** remains unchanged.

Infinitive	Present	Future	
acheter	j'achète	j'**achèterai**	*I will buy*
employer	j'emploie	j'**emploierai**	*I will use*
jeter	je jette	je **jetterai**	*I will throw*
préférer	je préfère	je **préférerai**	*I will prefer*

EXERCISE 8-1: Answer the following questions using the adverbial expression given in parentheses and the formal future tense. Answers and translations are at the end of the chapter.

Example: Quand les cours reprennent-ils? *When do classes start again?*
(en septembre) *(in September)*
Les cours reprendront en *Classes start up again in*
septembre. *September.*

1. Quand est-ce que nous partons? (ce soir)
2. En quelle année finis-tu tes études? l'année prochaine)
3. Quand vend-on ses livres? (à la fin du semestre)
4. En quel mois finis-tu tes études? (au mois de mai)
5. Quand mange-t-on? (dans quelques minutes)
6. Combien de temps le voyage prend-il? (trois jours)
7. Quand se marient-ils? (dans deux mois)
8. A quelle heure lisent-elles la liste? (à cinq heures)
9. Quand annoncez-vous les résultats? (demain matin)
10. Dans combien de minutes l'avion atterrit-il? (cinq minutes)

3. All verbs—regular and irregular—use the same future endings. BUT a few irregular verbs and their compounds have irregular future stems.

aller, *to go*   stem: **ir-**

j'**irai**   nous **irons**
tu **iras**   vous **irez**   *I, you, one, we, they will go*
on **ira**   ils **iront**

s'asseoir, *to sit down*	stem: **assiér-**	je m'**assiérai**	*I will sit down*
avoir, *to have*	stem: **aur-**	tu **auras**	*you will have*
courir, *to run*	stem: **courr-**	il **courra**	*he will run*
cueillir, *to pick*	stem: **cueiller-**	nous **cueillerons**	*we will pick*
devoir, *to have to, must*	stem: **devr-**	vous **devrez**	*you will have to*
être, *to be*	stem: **ser-**	ils **seront**	*they will be*
faire, *to do, make*	stem: **fer-**	je **ferai**	*I will do, will make*
falloir, *it is necessary*	stem: **faudr-**	il **faudra**	*it will be necessary (one will have to)*
mourir, *to die*	stem: **mourr-**	tu **mourras**	*you will die*
pleuvoir, *to rain*	stem: **pleuvr-**	il **pleuvra**	*it will rain*
pouvoir, *to be able*	stem: **pourr-**	elle **pourra**	*she will be able*
recevoir, *to receive*	stem: **recevr-**	nous **recevrons**	*we will receive*
savoir, *to know*	stem: **saur-**	vous **saurez**	*you will know*
tenir, *to hold*	stem: **tiendr-**	elles **tiendront**	*they will hold*
venir, *to come*	stem: **viendr-**	je **viendrai**	*I will come*
voir, *to see*	stem: **verr-**	tu **verras**	*you will see*
vouloir, *to want, wish*	stem: **voudr-**	on **voudra**	*one, we, they, people will want*

NOTE: American English translates the future tense by *will* or *'ll*—even though British or formal usage sometimes translates it as *shall*.

Nous **serons** contents de vous *We will (we'll) be happy to*
accueillir. *welcome you.*
(British: We shall be happy to welcome you.)

EXERCISE 8-2: Answer the following questions in the affirmative with a single, future tense verb in place of the double verb phrase. Answers and translations are at the end of the chapter.

Example: Est-ce que je dois recevoir la *Am I to get the list of names?*
liste des noms?
Oui, tu recevras la liste des *Yes, you will receive the list of names.*
noms.

1. Allons-nous être à l'heure?
2. Penses-tu pouvoir venir avec nous?
3. Est-ce qu'elle va avoir assez de temps?
4. Est-ce que je peux savoir votre nouvelle adresse?
5. Pensez-vous voir ce film?
6. Doit-on lui envoyer son argent la semaine prochaine?
7. Comptent-ils faire ce voyage avec vous?
8. Est-ce qu'on va retenir des places pour le concert?
9. Espères-tu devenir médecin?
10. Est-ce qu'il va pleuvoir cet après-midi?

B. Use of the future tense

1. Use the future tense to express what will take place in the future.

Le congrès **aura** lieu à Paris.	*The convention will take place in Paris.*
Guy et Marie **reviendront** en Septembre	*Guy and Marie will come back in September.*

2. In contrast to English, use a future tense whenever a subordinate clause following one of these time conjunctions refers to a future event or situation.

quand	*when*	**après que**	*after*
lorsque	*when*	**pendant que**	*while*
dès que	*as soon as*	**tant que**	*as long as*
aussitôt que	*as soon as*		

Appelez-moi quand il viendra.	*Call me when he comes.*
Tant qu'il y aura des hommes il y a aura des guerres.	*As long as there are men there will be wars.*

EXERCISE 8-3:   Answer the following questions, replacing the conjunction **si** with a future time conjunction. Then translate your sentence into English. Answers and translations are at the end of the chapter.

Example:	Viendras-tu si tu as le temps?	*Will you come if you have the time?*
	Oui, je viendrai quand j'aurai le temps.	*Yes, I'll come when I have the time.*

1. Répondra-t-elle au téléphone s'il sonne?

2. Les gens monteront-ils dans le train s'il s'arrête?

3. Me comprendrez-vous si je parle français?

4. Ouvriras-tu ton parapluie s'il pleut?

5. Les reconnaîtrons-nous si elles viennent?

6. Ferons-nous une promenade s'il fait beau?

7. Serez-vous prêt s'il faut partir?

8. Nous aidera-t-elle si elle peut?

9. Est-ce que je l'aurai si je le veux?

10. Lui parleront-ils s'ils le voient?

8-2. The Conditional

The conditional is not associated with any particular time or tense, so you may use it in both present and past time. The meaning of the conditional depends upon its context.

A. Formation of the present conditional

1. To form the present conditional of regular verbs, add the imparfait endings to the entire infinitive—without the final **-e**.

	Singular	Plural
	-ais	-ions
	-ais	-iez
	-ait	-aient

Infinitive	Conditional	
préférer	je préférer**ais**	*I would prefer*
établir	tu établir**ais**	*you would establish*
rompre	il rompr**ait**	*she would break*
danser	nous danser**ions**	*we would dance*
comprendre	vous comprendr**iez**	*you would understand*
finir	ils finir**aient**	*they would finish*

2. Verbs that have an irregular stem in the future tense (see Sec. 8-1) have the same stem in the conditional. Add the imparfait endings to these stems to form the conditional.

Infinitive	Conditional	
aller	j'**irais**	*I would go*
s'asseoir	tu **t'assiérais**	*you would sit down*
avoir	il **aurait**	*he would have*
parcourir	nous **parcourrions**	*we would run through*
accueillir	vous **accueilleriez**	*you would welcome*
devoir	ils **devraient**	*they ought to (should)*

> **NOTE:** Although British English sometimes uses *should* for the conditional, in American English *should* usually means *ought to*. Use the conditional when you want to say *would* _____, and the conditional of **devoir** followed by an infinitive when you want to say *should* _____.

J'aurais honte à votre place.	*I would be ashamed if I were you.*
Nous **devrions** respecter la loi.	*We should (ought to) respect the law.*

être	je **serais**	*I would be*
faire	tu **ferais**	*you would do*
falloir	il **faudrait**	*it would be necessary*
mourir	nous **mourrions**	*we would die*
pleuvoir	il **pleuvrait**	*it would rain*
pouvoir	vous **pourriez**	*you would be able (could)*
recevoir	ils **recevraient**	*they would receive*
savoir	je **saurais**	*I would know*
tenir	tu **tiendrais**	*you would hold*
venir	elle **viendrait**	*she would come*
voir	nous **verrions**	*we would see*
vouloir	vous **voudriez**	*you would want*

> **NOTE:** In some English sentences *would* means *used to*. This is *not* the conditional use—translate it with the French imparfait.

*We **would** often take walks after dinner.*	Nous **faisions** souvent des promenades après dîner.

B. Use of the present conditional

1. Use the conditional in the present time to ask a polite question or make a request.

Voudriez-vous un verre de vin?	*Would you like a glass of wine?*
J'aimerais les voir une autre fois.	*I would like to see them at some other time.*

EXERCISE 8-4:   Make the following requests or ask the questions in a more polite manner. Then translate your sentence into English. Answers and translations are at the end of the chapter.

Example: Désirez-vous autre chose?   *Do you want anything else?*
Désireriez-vous autre chose?   *Would you like anything else?*

1. Est-ce que ces Messieurs veulent s'asseoir?

2. Je prends volontiers un morceau de ce gâteau-là.

3. Vous devez faire attention à moi!

4. Peux-tu me rendre ce service?

5. Nous aimons nous reposer ici une minute.

6. Passez-moi le sel, s'il vous plaît.

7. Ouvres-tu cette porte?

8. Je veux avoir ta réponse.

9. Me rendez-vous un petit service?

10. Aimes-tu danser avec moi?

2. Use the conditional in the present time to make contrary-to-fact statements—what would happen if something imaginary were true.

S'il y avait un incendie on **appellerait** les pompiers.
If there were a fire, we would call the firemen.

Je **serais** très vexé si tu ne venais pas.
I would be very cross if you didn't come.

> **REMEMBER:** Even though you express the imaginary situation in the imparfait, you are referring to time in the present or future.

EXERCISE 8-5:   Tell what would happen if the following things were true rather than false. Answers and translations are at the end of the chapter.

Example: La France n'est pas une monarchie, donc elle n'a pas de roi.
France is not a monarchy so it doesn't have a king.

Si la France était une monarchie, elle aurait un roi.
If France were a monarchy, it would have a king.

Je ne mange pas parce que je n'ai pas faim.
I'm not eating because I'm not hungry.

Je mangerais si j'avais faim.
I would eat if I were hungry.

1. Je ne parle pas espagnol donc je ne visite pas le Pérou.
2. Il ne fait pas beau parce qu'il y des nuages.
3. Votre maison ne me plaît pas parce qu'elle n'a pas d'étage.
4. Ces voitures ne sont pas bon marché donc je n'en achète pas une.
5. Vous ne savez pas nager donc vous ne faites pas de bateau.
6. Je n'ai pas de bonnes notes parce que je n'étudie pas.
7. Ils ne viennent pas me chercher donc je reste à la maison.
8. Les émissions ne nous intéressent pas donc nous ne regardons pas la télévision.
9. Il n'y a pas de soleil donc les jeunes ne vont pas à la plage.
10. Elle ne se sent pas bien donc elle ne sort pas ce soir.

3. Use the conditional in past narration to tell about things that were supposed to happen later.

Il a dit qu'il **aurait** l'argent le lendemain.
He said he would have the money the next day.

| Les journaux annonçaient que les banques **fermeraient**. | *The papers announced that the banks would close.* |

EXERCISE 8-6: Change the double verb phrases in the following sentences to a single verb in the conditional. Then translate your sentence into English. Answers and translations are at the end of the chapter.

| Example: | Il insistait qu'il allait y avoir une tempête. | *He insisted that there was going to be a storm.* |
| | Il insistait qu'il y aurait une tempête. | *He insisted that there would be a storm.* |

1. Robert a dit que son équipe allait gagner.

2. Les commerçants savaient que les prix allaient monter.

3. Les journaux ont prédit que tu allais perdre l'élection.

4. Tu espérais qu'elle n'allait pas s'en rendre compte.

5. Je vous ai dit que j'allais vous envoyer cet argent.

6. Qui disait que l'hiver allait être pénible?

7. Tout le monde pensait que nous allions faire faillite.

8. Les chercheurs ont annoncé qu'ils allaient abandonner leurs recherches.

9. Ses amis lui ont écrit qu'ils allaient venir la voir.

10. Le roi a proclamé qu'il allait choisir son propre ministre.

8-3. The Perfect Tenses

The perfect tenses indicate the relative order of two events in the past or in the future.

A. Plus-que-parfait, *pluperfect*

The **plus-que-parfait** consists of the imparfait of **être** or **avoir** plus the past participle of the main verb. Use the plus-que-parfait to refer to something that had happened before something else in the past.

Il n'**avait** jamais **vu** une chose pareille!	*He had never seen anything like it!*
Il paraissait que les camions **étaient** déjà **passés**.	*It appeared that the trucks had already gone by.*
Le speaker a dit que la séance **était** **levée**.	*The announcer said that the session had come to a close.*

> *NOTE:* Form the compound tenses of transitive verbs and the copulative verb **être** with **avoir**. Form the compound tenses of reflexive verbs and change-of-place or -state verbs with **être**. Be sure to make all necessary past participle agreements (see Sec. 7-1).

EXERCISE 8-7: Answer the following questions in the negative, substituting the plus-que-parfait for the double verb phrase. Then translate your sentence into English. Answers and translations are at the end of the chapter.

| Example: | A-t-elle dit qu'elle allait manger? | *Did she say she was going to eat?* |
| | Non, elle a dit qu'elle avait déjà mangé. | *No, she said she had already eaten.* |

1. As-tu dit que tu voulais te reposer?

2. Croyait-il que le téléphone allait sonner?

3. Disaient-ils qu'ils pensaient voir ce film?

4. A-t-on dit que je comptais emprunter de l'argent?

5. Disaient-elles qu'elles voulaient essayer ce restaurant?

6. Croyait-on que nous allions devenir riches?

7. Est-ce qu'on a annoncé que le Président allait venir?

8. As-tu dit que je devais me mettre à travailler?

9. Est-ce que je vous ai dit qu'il devait pleuvoir?

10. Pensiez-vous qu'il allait y avoir un défilé?

B. Passé surcomposé

1. Form the passé surcomposé with the passé composé of **être** or **avoir** plus the past participle of the main verb.

J'ai eu parlé.	*I had spoken.*	Nous **avons eu parlé**.	*We had spoken.*
J'ai été venu(e).	*I had come.*	Nous **avons été venus(es)**.	*We had come.*

2. Use the passé surcomposé to replace the plus-que-parfait after one of the following time conjunctions to refer to a single event in the past. These are some of the same conjunctions that require the future tense when future time is indicated (see Sec. 8-1).

quand	*when*	**aussitôt que**	*as soon as*
lorsque	*when*	**après que**	*after*
dès que	*as soon as*		

Dès que la famille **a eu mangé** hier soir, je suis rentré.

As soon as the family had eaten last night, I came back home.

> **NOTE:** After a time conjunction, the plus-que-parfait describes a continuing or habitual circumstance.

Chaque soir, **dès que** la famille **avait mangé**, je rentrais.

Every evening, as soon as the family had eaten, I used to come home.

3. You may also introduce a verb in the passé surcomposé with the adverbial phrase **à peine**, *hardly*. Invert the subject and verb after **à peine**.

A peine a-t-elle **eu fini** de parler quand on l'a vu.

She had hardly finished speaking when we saw him.

OR

Hardly had she finished speaking when we saw him.

> **REMEMBER:** Use the plus-que-parfait after a time conjunction or **à peine** to mean something *had happened repeatedly or continually*.

EXERCISE 8-8: Combine the two sentences logically with a time conjunction to show that one action took place just before the other. Answers and translations are at the end of the chapter.

Example:

Il a pris son revolver. Il a tiré quatre fois.

He took his gun. He fired four times.

Quand il a eu pris son revolver, il a tiré quatre fois.

When he had taken his gun he fired four times.

Napoléon remportait des victoires. Il faisait construire des monuments.

Napoleon achieved victories. He used to have monuments built.

Quand Napoléon avait remporté des victoires, il faisait construire des monuments.

Whenever Napoleon achieved victories he used to have monuments built.

1. Il a commence à pleuvoir. J'ai fermé les fenêtres.
2. L'avion a atterri. Les passagers se sont levés.
3. Nous faisions notre marché. Nous préparions le repas.
4. Ils ont mis les moteurs en marche. La course a commencé.
5. Ma mère a apporté le gâteau. J'ai soufflé les bougies.
6. Il ouvrait un livre. Il s'endormait.
7. Ces artistes ont monté une exposition. Ils ont terminé leur collection.
8. J'ai lâché le verre. Il est tombé par terre.
9. Elle est venue vous chercher. Vous êtes descendu.
10. Le guide parlait lentement. Je comprenais son français.

C. Past Infinitive

1. Combine the infinitive **être** or **avoir** with the past participle to form a past infinitive which means *having* _____.

<table>
<tr><td>Il a été condamné pour **avoir menti**.</td><td>*He was condemned for having lied.*</td></tr>
<tr><td>Nous vous remercions d'**être venu**.</td><td>*We thank you for having come.*</td></tr>
</table>

2. Use the past infinitive after a preposition—most frequently the preposition **après**, *after*, since the past infinitive always refers to a preceding action.

<table>
<tr><td>Ils sont partis **après s'être excusés**.</td><td>*They left after excusing themselves.*</td></tr>
</table>

EXERCISE 8-9: Answer the following questions in the negative, substituting **après**, *after*, for **avant**, *before*. Answers and translations are at the end of the chapter.

Example: Déjeunez-vous avant de vous habiller?   *Do you have breakfast before getting dressed?*

Non, je déjeune après m'être habillé.   *No, I have breakfast after getting dressed.*

1. S'est-il arrêté avant de voir le feu rouge?
2. Ont-ils acheté la maison avant de se marier?
3. Est-ce que je devrais lire le roman avant de voir le film?
4. Paieras-tu la facture avant de recevoir les marchandises?
5. Apprécie-t-on ses amis avant de les perdre?
6. Prendras-tu un café avant de manger?
7. Auraient-elles accepté avant de se renseigner?
8. Est-ce qu'elle était riche avant de devenir médecin?
9. Vous sentez-vous reposé avant de dormir?
10. As-tu regardé ta montre avant de partir?

D. Perfect progressive

Combine the present participle **étant** or **ayant** with a past participle to form an adjective phrase, which modifies the subject.

<table>
<tr><td>**Ayant fini** avant les autres, elle est partie.</td><td>*Having finished before the others, she left.*</td></tr>
<tr><td>**S'étant trompé**, il a perdu beaucoup de temps.</td><td>*By making a mistake he lost a lot of time.*</td></tr>
</table>

NOTE: Do not use the perfect progressive as a main verb or after a preposition.

EXERCISE 8-10: Change the clauses to the perfect progressive. Answers and translations are at the end of the chapter.

Example: Quand il a eu fini, il est sorti.   *When he had finished, he left.*

Ayant fini, il est sorti.   *Having finished, he left.*

1. Lorsque j'ai été arrivée, j'ai fait sa connaissance.
2. Dès qu'il a été parti, il a s'est senti mieux.

3. Aussitôt que nous l'avons eu vu, nous l'avons aimé.
4. Parce qu'il a eu de bonnes notes, il a eu un prix.
5. Quand vous avez eu mangé vous avez été content.

E. Future perfect

1. Combine the future of **avoir** or **être** with a past participle to form the future perfect which means *will have _____*.

Tu **auras fini** avant moi dans ces conditions-là.	*You will have finished before me if that keeps up.*
Les messagers **seront partis** avant l'aube.	*The messengers will have left before dawn.*
Elles **se seront mises** d'accord éventuellement.	*They will eventually have come to an agreement.*

2. If you use a time conjunction, translate an English verb in the present perfect by the French future perfect—if the action is in the future.

I'll be with you **as soon as** *I* **have finished** *here.*	Je serai à vous **aussitôt que** j'**aurai fini** ici.

EXERCISE 8-11: Combine each pair of sentences to indicate logically that one event will happen before the other. Answers and translations are at the end of the chapter.

Example:	J'arriverai devant la maison.	*I'll pull up in front.*
	Je klaxonnerai.	*I'll blow the horn.*
	Quand je serai arrivé devant la maison, je klaxonnerai.	*When I've pulled up in front, I'll blow the horn.*

1. Le speaker annoncera les résultats. On célébrera.
2. Ils se lèveront. Il prendront leurs valises.
3. Nous finirons cet article. Nous te l'expliquerons.
4. Tu auras de ses nouvelles. Le facteur arrivera.
5. Je mangerai. Je me laverai les dents.
6. Je m'habillerai. Je partirai pour l'université.
7. Tu finiras tes études. Tu chercheras du travail.
8. On roulera à cent kilomètres à l'heure. On prendra l'autoroute.
9. Vous lirez cette lettre. Vous vous rendrez compte de mes intentions.
10. Vous verrez mieux la page. Vous allumerez la lampe.

F. The past conditional

1. To form the past conditional, combine the conditional of **avoir** or **être** with the past participle of the main verb.

j'**aurais parlé**	*I would have spoken*	nous **aurions parlé**	*we would have spoken*
je **serais venu(e)**	*I would have come*	nous **serions venus(es)**	*we would have come*

> **REMEMBER:** The past participle of intransitive verbs conjugated with **être** agrees in gender and number with the subject of the verb (see Sec. 7-1).

2. Use the past conditional to express the sense of *would have _____*.

Ils **seraient rentrés** plus tôt s'il n'y avait pas eu de neige.	*They would have come home sooner if there hadn't been any snow.*
Deux mille francs **auraient suffi**.	*Two thousand francs would have been enough.*
Nous **nous serions moqués** d'une telle proposition.	*We would have scoffed at any such offer.*

> ***NOTE:*** Translate the verb **devoir** in the past conditional as *should have*, and the verb **pouvoir** as *could have*.

Vous **auriez dû** le laisser tranquille!
You should have left him alone!

Ils **auraient pu** faire un petit effort.
They could have put a little effort into it.

EXERCISE 8-12: Answer the following questions in the past conditional. Then translate your sentences into English. Answers and translation are at the end of the chapter.

Example: Avez-vous répondu à sa demande?
Did you answer his request?

J'aurais répondu à sa demande, mais c'était trop tard.
I would have answered his request but it was too late.

1. Voulait-il voyager en France?

2. Se sont-elles mises à faire des économies?

3. Nous aidiez-vous?

4. A-t-elle tenu sa promesse?

5. T'efforçais-tu à le faire?

6. Sont-ils retournés en Russie?

7. Leur avez-vous rendu cet argent?

8. Est-ce que j'ai eu le contrat?

9. Etions-nous les candidats?

10. Es-tu descendu à l'hôtel?

8-4. Conditional Sentences

A conditional **sentence** has two parts—the **si**, *if*, *clause* which expresses *a condition, a supposition,* or *an eventuality,* and the *main clause* which gives *a result* or *a conclusion.* A sentence that contains a clause introduced by **si** is called a *conditional statement*—whether it contains a verb in the conditional mood or not.

A. Si with the present tense

If the **si** clause supposes something within the realm of possibility, use the verb or its auxiliary in the present tense. In the main clause, you may use a verb in the present, the imperative, or the future—depending upon the sense of the sentence.

Si vous **étudiez** vous **faites** des progrès.
If you study you make progress.

Si vous **étudiez** vous **ferez** des progrès.
If you study you will make progress.

Ne m'en **voulez** pas si je **fais** une erreur.
Don't hold it against me if I make a mistake.

> *NOTE:* The **si** clause may come before or after the main clause.

Je **reste** au lit **si je suis malade**.
I stay in bed if I am ill.

OR

Si je suis malade, je **reste** au lit.
If I'm ill, I stay in bed.

EXERCISE 8-13: Answer the following questions, replacing the time conjunction with **si**. Answers and translations are at the end of the chapter.

Example: Est-ce que l'eau bout quand sa température atteint cents degrés?
Does water boil when its temperature reaches 100 degrees?

Oui, l'eau bout si sa température atteint cents degrés.
Yes, water boils if its temperature reaches 100 degrees.

Est-ce que tu liras des romans quand tu seras en vacances?
Will you read novels when you are on vacation?

Oui, je lirai des romans si je suis en vacances.
Yes, I'll read novels if I'm on vacation.

1. Verras-tu ce film aussitôt qu'il passera au cinéma?
2. Est-ce que nous rentrerons aussitôt qu'il pleuvra?
3. Le mangera-t-on dès qu'il sera prêt?
4. Construirez-vous votre maison lorsque vous achetèrez le terrain?
5. Prends-tu des aspirines quand tu as mal à la tête?
6. Quand je te le demanderai, m'aideras-tu?
7. Après qu'on rentre tard, est-ce qu'on se couche tout de suite?
8. Réfléchissez-vous lorsqu'on vous pose une question?
9. Le taxi s'arrêtera-t-il aussitôt qu'on appellera?
10. Les ouvriers démoliront-ils le bâtiment dès qu'ils en recevront l'ordre?

B. Si with imparfait

If the **si** clause states something imaginary or contrary-to-fact, use the verb or its auxiliary in the imparfait. In the main clause, you may use a verb in the conditional or the past conditional — depending upon the sense of the sentence.

Si j'étais vous je ne **dirais** rien à personne.	*If I were you I wouldn't say anything to anyone.*
OR	
Si j'étais vous je n'**aurais** rien **dit** à personne.	*If I were you I wouldn't have said anything to anyone.*
OR	
Si j'avais été vous je n'**aurais** rien **dit** à personne.	*If I had been you I wouldn't have said anything to anyone.*

EXERCISE 8-14:   Tell what would have happened in each instance if the situation had been the contrary. Then translate your sentence into English. Answers and translations are at the end of the chapter.

Example:	Nous ne pouvons pas partir maintenant parce qu'il n'y a pas de train.	*We can't leave now because the train doesn't run.*
	S'il y avait un train, nous pourrions partir maintenant.	*If the train ran we could leave now.*
	Il n'a pas téléphoné donc nous ne sommes pas sortis.	*He didn't call so we didn't go out.*
	S'il avait téléphoné, nous serions sortis.	*If he had called we would have gone out.*

1. Je suis arrivé en retard parce que ma montre ne marchait pas.
2. Leurs parents sont nés au Mexique, donc ils parlent espagnol.
3. Elle est fatiguée aujourd'hui parce qu'elle s'est couchée tard hier soir.
4. Nous n'avons pas payé la note, donc ils ont coupé l'électricité.
5. Tu grossis parce que tu ne fais pas d'exercice.
6. Vous chantez faux parce que vous n'entendez pas bien.
7. Paul dépense tout son argent, donc il n'a pas d'économies.
8. Il n'y avait rien à manger donc nous sommes partis tôt.
9. Il ne neige pas, donc nous ne pouvons pas faire de ski.
10. Ils nous ont trouvés sympathiques parce que nous nous sommes efforcés à être gentils.

SUMMARY

1. The future tense is based on the entire infinitive or an irregular future stem to which the last syllable of the present tense of **avoir** is added. It is translated *will* _____.
2. The conditional is based on the entire infinitive or the future stem to which the endings of the imparfait are added. It is translated *would* _____.

3. A perfect tense combines the verb **être** or **avoir** and the past participle of the main verb. Perfect tenses indicate the relative order in which two things take place when both are in the present, past, or future.

4. The plus-que-parfait combines the imparfait of **être** or **avoir** with the past participle of the main verb and means *had* _____.

5. The passé surcomposé is a spoken tense composed of the passé composé of **être** or **avoir** and the past participle of the main verb. It means *had* _____, and replaces the plus-que-parfait after time conjunctions if an event happened just once.

6. A past infinitive denotes prior actions after prepositions and means *having* _____.

7. The future perfect combines the future of **être** or **avoir** with the past participle of the main verb and means *will have* _____.

8. The past conditional combines the conditional of **être** or **avoir** with the past participle of the main verb and means *would have* _____.

9. When a clause introduced by **si** describes something within the realm of possibility, its verb or auxiliary is in the present tense. The main clause may be in the present, future, or imperative, depending upon the meaning of the sentence.

10. When a clause introduced by **si** describes something imaginary or contrary-to-fact, its verb or auxiliary is in the imparfait. The main clause may be in the conditional or past conditional, depending upon the meaning of the sentence.

RAISE YOUR GRADES

Identification: Time and Tense

Identify the time and tense of the verb in parentheses by writing the corresponding letters in the spaces provided. Answers and translations are at the end of the chapter.

P = past   **Pr** = present   **C** = conditional   **F** = future

Example: **Pr**   **C**   J'(aimerais) vous voir demain.

Time   Tense

_____ _____ 1. Nous (restons) à la maison demain.
_____ _____ 2. Si j'(étais né) en Chine je parlerais chinois.
_____ _____ 3. Nos parents nous (invitent) chez eux.
_____ _____ 4. (Voudriez)-vous encore un peu de café?
_____ _____ 5. Il ne se plaindrait pas s'il (était) riche.
_____ _____ 6. Descends dès que je (sonnerai) à la porte!
_____ _____ 7. Elle ne sait pas si elle (vient) lundi prochain.
_____ _____ 8. Si nous (finissons) nous célébrerons.
_____ _____ 9. Quand il (viendra) nous le verrons.
_____ _____ 10. Si j'(avais) mille dollars je les dépenserais.

Fill in the blanks with the appropriate form and tense of **être** or **avoir** as called for by the meaning and structure of the sentence. Answers and translations are at the end of the chapter.

11. Je ne me plaindrais pas si j' _____ à votre place.
12. Il ne voulait pas dîner parce qu'il _____ déjà mangé.
13. Dès que nous _____ fait nos adieux nous sommes partis.
14. Elle n'est jamais là quand on _____ besoin d'elle.
15. Nous viendrons aussitôt que nous nous _____ habillés.
16. Si tu _____ le temps tu pourras lui rendre visite.
17. Quand tu _____ le temps tu liras cet article.
18. Après qu'il _____ lu ce livre, il en commencera un autre.
19. Tu ne te _____ pas trompée, si tu avais suivi ton instinct.
20. S'il _____ fait beau aujourd'hui, nous serions allés à la plage.
21. Si elles _____ assez de courage elles auraient protesté.
22. Ils avaient l'intention de partir après s' _____ excusés.

CHAPTER ANSWERS

EXERCISE 8-1:

1. Nous partirons ce soir. *We will leave this evening.*
2. Je finirai mes études l'année prochaine. *I will finish my studies next year.*
3. On vendra ses livres à la fin du semestre. *They will sell their books at the end of the semester.*
4. Je finirai mes études au mois de mai. *I will finish my studies in May.*
5. On mangera dans quelques minutes. *We will eat in a few minutes.*
6. Le voyage prendra trois jours. *The trip will take three days.*
7. Ils se marieront dans deux mois. *They will be married in two months.*
8. Elles liront la liste à cinq heures. *They will read the roll at five o'clock.*
9. J'annoncerai (nous annoncerons) les résultats demain matin. *I will announce (we will announce) the results tomorrow morning.*
10. L'avion atterrira dans cinq minutes. *The airplane will land in five minutes.*

EXERCISE 8-2:

1. Oui, nous serons à l'heure. *Yes, we will be on time.*
2. Oui, je pourrai venir avec vous. *Yes, I will be able to come with you.*
3. Oui, elle aura assez de temps. *Yes, she will have enough time.*
4. Oui, vous saurez ma nouvelle adresse. *Yes, you will know my new address.*
5. Oui, je verrai ce film. *Yes, I will see that movie.*
6. Oui, on lui enverra son argent la semaine prochaine. *Yes, we'll bring his money next week.*
7. Oui, ils feront ce voyage avec moi (avec nous). *Yes, they will take this trip with me (with us).*
8. Oui, on retiendra des places pour le concert. *Yes, they'll reserve seats for the concert.*
9. Oui, je deviendrai médecin. *Yes, I will become a doctor.*
10. Oui, il pleuvra cet après-midi. *Yes, it will rain this afternoon.*

EXERCISE 8-3:

1. Oui, je répondrai au téléphone aussitôt qu' (dès qu') il sonnera. *Yes, I'll answer the phone as soon as it rings.* Oui, je répondrai au téléphone après qu'il sonnera. *Yes, I'll answer the phone after it rings.* Oui, je répondrai au téléphone quand (lorsqu') il sonnera. *Yes, I'll answer the phone when it rings.*
2. Oui, les gens monteront dans le train quand (lorsqu') il s'arrêtera. *Yes, the people will board the train when it stops.* Oui, les gens monteront dans le train après qu'il s'arrêtera. *Yes, the people will board the train after it stops.*

Oui, les gens monteront dans le train aussitôt qu' (dès qu') il s'arrêtera. *Yes, the people will board the train as soon as it stops.*
3. Oui, je vous comprendrai quand (lorsque) vous parlerez français. *Yes, I will understand you when you speak French.*
4. Oui, j'ouvrirai mon parapluie dès qu' (aussitôt qu') il pleuvra. *Yes, I'll open my umbrella as soon as it rains (begins raining).*
5. Oui, nous les reconnaîtrons quand (lorsqu') elles viendront. *Yes, we'll recognize them when they come.*
6. Oui, nous ferons une promenade dès qu' (aussitôt qu') il fera beau. *Yes, we'll take a walk as soon as the weather clears up.*
7. Oui, je serai (nous serons) prêt(s) lorsqu' (quand) il faudra partir. *Yes, I (we) will be ready when it's time to leave.*
8. Oui, elle nous (vous) aidera quand (lorsqu') elle pourra. *Yes, she'll help us (you) when she can.*
9. Oui, vous l'aurez (tu l'auras) dès que (aussitôt que) vous le voudrez (tu le voudras). *Yes, you'll have it as soon as you want it.*
10. Oui, ils lui parleront quand (lorsqu') ils le verront. *Yes, they'll speak to him when they see him.*

EXERCISE 8-4:

1. Est-ce que ces Messieurs voudraient s'asseoir? *Would the gentlemen like to sit down?*
2. Je prendrais volontiers un morceau de ce gâteau-là. *I would gladly take a piece of that cake.*
3. Vous devriez faire attention à moi! *You ought to (should) pay attention to me!*
4. Pourrais-tu me rendre ce service? *Would you be able to (Could you) do me a favor?*
5. Nous aimerions nous reposer ici une minute. *We would like to rest here a minute.*
6. Me passeriez-vous le sel, s'il vous plait? *Would you pass the salt, please?*
7. Ouvrirais-tu cette porte? *Would you open that door?*
8. Je voudrais avoir ta réponse. *I would like to have your answer.*
9. Me rendriez-vous un petit service? *Would you do me a small favor?*
10. Aimerais-tu danser avec moi? *Would you like to dance with me?*

EXERCISE 8-5:

1. Si je parlais espagnol, je visiterais le Pérou. *If I spoke Spanish, I would visit Peru.* OR Je visiterais le Pérou si je parlais espagnol. *I would visit Peru if I spoke Spanish.*
2. Il ferait beau s'il n'y avait pas de nuages. *It would be beautiful if there weren't any clouds.*

3. Votre maison me plairait si elle avait un étage. *I would like your house if it had a second story.*

4. Si ces voitures étaient bon marché, j'en achèterais une. *If those cars were cheap, I would buy one of them.*

5. Si vous saviez nager, vous feriez du bateau. *If you knew how to swim, you would go boating.*

5. J'aurais de bonnes notes si j'étudiais. *I would have good grades if I would study.*

7. S'ils venaient me chercher, je ne resterais pas à la maison. *If they would come to get me, I would not stay at home.*

8. Si les émissions nous intéressaient, nous regarderions la télévision. *If the programs interested us, we would watch television.*

9. S'il y avait du soleil, les jeunes iraient à la plage. *If it were sunny, the young people would go to the beach.*

10. Si elle se sentait bien, elle sortirait ce soir. *If she felt well, she would go out this evening.*

EXERCISE 8-6:

1. Robert a dit que son équipe gagnerait. *Robert said that his team would win.*

2. Les commerçants savaient que les prix monteraient. *The salesmen knew that the prices would go up.*

3. Les journaux ont prédit que tu perdrais l'élection. *The papers predicted that you would lose the election.*

4. Tu espérais qu'elle ne s'en rendrait pas compte. *You hoped she would not be aware of it.*

5. Je vous ai dit que je vous enverrais cet argent. *I told you that I would send you that money.*

6. Qui disait que l'hiver serait pénible? *Who said that winter would be painful?*

7. Tout le monde pensait que nous ferions faillite. *Everyone thought that we would go bankrupt.*

8. Les chercheurs ont annoncé qu'ils abandonneraient leurs recherches. *The investigators announced that they would abandon their inquiries.*

9. Ses amis lui ont écrit qu'ils viendraient la voir. *His friends told him that they would come to see her.*

10. Le roi a proclamé qu'il choisirait son propre ministre. *The king proclaimed that he would choose his own minister.*

EXERCISE 8-7:

1. Non, j'ai dit que je m'étais déjà reposé(e). *No, I said that I had already rested.*

2. Non, il croyait que le téléphone avait déjà sonné. *No, he thought the telephone had already rung.*

3. Non, ils disaient qu'ils avaient déjà vu ce film. *No, they said they had already seen that movie.*

4. Non, on a dit que tu avais déjà emprunté cet argent. *No, they said you had already borrowed that money.*

5. Non, elles disaient qu'elles avaient déjà essayé ce restaurant. *No, they said they had already tried that restaurant.*

6. Non, on croyait que nous étions déjà devenue(e)s riches. *No, people believed we had already gotten rich.*

7. Non, on a annoncé que le Président était déjà venu. *No, they announced that the President had already been there.*

8. Non, j'ai dit que tu t'étais déjà mis(e) à travailler. *No, I said you had already begun to work.*

9. Non, vous m'avez dit qu'il avait déjà plu. *No, you told me it had already rained.*

10. Non, je pensais qu'il y avait déjà eu un défilé. *No, I thought there had already been a parade.*

EXERCISE 8-8:

1. Quand (lorsqu', dès qu', aussitôt qu', après qu') il a eu commencé à pleuvoir, j'ai fermé les fenêtres. *When (as soon as, after) it had begun to rain I closed the windows.*

2. Dès que l'avion a eu atterri, les passagers se sont levés. *As soon as the plane had landed the passengers got up.*

3. Après que nous avions fait notre marché, nous préparions le repas. *Whenever we had finished our marketing we always prepared the meal.*

4. Aussitôt qu'ils ont eu mis les moteurs en marche, la course a commencé. *As soon as they had started the motors the race began.*

5. Lorsque ma mère a eu apporté le gâteau, j'ai soufflé les bougies. *When my mother had brought the cake I blew out the candles.*

6. Dès qu'il a eu ouvert un livre, il s'est endormi. *As soon as he had opened a book he fell asleep.*

7. Ces artistes ont monté une exposition aussitôt qu'ils ont eu terminé leur collection. *Those artists hung a show as soon as they had completed their collection.*

8. Aussitôt que j'ai eu lâché le verre, il est tombé par terre. *As soon as I had let go of the glass, it fell to the floor.*

9. Quand elle a été venue vous chercher, vous êtes descendu. *When she had come to get you, you went downstairs.*

10. Lorsque le guide avait parlé lentement, je comprenais son français. *Whenever the guide had spoken slowly I understood his French.*

EXERCISE 8-9:

1. Non, il s'est arrêté après avoir vu le feu rouge. *No, he stopped after having seen the red light.*

2. Non, ils ont acheté la maison après s'être mariés. *No, they bought the house after they were married.*

3. Non, vous devriez lire le roman après avoir vu le film. *No, you should read the book after having seen the film.*

4. Non, je paierai la facture après avoir reçu les marchandises. *No, I will pay the bill after having received the goods.*

5. Non, on apprécie ses amis après les avoir perdus. *No, we appreciate our friends after having lost them.*

6. Non, je prendrai du café après avoir mangé. *No, I will take some coffee after having eaten.*

7. Non, elles auraient accepté après s'être renseignées. *No, they would have accepted after having made inquiries.*

8. Non, elle était riche après être devenue médecin. *No, she was rich after having become a doctor.*

9. Non, je me sens reposé après avoir dormi. *No, I feel rested after having slept.*

10. Non, j'ai regardé ma montre après être parti. *No, I looked at my watch after having left.*

EXERCISE 8-10:

1. Etant arrivée, j'ai fait sa connaissance. *Having arrived, I met him.*

2. Etant parti, il s'est senti mieux. *Having left, he felt better.*

3. L'ayant vu, nous l'avons aimé(e). *Having seen it (him, her), we loved it (him, her).*

4. Ayant eu de bonnes notes, il a eu un prix. *By having good grades, he got a prize.*

5. Ayant mangé, vous avez été content. *Having eaten, you were happy.*

EXERCISE 8-11:

1. Dès que (aussitôt que, quand, lorsque, après que) le speaker aura annoncé les résultats, on célébrera. *As soon as (when, after) the announcer has announced the results we'll celebrate.*

2. Aussitôt qu'ils se seront levés, ils prendront leurs valises. *As soon as they have gotten up, they'll get their suitcases.*

3. Quand nous aurons fini cet article, nous te l'expliquerons. *When we have finished this article we'll explain it to you.*

4. Tu auras de ses nouvelles aussitôt que le facteur sera arrivé. *You'll have news from him as soon as the mailman has arrived.*

5. Après que j'aurai mangé, je me laverai les dents. *As soon as I have eaten I'll brush my teeth.*

6. Dès que je me serai habillé(e), je partirai pour l'université. *As soon as I have gotten dressed, I'll leave for the university.*

7. Quand tu auras fini tes études, tu chercheras du travail. *When you have finished school you'll look for work.*

8. On roulera à cent kilomètres à l'heure quand on aura pris l'autoroute. *We'll go a hundred kilometers an hour when we've turned onto the freeway.*

9. Quand vous aurez lu cette lettre, vous vous rendrez compte de mes intentions. *When you have read this letter, you will understand my intentions.*

10. Vous verrez mieux la page quand vous aurez allumé la lampe. *You'll see the page better when you have lit the lamp.*

EXERCISE 8-12:

1. Il aurait voulu voyager en France, mais c'était trop tard. *He would have liked to travel to France, but it was too late.*

2. Elles se seraient mises à faire des économies, mais c'était trop tard. *They would have begun to save money, but it was too late.*

3. Je vous aurais aidés, mais c'était trop tard. *I would have liked to help you, but it was too late.*

4. Elle aurait tenu sa promesse, mais c'était trop tard. *She would have kept her promise, but it was too late.*

5. Je me serais efforcé à le faire, mais c'était trop tard. *I would have forced myself to do it, but it was too late.*

6. Ils seraient retournés en Russie, mais c'était trop tard. *They would have gone back to Russia, but it was too late.*

7. Je leur aurais rendu cet argent, mais c'était trop tard. *I would have given them back that money, but it was too late.*

8. Vous auriez (tu aurais) eu le contrat, mais c'était trop tard. *You would have had the contract, but it was too late.*

9. Vous auriez été les candidats, mais c'était trop tard. *You would have been the candidates, but it was too late.*

10. Je serais descendu(e) à l'hôtel, mais c'était trop tard. *I would have gone to a hotel, but it was too late.*

EXERCISE 8-13:

1. Oui, je verrai ce film s'il passe au cinéma. *Yes, I'll see that movie if it plays at the theater.*

2. Oui, nous rentrerons s'il pleut. *Yes, we'll go back into the house if it rains.*

3. Oui, on le mangera s'il est prêt. *Yes, we'll eat it if it's ready.*

4. Oui, je construirai ma maison si j'achète le terrain. *Yes, I'll build my house if I buy the lot.*

5. Oui, je prends des aspirines si j'ai mal à la tête. *Yes, I take aspirin if I have a headache.*

6. Oui, je t'aiderai si tu me le demandes. *Yes, I'll help you if you ask me to.*

7. Oui, on se couche tout de suite si on rentre tard. *Yes, you go to bed right away if you come home late.*

8. Oui, je réfléchis si on me pose une question. *Yes, I think carefully if someone asks me a question.*

9. Oui, le taxi s'arrêtera si on appelle. *Yes, the taxi will stop if you call.*

10. Oui, les ouvriers démoliront le bâtiment s'ils en reçoivent l'ordre. *Yes, the workers will demolish the building if they receive the order.*

EXERCISE 8-14:

1. Je ne serais pas arrivé en retard si ma montre avait marché. *I wouldn't have arrived late if my watch had worked.*

2. Si leurs parents n'étaient pas nés au Mexique, ils ne parleraient pas espagnol. *If their parents*

hadn't been born in Mexico, they wouldn't speak Spanish.

3. Elle ne serait pas fatiguée aujourd'hui si elle ne s'était pas couchée tard hier soir. *She wouldn't be tired today if she hadn't gone to bed late last night.*

4. Si nous avions payé la note, ils n'auraient pas coupé l'électricité. *If we had paid the bill, they wouldn't have turned off the electricity.*

5. Tu ne grossirais pas si tu faisais de l'exercice. *You wouldn't put on weight if you exercised.*

6. Vous ne chanteriez pas faux si vous entendiez bien. *You wouldn't sing off key if you heard well.*

7. Si Paul ne dépensait pas tout son argent, il aurait des économies. *If Paul didn't spend all his money, he would have some savings.*

8. S'il y avait eu quelque chose à manger, nous ne serions pas partis si tôt. *If there had been something to eat, we wouldn't have left so early.*

9. S'il neigeait, nous pourrions faire du ski. *If it snowed, we could go skiing.*

10. Ils ne nous auraient pas trouvés sympathiques si nous ne nous étions pas éfforcés à être gentils. *They wouldn't have liked us if we hadn't gone out of our way to be nice.*

RAISE YOUR GRADES

Identification: Time and Tense

F   Pr   1. *We will stay home tomorrow.*

P   P   2. *If I had been born in China, I would speak Chinese.*

Pr   Pr   3. *Our parents invite us to their house.*

Pr   C   4. *Would you like a little more coffee?*

P   Pr   5. *He wouldn't complain if he were rich.*

F   F   6. *Come down as soon as I ring the doorbell.*

F   Pr   7. *She doesn't know if she will come next Monday.*

F   Pr   8. *If you finish, we will celebrate.*

F   F   9. *When he comes, we will see him.*

Pr   P   10. *If I had a million dollars, I would spend it.*

11. Je ne me plaindrais pas si j'étais à votre place. *I wouldn't complain if I were in your place.*

12. Il ne voulait pas dîner parce qu'il avait déjà mangé. *He didn't want to have dinner because he had already eaten.*

13. Dès que nous avons eu fait nos adieux nous sommes partis. *As soon as we had said our goodbyes we left.*

14. Elle n'est jamais là quand on a besoin d'elle. *She's never there when you need her.*

15. Nous viendrons aussitôt que nous nous serons habillés. *We'll come as soon as we have gotten dressed.*

16. Si tu as le temps tu pourras lui rendre visite. *If you have time you can visit him (her).*

17. Quand tu auras le temps tu liras cet article. *When you have time you'll read this article.*

18. Après qu'il aura lu ce livre, il en commencera un autre. *After he has finished that book, he'll begin another.*

19. Tu ne te serais pas trompé(e) si tu avais suivi on instinct. *You wouldn't have made a mistake if you had followed your instinct.*

20. S'il avait fait beau aujourd'hui, nous serions allés à la plage. *If the weather had been nice today, we would have gone to the beach.*

21. Si elles avaient eu assez de courage, elles auraient protesté. *If they had had enough courage, they would have protested.*

22. Ils avaient l'intention de partir après s'être excusés. *They intended to leave after excusing themselves.*

9 INTERROGATIVES AND RELATIVES

THIS CHAPTER IS ABOUT

☑ **Question Formation**
☑ **Indefinite Interrogatives**
☑ **Interrogative Adjectives**
☑ **Interrogative Pronouns**
☑ **Relative Pronouns**

9-1. Question Formation

There are several ways to ask questions in French, depending on whether the situation is formal or informal, whether the subject is a pronoun or a noun, and whether or not a question word is used.

A. The interrogative phrase Est-ce que . . . ?

In informal spoken French, you may ask a yes/no question by saying **Est-ce que . . .** before the subject noun or pronoun.

Notre opinion est valable.	*Our opinion is valid.*
Est-ce que notre opinion est valable?	*Is our opinion valid?*
Elles ont commandé un deuxième dessert.	*They ordered a second dessert.*
Est-ce qu'elles ont commandé un deuxième dessert?	*Did they order a second dessert?*

> *NOTE:* You may simply use a rising, questioning intonation alone to ask a yes/no question.
>
> | | |
> |---|---|
> | Vous descendez ici? | *Are you getting off here?* |
> | Il fait trop chaud? | *Is it too hot here?* |

EXERCISE 9-1: Use **Est-ce que . . .** with the following sentences to ask yes/no questions. Answers and translations are at the end of the chapter.

1. Leur sincérité est en question.
2. Nous étions ici pour écouter la conférence.
3. Elle promet son aide pour le dîner.
4. Il y a des erreurs dans son examen.
5. C'est aujourd'hui le 3 juillet.
6. Quelqu'un a sonné à la porte.
7. Françoise est retournée en France cet été.
8. Un autre répondrait à sa place.
9. La valise contiendra des papiers importants.
10. Tu sais ce que tu fais.

B. Subject pronoun/verb inversion

1. In written and formal French, you may ask both yes/no and information questions by saying the subject pronouns—except **je**—after the verb.

Avez- vous le temps de regarder ceci?   *Do you have time to look at this?*

Pourquoi **refuseront-ils** de participer?   *Why will they refuse to participate?*

2. Always use **Est-ce que . . .** to ask questions in the first person singular. It is extremely formal—if not pretentious—to say **je** after its verb.

Est-ce que j'ai votre numéro de téléphone?   *Do I have your phone number?*

3. The dash which connects the following subject pronoun to its verb shows that the two words are linked as a single word. In most cases this means that the final **-t** or **-d** of the third person singular will be pronounced **t** as the first consonant of the following syllable.

Dort-**il** toujours?   *Is he still sleeping?*

Prenai**t-elle** des vitamines?   *Did she used to take vitamins?*

Insert a **-t-** after verbs that do not end in final **-t** or **-d** in the third person singular if they precede **il**, **elle**, or **on**.

Retournera-t-elle bientôt?   *Will she return soon?*

Y **a-t-il** un téléphone?   *Is there a telephone?*

Quand **ira-t-on** à la montagne?   *When will we go to the mountains?*

EXERCISE 9-2: Ask the following questions in a more formal way by omitting **Est-ce que . . .** and using inverted question order. Answers and translations are at the end of the chapter.

1. Est-ce que vous comprenez tout cela?
2. Est-ce qu'il paiera à la fin du mois?
3. Quand est-ce que tu as passé tes examens semestriels?
4. Est-ce qu'elle regarde beaucoup la télévision?
5. Est-ce qu'on irait au mariage?
6. Avec qui est-ce que vous sortirez ce soir?
7. Est-ce que nous buvons du champagne?
8. Est-ce qu'elles lisent les journaux tous les jours?
9. Pourquoi est-ce que vous avez dit ceci?
10. Où est-ce qu'il étudiait la musique?

C. Noun subjects

To ask a formal question when the subject of the sentence is a noun phrase or a proper noun, repeat the subject after the verb as a third person pronoun of the same number and gender.

Jean-Pierre est-il un acteur célèbre?   *Is Jean-Pierre a famous actor?*

Vos cousines étaient-elles en visite?   *Were your cousins visiting?*

Pourquoi **son mari travaillera-t-il** cet été?   *Why will her husband be working this summer?*

EXERCISE 9-3: Ask the following questions in a more formal way by omitting **Est-ce que . . .** and using inverted question order. Answers and translations are at the end of the chapter.

1. Est-ce que Lucie et Jérôme connaissent vos parents?
2. Pourquoi est-ce que votre ami était si timide?
3. Est-ce que la France est plus grande que l'Italie?
4. Est-ce que la définition serait dans le dictionnaire?
5. Est-ce que ce restaurant sera ouvert lundi?
6. Quand est-ce que les feuilles jaunissent?
7. Comment est-ce que la cuisinière a préparé ce plat?
8. Est-ce que leur permis est toujours valable?
9. Est-ce qu'Henri est parti avant vous?
10. Qui est-ce que votre frère accompagne ce soir?

9-2. Indefinite Interrogatives

You can ask information questions by substituting interrogatives for subject or object nouns—including those that are objects of prepositions. When a question concerns someone or something not yet introduced into the conversation, the interrogative is neutral in gender and takes a third person singular verb.

A. Short interrogatives

The short interrogatives are

qui	*who(m)*
que	*what*
quoi	*what*

1. Use **qui**, *who*, whenever the question concerns a person.

Qui êtes-vous? (subject)	*Who are you?*
Qui voulez-vous voir? (direct object)	*Who(m) do you want to see?*
A qui adressez-vous cette question? (indirect object)	*To whom are you directing that question?*
Avec qui sortez-vous? (object of a preposition)	*Who(m) do you go out with?*
Qui? Je n'ai pas saisi le nom.	*Who? I didn't catch the name.*

2. Use **que**, *what*, to ask a question concerning something other than a person. **Que** is *always* the direct object of the verb.

Que faisais-tu là?	*What were you doing there?*

> **REMEMBER:** Never use **Que ...?** as the subject of a sentence or as the object of a preposition.

3. Use the stressed form **quoi**, *what*, as the object of a preposition and in one-word questions or exclamations.

Avec quoi comptes-tu acheter ce vélo?	*With what do you plan to buy that bike?*
Quoi? Nulle trahison?	*What? No treason?*

EXERCISE 9-4: Ask the questions for which these are the answers replacing the indefinites **quelque chose**, **personne**, etc., with a short interrogative. Answers and translations are at the end of the chapter.

Example:	Nous voyons quelque chose en haut.	*We see something up above.*
	Que voyons-nous en haut?	*What do we see up above?*

1. Quelqu'un va venir demain.
2. Je voulais voir quelque chose.
3. On s'est occupé des enfants.
4. Elle a voyagé avec quelqu'un.
5. Ils ont besoin de quelque chose.
6. Nous ne verrions rien.
7. Personne ne nous aidera.
8. Elles ne pensent à rien.
9. Quelqu'un avait laissé un message.
10. Nous n'aurions fait attention à personne.

B. Long interrogatives

1. The long forms of interrogatives consist of the words **qui**, *who, whom,* or **que**, *what,* followed by **est-ce qui**—for the sentence subject—or **est-ce que**—for its direct object.

Qui (*Who, Whom*)	**qui**	(subject)
	est-ce	
Qu' (*What*)	**qu(e)**	(object)

Qu'est-ce qui est dans ce sac?   *What's in that bag?*

Qu'est-ce que vous voulez dire?   *What do you mean?*
    Que voulez-vous dire?

Qui est-ce qu'il appelle?   *Who(m) is he calling?*
    Qui appelle-t-il?

Qui est-ce qui arrive?   *Who's coming?*
    Qui arrive?

> *NOTE:* Do not invert the order of subject and verb after a long interrogative.

2. Always use the long form **Qu'est-ce qui . . . ?** *What . . . ?* as the subject of a sentence.

    Qu'est-ce qui se passe?   *What's going on?*

3. Use the long forms **Qui est-ce qu(e)** and **Qu'est-ce que** when **je** is the subject of the sentence.

    Qu'est-ce que je vais faire?   *What am I going to do?*
NOT Que vais-je faire?
    Qui est-ce que je devrais remercier?   *Who(m) should I thank?*
NOT Qui devrais-je remercier?

4. In all other cases, you may use either the long or short form.

Long form	Short form	Function
Qu'est-ce qu(e)	OR Qu(e) . . . ?	direct object
Qui est-ce qu(e)	OR Qui . . . ?	direct object
Qui est-ce qui	OR Qui . . . ?	subject

EXERCISE 9-5: Give the short form of each of the following questions. If there is no appropriate short form, repeat the sentence as it is given. Answers and translations are at the end of the chapter.

    1. Qui est-ce qu'il faut voir?
    2. Qu'est-ce que nous devrions apporter?
    3. Qui est-ce qui favorise cette solution?
    4. A qui est-ce que je ressemble?
    5. Avec quoi est-ce qu'on arrose les plantes?
    6. Qu'est-ce qui ne va pas?
    7. Qu'est-ce que je ferai la prochaine fois?
    8. Pour qui est-ce que tu as fait tout ce travail?
    9. Qu'est-ce que cela vous fait?
   10. Qui est-ce que Pierre accompagnait?

EXERCISE 9-6: Ask the following questions using the long form of the interrogative pronoun. Answers and translations are at the end of the chapter.

    1. Que dis-tu?
    2. Qui a la balle?
    3. Qui accuse-t-il?
    4. Que devient-elle?
    5. Qui l'aurait cru?
    6. Que ferons-nous?
    7. Qui proposent-ils?
    8. Que suggérez-vous?
    9. Qui est venu te chercher?
   10. Que mangerons-nous?

9-3. Interrogative Adjectives

The interrogative adjective **quel**, *which*, *what*, agrees in gender and number with a following noun, or stands in its place as a pronoun when the subject noun follows a form of **être**.

A. Forms of the interrogative adjective

	Singular	Plural	
Masculine	quel	quels	*which, what*
Feminine	quelle	quelles	

EXERCISE 9-7:   Use interrogative adjectives to ask the questions for which these are the answers. Answers and translations are at the end of the chapter.

Example: Nous prenons ce livre-là.   *We're taking that book.*

Quel livre prenez-vous?   *Which book are you taking?*

1. Nous suivons l'autoroute du sud.
2. Ils ont pris ma clé.
3. Le chapitre 10 présente le subjonctif.
4. Il est 8 heures.
5. Je note la différence.
6. Mes examens sont les meilleurs.
7. Napoléon 1er est mort en 1821.
8. Elle avait envie de visiter les pays scandinaves.
9. On regarde les émissions culturelles à la télévision.
10. Cet autre train part pour Marseille.

B. Exclamations with quel

Use **quel** in exclamations with the same meaning as *What (a)...!* in English. In an exclamation, **quel** cannot be followed by an article.

Quelle pagaïe!	*What a mess!*
Quel pessimisme insensé!	*What senseless pessimism!*
Quel toupet!	*What (a) nerve!*

EXERCISE 9-8:   Make an appropriate exclamation in response to each of the following statements. Answers and translations are at the end of the chapter.

Example: Cet examen est impossible!   *This test is impossible!*

Quel examen impossible!   *What an impossible test!*

1. Mon père est formidable!
2. Ces enfants sont adorables!
3. Le temps est splendide!
4. Votre énergie est impressionante!
5. Cet exercice est facile!

C. Quel as an interrogative pronoun

Quel may stand alone as an interrogative pronoun in subject position if the subject noun follows the verb **être**. In this case, **quel** takes its gender and number from the subject noun.

| **Quels** seront les **résultats**? | *What will the results be?* |
| **Quelle** est la **différence**? | *What's the difference?* |

EXERCISE 9-9:   Replace the expression **il y a** with the appropriate form of the verb **être** and a following subject. Answers and translations are at the end of the chapter.

Example: Quelle différence y aura-t-il?   *What difference will there be?*

Quelle sera la différence?   *What will be the difference?*

1. Quels vins y avait-il?
2. Quelles objections y aurait-il?
3. Quelle atmosphère y a-t-il?
4. Quel menu y aura-t-il?
5. Quelle réponse y avait-il?

9-4. Interrogative Pronouns

When you ask a question about someone or something already referred to by a specific noun, use a form of the pronoun **lequel**, *which, which one*. Unlike quel, **lequel** may function as a subject, a direct or indirect object, or the object of a preposition.

A. Formation of interrogative pronouns

The interrogative pronoun **lequel** is a combination of the definite article—**le**, **la**, or **les**—and the interrogative adjective **quel**.

	Singular	Plural	
Masculine	**lequel**	**lesquels**	*which, which one(s)*
Feminine	**laquelle**	**lesquelles**	*which, which one(s)*

The preposition **à** or **de** immediately preceding **lequel** or **lesquel(le)s** forms the following contractions:

à + lequel = **auquel**
à + lesquels = **auxquels**
à + lesquelles = **auxquelles**
de + lequel = **duquel**
de + lesquels = **desquels**
de + lesquelles = **desquelles**

B. Use of interrogative pronouns

Use the interrogative pronoun to ask a question concerning someone or something referred to by a specific noun:

1. as the subject

   Je vois **des voitures**.   *I see some cars.*
       Laquelle t'appartient?   *Which one belongs to you?*

2. as the direct object

   Il nous offre **des billets**.   *He's offering us tickets.*
       Lesquels prend-on?   *Which ones do we take?*

3. as the indirect object

   Tes parents sont grands.   *Your parents are tall.*
       Auquel ressembles-tu?   *Which one do you take after?*

4. as the object of a preposition

   Il y a trop **de tiroirs**.   *There are too many drawers.*
       Dans lequel met-il ses papiers?   *Which one does he put his papers in?*

   NOTE: Even in casual spoken French—which does allow some stranded prepositions—never end a sentence with **à** or **de**.

EXERCISE 9-10: Replace the interrogative noun phrase with the appropriate interrogative pronoun. Answers and translations are at the end of the chapter.

   Example: Quelles difficultés prévoyez-vous?   *What difficulties do you foresee?*
          Lesquelles prévoyez-vous?   *Which (ones) do you foresee?*

1. Quel vin désirez-vous?
2. Quelle était la classe qu'ils préféraient?
3. Quels journaux ont publié les résultats?
4. Quelle est la plus grande ville des Etats-Unis?
5. A quel restaurant dinerions-nous?
6. De quels articles parle-t-il?
7. Pour quelles raisons a-t-elle refusé de parler?
8. A quels étudiants donnerons-nous les prix?
9. De quel siècle est ce tableau?
10. Quelle question ne comprenez-vous pas?

9-5. Relative Pronouns

A relative pronoun introduces a relative clause—a subordinate clause which modifies a noun in the main clause. Study the following table of relative pronouns.

Relative pronoun		Function
qui	*who, which, that*	subject of the verb
que	*whom, which, that*	direct object of the verb
quoi	*whom, which*	object of a preposition
lequel, laquelle	*whom, which*	object of a preposition
lesquels, lesquelles	*whom, which*	object of a preposition
dont	*whose, of whom, of which*	

A. Relative pronouns with adjective clauses

An adjective clause describes an immediately preceding noun. The form of the relative pronoun that introduces the adjective clause varies according to its function.

1. The relative pronoun **qui**, *who, which, that*, introduces an adjective clause as the subject of that clause. **Qui** is invariable—standing for persons or things, masculine or feminine, singular or plural.

> Elle porte des bottes **qui ont coûté dix mille francs.**
>
> *She's wearing boots that cost ten thousand francs.*
>
> J'ai vu un acteur **qui jouait extrêmement bien dans cette pièce.**
>
> *I saw an actor who acted extremely well in that play.*

> **NOTE:** The relative pronoun **qui** usually comes right before its verb.

> J'aime regarder les trains **qui passent**.
>
> *I like to watch passing trains.*

> **REMEMBER:** Do not confuse the interrogative **Qui ... ?** meaning *Who(m) ... ?* with the relative pronoun **qui** which simply refers to any preceding noun.

EXERCISE 9-11: Combine each pair of sentences into a single sentence with an adjective clause. Answers and translations are at the end of the chapter.

> Example: J'admire sa secrétaire. Elle tape cents mots à la minute.
>
> *I admire her secretary. She types a hundred words a minute.*
>
> J'admire sa secrétaire qui tape cents mots à la minute.
>
> *I admire her secretary who types a hundred words a minute.*

1. Cet exercice prend dix minutes. Il n'est pas difficile.
2. On admire beaucoup mon père. Il parle cinq langues.
3. J'ai donné une montre à ma soeur. Elle est en or.
4. La radio est en réparation. Elle faisait du bruit.
5. Madrid est la plus grande ville d'Espagne. C'est la capitale.
6. Regarde toutes ces voitures! Elles circulent à toute vitesse.
7. Tu feras la queue devant le restaurant. Il est plein de monde.
8. Nous aimerions annoncer les nouvelles à la famille. Elles sont excellentes.
9. Les responsables ont refusé de faire la grève. Ils sont très bien payés.
10. Il y a un nouveau film en ville. Il est en anglais.

2. The relative pronoun **que**, *who, which, that*, introduces an adjective clause and is itself the direct object of that clause.

> C'est la seule chose **que je ne comprends pas**.
>
> *It's the only thing (that) I don't understand.*

> **NOTE:** Never omit **que** in French—even though we often omit *that* in English.

Le jeune homme **que** je vous ai presenté s'appelle Paul.	*The young man (that) I introduced to you is named Paul.*
C'est le restaurant **que** je vous ai recommandé.	*It is the restaurant (that) I recommended to you.*

> *NOTE:* The subject of the adjective clause *usually*—but not always—follows the relative pronoun **que**.

C'est le même modèle
que mon père conduit.

OR

It's the same model (that) my father drives.

C'est le même modèle
que conduit **mon père**.

In French, the choice of **que** rather than the word order makes the meaning of the second version clear.

> *REMEMBER:* Do not confuse the relative pronoun **que**, *that*, which can refer to persons and to things, with the interrogative **Que . . . ?**, *What . . . ?* which never refers to persons.

EXERCISE 9-12: Combine each pair of sentences into a single sentence with an adjective clause. Answers and translations are at the end of the chapter.

Example:	Le rendez-vous est déjà annulé.	The date is already off.
	Je l'ai pris hier.	I made it yesterday.
	Le rendez-vous que j'ai pris hier est déjà annulé.	The date (that) I made yesterday is already off.

1. Cette montre ne marche pas. Je l'ai achetée en solde.
2. Les gens sont sympathiques. Nous les inviterons.
3. Ils ont annoncé des réformes. On les attendait depuis longtemps.
4. Un monsieur vous attend dehors. Je ne le connais pas.
5. Le train est parti à midi. Nous l'avons manqué.
6. Ce bâtiment va être démoli. Tu le vois au coin de la rue.
7. La jeune fille s'appelle Odette. Il la voit beaucoup.
8. Notre jardin produit des légumes. Nous les vendons.
9. Ce poste transmet de la musique classique. Je l'adore.
10. L'exercice était bien clair. Vous venez de le terminer.

EXERCISE 9-13: Combine each pair of sentences into a single sentence with an adjective clause introduced by **qui** or **que**, depending on whether the relative is the *subject* or *direct object* of the following clause. Answers and translations are at the end of the chapter.

1. Un journal paraît une fois par semaine. Il s'appelle un hebdomadaire.
2. Ce tableau représente les horreurs de la guerre. Picasso l'a peint.
3. Le café est trop fort. Ma belle-soeur nous le sert.
4. J'ai passé un coup de téléphone transatlantique. Il m'a coûté 32 dollars.
5. Ce manuel explique la grammaire française. Tu devrais l'acheter.
6. L'anglais britannique n'est pas pareil à l'américain. On le parle en Angleterre.
7. La musique moderne est quelquefois dissonante. Je ne l'apprécie pas beaucoup.
8. Mes parents ont une grande piscine. Elle est derrière leur maison.
9. La politique est un art. Il n'a pas de règles.
10. Mon amie Anne m'a donné une plante. Je l'arrose régulièrement.

3. Use the relative pronoun **lequel**—**lesquels, laquelle, lesquelles**—to introduce an adjective clause preceded by a preposition.

Un crayon, c'est un instrument **avec lequel on écrit.**	*A pencil is an instrument you write with.*
Ce sont des produits **desquels on dit beaucoup de bien.**	*These are products they say a lot of good things about.*
Tu parles de choses **auxquelles je préfère ne pas penser.**	*You're talking about things I'd rather not think about.*
Il a une fiancée **sans laquelle il ne peut pas vivre.**	*He has a fiancee he can't live without.*

EXERCISE 9-14: Combine each pair of sentences into a single sentence with an adjective clause preceded by a preposition. Answers and translations are at the end of the chapter.

Example: Je vois souvent mon beau frère.	*I see my brother-in-law often.*
J'ai beaucoup de respect pour lui.	*I have a lot of respect for him.*
Je vois souvent mon beau frère pour qui j'ai beaucoup de respect.	*I often see my brother-in-law for whom I have a lot of respect.*

1. Il y a un grand bâtiment en briques rouges. Derrière ce bâtiment vous trouverez des garages.
2. Je vous présente mon professeur. Grâce à lui j'ai eu une bourse d'études.
3. Les enfants font des bêtises. Ils sont punis pour ces bêtises.
4. Nous avons plusieurs camarades canadiens. Leur langue maternelle est le français.
5. Paris est une grande capitale. Dans cette capitale, il y a toujours des étrangers.
6. Stendhal est un nom de plume. Henri Beyle écrivait sous ce nom.
7. C'était la même année. Dans cette année il n'y a pas eu de neige.
8. L'amour est une émotion positive. Sans l'amour la vie n'a pas beaucoup de sens.
9. J'ai des cousins au Canada. Je leur envoie des journaux français.
10. Nous habitons près d'un lac. Sur les bords de ce lac, il y a de belles villas.
11. Dans notre rue il y a une église. A côté de l'église il y a un parc.
12. C'est mon bistro favori. Je m'assieds devant ce bistro pour prendre mon café.
13. On voit toutes sortes de gens. La raison d'être de ces gens, c'est l'argent.
14. Ils sont enfin arrivés au cinéma. Devant le cinéma il y avait une foule énorme.
15. C'est un petit exercice pratique. A la fin de cet exercice je comprends mieux les pronoms relatifs.

4. You may use the relative pronouns **qui**, *who(m)*, **dont**, *whose*, *of whom*, *of which*, or the adverb **où**, *where*, *when*, as less precise—but equally correct—alternatives to **lequel** in certain instances.

- You may use **qui** after a preposition to introduce an adjective clause describing a person.

Il admire son **beau-père pour lequel / qu'** il travaille.	*He admires his father-in-law for whom he works.*
C'est le seul **ami auquel / à qui** je n'ai rien à dire.	*He's the only friend I have nothing to say to.*

- You may use **dont**, *whose*, *of whom*, *of which*, as a synonym for the relative pronouns **de laquelle**, **duquel**, **desquels**, **desquelles**, or **de qui**. Since **dont** is invariable, it is used more frequently than the longer forms.

J'ai un **ami de qui / dont** le père est banquier.	*I have a friend whose father is a banker.*
Nous apporterons les **livres desquels / dont** vous avez besoin.	*We'll bring the books you need.*

• You may use the adverbial of time and place **où**, *where, when,* in place of a relative pronoun before an adjective clause referring either to time or place.

C'est un endroit **où** nous voyageons beaucoup.	*It's a place we travel to (where we travel) a lot.*
On ne l'a pas vu le jour **où** il est revenu.	*We didn't see him the day he returned.*

EXERCISE 9-15: Repeat Exercise 9-14, but this time use alternatives to the different forms of **lequel** whenever possible. Answers and translations at the end of the chapter.

B. Relative pronouns with noun clauses

A relative clause that is not preceded by a noun functions as a noun phrase. In this case, use one of the demonstrative pronouns—**ce**, **celui**, **ceux**, **celle(s)**—before the relative pronoun in place of the noun, unless the relative pronoun means *who.*

1. Use **qui** followed by a singular verb to introduce a noun clause referring to an indefinite person or persons.

Il est impossible de prévoir **qui gagnera**.	*It's impossible to foresee who will win.*
Nous ne savons pas à **qui** nous **fier**.	*We don't know whom to trust.*

2. Use **ce** before the relative pronoun if the noun clause refers to something indefinite.

Je ne comprends pas **ce que** vous voulez dire.	*I don't understand what you mean.*
Prenez **ce qui** reste pour vos enfants.	*Take what's left for your children.*
Personne ne savait **ce dont** il avait besoin.	*Nobody knew what he needed.*

EXERCISE 9-16: Answer each of the following questions by saying **je ne sais pas**, *I don't know*, before each response. Answers and translations are at the end of the chapter.

Example: Que font ces enfants?	*What are those children doing?*
Je ne sais pas ce que font ces enfants.	
OR	*I don't know what those children are doing.*
Je ne sais pas ce que ces enfants font.	

1. Qui est cette dame?
2. Qu'est-ce que ce mot veut dire?
3. Qu'est-ce qui irrite le professeur?
4. Qui est-ce qui gagnera les élections?
5. Que ferons-nous ensuite?
6. Qu'y a-t-il dans le réfrigérateur?
7. Qui accompagne-t-il?
8. Qu'est-ce qu'on devrait répondre?
9. Qui est-ce qui est assis là-bas?
10. Qu'est-ce qui suit cet exercice?

3. Use a demonstrative pronoun—**celui**, **ceux**, **celle(s)**—of the appropriate gender and number before a relative pronoun if the noun clause refers to a person or thing whose gender and number is specified.

Le disque que j'ai est meilleur **que celui** qui va suivre.	*The record I have is better than the one coming out.*
Cette photo est **celle** **de laquelle** / **dont** tout le monde parle.	*This picture is the one everyone is talking about.*

Ceux qui ne veulent pas travailler sont paresseux.

Those (men and women) who refuse to work are lazy.

Nous avons offert nos places **à celles qui entraient**.

We offered our seats to those (females) who came in.

> *NOTE:* Use **qui**, *who(m)*, alone to introduce a noun clause with a broader meaning.

Qui ne veut pas travailler est paresseux.

Whoever refuses to work is lazy.

Nous avons offert nos places à **qui** entrait.

We offered our seats to whoever entered.

EXERCISE 9-17: Replace the noun or noun phrase before each adjective clause with the appropriate form of the demonstrative pronoun. Answers and translation are at the end of the chapter.

Example: Je préfère les fleurs qui sentent bon.   *I prefer flowers that smell good.*

Je préfère celles qui sentent bon.   *I like the ones that smell good (good smelling ones).*

1. Quel est ce bâtiment que je vois?
2. Il m'a apporté tous ses livres qui sont en français.
3. On aura les avantages dont les autres étaient privés.
4. C'est la femme de laquelle on a fait tant de portraits.
5. Ma tante est la personne à qui je ressemble le plus.
6. Il faudra répéter la phrase que je n'ai pas comprise.
7. J'aimerais bien voir la maison dans laquelle elle est née.
8. Connaissez-vous ce monsieur dont l'épouse est chilienne?
9. Je crois que c'est le film auquel je pense.
10. Répétez les questions auxquelles vous avez mal répondu!

EXERCISE 9-18: Answer the questions with a form of **celui qui**, **celui que**, or **celui dont**. Answers and translations are at the end of the chapter.

Example: Je le connais, et vous?   *I know him, and you?*

Non, je ne connais pas celui que vous connaissez.   *No, I don't know the one you know.*

J'ai besoin de cette carte, et vous?   *I need this map, and you?*

Non, je n'ai pas besoin de celle dont vous avez besoin.   *No, I don't need the one you need.*

Ce problème m'intrigue, et vous?   *That problem intrigues me, and you?*

Non, celui qui vous intrigue ne m'intrigue pas.   *No, the one that intrigues you doesn't intrigue me.*

1. Nous avons peur de ces chiens, et vous?
2. Il verra ce film, et toi?
3. Ces habitudes m'agacent, et vous?
4. Je m'occuperai de cette affaire, et vous?
5. Sa soeur me fascine, et toi?

SUMMARY

1. Question formation varies according to the situation—use **Est-ce que** . . . or a rising intonation in an informal situation, and subject pronoun/verb inversion in written or formal French.
2. When the subject of a question is a noun, repeat the subject after the verb using a third person pronoun of the same number and gender.

3. Indefinite interrogative pronouns include short forms—**qui** (subject), **que** (object), **quoi** (after a preposition)—and long forms—**qui est-ce qui** (subject), **qui est-ce que, qu'est-ce que** (object). These forms are interchangeable unless the subject is **je**, when the long form must be used.
4. An interrogative adjective—**quel, quels, quelle, quelles**—agrees in number and gender with the noun it qualifies.
5. An interrogative pronoun—**lequel, lesquels, laquelle, lesquelles**—replaces **quel** plus a noun already mentioned. The interrogative pronoun agrees with this noun in number and gender. **Lequel** is contracted to **auquel** when used with **à**, and to **duquel** when used with **de**.
6. Interrogative pronouns may be subjects, direct or indirect objects, and objects of prepositions.
7. Relative pronouns introduce an adjective clause. **Qui** is used as subject for persons or things, and **que** as object for persons or things.
8. A demonstrative pronoun—**ce, celui, ceux, celles**—precedes a relative pronoun if the noun clause refers to a person or thing whose number and gender is specified.

RAISE YOUR GRADES

Interrogatives

Fill in the blanks with a one-word interrogative. Answers and translations are at the end of the chapter.

1. J'ai deux oranges? _____ des deux veux-tu?
2. _____ est l'importance de cette idée?
3. _____ préparez-vous pour manger ce soir?
4. _____ gentille petite fille!
5. _____ aurait-cru qu'elle réussirait?
6. Avec _____ se lave-t-on les dents?
7. Ce sont de beaux jeunes gens! _____ est ton cousin?
8. _____ est le meilleur livre de l'année?
9. _____? Cela, c'est une grande surprise!
10. _____ boit-on normalement après un repas.
11. _____ est ce monsieur sur la photo?
12. De _____ parlez-vous maintenant?
13. _____ est la date de demain?
14. _____ de tous ces gens sont tes parents?
15. _____ chemin serait le plus court?

Rewrite the following questions, replacing the short interrogatives with the long forms. Answers and translations are at the end of the chapter.

16. Avec qui sortez-vous ce week-end?
17. Qu'allons-nous faire sans voiture?
18. Qui s'occupera des enfants?
19. Qu'en penses-tu?
20. Qui achètera cette monstruosité?
21. Que reste-t-il de cette salade?
22. Qu'y a-t-il dans cette soupe?
23. Pour qui faites-vous toute cette parade?
24. Qui ira chercher les journaux pour nous?
25. A quoi rêves-tu?

Relative pronouns

Fill in the blanks with the correct relative or demonstrative pronoun. Answers and translations are at the end of the chapter.

26. On ne peut pas savoir _____ les jeunes pensent.
27. C'est le seul désavantage _____ je vois.
28. J'admire la patience avec _____ il travaille.

29. Tu n'auras pas la meilleure note; tu auras _____ tu mérites.
30. J'habite un appartement _____ les propriétaires sont à Paris.
31. Il y a toujours quelque chose _____ sent mauvais chez lui.
32. C'est une famille dans _____ tout le monde travaille.
33. Il vaut mieux dire _____ l'on pense.
34. Si tu ne fais pas attention, il mangera _____ en reste.
35. Il était difficile de prévoir _____ nous aurions besoin.
36. Parmi ses amis elle préfère _____ sont sportifs.
37. Les vêtements _____ j'ai achetés étaient bon marché.
38. _____ vous voyez dans la photo sont mes cousines.
39. Ce professeur est _____ tout le monde a peur.
40. Est-ce que c'est le téléphone _____ sonne?
41. On fait _____ on peut!
42. Tout _____ brille n'est pas d'or.
43. Les meilleurs vins sont _____ l'appelation est contrôlée.
44. Tu passeras devant deux bâtiments entre _____ tu verras une allée.
45. Il est certain que cet exercice est plus facile que _____ vous avez vus dans la leçon précédente.

Replace the words in parentheses in each sentence with one word without changing the meaning of the sentence. Answers and translations are at the end of the chapter.

46. (Les gens) qui se plaignent tout le temps ont tort.
47. On tient à connaître cette dame (de laquelle) le mari est un artiste.
48. C'est un célèbre musée (à l'intérieur duquel) il y a une collection impressionante.
49. (La chose) qui me fascine, c'est son enthousiasme.
50. Voilà un étudiant (de qui) on aura des nouvelles un jour.
51. Parmi ces femmes, (les femmes) qui ont fini leurs études sont les plus heureuses.
52. C'est un endroit (auquel) je vais régulièrement.
53. Ses parents ne sont pas irrités par (les choses) qu'il fait.
54. (Celui qui) vivra, verra.
55. Il faut choisir des dates (auxquelles) il n'y aura pas de conflit.

Yes/no questions

Ask all the yes/no questions for which these sentences are logical answers. Answers and translations are at the end of the chapter.

Example:	Nous déjeunons à onze heures.	*We have lunch at eleven o'clock.*
	Est-ce que vous déjeunez à onze heures?	*Do you have lunch at eleven o'clock?*
	Déjeunez-vous à onze heures?	
	Vous déjeunez à onze heures?	

56. Anne est allée à la plage avec son petit neveu.
57. La lettre **n** suit la lettre **m** dans l'alphabet.
58. Je vois le lac par la fenêtre de mon appartement.
59. Le locataire allumait la lampe pour lire.
60. Le manuscrit arrivera demain matin.

CHAPTER ANSWERS

EXERCISE 9-1:

1. Est-ce que leur sincérité est en question? *Is their sincerity in question?*
2. Est-ce que nous étions ici pour écouter la conférence? *Were we here in order to listen to the lecture?*
3. Est-ce qu'elle promet son aide pour le dîner? *Does she promise her help for dinner?*
4. Est-ce qu'il y a des erreurs dans son examen? *Are there some mistakes on his (her) test?*
5. Est-ce que c'est aujourd'hui le 3 juillet? *Is today the third of July?*

6. Est-ce que quelqu'un a sonné à la porte? *Did someone knock at the door?*

7. Est-ce que Françoise est retournée en France cet été? *Has Françoise returned to France this summer?*

8. Est-ce qu'un autre répondrait à sa place? *Would another answer in his (her) place? Would someone answer for him (her)?*

9. Est-ce que la valise contiendra des papiers importants? *Will the suitcase contain some important papers?*

10. Est-ce que tu sais ce que tu fais? *Do you know what you are doing?*

EXERCISE 9-2:

1. Comprenez-vous tout cela? *Do you understand all this?*

2. Paiera-t-il à la fin du mois? *Will he pay at the end of the month?*

3. Quand as-tu passé tes examens semestriels? *When did you finish your final exams?*

4. Regarde-t-elle beaucoup la télévision? *Does she watch a lot of television?*

5. Irait-on au mariage? *Would they go to the wedding?*

6. Avec qui sortirez-vous ce soir? *Who will you go out with this evening?*

7. Buvons-nous du champagne? *Do we drink some champagne?*

8. Lisent-elles les journaux tous les jours? *Do they read the paper every day?*

9. Pourquoi avez-vous dit ceci? *Why did you say that?*

10. Où étudiait-il la musique? *Where did he study music?*

EXERCISE 9-3:

1. Lucie et Jérôme connaissent-ils vos parents? *Do Lucie and Jerome know your parents?*

2. Pourquoi votre ami était-il si timide? *Why was your friend so shy?*

3. La France est-elle plus grande que l'Italie? *Is France larger than Italy?*

4. La définition serait-elle dans le dictionnaire? *Would the definition be in the dictionary?*

5. Ce restaurant sera-t-il ouvert lundi? *Will this restaurant open Monday?*

6. Quand les feuilles jaunissent-elles? *When do the leaves turn yellow?*

7. Comment la cuisinière a-t-elle préparé ce plat? *How did the chef prepare this dish?*

8. Leur permis est-il toujours valable? *Is their pass always valid?*

9. Henri est-il parti avant vous? *Did Henry leave before you?*

10. Qui votre frère accompagne-t-il ce soir? *Who is your brother going with this evening?*

EXERCISE 9-4:

1. Qui va venir demain? *Who is going to come tomorrow?*

2. Que vouliez-vous voir? *What did you want to see?*

3. Qui s'est occupé des enfants? *Who took care of the children?*

4. Avec qui a-t-elle voyagé? *Who did she travel with?*

5. De quoi ont-ils besoin? *What do they need?*

6. Que verriez-vous? *What would you see?*

7. Qui vous aidera? *Who will help you?*

8. A quoi pensent-elles? *What are they thinking about?*

9. Qui avait laissé un message? *Who left a message?*

10. A qui auriez-vous fait attention? *To whom would you pay attention?*

EXERCISE 9-5:

1. Qui faut-il voir? *Who is it necessary to see? Who must you see?*

2. Que devrions-nous apporter? *What should we bring?*

3. Qui favorise cette solution? *Who is in favor of this solution?*

4. A qui est-ce que je ressemble? *Who(m) do I resemble?*

5. Avec quoi arrose-t-on les plantes? *What do they water thee plants with?*

6. Qu'est-ce qui ne va pas? *What isn't going well?*

7. Qu'est-ce que je ferai la prochaine fois? *What will I do next time?*

8. Pour qui as-tu fait tout ce travail? *For whom have you done all this work?*

9. Qu'est-ce que cela vous fait? *What is that you are doing?*

10. Qui Pierre accompagnait-il? *Who was Pierre accompanying?*

EXERCISE 9-6:

1. Qu'est-ce que tu dis? *What are you saying?*

2. Qui est-ce qui a la balle? *Who has the ball?*

3. Qui est-ce qu'il accuse? *Who is he accusing?*

4. Qu'est-ce qu'elle devient? *What is she becoming?*

5. Qui est-ce qui l'aurait cru? *Who would have believed it?*

6. Qu'est-ce que nous ferons? *What will we do?*

7. Qui est-ce qu'ils proposent? *Who are they proposing?*

8. Qu'est-ce que vous suggérez? *What are you suggesting?*

9. Qui est-ce qui est venu te chercher? *Who is coming to get you?*

10. Qu'est-ce que nous mangerons? *What will we eat?*

EXERCISE 9-7:

1. Quelle autoroute suivez-vous? *Which highway are we taking?*

2. Quelle clé ont-ils prise? *Which key have they taken?*

3. Quel chapitre présente le subjonctif? *Which chapter presents the subjunctive?*

4. Quelle heure est-il? *What time is it?*

5. Quelle différence notez-vous? *What difference do you notice?*

6. Quels examens sont les meilleurs? *Which tests are the best?*

7. En quelle année Napoléon 1ᵉʳ est-il mort? *In what year did Napoleon I die?*

8. Quel pays avait-elle envie de visiter? *Which country did she want to visit?*

9. Quelles émissions regarde-t-on à la télévision? *Which programs do they watch on television?*

10. Quel train part pour Marseille? *Which train leaves for Marseilles?*

EXERCISE 9-8:

1. Quel père formidable! *What a formidable father!*

2. Quels enfants adorables! *What adorable children!*

3. Quel temps splendide! *What splendid weather!*

4. Quelle énergie impressionante! *What impressive energy!*

5. Quel exercice facile! *What an easy exercise!*

EXERCISE 9-9:

1. Quels étaient les vins? *Which were the wines?*

2. Quelles seraient les objections? *What were the objections?*

3. Quelle est l'atmosphère? *What is the atmosphere?*

4. Quel sera le menu? *What will the menu be?*

5. Quelle était la réponse? *What was the response?*

EXERCISE 9-10:

1. Lequel désirez-vous? *Which one do you desire?*

2. Laquelle préféraient-ils? *Which one do they prefer?*

3. Lesquels ont publié les résultats? *Which ones published the results?*

4. Laquelle est la plus grande des Etats-Unis? *Which one is the largest in the United States?*

5. Auquel dînerions-nous? *At which one shall we dine?*

6. Desquels parle-t-il? *Which ones does he talk about?*

7. Pour lesquelles a-t-elle refusé de parler? *For which ones has she refused to speak?*

8. Auxquels donnerons-nous les prix? *To which ones shall we give the prizes?*

9. Duquel est ce tableau? *From which is this painting?*

10. Laquelle ne comprenez-vous pas? *Which one don't you understand?*

EXERCISE 9-11:

1. Cet exercice, qui n'est pas difficile, prend dix minutes. *This exercise, which is not difficult, takes ten minutes.*

2. On admire beaucoup mon père qui parle cinq langues. *People very much admire my father who speaks five languages.*

3. J'ai donné une montre qui est en or à ma soeur. *I gave a watch, which is gold, to my sister.*

4. La radio, qui faisait du bruit, est en réparation. *The radio that made noise is being repaired.*

5. Madrid, qui est la capitale, est la plus grande ville d'Espagne. *Madrid, which is the capital, is the largest city in Spain.*

6. Regarde toutes ces voitures qui circulent à toute vitesse! *Look at all these cars that travel so fast!*

7. Tu feras la queue devant le restaurant qui est plein de monde. *Form a line in front of the restaurant which is full of people.*

8. Nous aimerions annoncer les nouvelles, qui sont excellentes, à la famille. *We would like to announce the news, which is excellent, to the family.*

9. Les responsables, qui sont très bien payés, ont refusé de faire le grève. *Those responsible, who are very well paid, refused to strike.*

10. Il y a un nouveau film, qui est en anglais, en ville. *There is a new film, which is in English, in town.*

EXERCISE 9-12:

1. Cette montre que j'ai achetée en solde ne marche pas. *This watch (that) I bought on sale doesn't work.*

2. Les gens que nous inviterons sont sympathiques. *The people that we are going to invite are pleasing.*

3. Ils ont annoncé des réformes qu'on attendait depuis longtemps. *They announced reforms that we waited a long time for.*

4. Un monsieur que je ne connais pas vous attend dehors. *A gentleman that I don't know is waiting for you outside.*

5. Le train que nous avons manqué est parti à midi. *The train that we missed left at noon.*

6. Ce bâtiment que tu vois au coin de la rue va être démoli. *That building that you saw at the corner of the street is going to be demolished.*

7. La jeune fille qu'il voit beaucoup s'appelle Odette. *The young woman that he sees a lot is called Odette.*

8. Notre jardin produit des légumes que nous vendons. *Our garden produces vegetables that we sell.*

9. Ce poste transmet de la musique classique que j'adore. *This station broadcasts classical music that I adore.*

10. L'exercice que vous venez de terminer était bien clair. *The exercise that you have just finished is very clear.*

EXERCISE 9-13:

1. Un journal qui paraît une fois par semaine s'appelle un hebdomadaire. *A journal that comes out once a week is called a weekly.*

2. Ce tableau, que Picasso a peint, représente les horreurs de la guerre. *This painting, which Picasso painted, represents the horrors of war.*

3. Le café que ma belle soeur nous sert est trop fort. *The coffee that my sister-in-law serves us is too strong.*

4. J'ai passé un coup de téléphone transatlantique qui m'a coûté 32 dollars. *I made a transatlantic telephone call that cost me 32 dollars.*

5. Ce manuel, que tu devrais acheter, explique la grammaire française. *This handbook, which you ought to buy, explains French grammar.*

6. L'anglais britannique qu'on parle en Angleterre n'est pas pareil à l'américain. *The British English that one speaks in England is not the same as American English.*

7. La musique moderne, que je n'apprécie pas beaucoup, est quelquefois dissonante. *Modern music, which I don't appreciate very much, is sometimes dissonant.*

8. Mes parents ont une grande piscine qui est derrière leur maison. *My parents have a large swimming pool which is behind their house.*

9. La politique est un art qui n'a pas de règles. *Politics is an art that has no rules.*

10. Mon amie Anne m'a donné une plante que j'arrose régulièrement. *My friend Anne gave me a plant that I water regularly.*

EXERCISE 9-14:

1. Il y a un grand bâtiment en briques rouges derrière lequel vous trouverez des garages. *There is a large red-brick building behind which you will find some garages.*

2. Je vous présente mon professeur grâce auquel j'ai eu une bourse d'études. *I would like to present my professor, thanks to whom I got a scholarship.*

3. Les enfants font des bêtises pour lesquelles ils sont punis. *Children make mistakes for which they are punished.*

4. Nous avons plusieurs camarades canadiens desquels la langue maternelle est le français. *We have several Canadian friends whose mother tongue is French.*

5. Paris est une grande capitale dans laquelle il y a toujours des étrangers. *Paris is a great capital in which there are always foreigners.*

6. Stendhal est le nom de plume sous lequel Henri Beyle écrivait (OR ... sous lequel écrivait Henri Beyle). *Stendhal is the pen name under which Henri Beyle wrote.*

7. C'était la même année dans laquelle il n'y a pas eu de neige. *It was the same year in which there was no snow.*

8. L'amour est une émotion positive sans laquelle la vie n'a pas beaucoup de sens. *Love is a positive emotion without which life hasn't a lot of sense.*

9. J'ai des cousins au Canada auxquels j'envoie des journaux français. *I have cousins in Canada to whom I send French papers.*

10. Nous habitons près d'un lac sur les bords duquel il y a de belles villas. *We live near a lake on the banks of which there are beautiful villas.*

11. Dans notre rue il y a une église à côté de laquelle il y a un parc. *On our street there is a church next to which there is a park.*

12. C'est mon bistro favori devant lequel je m'assieds pour prendre mon café. *It is my favorite cafe in front of which I sit to have my coffee.*

13. On voit toutes sortes de gens pour lesquels la raison d'être, c'est l'argent. *One sees all sorts of people whose reason to live is money.*

14. Ils sont enfin arrivés au cinéma devant lequel il y avait une foule énorme. *They finally arrived at the theater in front of which there was an enormous crowd.*

15. C'est un petit exercice pratique à la fin duquel je comprends mieux les pronoms relatifs. *This is a short, practical exercise at the end of which I understand relative pronouns better.*

EXERCISE 9-15:

1. Il y a un grand bâtiment en briques rouges derrière lequel vous trouverez des garages. *There is a large building of red brick behind which you will find some garages.*

2. Je vous présente mon professeur grace à qui j'ai eu une bourse d'études. *I would like you to meet my professor thanks to whom I got a scholarship.*

3. Les enfants font des bêtises pour lesquelles ils sont punis. *Children make mistakes for which they are punished.*

4. Nous avons plusieurs camarades canadiens dont (de qui) la langue maternelle est le français. *We have several Canadian friends whose mother tongue is French.*

5. Paris est une grande capitale où il y a toujours des étrangers. *Paris is a great capital where there are always foreigners.*

6. Stendhal est le nom de plume sous lequel Henri Beyle écrivait (OR ... sous lequel écrivait Henri Beyle). *Stendhal is a pen name under which Henri Beyle wrote.*

7. C'était la même année où il n'y a pas eu de neige. *It was the same year when there was no snow.*

8. L'amour est une émotion positive sans laquelle la vie n'a pas beaucoup de sens. *Love is a positive emotion without which life hasn't a lot of sense.*

9. J'ai des cousins au Canada à qui j'envoie des journaux français. *I have cousins in Canada to whom I send French papers.*

10. Rabelais est un célèbre auteur français dont (de qui) le Gargantua fait rire tout le monde.

Rabelais is a famous French author whose Gargantua made everyone laugh.

11. Dans notre rue il y a une église à côté de laquelle il y a un parc. *On our street there is a church next to which there is a park.*

12. C'est mon bistro favori devant lequel je m'assieds pour prendre mon café. *It is my favorite cafe in front of which I sit to have my coffee.*

13. On voit toutes sortes de gens dont (de qui) la raison d'être, c'est l'argent. *One sees all sorts of people whose reason to live is money.*

14. Ils sont enfin arrivés au cinéma devant lequel il y avait une foule énorme. *They finally arrived at the theater in front of which there was an enormous crowd.*

15. C'est un petit exercice pratique à la fin duquel je comprends mieux les pronoms relatifs. *It is a short, practical exercise at the end of which I understand relative pronouns better.*

EXERCISE 9-16:

1. Je ne sais pas qui est cette dame. *I don't know who that woman is.*

2. Je ne sais pas ce que ce mot veut dire. *I don't know what this word means.*

3. Je ne sais pas ce qui irrite le professeur. *I don't know who irritates the professor.*

4. Je ne sais pas qui gagnera les élections. *I don't know who will win the elections.*

5. Je ne sais pas ce que nous ferons ensuite. *I don't know what we will do next.*

6. Je ne sais pas ce qu'il y a dans le réfrigérateur. *I don't know what there is in the refrigerator.*

7. Je ne sais pas qui il accompagne. *I don't know who he escorts.*

8. Je ne sais pas ce qu'on devrait répondre. *I don't know what one should answer.*

9. Je ne sais pas qui est assis là-bas. *I don't know who sat down there.*

10. Je ne sais pas ce qui suit cet exercice. *I don't know what follows this exercise.*

EXERCISE 9-17:

1. Quel est celui que je vois? *Which is the one that I see?*

2. Il m'a apporté tous ceux qui sont en français. *He brings me all those that are in French.*

3. On aura ceux dont les autres étaient privés. *One will have those (of) which the others are privileged (to have).*

4. C'est celle dont on a fait tant de portraits. *She is the one of whom many portraits were made.*

5. Ma tante est celle à qui je ressemble le plus. *My aunt is the one whom I resemble the most.*

6. Il faudra répéter celle que je n'ai pas comprise. *I will have to repeat those that I don't understand.*

7. J'aimerais bien voir celle dans laquelle elle est née. *I would like very much to see the one in which she was born.*

8. Connaissez-vous celui dont l'épouse est chilienne? *Do you know the one whose wife is from Chile?*

9. Je crois que c'est celui auquel je pense. *I believe that this is the one I'm thinking of.*

10. Répétez celles auxquelles vous avez mal répondu! *Repeat the ones that you answered incorrectly!*

EXERCISE 9-18:

1. Non, je n'ai pas peur de ceux dont vous avez peur. *No, I'm not afraid of the ones that you are afraid of.*

2. Non, je ne verrai pas celui qu'il verra. *No, I will not see the one that he will see.*

3. Non, celles qui vous agacent ne m'agacent pas. *No, the ones that annoy you don't annoy me.*

4. Non, je ne m'occuperai pas de celle dont vous vous occuperez. *No, I don't take care of the one that you take care of.*

5. Non, celle qui te fascine ne me fascine pas. *No, the one who fascinates you doesn't fascinate me.*

RAISE YOUR GRADES

Interrogatives

1. J'ai deux oranges. Laquelle des deux veux-tu? *I have two oranges. Which one of the two do you want?*

2. Quelle est l'importance de cette idée? *What is the importance of this idea?*

3. Que préparez-vous pour manger ce soir? *What are you making to eat this evening?*

4. Quelle gentille petite fille! *What a nice little girl!*

5. Qui aurait-cru qu'elle réussirait? *Who would have believed that she would succeed?*

6. Avec quoi se lave-t-on les dents? *What do we brush our teeth with?*

7. Ce sont de beaux jeunes gens! Lequel est ton cousin? *They are beautiful young people! Which one is your cousin?*

8. Quel est le meilleur livre de l'année? *Which one is the best book of the year?*

9. Quoi? Cela, c'est une grande surprise! *What? That's a big surprise!*

10. Que boit-on normalement après un repas? *What do we normally drink after a meal?*
11. Qui est ce monsieur sur la photo? *Who is that gentleman in the picture?*
12. De qui (quoi) parlez-vous maintenant? *Whom (what) are you talking about now?*
13. Quelle est la date de demain? *What is the date tomorrow?*
14. Lesquels de tous ces gens sont tes parents? *Which (ones) of all those people are your parents?*
15. Quel chemin serait le plus court? *Which road will be the shortest?*
16. Avec qui est-ce que vous sortez ce week-end? *Who are you going out with this weekend?*
17. Qu'est-ce que nous allons faire sans voiture? *What are we going to do without a car?*
18. Qui est-ce qui s'occupera des enfants? *Who will take care of the children?*
19. Qu'est-ce que tu en penses? *What do you think of it?*
20. Qui est-ce qui achètera cette monstruosité? *Who will buy this monstrosity?*
21. Qu'est-ce qu'il reste de cette salade? *What's left of that salad?*
22. Qu'est-ce qu'il y a dans cette soupe? *What is there in this soup?*
23. Pour qui est-ce que vous faites toute cette parade? *Who are you making all this show for?*
24. Qui est-ce qui ira chercher les journaux pour nous? *Who will get the papers for us?*
25. A quoi est-ce que tu rêves? *What do you dream of?*

Relative pronouns

26. On ne peut pas savoir ce que les jeunes pensent. *One can't know what young people think.*
27. C'est le seul désavantage que je vois. *It's the only disadvantage that I see.*
28. J'admire la patience avec laquelle il travaille. *I admire the patience with which he works.*
29. Tu n'auras pas la meilleure note; tu auras celle que tu mérites. *You will not have the best grade; you will have the one you deserve.*
30. J'habite un appartement dont les propriétaires sont à Paris. *I live in an apartment whose owners are in Paris.*
31. Il y a toujours quelque chose qui sent mauvais chez lui. *There is always something that smells bad at his house.*
32. C'est une famille dans laquelle tout le monde travaille. *It's a family in which everyone works.*
33. Il vaut mieux dire ce que l'on pense. *It's best to say what you think.*
34. Si tu ne fais pas attention, il mangera ce qui en reste. *If you don't pay attention, he will eat what is left of it.*
35. Il était difficile de prévoir ce dont nous aurions besoin. *It was difficult to predict what we would have needed.*
36. Parmi ses amis, elle préfère ceux qui sont sportifs. *Among her friends, she prefers the ones who are athletic.*
37. Les vêtements que j'ai achetés étaient bon marché. *The clothes that I bought were cheap.*
38. Celles que voyez dans la photo sont mes cousines. *The ones that you see in the picture are my cousins.*
39. Ce professeur est celui de qui (celui dont) tout le monde a peur. *That professor is the one everyone is afraid of.*
40. Est-ce que c'est le téléphone qui sonne? *Is it the telephone that is ringing?*
41. On fait ce qu'on peut! *One does what one can!*
42. Tout ce qui brille n'est pas d'or. *All that glitters is not gold.*
43. Les meilleurs vins sont ceux dont l'appelation est contrôlée. *The best wines are those whose trademarks are controlled.*
44. Tu passeras devant deux bâtiments entre lesquels tu verras une allée. *You will pass in front of two buildings between which you will see a path.*
45. Il est certain que cet exercice est plus facile que ceux que vous avez vus dans la leçon précédente. *It's certain that this exercise is easier than the ones you have seen in the preceding lesson.*
46. Ceux qui se plaignent tout le temps ont tort. *Those who complain all the time are wrong.*
47. On tient à connaître cette dame dont le mari est un artiste. *We'd like to know that woman whose husband is an artist.*
48. C'est un célèbre musée où il y a une collection impressionante. *That's a famous museum where there is an impressive collection.*
49. Ce qui me fascine, c'est son enthousiasme. *What fascinates me is his (her) enthusiasm.*

50. Voilà un étudiant dont on aura des nouvelles un jour. *Here's a student you'll hear a lot about one day.*
51. Parmi ces femmes, celles qui ont fini leurs études sont les plus heureuses. *Among these women, the ones who finished their studies are the happiest.*
52. C'est un endroit où je vais régulièrement. *It's a place where I go regularly.*
53. Ses parents ne sont pas irrités par ce qu'il fait. *His parents are not bothered by what he does.*
54. Qui vivra, verra. *Whoever will live, will see.*
55. Il faut choisir des dates où il n'y aura pas de conflit. *You must choose some dates when there will not be a conflict.*

Yes/no questions

56. Anne est allée à la plage avec son petit neveu? Anne est-elle allée à la plage avec son petit neveu? Est-ce qu'Anne est allée à la plage avec son petit neveu? *Did Anne go to the beach with her little nephew?*
57. La lettre **n** suit la lettre **m** dans l'alphabet? Est-ce que la lettre **n** suit la lettre **m** dans l'alphabet? La lettre **n** suit-il la lettre **m** dans l'alphabet? *Does the letter n follow the letter m in the alphabet?*
58. Voyez-vous (vois-tu) le lac par la fenêtre de votre (ton) appartement? Est-ce que tu vois le lac par la fenêtre de ton appartement? Tu vois le lac par la fenêtre de ton appartement? *Do you see the lake from the window of your apartment?*
59. Le locataire allumait-il la lampe pour lire? Est-ce que le locataire allumait la lampe pour lire? Le locataire allumait la lampe pour lire? *Did the tenant light the lamp in order to read?*
60. Le manuscrit arrivera demain matin? Est-ce que le manuscrit arrivera demain matin? Le manuscrit arrivera-t-il demain matin? *Will the manuscript arrive tomorrow morning?*

UNIT EXAM III

PASSÉ COMPOSÉ

Write each of the following sentences in the passé composé. Be sure to use the correct auxiliary and make all necessary agreements.

1. Qui choisit la glace au chocolat?
2. Il ne réalise pas les implications.
3. Les élèves restent debout devant la classe.
4. Ils partent pour l'Italie par bateau.
5. Nous possédons un chalet à la montagne.
6. Vous vous préparez un sandwich et une salade.
7. Ces demoiselles arrivent un peu plus tard.
8. Je compose une lettre sur mes derniers exploits.
9. Pourquoi racontez-vous ces histoires aux enfants?
10. Mes grands-parents fréquentent les Cléry.
11. Elle habite au Caire avec son mari.

Rewrite sentences 1–11 using an irregular verb with the same meaning, also in the passé composé.

IMPARFAIT/PASSÉ COMPOSÉ

Rewrite the following sentences, if necessary, to indicate that

(a) the second event interrupted the first
(b) the two events were simultaneous
(c) the events occurred one after another

23. Ils fumaient quand l'avion arrivait.
    a.
    b.
    c.

24. La musique a commencé lorsque le rideau s'est levé.
    a.
    b.
    c.

25. Nous jouions et vous vous amusiez.
    a.
    b.
    c.

FUTURE AND CONDITIONAL TENSES

Complete the following sentences with the appropriate verb in the future or the conditional, as required.

26. Si j'étais né en 1950, j' _____ plus de 35 ans maintenant.

27. Lorsque tu auras très soif, tu _____ de l'eau.

28. Demain matin nous nous _____ à 5:00 heures.

29. Robert m'a dit qu'il m' _____ une longue lettre.

30. Garçon, s'il vous plaît, je _____ voir le menu.

31. Mardi prochain ce _____ le 10 octobre.

32. Elle se _____ mal si elle tombait sur la tête.

33. Quand vous _____ la fenêtre, vous aurez un peu d'air.

34. Même si nous les invitons, ils ne _____ pas à la fête.

35. Elles _____ toutes les portes à clé s'il y avait du danger.

36. Si tu avais une machine à écrire tu _____ taper tes devoirs.

37. S'il y avait un feu rouge nous _____ l'auto.

PERFECT TENSES

Complete the following sentences by supplying the appropriate auxiliary verb for one of the perfect tenses—future perfect, conditional perfect, pluperfect, or the double compound past.

38. Elle ne voulait pas aller au restaurant parce qu'elle _____ déjà mangé.

39. Ils se _____ fait mal s'ils avaient essayé de grimper ce mur.

40. Aussitôt que nous _____ fini, nous sommes partis.

41. Si Jeanne s'était levée de bonne heure elle n' _____ pas manqué son train.

42. Dès que tu _____ arrivé, téléphone-moi!

43. L'inspecteur n'aurait rien dit si vous _____ fait un effort.

44. Les journalistes promettent qu'ils _____ revenus demain.

45. Quand je me _____ habillée, je descendrai les voir.

EXAM ANSWERS

Passé composé

1. Qui a choisi la glace au chocolat? *Who had the chocolate ice cream?*
2. Il n'a pas réalisé les implications. *He did not realize the implications.*
3. Les élèves sont resté(e)s debout devant la classe. *The students remained standing in front of the class.*
4. Ils sont partis pour l'Italie en bateau. *They left for Italy by boat.*
5. Nous avons possédé un chalet à la montagne. *We owned a cabin in the mountains.*
6. Vous vous ête préparé un sandwich et une salade. *You prepared a sandwich and a salad for yourself.*
7. Ces demoiselles sont arrivées un peu plus tard. *The young ladies arrived a little later.*
8. J'ai composé une lettre sur mes derniers exploits. *I wrote a letter about my latest adventures.*
9. Mes grands-parents ont frequenté les Cléry. *My grandparents spent a lot of time with the Clerys.*
10. Elle a habité au Caire avec son mari. *She lived in Cairo with her husband.*
11. Pourquoi avez-vous raconté ces histoires aux enfants? *Why did you tell those stories to the children?*
12. Qui a pris de la glace au chocolat? *Who had the chocolate ice cream?*
13. Il ne s'est pas rendu compte des implications. *He did not realize the implications.*
14. Les élèves sont restés debout devant la classe. *The students remained standing in front of the class.*
15. Ils sont allés en Italie en bateau. *They left for Italy by boat.*
16. Nous avons eu un chalet à la montagne. *We owned a cabin in the mountains.*

17. Vous vous êtes fait un sandwich et une salade. *You prepared a sandwich and a salad for yourself.*
18. Ces demoiselles sont venues un peu plus tard. *The young ladies arrived a little later.*
19. J'ai écrit une lettre sur mes derniers exploits. *I wrote a letter about my latest adventures.*
20. Mes grands-parents ont connu les Clèry. *My grandparents spent a lot of time with the Clerys.*
21. Elle a vécu au Caire avec son mari. *She lived in Cairo with her husband.*
22. Pourquoi avez-vous dit ces histoires aux enfants? *Why did you tell those stories to the children.*

Imparfait/passé composé

23. a) Ils fumaient quand l'avion est arrivé. *They were smoking when the plane arrived.* b) Ils fumaient quand l'avion arrivait. *They were smoking while the plane was arriving.* c) Ils ont fumé et l'avion est arrivé. *They smoked a cigarette and then the plane arrived.*
24. a) La musique commençait lorsque le rideau s'est levé. *The music was starting when the curtain rose.* b) La musique commençait lorsque le rideau se levait. *The music was starting while the curtain was being raised.* c) La musique a commencé lorsque le rideau s'est levé. *The music started when the curtain rose.*
25. a) Nous jouions et vous vous êtes amusés. *We were playing and you had fun.* b) Nous jouions et vous vous amusiez. *We were playing and you were having fun.* c) Nous avons joué et vous vous êtes amusés. *We played and you had fun.*

Future and conditional tenses

26. Si j'étais né en 1950, j'aurais plus de 35 ans maintenant. *If I had been born in 1950, I would be over 35 years old now.*
27. Lorsque tu auras soif, tu boiras de l'eau. *When you're thirsty, you'll drink water.*
28. Demain, nous nous lèverons à 5 heures. *Tomorrow morning we will get up at 5:00 A.M.*
29. Robert m'a dit qu'il m'avait écrit une longue lettre. *Robert told me that he had written a long letter.*

30. Garçon, s'il vous plaît, je voudrais voir le menu. *Waiter, please, I'd like to see the menu.*
31. Mardi prochain, ce sera le 10 octobre. *Next Tuesday it will be the 10th of October.*
32. Elle se ferait mal si elle tombait sur la tête. *She would hurt herself if she fell on her head.*
33. Quand vous ouvrirez la fenêtre, vous aurez un peu d'air. *When you open the window, you'll get a little fresh air.*
34. Même si nous les invitons, ils ne viendront pas à la fête. *Even if we invite them, they will not come to the party.*
35. Elles fermeraient toutes les portes à clé s'il y avait du danger. *They would lock all the doors if there were any danger.*
36. Si tu avais une machine à écrire, tu taperais tes devoirs. *If you had a typewriter, you would type your homework.*
37. S'il y avait un feu rouge, nous arrêterions l'auto. *If there were a red light, we would stop the car.*

Perfect tenses

38. Elle ne voulait pas aller au restaurant parce qu'elle avait déjà mange. *She did not want to go to the restaurant because she had already eaten.*
39. Ils se seraient fait mal s'ils avaient essayé de grimper ce mur. *They would have hurt themselves if they had tried to climb this wall.*
40. Aussitôt que nous avons eu fini, nous sommes partis. *As soon as we had finished, we left.*
41. Si Jeanne s'était levée de bonne heure, elle n'aurait pas manqué son train. *If Jeanne had gotten up early, she would not have missed her train.*
42. Dès que tu seras arrivé, téléphone-moi! *Call me as soon as you have arrived.*
43. L'inspecteur n'aurait rien dit si vous aviez fait un effort. *The inspector would not have said anything if you had made an effort.*
44. Les journalistes promettent qu'ils seront revenus demain. *The reporters promise that they will be back tomorrow.*
45. Quand je me serai habillée, je descendrai les voir. *When I am dressed, I'll come down to see them.*

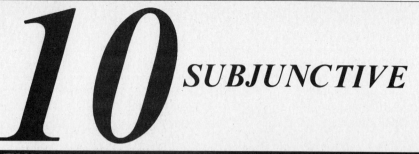

10 SUBJUNCTIVE

THIS CHAPTER IS ABOUT

☑ **The Present Subjunctive**
☑ **The Perfect Subjunctive**

Like the infinitive, the subjunctive is timeless—whether it describes past, present, or future events depends upon the time or tense of the main verb. Unlike the infinitive, however, the subjunctive is not used in main clauses, and has a subject different from that of the main verb.

10-1. The Present Subjunctive

A. Formation of the subjunctive

1. Form the subjunctive of most verbs by adding the following endings to the plural stem—that is, the first person plural of the present tense minus the -**ons** ending.

Person	Singular	Plural
1st	-e	-ions
2nd	-es	-iez
3rd	-e	-ent

> *NOTE:* The unpronounced subjunctive endings—**je, tu, il,** and **ils** forms—of all verbs except **être** and **avoir** are the same as those of the present tense of -**er** verbs. The pronounced subjunctive endings—**nous** and **vous** forms—are the same as the **nous** and **vous** endings of the **imparfait**.

Infinitive	Plural Stem	Subjunctive	
danser	nous **dans**ons	que je **danse**	*that I dance*
grandir	nous **grandiss**ons	que tu **grandisses**	*that you grow*
perdre	nous **perd**ons	qu'il **perde**	*that he lose*
prendre	nous **pren**ons	que nous **prenions**	*that we take*
mettre	nous **mett**ons	que vous **mettiez**	*that you put*
ecrire	nous **écriv**ons	qu'elles **écrivent**	*that they write*

> *NOTE:* Subjunctive forms are often listed with the conjunction **que** to reinforce the fact that they are not used as main verbs.

Mes parents veulent **que je rentre** avant minute.
My parents want me to come home before midnight.

J'ai peur **que cela finisse** mal.
I'm afraid that it's going to end badly.

Il fallait **que nous vendions** ce terrain.
We had to sell that lot.

Il sera nécessaire **qu'il prenne** des précautions.
It will be necessary for him to take precautions.

> *NOTE:* Most often you'll translate the subjunctive as an English infinitive.

2. Verbs whose stems undergo minor spelling changes in the present tense (see Sec. 4-5) have those same spelling changes in the subjunctive.

acheter	*to buy*	que j'**achète**	BUT	que nous **achetions**
appeler	*to call*	que tu **appelles**		que nous **appelions**
croire	*to believe*	que je **croie**		que nous **croyions**
préférer	*to prefer*	que je **préfère**		que nous **préférions**

EXERCISE 10-1: Replace the infinitive in parentheses with a second clause containing a new subject and a verb in the subjunctive. Answers and translations are at the end of the chapter.

Example: Il lui faut (terminer) son examen.   *It is necessary for him (her) to finish his (her) test.*

Il faut qu'il termine son examen.   *He must finish his test.* (Literally, *"It is necessary that he finish his test."*)

1. Il me faut (réfléchir) avant de parler.
2. Il vous faut (attendre) encore cinq minutes.
3. Il leur faut (acheter) des billets.
4. Il nous faut (rentrer) immédiatement.
5. Il faut (finir) tout cela.
6. Il te faut (ouvrir) les fenêtres.
7. Il me faut (m'exercer) de temps en temps.
8. Il vous faut (dormir) huit heures par nuit.
9. Il lui faut (répondre) correctement.
10. Il te faut (commencer) un autre exercice.

EXERCISE 10-2: Replace the infinitive in parentheses in the following sentences with a second clause containing a new subject and a verb in the subjunctive. Answers and translations are at the end of the chapter.

Example: Il ne nous permet pas de (fumer).   *He doesn't permit us to smoke.*

Il ne permet pas que nous fumions.   *He doesn't permit us to smoke (that we smoke).*

1. Nous leur disons de (rester) tranquilles.
2. Vos camarades vous demandent de leur (prêter) de l'argent.
3. Le capitaine me commande de (suivre) les ordres.
4. Ta conscience ne te permet pas de (mentir).
5. Le juge lui ordonne de (rendre) les documents.

3. Only the verbs **être**, *to be*, and **avoir**, *to have*, have irregular subjunctive stems and irregular endings.

être, *to be*

que je **sois**	*that I am*	que nous **soyons**	*that we are*
que tu **sois**	*that you are*	que vous **soyez**	*that you are*
qu'on **soit**	*that one is*	qu'ils **soient**	*that they are*

avoir, *to have*

que j'**aie**	*that I have*	que nous **ayons**	*that we have*
que tu **aies**	*that you have*	que vous **ayez**	*that you have*
qu'il **ait**	*that he has*	qu'elles **aient**	*that they have*

Il est dommage **que tu sois** si sensible.	*It's too bad you're so sensitive.*
Il faut qu'**il y ait** un compromis.	*There must be a compromise.*
Je ne crois pas **qu'elles soient** impliquées.	*I don't believe they have anything to do with it.*

4. Some verbs have irregular stems before the unpronounced subjunctive endings, but regular **nous** and **vous** forms.

aller	*to buy*	que tu **ailles**	BUT	que vous **alliez**
acquérir	*to acquire*	qu'elle **acquière**		que nous **acquérions**
apercevoir	*to glimpse*	qu'ils **aperçoivent**		que nous **apercevions**
boire	*to drink*	qu'elle **boive**		que nous **buvions**
conquérir	*to conquer*	qu'on **conquière**		que nous **conquérions**
devenir	*to become*	qu'elles **deviennent**		que nous **devenions**
devoir	*to owe, must*	que je **doive**		que vous **deviez**
falloir	*to be necessary*	qu'il **faille**		
mourir	*to die*	qu'on **meure**		que vous **mouriez**
prendre	*to take*	qu'elle **prenne**		que vous **preniez**
recevoir	*to receive*	que je **reçoive**		que nous **recevions**
tenir	*to hold*	que tu **tiennes**		que nous **tenions**
valoir	*to be worth*	qu'il(s) **vaille(nt)**		
venir	*to come*	qu'elles **viennent**		que vous **veniez**
vouloir	*to want*	que je **veuille**		que nous **voulions**

5. A few verbs have a single irregular stem in all forms of the subjunctive.

Infinitive		Stem	Subjunctive
faire	*to make, do*	**fass-**	que je **fasse**
pouvoir	*to be able*	**puisse-**	que tu **puisses**
savoir	*to know*	**sach-**	qu'il **sache**
résoudre	*to resolve*	**résolv-**	que nous **résolvions**

EXERCISE 10-3: Combine each pair of sentences into a single sentence with two subjects and a subordinate verb in the subjunctive. Translate your sentence into English. Answers and translations are at the end of the chapter.

Example: Paul est absent? C'est dommage! *Paul is absent? That's too bad!*

Il est dommage que Paul soit absent. *It's too bad that Paul is absent.*

1. Tu as froid? C'est intolérable!

2. Nous serons en retard? C'est possible!

3. Le bâtiment a 50 étages? C'est impressionant!

4. Vous êtes socialiste? C'est intéressant!

5. J'aurai une mauvaise note? C'est impossible!

6. Les journaux sont conservateurs? C'est faux!

7. Nous aurions tort? C'est impardonnable!

8. Je suis en retard? C'est inimaginable!

9. Tes parents ont une Mercedes? C'est splendide!

10. Alexandre est fatigué? C'est compréhensible!

11. Tu es au courant? C'est incroyable!

12. Vous aurez ma place? C'est malheureux!

EXERCISE 10-4: Replace the infinitive in parentheses in the following sentences with a verb in the subjunctive and its own subject pronoun. Answers and translations are at the end of the chapter.

Example: Il m'est difficile de savoir la vérité. *It is difficult for me to know the truth.*

Il est difficile que je sache   *It is unlikely that I (will) know*
    la vérité.   *the truth.*

1. Il leur est facile de (prendre) l'autoroute.
2. Il nous est impossible de (boire) autant.
3. Il m'est nécessaire de (recevoir) ce chèque.
4. Il t'est essentiel d'(acquérir) le français.
5. Il lui est difficile de (venir) si tôt.
6. Il m'est naturel de (faire) des erreurs.
7. Il nous est important d'(aller) à la réunion.
8. Il leur est normal de vouloir (se retirer).
9. Il lui est obligatoire de (pouvoir) résister.
10. Il vous est exceptionnel de (devenir) nerveux.

B. Use of the subjunctive

There must be a new clause whose verb agrees in person and number with each new subject noun or pronoun introduced into a sentence. When the main clause indicates that the events and situations described in the next clause are factual, probable, or hoped for, the second verb is in a specific tense—if not, the second verb is in the subjunctive.

1. Use the subjunctive when

- there is a change of subject
     AND
- there is no declaration of fact, probability, hope, or belief.

    Ses amis ne croient pas que **vous ayez**   *Her friends don't believe you*
      son adresse.   *have her address.*
    (The subject of the dependent clause **vous** differs from that of the main clause **ses amis** AND the main clause expresses disbelief.

BUT when there is *no change of subject* in the dependent clause, use an infinitive—not the subjunctive.

    Ses amis croient avoir son adresse.   *Her friends believe they have*
        her address.

    Ses amis ne croient pas avoir   *Her friends don't believe they have*
      son adresse.   *her address.*

AND when the main clause *expresses a fact, a hope, a probability, or a belief*, do not use the subjunctive.

    Ses amis croient que vous **avez**   *Her friends believe that you have*
      son adresse.   *her address.*

> *NOTE:* *Never* use the subjunctive after the verb **espérer**, *to hope*—it might bring bad luck!

> *NOTE:* *Always* use the subjunctive after the negative of **douter**, *to doubt*—il **ne doute pas** que . . . , *he doesn't doubt that . . .*—it is far from an affirmation of fact!

2. Use either an infinitive or a new subject followed by a verb in the subjunctive with verbs that permit personal indirect objects (see Sec. 6-4).

    Je permets des privilèges à mon frère.   *I allow my brother privileges.*
    Je lui permets de **conduire** ma voiture.

OR

    Je permets qu'**il conduise** ma voiture.   *I allow him to drive my car.*

BUT

    Nous **voulons** que tu **sois** gentil avec eux.   *We want you to be nice to them.*
    (The verb **vouloir**, *to want, wish*, does not take an indirect object.)

EXERCISE 10-5: Write **O** (*Oui*) or **N** (*Non*) in the space provided before each of the following phrases according to whether or not you think it should be followed by a verb in the subjunctive. Answers and translations are at the end of the chapter.

_____ 1. Nous insistons que tu . . .
_____ 2. La police craint que le voleur . . .
_____ 3. J'espérais qu'il . . .
_____ 4. Cette lettre vérifiera que nous . . .
_____ 5. Tout le monde savait qu'elle . . .
_____ 6. Nous doutons que les autres . . .
_____ 7. Il ne doute pas que je . . .
_____ 8. Mes parents ne se doutent pas que je . . .
_____ 9. Danielle a voulu que nous . . .
_____ 10. Cela prouve que les hommes . . .
_____ 11. Cela suggère que les femmes . . .
_____ 12. J'ai remarqué que le climat . . .
_____ 13. Les journaux annonceraient que le gouvernement . . .
_____ 14. Le gouvernement nierait que les journaux . . .
_____ 15. Vous désirez que les choses . . .
_____ 16. Le peuple a peur que les monarchistes . . .
_____ 17. Les monarchistes pensent que le peuple . . .
_____ 18. J'observe que les impôts . . .
_____ 19. Le colonel commandait que ses troupes . . .
_____ 20. Ils se réjouissent que vous . . .
_____ 21. Le metteur en scène ne pense pas que les acteurs . . .
_____ 22. Croyez-vous que cette robe . . . ?
_____ 23. Nous regrettons que vos notes . . .
_____ 24. Nous espérerions que vous . . .
_____ 25. La règle du jeu exige que . . .

EXERCISE 10-6: Combine each pair of sentences into a single sentence with the second verb in the infinitive, the subjunctive, or a specific tense. Answers and translations are at the end of the chapter.

Example:

Les animaux sont bêtes? / Nous ne le croyons pas!
Nous ne croyons pas que les animaux soient bêtes!

Animals are stupid? / We don't believe it!
We don't believe animals are stupid!

Tu pars tout de suite? / Tu le veux?
Tu veux partir tout de suite?

You're leaving right away? / That's what you want?
You want to leave right away?

Les ordinateurs sont chers? / Il le sait!
Il sait que les ordinateurs sont chers.

Computers are expensive? / He knows it!
He knows computers are expensive.

1. Il viendra demain? Je l'espère!
2. Nous nous amusons? Nous le désirons!
3. Tu réussis à tes examen? Qui le voudrait?
4. On se sert du subjonctif? Qu'est-ce qui l'exige?
5. Les libéraux gagneront? Nous le pensons.
6. Il faisait beau temps? Tout le monde le voulait.
7. Admettraient-ils leur erreur? J'en doute!
8. Aimerait-elle dîner en ville? Je le crois.
9. Vous maltraitez les serveurs? On l'a déploré!
10. Les notes sont mauvaises? Nous nous en plaignons!
11. On choisit un autre sujet? Il le fallait.
12. Tu as un si bon accent français. Je m'en émerveille!
13. Voit-elle beaucoup de monde? Elle l'évite!

14. Est-ce qu'on lui garantit une place? Elle le mérite!
15. Nous ne disons pas ce que nous pensons. On le préférait.

3. Use a verb in the subjunctive following impersonal verbs if
   - there is a change of subject
          AND
   - there is no declaration of fact, probability, hope, or belief.

> *NOTE:* The adjective **probable**, *probable*, is closer in meaning to *provable* in French than its English cognate. **Il est probable** is a declaration of belief — use a verb in a specific tense following it.

EXERCISE 10-7: Write **O** (*Oui*) or **N** (*Non*) in the space provided before the following impersonal expressions according to whether or not you think their meaning requires that they be followed by the subjunctive. Answers and translations are at the end of the chapter.

_____ 1. Il est certain que . . .
_____ 2. Il est rare que . . .
_____ 3. Il était possible que . . .
_____ 4. Il sera impossible que . . .
_____ 5. Il est sûr que . . .
_____ 6. Il était important que . . .
_____ 7. Il est vrai que . . .
_____ 8. Il n'est pas vrai que . . .
_____ 9. Il est surprenant que . . .
_____ 10. Il vaudrait mieux que . . .
_____ 11. Il ne fallait pas que . . .
_____ 12. Il a été choquant que . . .
_____ 13. Il était probable que . . .
_____ 14. Il est super que . . .
_____ 15. Il sera urgent que . . .
_____ 16. Il est écrit que . . .
_____ 17. Il faut que . . .
_____ 18. Il est démontrable que . . .
_____ 19. Il était amusant que . . .
_____ 20. Il serait dommage que . . .

EXERCISE 10-8: Combine each pair of sentences into a single sentence containing an impersonal expression followed by a verb in a specific tense or the subjunctive. Answers and translations are at the end of the chapter.

Example: Tu te marieras? C'est épatant! *You're going to get married?*
                                        That's swell!

Il est épatant que tu te maries! *It's swell that you're getting married!*

1. Il finit ses études? C'est essentiel!
2. Vous venez nous voir? C'est sûr!
3. Il fera beau demain? Ce n'est pas certain!
4. Elle étudiera la chimie? C'est vrai!
5. Elle étudiera le chinois? Ce n'est pas vrai!
6. Nous choisissons un président? C'est nécessaire!
7. La presse a une responsabilité. C'est évident!
8. Tu peux avoir confiance en lui. Ce n'est pas sûr!
9. La société doit punir les malfaiteurs. C'est dommage!
10. Nous faisons tous des erreurs. C'est malheureux!

4. After certain prepositions and conjunctions indicating that the second of two situations or events has not yet happened or is not expected to happen, you cannot use a verb tense.

- If there is *no change of subject*, use an *infinitive* after the preposition.

BUT

- If there is a *new subject*, use the *subjunctive* after the conjunction form.

The following is a list of these prepositions and their derived conjunctions:

Prepositions	Conjunctions	
pour	**pour que**	*in order that*
afin de	**afin que**	*in order that*
à condition de	**à condition que**	*on condition (that)*
sans	**sans que**	*without (his) _____ ing*
à moins de	**à moins que**	*unless*
avant de	**avant que**	*before*
de peur de	**de peur que**	*for fear (that)*

Je reste **à moins de changer** d'avis.   *I'll stay unless I change my mind.*

Je reste **à moins que vous changiez** d'avis.   *I'll stay unless you change your mind.*

Les gens travaillent **pour avoir** une bonne vie.   *People work (in order) to have a good life.*

Les gens travaillent **pour que leurs enfants aient** une bonne vie.   *People work for their children to have a good life. (Literally: People work so that their children (may, will) have a good life.)*

The following common conjunctions have no equivalent prepositions—you may use them with a specific tense or the subjunctive, according to the meaning of the sentence.

bien que	*although*
quoique	*although*
jusqu'à ce que	*until*
pourvu que	*provided that*
malgré que	*in spite of the fact that*

Je l'ai réveillé **bien qu'il dormait**.   *I woke him up although he was sleeping. (fact)*

Je le réveillerai **bien qu'il dorme**.   *I'll wake him up although he may be sleeping. (conjecture)*

> *REMEMBER:* Use a verb in the subjunctive after a conjunction if
>
> - there is a change of subject
>
> AND
>
> - there is no declaration of fact, probability, hope, or belief.

EXERCISE 10-9: Join each pair of sentences with a conjunction or preposition from the preceding lists to make a logical sentence. Answers and translations are at the end of the chapter.

Example: Nous prenons son crayon. Il ne nous voit pas.   *We take his pencil. He doesn't see us.*

Nous prenons son crayon sans qu'il nous voie.   *We take his pencil without his seeing us.*

1. J'achèterai une nouvelle voiture. J'aurai assez d'argent.
2. Nous l'attendrons ici. Il viendra nous chercher.
3. Il est très beau. Il a des yeux bizarres!
4. Yves s'en va. Il ne nous dit pas au revoir.
5. Les bons élèves étudient. Ils recevront de bonnes notes.
6. Le professeur fait des efforts. Ses étudiants comprennent.
7. Nous lisons le roman. Nous allons voir le film.

    8. La famille fera un pique-nique. Il ne pleuvra pas.
    9. Ma mère prépare le dîner. Mon père rentre du travail.
  10. Je ne fume pas au lit. Je ne mets pas le feu à la maison.

5. Use a verb in the subjunctive mode in a clause that follows and modifies a noun or pronoun referring to someone or something indefinite, imaginary, or singled out in a figure of speech.

Connaissez-vous **quelqu'un** qui **puisse** m'aider?	*Do you know someone who can (could, might) help me?*
Je ne vois **rien** qui **aille** avec cette robe.	*I don't see anything that goes (would go) with that dress.*
C'est **la plus belle maison** qui **soit** à vendre.	*It's the most beautiful house that is for sale.*

EXERCISE 10-10: Answer the following questions in both the affirmative and the negative. Answers and translations are at the end of the chapter.

Example:	As-tu une bicyclette que tu puisses me prêter?	*Do you have a bicycle you can lend me?*
	Oui, j'ai une bicyclette que je peux te prêter.	*Yes, I have a bicycle I can lend you.*
	Non, je n'ai pas de bicyclette que je puisse te prêter.	*No, I don't have a bicycle I can lend you.*

    1. Connaissez-vous quelqu'un qui veuille m'accompagner?
    2. Auriez-vous quelque chose que je puisse lire?
    3. Est-ce que c'est le seul modèle que vous ayez?
    4. Pouvez-vous me montrer une valise qui soit moins lourde?
    5. A-t-elle besoin d'un appartement qui ait deux chambres?
    6. Monique est-elle la plus belle fille que tu connaisses?
    7. Est-ce que cet avion est le dernier qui atterrira ce soir?
    8. Avez-vous trouvé des mots que vous ne compreniez pas?
    9. Cherche-t-elle une robe qui ait des manches longues?
  10. A-t-elle trouvé une robe qui ait des manches longues?

10-2. The Perfect Subjunctive

Use the perfect subjunctive to indicate that the event or situation in the subjunctive clause happened before that of the main clause. The perfect subjunctive is neither past, present, nor future—you may use it with all three tenses to indicate the relative order of two events.

A. Formation of the perfect subjunctive

The perfect subjunctive consists of the appropriate form of the subjunctive of **être** or **avoir** followed by the past participle of the verb.

arriver, *to arrive*

que je **sois arrivé(e)**	que nous **soyons arrivé(e)s**
que tu **sois arrivé(e)**	que vous **soyez arrivé(e)s**
qu'il **soit arrivé**	qu'elles **soient arrivées**

mentir, *to lie*

que j'**aie menti**	que nous **ayons menti**
que tu **aies menti**	que vous **ayez menti**
qu'on **ait menti**	qu'ils **aient menti**

> ***NOTE:*** The choice of the auxiliary verb depends on whether the verb is transitive, intransitive, or reflexive. The endings on the past participle depend on the auxiliary and the position of the direct object.

B. Use of the perfect subjunctive

1. After a main verb in the present, future, or conditional tense, the perfect subjunctive has a present perfect or past meaning.

Elle est **contente** que nous **soyons venus**.	She is glad that we have come (came).
Paul **niera** qu'il **ait** tout **mangé**.	Paul will deny having eaten everything.
Il **vaudrait** mieux que tu n'**aies** rien **compris**.	It would be better for you not to have understood anything.

EXERCISE 10-11: Change each of the following sentences to indicate that the action of the second clause preceded that of the first. Then translate your sentence into English. Answers and translations are at the end of the chapter.

Example:	Il est impossible qu'il fasse cela!	It's impossible for him to do that!
	Il est impossible qu'il ait fait cela!	It's impossible that he did that!

1. Tout le monde doute que nous comprenions.

2. Leurs parents ne croiront pas qu'ils se marient.

3. Je ne pense pas que tu paies l'addition.

4. Il est possible que cela soit vrai.

5. Tout sera en ordre à moins qu'il refuse.

6. Il semble que nous ayons les meilleures places.

7. Nous avons bien peur que l'avion descende trop vite.

8. Il se pourrait que son grand-père meure avant son arrivée.

9. Je t'aime bien quoique tu te moques de moi.

10. Elles seront surprises que cela prenne si longtemps.

2. After a verb in any past tense—including the past conditional—the perfect subjunctive has a pluperfect meaning.

Les spectateurs **regrettaient** que leur équipe **ait perdu**.	The spectators regretted that their team had lost.
On **s'est réjoui** que les soldats **soient revenus**.	They rejoiced that the soldiers had come back.
Il n'**avait** pas **cru** que nous **nous** en **soyons souvenus**.	He hadn't believed that we had remembered it.
Il **aurait** mieux valu qu'il **soit resté** chez lui.	It would have been better for him to stay home (had he stayed home).

EXERCISE 10-12: Change each of the following sentences to indicate that the action of the second clause preceded that of the first. Then translate your sentence into English. Answers and translations are at the end of the chapter.

Example:	Il aurait été impossible qu'il l'oublie.	It would have been impossible for him to forget it.
	Il aurait été impossible qu'il l'ait oublié.	It would have been impossible that he had forgotten it.

1. Cela m'ennuyait que tu parles en mangeant.

2. Peu importait que la bourse soit fermée.

3. Nous nous sommes étonnés qu'il prenne son temps.

4. Les officiers craignaient que nous ne revenions pas.

5. Elle était furieuse qu'on mette la stéréo à minuit.

6. Les parents déploraient qu'il n'y ait plus de discipline.

7. Tu avais détesté qu'on t'appelle par ton surnom.

8. Qui aurait douté qu'ils rendent cette somme d'argent?

9. Il a mérité qu'on se moque de lui.

10. Il avait été inadmissable qu'on perde tant de temps.

SUMMARY

1. The subjunctive is not a tense, but a timeless verb form like the infinitive except that it has personal endings and occurs in a separate clause with its own subject.
2. The subjunctive is regularly formed from the plural (**nous**) stem of the verb.
3. Only **être** and **avoir** have irregular subjunctive endings as well as irregular stems.
4. If there is only one subject in a sentence, all subsequent verbs are in the infinitive form.
5. If the main clause constitutes a declaration of fact, probability, hope or belief, the verb in the following clause must be in a specific tense—if not, the second verb must be in the subjunctive.
6. The past subjunctive consists of the appropriate form of the subjunctive or **avoir** or **être** combined with the past participle.
7. The past subjunctive is used when the situation or event described by the subjunctive clause happened before that of the main clause.
8. When the past subjunctive is used after a present, future, or conditional in the main clause, it has a past meaning; when the past subjunctive is used after any past tense, it has a past perfect or pluperfect meaning (*had* _____).

RAISE YOUR GRADES

Present subjunctive

From the following list, find the reason for the particular form of the second verb in each sentence. Then write its corresponding letter in the space provided. Answers and translations are at the end of the chapter.

    A Infinitive—there is only one subject
    B Subjunctive—no declaration of fact or belief
    C Specific tense—main clause declares fact
    D Specific tense—main clause expresses hope
    E Specific tense—main clause declares probability
    F Specific tense—main clause expresses belief

_____ 1. Nous sommes tous contents d'être ici.
_____ 2. Je vous dis qu'il y a trop de circulation.
_____ 3. Paulette est furieuse qu'elles aient refusé.
_____ 4. Est-ce que tu veux que je ferme les volets?
_____ 5. Tout le monde sait qu'il ne boit pas d'alcool.
_____ 6. Il me dit de ne pas y faire attention.
_____ 7. Mes parents voulaient que nous continuions nos études.
_____ 8. C'est le plus joli tableau que j'aie jamais vu!
_____ 9. Que désires-tu que j'en fasse?
_____ 10. Les cyclistes comptent arriver à Rouen à midi.
_____ 11. Il est important que vous compreniez ce principe.
_____ 12. Il est essentiel de garder son sang-froid.
_____ 13. Il est certain que nous ne nous reverrons plus.
_____ 14. Nous nous réjouissons que tout se soit bien passé!
_____ 15. On demandera seulement qu'il nous dise la vérité.

_____ 16. J'apporterai l'addition à moins que vous ne désiriez autre chose.

_____ 17. Elles espèrent que tout ira bien.

_____ 18. Il cherche une secrétaire qui sache parler français.

_____ 19. Il n'est pas impossible qu'on vous en trouve une.

_____ 20. Il faut qu'on fasse très attention.

_____ 21. Vous êtes le premier client qui ait posé cette question.

_____ 22. Faisons quelque chose avant qu'il découvre l'erreur!

_____ 23. Cela fait plaisir de rencontrer des gens pareils.

_____ 24. Personne ne croit que nous puissions continuer.

_____ 25. Il est probable qu'on aura le chèque à la fin du mois.

_____ 26. On espérait que nos efforts auraient des résultats.

_____ 27. J'ai insisté qu'ils viennent sans cérémonie.

_____ 28. Elle est sortie sans que je la voie.

_____ 29. Il est regrettable que ce soit le dernier exemplaire.

_____ 30. Les adultes sont sûrs d'avoir toujours raison.

Etre and avoir

Fill in the blanks with the appropriate form of **être** or **avoir**, according to the meaning and structure of each sentence. Then translate the entire sentence into English. Answers and translations are at the end of the chapter.

31. Tu es le meilleur ami que nous _____ .

32. Il ne faut pas _____ peur.

33. Tout le monde l'aime bien malgré qu'il _____ bête.

34. La directrice veut que nous _____ à l'heure.

35. Ma famille pense que mon frère _____ des idées bizarres.

36. Nous attendrons ici jusqu'à ce que nous _____ une réponse.

37. Tout cela s'est passé avant que je _____ né.

38. Il _____ difficile de prévoir toutes les possibilités.

39. C'est le meilleur film que je _____ vu cet été.

40. Il est probable que tu _____ ton diplôme à la fin de l'année prochaine.

41. J'espère qu'il _____ impressionné par ton dernier cadeau.

42. Il faut trouver un speaker qui _____ une bonne prononciation.

43. J'ai un ami qui _____ moitié français et moitié américain.

44. Les diplomates doutent que l'ambassadeur se _____ engagé dans l'affaire.

45. Il est malheureux que nos hôtes _____ invité tant de monde.

46. Il est vrai que l'autoroute _____ dangereuse.

47. J'ai tout fini malgré que je _____ de la difficulté.

48. Il fallait absolument qu'on _____ cette référence.

49. Elle aurait été contente que tu _____ avec nous.

50. Cela nous aurait fait plaisir qu'elle se _____ servie de notre appartement.

Faire

Fill in the blanks with the appropriate form of the verb **faire**, according to the meaning and structure of each sentence. Then translate the entire sentence into English. Answers and translations are at the end of the chapter.

51. J'espère qu'il _____ beau demain.

52. Que voulez-vous que j'en _____?

53. Il est évident que nous _____ moins de fautes.

54. C'est agaçant qu'elle _____ cela maintenant.

55. Voulez-vous _____ une promenade avec moi?

56. Il faut absolumment que tu _____ sa connaissance.

57. Il est probable qu'elles _____ plus d'effort la prochaine fois.

58. Nous serons contents si tu _____ cela.

59. Nous serons contents quand tu _____ cela.

60. Nous serons contents que tu _____ cela.

61. Nous serons contents de _____ cela.

62. Nous serons contents de _____ déjà _____ cela.

CHAPTER ANSWERS

EXERCISE 10-1:

1. Il faut que je réfléchisse avant de parler. *I must think before speaking.*
2. Il faut que vous attendiez encore cinq minutes. *You must wait another five minutes.*
3. Il faut qu'ils achètent des billets. *They must buy (some) tickets.*
4. Il faut que nous rentrions immédiatement. *We must come in again immediately.*
5. Il faut qu'on finisse tout cela. *They must finish all that.*
6. Il faut que tu ouvres les fenêtres. *You must open the windows.*
7. Il faut que je m'exerce de temps en temps. *I must exercise from time to time.*
8. Il faut que vous dormiez huit heures par nuit. *You must sleep eight hours each night.*
9. Il faut qu'il réponde correctement. *He must answer correctly.*
10. Il faut que tu commences un autre exercice. *You must begin another exercise.*

EXERCISE 10-2:

1. Nous leur disons qu'ils restent tranquilles. *We tell them to stay quiet.*
2. Vos camarades demandent que vous leur prêtiez de l'argent. *Your friends ask you to loan them some money.*
3. Le capitaine commande que je suive les ordres. *The captain commands me to follow orders.*
4. Ta conscience ne permet pas que tu mentes. *Your conscience doesn't allow you to lie.*
5. Le juge ordonne qu'il rende les documents. *The judge ordered him to give up the documents.*

EXERCISE 10-3:

1. Il est intolérable que tu aies froid. *It is unbearable that you are cold.*

2. Il est possible que nous soyons en retard. *It is possible that we are late.*
3. Il est impressionant que le bâtiment ait 50 étages. *It is impressive that the building has 50 stories.*
4. Il est intéressant que vous soyez socialiste. *It is interesting that you are a socialist.*
5. Il est impossible que j'aie une mauvaise note. *It is impossible that I got a bad grade.*
6. Il est faux que les journaux soient conservateurs. *It is not true that the papers are conservative.*
7. Il est impardonnable que nous ayons tort. *It is inexcusable that we are wrong.*
8. Il est inimaginable que je sois en retard. *It is unimaginable that I am late.*
9. Il est splendide que tes parents aient une Mercedes. *It is splendid that your parents have a Mercedes.*
10. Il est compréhensible qu'Alexandre soit fatigué. *It is understandable that Alexander is tired.*
11. Il est incroyable que tu sois au courant. *It is unbelievable that you are up-to-date.*
12. Il est malheureux que vous ayez ma place. *It is unfortunate that you have my seat.*

EXERCISE 10-4:

1. Il est facile qu'ils prennent l'autoroute. *It is easy for them to take the freeway.*
2. Il est impossible que nous buvions autant. *It is impossible that we drink so much.*
3. Il est nécessaire que je reçoive ce chèque. *It is necessary that I receive that check.*
4. Il est essentiel que tu acquières le français. *It is essential that you acquire French.*
5. Il est difficile qu'il vienne si tôt. *It is difficult that he comes so early.*
6. Il est naturel que je fasse des erreurs. *It is natural that I make some errors.*

7. Il est important que nous allions à la réunion. *It is important that we go to the meeting.*

8. Il est normal qu'ils veuillent se retirer. *It is normal that they want to go to bed.*

9. Il est obligatoire qu'il puisse résister. *It is obligatory that he be able to endure.*

10. Il est exceptionnel que vous deveniez nerveux. *It is unusual that you became nervous.*

EXERCISE 10-5:

O 1. *We insist that you . . .*
O 2. *The police fear that the thief . . .*
N 3. *I hoped that it . . .*
N 4. *This letter will verify that we . . .*
N 5. *Everybody knew that she . . .*
O 6. *We doubt that the others . . .*
O 7. *He doesn't doubt that I . . .*
O 8. *My parents don't suspect that I . . .*
O 9. *Danielle wanted us to . . .*
N 10. *That proves that men . . .*
O 11. *That suggests that women . . .*
N 12. *I've noticed that the climate . . .*
N 13. *The newspapers would announce that the government . . .*
O 14. *The government would deny that the newspapers . . .*
O 15. *You want things to . . .*
O 16. *The people are afraid that the monarchists . . .*
N 17. *The monarchists think that the people . . .*
N 18. *I point out that taxes . . .*
O 19. *The colonel commanded his troops to . . .*
O 20. *They are delighted that you . . .*
O 21. *The film director doesn't think that actors . . .*
O 22. *Do you believe that this dress . . . ?*
O 23. *We're sorry that your grades . . .*
N 24. *We would hope that you . . .*
O 25. *The rules of the game require that . . .*

EXERCISE 10-6:

1. J'espère qu'il viendra demain. *I hope that he will come tomorrow.*

2. Nous désirons nous amuser. *We want to have fun.*

3. Qui voudrait que tu réussisses à tes examens? *Who would like you to pass your tests?*

4. Qu'est-ce qui exige qu'on se serve du subjonctif? *What makes it necessary to use the subjunctive?*

5. Nous pensons que les libéraux gagneront. *We think that the liberals will win.*

6. Tout le monde voulait qu'il fasse beau temps. *Everyone wished the weather would be beautiful.*

7. Je doute qu'ils admettent leur erreur. *I doubt that they will admit their mistake.*

8. Je crois qu'elle aimerait dîner en ville. *I believe that she would like to eat in town.*

9. On a déploré que vous maltraitiez les serveurs! *We deplored that you mistreated the waiters.*

10. Nous nous plaignons que les notes soient mauvaises. *We complain that the grades were bad.*

11. Il fallait choisir un autre sujet. *We have to choose another subject.*

12. Je m'émerveille que tu aies un si bon accent français. *I'm amazed that you have such a good French accent.*

13. Elle évite de voir beaucoup de monde. *She avoids seeing a lot of people.*

14. Elle mérite qu'on lui garantisse une place. *She deserves our saving her a seat.*

15. On préférerait que nous ne disions pas ce que nous pensons. *They would prefer that we not say what we think.*

EXERCISE 10-7:

N 1. *It is certain that . . .*
O 2. *It is rare that . . .*
O 3. *It was possible that . . .*
O 4. *It'll be impossible that . . .*
N 5. *It is sure that . . .*
O 6. *It was important that . . .*
N 7. *It's true that . . .*
O 8. *It isn't true that . . .*
O 9. *It is surprising that . . .*
O 10. *It would be better that . . .*
O 11. *It was necessary not to . . .*
O 12. *It was shocking that . . .*
N 13. *It was probable that . . .*
O 14. *It's super that . . .*
O 15. *It will be urgent that . . .*
N 16. *It is written that . . .*
O 17. *It is necessary that . . .*
N 18. *It is demonstrable that . . .*
O 19. *It was amusing that . . .*
N 20. *It would be too bad for . . .*

EXERCISE 10-8:

1. Il est essentiel qu'il finisse ses études. *It is essential for him to finish his studies.*

2. Il est sûr que vous venez me voir. *It is sure that you will come to see me.*

3. Il n'est pas certain qu'il fasse beau demain. *It is not certain that it will be beautiful tomorrow.*

4. Il est vrai qu'elle étudiera la chimie. *It is true that she will study chemistry.*

5. Il n'est pas vrai qu'elle étudiera le chinois. *It is not true that she will study Chinese.*

6. Il est nécessaire que nous choisissions un président. *It is necessary that we choose a president.*

7. Il est évident que la presse a une responsabilité. *It is evident that the press has a responsibility.*

8. Il n'est pas sûr que tu puisses avoir confiance en lui. *It is not certain that you can have confidence in him.*

9. Il est dommage que la société doive punir les malfaiteurs. *It is a pity that society must punish scoundrels.*

10. Il est malheureux que nous fassions tous des erreurs. *It is too bad that we made all these errors.*

EXERCISE 10-9:

1. J'achèterai une nouvelle voiture pourvu que j'aie assez d'argent. *I will buy a new car provided (that) I have enough money.*
2. Nous l'attendrons ici jusqu'à ce qu'il vienne nous chercher. *We'll wait for him here until he comes to get us.*
3. Il est très beau quoiqu' (bien qu', malgré qu') il a (ait) des yeux bizarres! *He is very handsome although (in spite of the fact that) he has strange eyes!*
4. Yves s'en va sans nous dire au revoir. *Yves left without telling us good-bye.*
5. Les bons élèves étudient pour (afin de) recevoir de bonnes notes. *Good students study in order to get good grades.*
6. Le professeur fait des efforts pour que (afin que) ses étudiants comprennent. *The professor makes some effort in order that his students understand.*
7. Nous lisons le roman avant que nous allions voir le film. *We read the novel before we go to see the movie.*
8. La famille fera un pique-nique pourvu qu'il ne pleuve pas. *The family will have a picnic provided that it doesn't rain.*
9. Ma mère prépare le dîner avant que mon père rentre du travail. *My mother makes dinner before my father comes home from work.*
10. Je ne fume pas au lit pour (afin de) ne pas mettre le feu à la maison! *I don't smoke in bed in order not to set the house on fire!*

EXERCISE 10-10:

1. Oui, je connais quelqu'un qui veut vous accompagner. *Yes, I know someone who wants to go with you.* Non, je ne connais personne qui veuille vous accompagner. *No, I don't know anyone who wants to go with you.*
2. Oui, j'ai quelque chose que vous pouvez lire. *Yes, I have something that you can read.* Non, je n'ai rien que vous puissiez lire. *No, I don't have anything that you can read.*
3. Oui, c'est le seul modèle que j'ai. *Yes, it's the only model that I have.* Non, ce n'est pas le seul modèle que j'aie. *No, it's not the only model that I have.*
4. Oui, je peux vous montrer une valise qui est moins lourde. *Yes, I can show you a suitcase that is not as heavy.* Non, je ne peux pas vous montrer une valise qui soit moins lourde. *No, I can't show you a suitcase that is not as heavy.*
5. Oui, elle a besoin d'un appartement qui ait deux chambres. *Yes, she needs an apartment that has two rooms.* Non, elle n'a pas besoin d'un appartement qui ait deux chambres. *No,*

she doesn't need an apartment that has two rooms.
6. Oui, Monique est la plus belle fille que je connais. *Yes, Monique is the prettiest girl that I know.* Non, Monique n'est pas la plus belle fille que je connaisse. *No, Monique is not the prettiest girl that I know.*
7. Oui, cet avion est le dernier qui atterrira ce soir. *Yes, that plane is the last that will land this evening.* Non, cet avion n'est pas le dernier qui atterrira ce soir. *No, that plane is not the last that will land this evening.*
8. Oui, j'ai trouvé des mots que je ne comprends pas. *Yes, I found some words that I don't understand.* Non, je n'ai pas trouvé de mots que je ne comprends pas. *No, I didn't find any words that I don't understand.*
9. Oui, elle cherche une robe qui ait des manches longues. *Yes, she's looking for a dress that has long sleeves.* Non, elle ne cherche pas une robe qui ait des manches longues. *No, she isn't looking for a dress that has long sleeves.*
10. Oui, elle a trouvé une robe qui a des manches longues. *Yes, she found a dress that has long sleeves.* Non, elle n'a pas trouvé une robe qui ait des manches longues. *No, she hasn't found a dress that has long sleeves.*

EXERCISE 10-11:

1. Tout le monde doute que nous ayons compris. *Everyone doubts that we have understood.*
2. Leurs parents ne croiront pas qu'ils se soient mariés. *Their parents don't believe that they will get married.*
3. Je ne pense pas que tu aies payé l'addition. *I don't think that you paid the bill.*
4. Il est possible que cela ait été vrai. *It is possible that this was true.*
5. Tout sera en ordre à moins qu'il ait refusé. *All will be in order unless he refused.*
6. Il semble que nous ayons eu les meilleures places. *It seems that we have the best seats.*
7. Nous avons bien peur que l'avion ne soit descendu trop vite. *We're very afraid that the airplane will come down too fast.*
8. Il se pourrait que son grand-père soit mort avant son arrivée. *It is possible that his grand-father will die before his arrival.*
9. Je t'aime bien quoique tu te sois moqué(e) de moi. *I like you even though you make fun of me.*
10. Elles seront surprises que cela ait pris si longtemps. *They were surprised that this took so long.*

EXERCISE 10-12:

1. Cela m'ennuyait que tu aies parlé en mangeant. *It bothers me that you talked while eating.*
2. Peu importait que la bourse ait été fermée. *It didn't matter that the stock exchange was closed.*

3. Nous nous sommes étonnés qu'il ait pris son temps. *We were astonished that he took his time.*
4. Les officiers craignaient que nous ne soyons pas revenus. *The officers were afraid that we had not returned.*
5. Elle était furieuse qu'on ait mis la stéréo à minuit. *She was furious that they played the stereo at midnight.*
6. Les parents déploraient qu'il n'y ait plus eu de discipline. *Parents deplored that there was no longer any discipline.*
7. Tu avais détesté qu'on t'ait appellé par ton surnom. *You hated that they called you by your nickname.*
8. Qui aurait douté qu'ils aient rendu cette somme d'argent? *Who would have doubted that they repaid that sum of money?*
9. Il a mérité qu'on se soit moqué de lui. *He deserved to be made fun of.*
10. Il avait été inadmissible qu'on ait perdu tant de temps. *It was unacceptable that they wasted so much time.*

RAISE YOUR GRADES
Present subjunctive

A 1. *We are all happy to be here.*
C 2. *I tell you that there is too much traffic.*
B 3. *Paulette is furious that they refused.*
B 4. *Do you want me to close the shutters?*
C 5. *Everyone knows (that) he doesn't drink alcohol.*
A 6. *He tells me not to pay attention to it.*
B 7. *My parents wanted us to continue our studies.*
B 8. *It's the prettiest painting that I've ever seen!*
B 9. *What do you want me to do with it?*
A 10. *The cyclists plan to arrive in Rouen at noon.*
B 11. *It is important that you understand this principle.*
A 12. *It is essential that they keep their composure.*
C 13. *It is certain that we will not see one another again.*
B 14. *We rejoice that all went very well!*
B 15. *They will demand only that he tell us the truth.*
B 16. *I will bring the bill unless you want something else.*
D 17. *She hopes that all will go well.*
B 18. *He is looking for a secretary who knows how to speak French.*
B 19. *It is not impossible that they will find you one of them.*
B 20. *One must pay close attention.*
B 21. *You are the first customer who asked that question.*
B 22. *Do something before he discovers the mistake!*
A 23. *It is pleasant to meet some similar people.*
B 24. *No one believes that we can continue.*
E 25. *It is probable that they will have the check at the end of the month.*
D 26. *One hoped that our efforts will have results.*
B 27. *I insisted that they come without ceremony.*
B 28. *She left without my seeing her.*
B 29. *It is regrettable that this will be the last copy.*
C 30. *Adults are sure always to be right.*

Etre and avoir

31. **ayons** *You are the best friend that we have.*
32. **avoir** *Do not be afraid.*
33. **soit** *Everyone likes him in spite of the fact that he is silly.*
34. **soyons** *The principal wants us to be on time.*
35. **a** *My family thinks that my brother has some strange ideas.*
36. **ayons** *We will wait here until we have an answer.*
37. **sois** *All that happened before I was born.*
38. **est** *It is difficult to predict all the possibilities.*
39. **aie** *It's the best movie that I've seen this summer.*
40. **auras** *It is probable that you will have your diploma at the end of next year.*
41. **a été (était)** *I hope that he was impressed by your last gift.*
42. **ait** *We must find a speaker who speaks clearly.*
43. **est** *I have a friend who is half-French and half-American.*
44. **soit** *The diplomats doubt that the ambassador has involved himself in the affair.*
45. **aient** *It is too bad that our hosts invited so many people.*
46. **est** *It is true that the freeway is dangerous.*
47. **aie eu** *I finished everything in spite of the fact that I have had some difficulty.*
48. **ait** *It was absolutely necessary that we have this reference.*
49. **sois (aies été)** *She would have been happy that you were with us.*
50. **soit** *That would have pleased us that she made use of our apartment.*

Faire

51. **fera**   *I hope that it will be beautiful tomorrow.*
52. **fasse**   *What do you want me to do with it?*
53. **faisons**   *It is evident that we make fewer mistakes.*
54. **fasse**   *It's aggravating that she does that now.*
55. **faire**   *Would you take a walk with me?*
56. **fasses**   *You absolutely must meet him (her).*

57. **feront**   *It is probable that they will try harder next time.*
58. **fais**   *We will be happy if you do that.*
59. **feras**   *We will be happy when you do that.*
60. **fasses**   *We will be happy that you do that.*
61. **faire**   *We will be happy to do that.*
62. **avoir, fait**   *We will be happy to have already done that.*

11 IDIOMATIC VERB USAGE

THIS CHAPTER IS ABOUT

☑ **Idiomatic Use of Present and Imparfait**
☑ **Aspectual Idioms**
☑ **Causative Verb Phrases**
☑ **Reflexive Passives**
☑ **Meanings of the Verb Devoir**

Some tenses and combinations of verbs have unpredictable or *idiomatic* meanings that you can't deduce from the root meaning of the verb combined with its tense ending.

11-1. Idiomatic Use of Present and Imparfait

French and English both use the present tense to describe situations that are connected with the present but take place in the future. However, the two languages differ in their treatment of situations that begin in one past time period and continue into another, or that begin in the past and continue into the present.

A. Past events continuing in the present

Use the *present tense* to tell about situations that begin in the past and continue in the present—where English uses a perfect tense.

Les socialistes **sont** au pouvoir depuis les élections.	*The socialists have been in power since the elections.*
Je **garde** ce vieilles lettres depuis des années.	
OR	*I have been saving these old letters for years.*
Il y a des années que je **garde** ces vieilles lettres.	

> *NOTE:* **Depuis**, *since*, *for*, indicates the beginning of a situation or the length of time it has been going on. **Il y a + time + que**, *for*, always indicates the length of time.
>
> | | |
> |---|---|
> | Nous sommes à Los Angeles **depuis** dix ans; **depuis** 1976. | *We have been in Los Angeles for ten years, since 1976.* |
>
> In casual spoken French, use **cela fait** or **ce fait** in place of **il y a + an expression of time**.
>
> | | |
> |---|---|
> | **Cela (ça) fait** un moment que tu es là? | *Have you been here long?* |

EXERCISE 11-1: Answer the following questions affirmatively, substituting **il y a . . . que** for **depuis**, and **depuis** for **il y a**. Then translate your sentence into English. Answers and translations are at the end of the chapter.

Example:	Y a-t-il longtemps que tu es ici?	*Have you been here long?*
	Oui, je suis ici depuis longtemps.	*Yes, I've been here for a long time.*

1. Est-ce qu'il y a un an que nous avons cette voiture?

2. Est-ce que le magasin est fermé depuis un mois?

3. Y a-t-il longtemps que vous vous connaissez?

4. Etes-vous mariés depuis dix ans?

5. Est-ce qu'ils étudient le français depuis un mois?

6. Est-ce qu'il y a quelque temps que ce film se joue en ville?

7. Est-ce qu'on ne voit plus ces gens depuis trois semaines?

8. Y a-t-il longtemps que personne n'habite cet appartement?

9. Prends-tu ces médicaments depuis que tu es malade?

10. Est-ce qu'il y a plusieurs mois qu'ils viennent régulièrement?

B. Remote past situations continuing in the past

Use the *imparfait* to tell about situations that begin in the remote past and were continuing at the past moment under consideration—where English uses a past perfect tense.

Ils **se connaissaient** depuis un an
   quand ils se sont mariés.

They had known each other for a
year when they got married.

Nous **vivions** là depuis longtemps quand
   nous avons acheté la maison.
         OR

We had been living there for a long
time when we bought the house.

Il y avait longtemps que nous **vivions**
   là quand nous avons acheté la maison. .

> *NOTE:* When you use **il y a** with a time expression in the passé composé or the imparfait—without **que**—it means *ago* rather than *for*.
>
> Ils **se sont connus il y a** trois ans.
>   OR   *They met three years ago.*
> **Il y a** trois ans qu'ils **se sont connus**.

EXERCISE 11-2: Answer the following questions in the affirmative, substituting **depuis** for **il y a . . . que**, and **il y a . . . que** for **depuis**. Then translate your sentence into English. Answers and translations are at the end of the chapter.

Example: Vos parents se connaissaient-ils
                depuis longtemps lorsqu'ils
                se sont mariés?

Had your parents known
one another long before
they got married?

Il y avait longtemps qu'ils se
connaissaient lorsqu'ils se
sont mariés.

They had known each other
for a long time when
they got married.

1. Y avait-il quelques mois qu'ils négociaient au commencement de la guerre?

2. Est-ce que ton fils marchait depuis des mois quand il a appris à parler?

3. Est-ce qu'il y avait longtemps qu'elle dormait quand le téléphone a sonné?

4. Y habitaient-ils depuis un mois au moment de l'incident?

5. Y avait-il longtemps que tu l'attendais?

11-2. Aspectual Idioms

You may use combinations of verbs as well as verb endings to indicate certain aspects of time or tense such as progressivity, perfectivity, or finality.

A. Progressive aspect

French does not have progressive tenses equivalent to those formed with *be + ing* in English. You may use the idiomatic verb phrase (**être**) **en train de + infinitive** to emphasize the *ongoing* nature of a situation.

Il **est en train de faire** une grosse bêtise.   *He's making a big mistake.*
Nous **étions en train de discuter** son avenir.   *We were discussing her future.*

REMEMBER: You can also translate the French present and imparfait to refer to ongoing situations.

Il **fait** une grosse bêtise.   *He's making a big mistake.*
OR
He makes a big mistake.

Nous **discutions** son avenir.   *We were discussing her future.*
OR
We discuss her future.

NOTE: **Etre en train de** is most often used in the present or imparfait.

EXERCISE 11-3: Emphasize the ongoing nature of the following events or situations. Answers and translations are at the end of the chapter.

Example: On prend un bain de soleil.   *We sun ourselves.*
OR
We're sunning ourselves.

On est en train de prendre un bain de soleil.   *We're sunning ourselves.*

1. Ce monsieur perd ses cheveux.
2. Nous transportions des marchandises dans des camions.
3. Ils annoncent le départ de votre vol.
4. Le gouvernement subit de grands changements.
5. Pourquoi faisaient-ils toutes ces grimaces?
6. Les diplomates résolvent les difficultés.
7. Elle écrit son autobiographie.
8. Il mourait de soif.
9. Nous dépensions tout notre argent.
10. Ne les interrompez pas quand ils parlent.

B. Immediate future aspect

Combine the present or imparfait of the verb **aller**, *to go*, **+ infinitive** to form the equivalent of the English expression (*to be*) *going to . . .* to tell what is, or was, going to happen next.

Ces avions **vont partir** de l'aéroport d'Orly.   *Those planes are going to leave from Orly airport.*
J'**allais dire** cela quand tu m'as interrompu.   *I was going to say that when you interrupted me.*

NOTE: Use **aller + infinitive** only with the *present* or *imparfait* of **aller**. If the meaning of the main clause requires the subjunctive, use the subjunctive of **devoir** with a progressive meaning.

Il **n'est pas certain** qu'ils **doivent** rester.   *It's not certain that they're going to stay.*

EXERCISE 11-4: Answer the following questions with a form of **aller** followed by the infinitive. Then translate your sentence into English. Answers and translations are at the end of the chapter.

Example: Nous sortons ce soir; et toi? *We're going out tonight; and you?*
      Je vais sortir ce soir aussi. *I'm going to go out tonight too.*

1. Je finis mes études cette année; et elle?
2. Cet acteur paraissait à la télévision; et sa femme?
3. Tu dînes en ville; et moi?
4. Les enfants restaient chez eux; et leurs parents?
5. Vous avez rendu visite à vos voisins; et vos frères?
6. Nous prendrons des aspirines; et vous?
7. La France aura des élections; et l'Italie?
8. Elle a repris ses études; et lui?
9. Nous avons commandé des escargots; et eux?
10. Je finis cet exercice; et toi?

C. Immediate Past

Use the expression **venir de + infinitive** to make it clear that something just happened or had just happened.

Nous **venons d'expliquer** tout cela. *We've just explained all that.*
Leur patron **venait de** leur **donner** *Their boss had just given them a raise.*
 une augmentation.

> *NOTE:* Use **venir de + infinitive** only in the *present, subjunctive,* and *imparfait.*

EXERCISE 11-5: Rewrite the following sentences to indicate that the events happened in the immediate past. Then translate your sentence into English. Answers and translations are at the end of the chapter.

  Example: Il avait mangé tous les restes. *He had eaten all the leftovers.*
      Il venait de manger tous les *He had just eaten all the*
       restes. *leftovers.*
      Nos grands-parents ont pris leur *Our grandparents have*
       retraite. *retired.*
      Nos grands-parents viennent de *Our grandparents have just*
       prendre leur retraite. *retired.*

1. J'ai commencé un nouvel exercice.

2. Ils avaient complètement rénové leur maison.

3. Nous sommes retournés de vacances.

4. Est-ce qu'ils ont consulté un médecin?

5. J'avais posé la même question.

6. Se sont-ils mariés?

7. Elle avait fermé le magasin pour la nuit.

8. A-t-il pris le train pour Lyon?

9. Qui a téléphoné?

10. J'ai fini cet exercice.

D. Terminal aspect

Use the idiomatic expression **finir par + infinitive** to indicate the terminal aspect of an event or situation—translate it in the sense of *finally.*

Les choses **ont fini par s'arranger**. *Things finally worked out*
              (worked out in the end).

Tu **finiras par** lui **donner** raison. *You'll wind up agreeing with him.*

> *NOTE:* You may use **finir par + infinitive** in all tenses.

EXERCISE 11-6: Tell what *finally* happened or happens in each instance. Answers and translations are at the end of the chapter.

Example:	Il a essayé, mais il a abandonné.	*He tried, but he gave up.*
	Il a essayé, mais il a fini par abandonner.	*He tried, but he finally gave up.*

1. Nous avons joué, mais nous avons perdu.
2. Il s'efforcera, mais il arrivera le dernier.
3. On le ferait, mais on se tromperait.
4. Si elle était, venue elle se serait amusée.
5. Je réussirai, si je fais un peu d'effort.

11-3. Causative Verb Phrases

The verb **faire**, **laisser**, or **envoyer** before an infinitive forms a causative verb phrase and means *to have, make, let, send, or cause someone (to) do something.* These causative phrases act as single verbs in respect to their various subjects and objects.

A. Single subject causative sentences

If a causative precedes an infinitive that has a direct and/or an indirect object, but no explicit subject, the objects of the infinitive function as the objects of the entire verb phrase.

Il **a fait construire sa maison**.	*He had his house built.*
Il **l'a fait construire**.	*He had it built.*
On **a fait téléphoner aux parents** des élèves. On **leur a fait téléphoner**.	*We had the students' parents called. We had them called.*
Jacques **a envoyé annoncer son arrivée à sa fiancée**. Jacques **la lui a envoyé annoncer**.	*Jacques sent someone to announce his arrival to his fiancee. Jacques sent someone to announce it to her.*

B. Two-subject causative sentences

1. If the infinitive in a causative verb phrase has an explicit subject different from that of the main verb, the infinitive subject functions as the direct object of the entire verb phrase.

Ne **laisse** pas **passer cette occasion**.	*Don't let this opportunity get away.*
Ne **la** laisse pas **passer**.	*Don't let it get away.*
Nous **avons envoyé chercher le courier**.	*We sent for the mail. (We sent to look for the mail.)*
Nous **l'avons envoyé chercher**.	*We sent for it.*

2. If the infinitive in a causative phrase has both a subject and a direct object, the subject becomes the object of a preposition:

   • **par**—if the person in question is performing a task

Il a **fait réparer** sa voiture **par le mécanicien**.	*He had his car repaired by a mechanic.*

   • **à**—if he (she) is actually having something done for him (her)

Les mères **font manger** les épinards **aux enfants**.	*Mothers make their children eat spinach.*

   NOTE: The preposition **à** makes the second subject an indirect object:

Les mères les **leur** font manger.	*Mothers make them eat it.*

   par simply makes the second subject the object of a preposition.

Il l'a fait réparer **par lui**.	*He had him repair it.*
La reine **a fait faire** la robe **à la princesse par la couturière**.	*The queen had the dressmaker make the dress for the princess.*
La reine la **lui a fait faire par elle**.	*The queen had her make it for her.*

NOTE: For the sake of clarity, try to avoid sentences like the preceding—which uses three object pronouns.

3. **Laissé** and **envoyé** agree in number and gender with a preceding direct object—if that object is the logical subject of the following infinitive.

Nous **l'avons envoyée** promener.   *We sent her packing.*

BUT

Nous **l'avons envoyé** promener.   *We sent for her.*

None of these agreements are heard in spoken French.

NOTE: The past participle **fait** is invariable in causative sentences.

C. Reflexive causatives

If one of the objects of a causative phrase is identical to its subject, refer to it with a reflexive pronoun.

Ils se font masser avant un match important.   *They have themselves massaged before a big game.*

Elle ne **se laisse** pas **teindre** les cheveux.   *She doesn't let anyone tint her hair.*

EXERCISE 11-7: Replace the main verb in the following sentences with the appropriate causative verb. Answers and translations are at the end of the chapter.

Example: La secrétaire a demandé aux clients d'attendre.   *The secretary asked the customers to wait.*

La secrétaire a fait attendre les clients.   *The secretary had the customers wait.*

Nous avons permis aux enfants de sortir.   *We allowed the children to go out.*

Nous avons laissé sortir les enfants.   *We let the children go out.*

1. Le directeur dira aux employés de faire attention.
2. Je ne permettrais pas à ma femme de travailler.
3. Mon père va demander à son dentiste d'arranger ses dents.
4. On leur écrira d'apporter du champagne de France.
5. Elle dit au coiffeur de lui couper les cheveux.
6. On ne permet pas aux passagers de fumer.
7. Le roi a commandé à ses soldats de résister aux attaques de l'ennemi.
8. Napoléon avait ordonné aux sculpteurs de décorer l'Arc.
9. Qui disait aux enfants de faire leurs devoirs?
10. Il demandera à sa femme de repasser ses chemises.

EXERCISE 11-8: Repeat EXERCISE 11-7, substituting pronouns for the subjects and objects of the infinitives. Answers and translations are at the end of the chapter.

11-4. Reflexive Passives

To say that *something* is done without specifying *who* does it, French usually uses a reflexive verb. The three following sentences are synonymous:

(1) Le français est parlé au Canada.
(2) On parle français au Canada.   *French is spoken in Canada.*
(3) Le français se parle au Canada.

BUT (1)—the structure closest to English usage—is the *least natural* in French.

A. Personal reflexive passives

1. If the meaning of a transitive verb—a verb requiring a direct object—demands that the subject and object be two different persons, but the true subject is omitted, use a reflexive pronoun (see Sec. 6-6).

Je **m'appelle** Oscar.	*They call me Oscar. I am called Oscar.* *My name is Oscar.* (Literally: *I call myself Oscar.*)
Nous **nous sommes** brutalement **désabusés**.	*We had our eyes opened brutally.* (Literally: *We disillusioned ourselves brutally.*)

> *NOTE:* You may also suggest the same indefiniteness by using the impersonal pronoun **on**.
>
> **On** m'appelle Oscar.
> **On** nous a brutalement désabusés.

2. When a verb has a reflexive meaning that makes sense when the subject *is* a person or persons, the **on** form is clearer in meaning.

Il s'est trouvé devant la porte.	*He found himself at the door.* (*He was found at the door.*)
On l'a trouvé devant la porte.	*They (We, One) found him at the door.* (*He was found at the door.*)

B. Impersonal reflexives

For a verb whose reflexive makes little sense when the subject is *not* a person, use the reflexive passive structure.

L'église se trouvait en face de la mairie.	*The church was (found) across from the city hall.*
A Paris, **les appartements** ne **se louent** pas; **ils s'achètent**.	*In Paris, apartments aren't rented; they're bought.*

EXERCISE 11-9: Make passive reflexive sentences from the following active sentences. If the reflexive form seems to have more than one meaning, write another sentence with **on** as its subject. Answers and translations are at the end of the chapter.

Example:	Quelqu'un a nommé les candidats.	*Someone nominated the candidates.*
	Les candidats se sont nommés.	*The candidates were nominated.*
		OR
		The candidates nominated themselves.
	On a nommé les candidats.	*The candidates were nominated.*

1. Les gens lisaient les journaux le soir.
2. Personne ne disputera cette opinion.
3. Vous trouvez la Bretagne au Nord de la France.
4. Ils ont choisi le nouveau président en Novembre.
5. Rien ne contredit les faits.
6. Tout le monde cacherait la vérité.
7. Quelqu'un a perdu un portefeuille.
8. Aucun événement ne changera son avis.
9. Vous ne gagnez rien en mentant.
10. Ils ont fermé les portes du magasin.

11-5. Meanings of the Verb Devoir

Although the forms of **devoir** are irregular, its meanings in the different tenses are predictable from its basic meaning combined with its tense endings. We perceive the different translations as irregularities because there is no equivalent English verb with a complete set of tenses.

A. Use of devoir, *to owe*

The verb **devoir** means *owe(d)* in all tenses

- when it is used with a noun or pronoun direct object:

La banque me **doit 5 mille francs**.   *The bank owes me 5 thousand francs.*

OR

- when it is used with a complement infinitive preceded by the preposition **de**:

Il me **devra de s'occuper** de mes affaires.   *He will owe it to me to take care of my affairs.*

B. Devoir followed directly by an infinitive

1. Translate the present tense of **devoir** as *must . . .*—in both the certain and conjectural senses—or *have to . . .*

Il **doit** être à l'école.   *He must be in school. (has to be/probably is)*

2. Translate the *passé composé* of **devoir** as *must have . . .*—in the conjectural sense—or *had to . . .*

Elle **a dû** remettre cela au lendemain.   *She must have put that off until the next day. (conjecture)*
She had to put that off until the next day.

NOTE: In the sense of *had to . . .*, **devoir** means that the action was actually undertaken.

3. Translate the *imparfait* of **devoir** as *was (were) supposed to . . .*—not specifying that the action was ever undertaken.

A l'âge de huit ans, je **devais** me coucher tôt.   *At eight years of age, I was supposed to go to bed early.*
Vous **deviez** venir me voir l'autre soir!   *You were supposed to come see me the other evening!*

In the conjectural sense, the *imparfait* of **devoir** means *was probably . . .*

Il **devait** être bien fatigué après ce long voyage.   *He was probably very tired after that long trip.*

4. Translate the *future tense* of **devoir** as *will have to . . .*

Nous **devrons** refaire tout cela.   *We'll have to do all that again.*
Les trains **devront** faire un petit détour.   *The trains will have to go a little out of their way.*

5. Translate the *conditional* of **devoir** as *should . . .* or *ought to . . .*—implying *probably won't*.

Vous **devriez** arrêter de fumer.   *You should (ought to) quit smoking.*
Mes parents **devraient** être plus indulgents.   *My parents should (ought to) be more indulgent.*

6. Translate the *past conditional* of **devoir** as *should have . . .* or *ought to have . . .*—implying *probably didn't*.

Le gouvernement **aurait dû** faire quelque chose.   *The government should have done something.*
Tu n'**aurais** pas **dû** lui dire cela!   *You shouldn't have told him that!*

EXERCISE 11-10: Fill in the blanks with the appropriate form and tense of the verb **devoir**, according to the meaning of the entire sentence. Then translate the sentence into English. Answers and translations are at the end of the chapter.

1. Vous _____ obtenir votre passeport avant votre départ.

2. Le mécanicien _____ réparer le carburateur, mais il n'avait pas le temps.

3. Il m'attendait devant le cinéma où nous _____ nous rencontrer.

4. Mon frère était si malade que nous _____ appeler le médecin.

5. Je _____ vous appeler cet après midi parce que je suis trop occupée en ce moment.

6. Ces enfants _____ étudier, mais ils préfèrent regarder la télévision.

7. Si elle a refusé de répondre elle ne _____ pas être seule.

8. Tu _____ le voir; il était assis en face de toi!

9. J' _____ me laver la tête ce matin, mais je n'avais plus de shampooing.

10. Vous _____ changer d'école, mais vous ne le ferez jamais.

11. Mes amis _____ déménager parce que leur appartement a été vendu.

12. Ma soeur me _____ de l'argent depuis deux mois.

13. Le gouvernement _____ annuler toutes les taxes un jour!

14. Les Etats-Unis _____ annexer le Canada en 1776.

15. Les colonies américaines _____ faire la guerre pour avoir leur indépendance.

SUMMARY

1. French uses the present tense to talk about past situations continuing into the present, and the imparfait to talk about remote past situations continuing into the closer past.
2. **Depuis**, *since*, *for*, is used with the imparfait or present tense to tell when a continuing action began or how long it had (has) been going on. **Il y a . . . que** is used in the same way, but tells only how long a situation continued.
3. When **il y a**—*without* **que**—is used with an expression of time and a past tense verb, it simply means *ago*.
4. To emphasize the progressive aspect of a situation in the present or imparfait, the verb phrase **être en train de + infinitive** may be used.
5. An action beginning in the immediate future or one that was about to begin in the past may be expressed by the present or imparfait of **aller + infinitive**, meaning *is (was) going to . . .*
6. In order to stress the immediate past aspect, the phrase **venir de + infinitive** is used to mean *have (had) just . . .* This phrase is used only in the present tense or imparfait.
7. The final aspect of a situation may be expressed by the phrase **finir par + infinitive**, which may be used in all tenses.
8. Causative verb phrases have **faire**, **laisser**, or **envoyer** as their main verb followed by an infinitive. Causatives function as a single verb in respect to all subjects and objects. Where the result would be two subjects, the second subject becomes a direct object. Where the result would be two direct objects, the second object becomes an indirect object or the object of the preposition **par** or **à**.
9. The past participle **fait** is invariable in causative sentences. **Laissé(e)(s)** and **envoyé(e)(s)** agree in gender and number with a preceding direct object—if that object is the logical subject of the infinitive.
10. The irregular verb **devoir** has a consistent meaning in all tenses. Pay special attention to the conditional meaning *should*, the past conditional meaning *should have*, and the passé composé meaning *had to* or *must have*—according to the context of the sentence.

RAISE YOUR GRADES

Il y a . . . que and depuis

Tell how long each situation has been going on using **il y a . . . que** wherever possible, and **depuis** where **il y a . . . que** is incorrect. Then translate your sentence into English. Answers and translations are at the end of the chapter.

    Example: Les satéllites sont dans l'espace.   *Satellites are in space.*
        /20 ans   */20 years*

        Il y a 20 ans que les satéllites   *Satellites have been in space for*
        sont dans l'espace.   *20 years.*

1. Les socialistes sont au pouvoir. /les dernières élections
2. Mes parents sont mariés. /40 ans
3. Ce magasin vend des ordinateurs. /l'été dernier
4. Nous attendons l'autobus. /une demi-heure
5. J'habite à Montréal. /1975
6. Ma voiture ne marche plus. /le dernier accident
7. La France est une république. /200 ans
8. Il enseigne à cette école. /la fin de ses études
9. Nous nous connaissons. /des années
10. Tu répètes la même chose. /le début de la discussion

Repeat the preceding ten sentences telling how long each situation *had* been going on. Translate your sentence into English. Answers and translations are at the end of the chapter.

Immediate future, immediate past, final or progressive aspect

Rewrite the following sentences using a phrase indicating immediate future, immediate past, final or progressive aspect, according to the meaning of each. Answers and translations are at the end of the chapter.

21. Je fais un exercice de français en ce moment.
22. Nous prendrons un café et un croissant.
23. Non merci, j'ai mangé.
24. Il faisait sa gymnastique.
25. Maintenant tout le monde saura la vérité.
26. Finalement le bateau est arrivé au Havre.
27. C'est gentil de nous inviter, mais nous avons vu ce film.
28. Excusez-moi, mais je parle au téléphone.
29. Mes parents seront très contents de mes notes.
30. Il était déjà très tard et les invités étaient arrivés un quart d'heure avant.
31. Nous arriverons finalement à répondre à cette question.
32. Qu'est-ce que tu lis?
33. A mon départ, ils regardaient fixement la télévision.
34. Il était parti juste avant la fin.
35. Malheureusement l'enfant ne verrait jamais sa mère.

Causative verbs

Change the main verb in the following sentences to the appropriate causative verb, making any other necessary changes. Answers and translations are at the end of the chapter.

36. Le directeur permet aux employés de manger à leur bureau.
37. Ma mère a demandé au pâtissier de me faire un gâteau.
38. J'expédierai un messager pour demander les renseignements.
39. Il t'a dit de nettoyer la chambre.

40. Le client a demandé au coiffeur de lui tailler la barbe.
41. Qui te permettra de t'absenter de l'école?
42. Les propriétaires ont dit aux jardiniers de planter des arbres pour eux.
43. Personne ne te permet de l'insulter comme cela.
44. Nous allons commander à la serveuse de nous le servir tout de suite.
45. Elles disent aux invités d'entrer par la grande porte.

Devoir

Fill in the blanks with the appropriate tense of the verb **devoir**. Then translate the complete sentence into English. Answers and translations are at the end of the chapter.

46. Nous _____ y penser avant.

47. On ne le voit plus; il _____ être amoureux.

48. Vous _____ vraiment vous arrêter de fumer.

49. Si vous ne le faites pas aujourd'hui vous _____ le faire demain.

50. Je n' _____ pas _____ lui répondre comme cela.

51. Nous _____ du respect et de la consideration à nos parents.

52. Les gouvernements _____ bannir les armes thermonucléaires.

53. Je ne pouvais être présent parce que je _____ assister à une autre classe.

54. Il y avait beaucoup d'absences la semaine dernière; il _____ y avoir une épidemie de grippe.

55. Les voitures _____ s'arrêter au feu rouge, mais elles ont continué sans ralentir.

CHAPTER ANSWERS

EXERCISE 11-1:
1. Oui, nous avons cette voiture depuis un an. *Yes, we've had this car for a year.*
2. Oui, il y a un mois que le magasin est fermé. *Yes, the store has been closed for a month.*
3. Oui, nous nous connaissons depuis longtemps. *Yes, we've known one another for a long time.*
4. Oui, il y a dix ans que nous sommes mariés. *Yes, we've been married for ten years.*
5. Oui, il y a un mois qu'ils étudient le français. *Yes, they've been studying French for a month.*
6. Oui, ce film se joue en ville depuis quelque temps. *Yes, that movie has been playing in town for a while.*
7. Oui, il y a trois semaines qu'on ne voit plus ces gens. *Yes, we haven't seen those people for three weeks.*
8. Oui, personne n'habite cet appartement depuis longtemps. *Yes, nobody has been living in that apartment for a long time.*
9. Oui, je prends ce médicament depuis que je suis malade. *Yes, I've been taking this medicine (ever) since I've been sick.*
10. Oui, ils viennent régulièrement depuis plusieurs mois. *Yes, they have been coming regularly for several months.*

EXERCISE 11-2:
1. Oui, ils négociaient depuis quelques mois au commencement de la guerre. *Yes, they had been negotiating for several months at the beginning of the war.*
2. Oui, il y avait des mois que mon fils marchait quand il a appris à parler. *Yes, my son had been walking for months when he learned to talk.*
3. Oui, elle dormait depuis longtemps quand le téléphone a sonné. *Yes, she had been sleeping for a long time when the telephone rang.*
4. Oui, il y avait un mois qu'ils y habitaient au moment de l'incident. *Yes, they had lived there for a month at the time of the incident.*
5. Oui, je l'attendais depuis longtemps. *Yes, I had been waiting for him for a long time.*

EXERCISE 11-3:
1. Ce monsieur est en train de perdre ses cheveux. *That gentleman is losing his hair.*
2. Nous étions en train de transporter des marchandises dans des camions. *We were transporting some merchandise in trucks.*
3. Ils sont en train d'annoncer le départ de votre vol. *They are announcing the departure of your flight.*

4. Le gouvernement est en train de subir de grands changements. *The government is undergoing some big changes.*

5. Pourquoi étaient-ils en train de faire toutes ces grimaces? *Why were they making all those faces?*

6. Les diplomates sont en train de résoudre les difficultés. *The diplomats are resolving the difficulties.*

7. Elle est en train d'écrire son autobiographie. *She is writing her autobiography.*

8. Il était en train de mourir de soif. *He was dying of thirst.*

9. Nous étions en train de dépenser tout notre argent. *We were spending all our money.*

10. Ne les interrompez pas quand ils sont en train de parler. *Don't interrupt them when they are speaking.*

EXERCISE 11-4:

1. Elle va finir ses études cette année aussi. *She is going to finish her studies this year too.*

2. Sa femme allait paraître à la télévision aussi. *His wife is going to appear on television too.*

3. Tu vas diner en ville aussi. *You are going to dine in town too.*

4. Leurs parents vont rester chez eux aussi. *Their parents are going to stay at their home too.*

5. Mes frères vont leur rendre visite aussi. *My brothers are going to visit them too.*

6. Je vais prendre des aspirines aussi. *I am going to take some aspirin too.*

7. L'Italie va avoir des elections aussi. *Italy is going to have (some) elections too.*

8. Il va reprendre ses études aussi. *He is going to resume his studies too.*

9. Ils vont commander des escargots aussi. *They are going to order snails too.*

10. Je vais finir cet exercice aussi. *I am going to finish this exercise too.*

EXERCISE 11-5:

1. Je viens de commencer un nouvel exercice. *I've just begun (I just began) a new exercise.*

2. Ils venaient de rénover complètement leur maison. *They had just completely renovated their house.*

3. Nous venons de retourner de vacances. *We('ve) just returned from vacation.*

4. Ils viennent de consulter un médecin. *They('ve) just consulted a doctor.*

5. Je venais de poser la même question. *I had just asked the same question.*

6. Est-ce qu'ils viennent de se marier? (Viennent-ils de se marier?) *Did they just get married? (Have they just got(ten) married?)*

7. Elle venait de fermer le magasin pour la nuit. *She had just closed the store for the night.*

8. Vient-il de prendre le train pour Lyon? *Has he just taken (Did he just take) the train for Lyons?*

9. Qui vient de téléphoner? *Who (has) just called?*

10. Je viens de finir cet exercice. *I have just finished this exercise.*

EXERCISE 11-6:

1. Nous avons joué, mais nous avons fini par perdre. *We played, but we finally lost.*

2. Il s'efforcera, mais il finira par arrivera. *He would strain himself, but he would finally arrive.*

3. On le ferait, mais on finirait par se tromper. *We would do it, but we would finally make a mistake.*

4. Si elle était venue, elle aurait fini par s'amuser. *If she would come, she would finally have a good time.*

5. Je finirai par réussir, si je fais un peu d'effort. *I would finally succeed if I made a little effort.*

EXERCISE 11-7:

1. Le directeur fera faire attention aux employés. *The boss made the employees pay attention.*

2. Je ne laisserais pas travailler ma femme. *I would not let my wife work.*

3. Mon père va se faire arranger les dents par son dentiste. *My father is going to have his dentist fix his teeth.*

4. On leur fera apporter du champagne de France. *They are going to bring them some champagne from France.*

5. Elle se fera couper les cheveux par le coiffeur. *She is going to have the hairdresser cut her hair.*

6. On ne laisse pas fumer les passagers. *Passengers are not allowed to smoke.*

7. Le roi a fait résister ses soldats aux attaques de l'ennemi. *The king had his soldiers resist the enemy attack.*

8. Napoléon avait fait décorer l'Arc par les sculpteurs. *Napoleon had the sculptors decorate the Arch.*

9. Qui faisait faire leurs devoirs aux enfants? *Who made the children do their homework?*

10. Il fera repasser ses chemises par sa femme. *He had his wife iron his shirts.*

EXERCISE 11-8:

1. Le directeur leur fera faire attention. *The boss made them pay attention.*

2. Je ne la laisserais pas travailler. *I would not let her work.*

3. Mon père va se les faire arranger par lui (son dentiste). *My father is going to have him fix them.*

4. On leur en fera apporter de France. *They are going to bring them some (of it) from France.*

5. Elle se les fera couper par lui (le coiffeur). *She is going to have him cut it.*

6. On ne les laisse pas fumer. *They do not let them smoke.*
7. Le roi les y a fait résister. *The king made them resist it.*
8. Napoléon l'avait fait décorer par eux. *Napoleon had them decorate it.*
9. Qui les leur faisait faire? *Who made them do it?*
10. Il les fera repasser par elle (sa femme). *He had her iron them.*

EXERCISE 11-9:

1. Les journaux se lisaient le soir. *The newspapers were read this evening.*
2. Cette opinion ne se disputera pas. *This opinion will not be disputed.*
3. La Bretagne se trouve au Nord de la France. *Brittany is found in the north of France.*
4. Le nouveau président se choisira en Novembre. On choisira le nouveau président en Novembre. *The new president will be chosen in November.*
5. Les faits ne se contredisent pas. *The facts are not contradicted.*
6. La vérité se cachera. *The truth will not be hidden.*
7. Un portefeuille s'est perdu. *A billfold was lost.*
8. Son avis ne se changera pas. *His advice will not change.*
9. Rien ne se gagne en mentant. *Nothing is gained by lying.*
10. Les portes du magasin se sont fermées. *The doors of the store are closed.*

EXERCISE 11-10:

1. **devrez** *You will have to get your passport before your departure.*
2. **devait** *The mechanic was supposed to repair the carburetor, but he didn't have time.*
3. **devions** *He waited for me in front of the theater where we were supposed to meet.*
4. **avons dû** *My brother was so sick that we had to call the doctor.*
5. **devrai** *I will have to call you this afternoon because I am too busy right now.*
6. **devraient** *These children should (ought to) study, but they prefer to watch television.*
7. **n'a pas dû** *If she refused to answer she must not have been alone.*
8. **as dû** *You had to see him; he was sitting in front of you!*
9. **aurais dû** *I should have washed my hair this morning, but I didn't have any more shampoo.*
10. **devriez** *You should (ought to) change after school, but you never do it.*
11. **ont dû (devront)** *My friends had to (will have to) move because their apartment was sold.*
12. **doit** *My sister has owed me money for six months.*
13. **devrait** *The government should (ought to) cancel all the taxes one day!*
14. **auraient dû** *The United States should have annexed Canada in 1776.*
15. **ont dû** *The American colonies had to make war in order to get their independence.*

RAISE YOUR GRADES

Il y a . . . que and depuis

1. Les socialistes sont au pouvoir depuis les dernières élections. *The socialiste have been in power since the last elections.*
2. Il y a 40 ans que mes parents sont mariés. *My parents have been married for 40 years.*
3. Ce magasin vend des ordinateurs depuis l'été dernier. *This store has been selling computers since last summer.*
4. Il y a une demi-heure que nous attendons l'autobus. *We've been waiting for the bus for half an hour.*
5. J'habite à Montréal depuis 1975. *I've been living in Montreal since 1975.*
6. Ma voiture ne marche plus depuis le dernier accident. *My car has not been running any more since the last accident.*
7. Il y a 200 ans que la France est une république. *France has been a republic for 200 years.*
8. Il enseigne à cette école depuis la fin de ses études. *He has been teaching at that school since the end of his studies.*
9. Il y a des années que nous nous connaissons. *We've known each other (one another) for years.*
10. Tu répètes la même chose depuis le début de la discussion. *You've been repeating the same thing since the beginning of the discussion.*
11. Les socialistes étaient au pouvoir depuis les dernières élections. *The socialists had been in power since the last (preceding) elections.*
12. Il y avait 40 ans que mes parent étaient mariés. *My parents had been married for 40 years.*
13. Ce magasin vendait des ordinateurs depuis l'été dernier. *That store had been selling computers since the previous summer.*
14. Il y avait une demi-heure que nous attendions l'autobus. *We had been waiting for the bus for a half hour.*
15. J'habitais à Montréal depuis 1975. *I had been living in Montreal since 1975.*
16. Ma voiture ne marchait plus depuis le dernier accident. *My car had not been working since the last accident.*
17. Il y avait 200 ans que la France était une république. *France had been a republic for 200 years.*
18. Il enseignait à cette école depuis la fin de ses études. *He had been teaching at that school since the end of his studies.*

19. Il y avait des années que nous nous connaissions. *We had known each other for years.*

20. Tu répétais la même chose depuis le début de la discussion. *You had been repeating the same thing since the beginning of the discussion.*

Immediate future, immediate past, final or progressive aspect

21. Je suis en train de faire un exercice de français. *I am doing an exercise in French.*

22. Nous allons prendre un café et un croissant. *I'm going to have coffee and a roll.*

23. Non merci, je viens de manger. *No thank you, I've just eaten.*

24. Il était en train de faire sa gymnastique. *He was doing his gymnastics.*

25. Maintenant tout le monde va savoir la vérité. *Now everyone is going to know the truth.*

26. Le bateau a fini par arriver au Havre. *The boat finally arrived at Havre.*

27. C'est gentil de nous inviter mais nous venons de voir ce film. *It is nice (of you) to invite us but we just saw that movie.*

28. Excusez-moi, mais je suis en train de parler au téléphone. *Excuse me, but I am speaking on the telephone.*

29. Mes parents vont être très contents de mes notes. *My parents are going to be very happy with my grades.*

30. Il était déjà très tard et les invités venaient d'arriver. *He was very late and the guests had just arrived.*

31. Nous finirons par arriver à répondre à cette question. *We will finally manage to answer that question.*

32. Qu'est-ce que tu es en train de lire? *What are you reading?*

33. A mon départ, ils étaient en train de regarder fixement la télévision. *When I left, they were staring fixedly at the television.*

34. Il venait de partir juste avant la fin. *He left just before the end.*

35. Malheureusement, l'enfant n'allait jamais voir sa mère. *Unfortunately, the child never saw his (her) mother.*

Causative verbs

36. Le directeur laisse les employés manger à leur bureau. *The boss let the employees eat at their desks.*

37. Ma mère m'a fait faire un gâteau par le pâtissier. *My mother had the pastry-cook make me a cake.*

38. J'enverrai chercher les renseignements par un messager. *I sent a messenger to look for the documents.*

39. Il a fait nettoyer la chambre par toi. *He made you clean the room.*

40. Le client s'est fait taillé la barbe par le coiffeur. *The customer had the barber trim his beard.*

41. Qui te laissera t'absenter de l'école? *Who will give you permission to be absent from school?*

42. Les propriétaires se sont fait planter des arbres par les jardiniers. *The owners had the gardeners plant some trees.*

43. Personne ne se laisse insulter comme cela par toi. *Nobody lets you insult them like that.*

44. Nous allons nous le faire servir par la serveuse tout de suite. *We are going to have the waitress serve it right away.*

45. Elles font entrer les invités par la grande porte. *They have the guests enter by the big door.*

Devoir

46. **aurions dû**   *We should have thought of it before today.*

47. **doit**   *We don't see him any more; he must be in love.*

48. **devriez**   *You should really stop smoking.*

49. **devrez**   *If you don't do it today, you will have to do it tomorrow.*

50. **n'aurais pas dû**   *I shouldn't have answered him (her) like that.*

51. **devons**   *We owe our parents respect and consideration.*

52. **devraient**   *Governments should ban thermonuclear weapons.*

53. **devais**   *I couldn't attend because I had to (was supposed to) attend another class.*

54. **a dû**   *There were a lot of absences last week; there must have been a flu epidemic.*

55. **auraient dû (devaient)**   *The cars should have stopped (were supposed to stop) at the red light, but they went on without stopping.*

12 LITERARY TENSES

THIS CHAPTER IS ABOUT

☑ **The Simple Past**
☑ **The Simple Past Perfect**
☑ **The Imperfect Subjunctive**
☑ **The Pluperfect Subjunctive**

French has past tenses and a past subjunctive used primarily on official or solemn occasions. Until quite recently, all serious writers used these formal tenses, which are also called **literary tenses**. The distinction between the literary and spoken past tenses has more to do with style than meaning, so you only have to recognize the literary tenses—and know that they have past or past perfect meanings.

12-1. The Simple Past

The *simple past* (**passé simple**) is a one-word verb form used in formal writing where the passé composé is normally used in spoken French (see Sec. 7-2).

A. Regular formation of the simple past tense

1. All verbs whose infinitives end in **-er** form the simple past from the infinitive stem by adding the following "**a**" endings.

Person	Singular	Plural
1st	-ai	-âmes
2nd	-as	-âtes
3rd	-a	-èrent

2. All regular **-ir** and **-re** verbs add the following "**i**" endings to the infinitive stem.

Person	Singular	Plural
1st	-is	-îmes
2nd	-is	-îtes
3rd	-it	-irent

Les attaques **finirent** quand l'ennemi
   se rendit.

The attacks ended when the
   enemy surrendered.

B. Irregular formation of the simple past tense

1. Irregular **-ir** verbs—except **courir, mourir, tenir, venir,** and their compounds—form the simple past with the "**i**" endings.

dormir, *to sleep*	il dorm**it**, *he slept*	ils dorm**irent**, *they slept*
ouvrir, *to open*	elle ouvr**it**, *she opened*	elles ouvr**irent**, *they opened*
acquérir, *to acquire*	il acquér**it**, *he acquired*	ils acquér**irent**, *they acquired*

222

2. Many irregular **-re** verbs form the simple past by adding the "**i**" endings to the plural (**nous**) stem.

* **écrire**, *to write*, and its compounds

(nous) **écriv**ons	ils écriv**it**,	ils écriv**irent**,
	he wrote	*they wrote*
(nous) **inscriv**ons	elle inscriv**it**,	elles inscriv**irent**,
	she inscribed	*they inscribed*

* **coudre**, *to sew*, and its compounds

(nous) **cous**ons	il cous**it**,	ils cous**irent**,
	he sewed	*they sewed*
(nous) **recous**ons	je recous**is**,	nous recous**îmes**,
	I restitched	*we restitched*

* **vaincre**, *to conquer*, and its compounds

(nous) **vainqu**ons	il vainqu**it**,	ils vainqu**irent**,
	he conquered	*they conquered*
(nous) **convainqu**ons	je convainqu**is**,	vous convainqu**îtes**,
	I convinced	*you convinced*

* **-indre** verbs

(nous) **craign**ons	il craign**it**, *he feared*	ils craign**irent**, *they feared*
(nous) **joign**ons	elle joign**it**, *she joined*	elles joign**irent**, *they joined*

* **-uire** verbs

(nous) **produis**ons	tu produis**is**,	vous produis**îtes**,
	you produced	*you produced*
(nous) **réduis**ons	il réduis**it**,	ils réduis**irent**,
	he reduced	*they reduced*

3. Many irregular verbs base the simple past on the stem and final vowel of the past participle. If that vowel is **-u-**, use the following "**u**" endings.

Person	Singular	Plural
1st	**-us**	**-ûmes**
2nd	**-us**	**-ûtes**
3rd	**-ut**	**-urent**

Infinitive	Past Participle	Simple past
apercevoir, *to glimpse*	aperçu	il aperç**ut**, *he glimpsed*
		ils aperç**urent**, *they glimpsed*
croire, *to believe*	cru	elle cr**ut**, *she believed*
		elles cr**urent**, *they believed*
dire, *to tell*	dit	nous d**îmes**, *we told*
		vous d**îtes**, *you told*
devoir, *must, have to*	dû	tu d**us**, *you must*
		vous d**ûtes**, *you must*
falloir, *to be necessary*	fallu	il fall**ut**, *it was necessary*
mettre, *to put, place*	mis	elle m**it**, *she put*
		elles m**irent**, *they put*
plaire, *to please*	plu	il pl**ut**, *it pleased*
		ils pl**urent**, *they pleased*
pleuvoir, *to rain*	plu	il pl**ut**, *it rained*
pouvoir, *to be able*	pu	nous p**ûmes**, *we were able*
		vous p**ûtes**, *you were able*
prendre, *to take*	pris	elle pr**it**, *she took*
		elles pr**irent**, *they took*
recevoir, *to receive*	reçu	il reç**ut**, *he received*
		ils reç**urent**, *they received*
résoudre, *to resolve*	résolu	il résol**ut**, *he resolved*
		ils résol**urent**, *they resolved*

Infinitive	Past Participle	Simple Past
savoir, *to know*	su	elle **sut**, *she knew*
		elles **surent**, *they knew*
vivre, *to live*	vécu	il **vécut**, *he lived*
		ils **vécurent**, *they lived*
vouloir, *to want*	voulu	elle voul**ut**, *she wanted*
		elles voul**urent**, *they wanted*

4. Some irregular verbs and their compounds have unpredictable simple past stems and vowels.

être, *to be*	je **fus**, *I was*	il **fut**, *he was*	nous **fûmes**, *we were*
avoir, *to have*	elle **eut**, *she had*	vous **eûtes**, *you had*	ils **eurent**, *they had*
courir, *to run*	je **courus**, *I ran*	tu **courus**, *you ran*	ils **coururent**, *they ran*
faire, *to do, make*	tu **fis**, *you did*	nour **fîmes**, *we did*	ils **firent**, *they did*
mourir, *to die*	il **mourut**, *he died*		ils **moururent**, *they died*
naître, *to be born*	je **naquis**, *I was born*	il **naquit**, *he was born*	elles **naquirent**, *they were born*
vivre, *to live*	il **vécut**, *he lived*	nous **vécûmes**, *we lived*	ils **vécurent**, *they lived*
voir, *to see*	je **vis**, *I saw*	elle **vit**, *she saw*	elles **virent**, *they saw*

> *NOTE:* The simple past stems of the verbs **tenir** and **venir** and their compounds follow the "î" pattern, but drop the vowel.

tenir, *to hold*	tu **tins**, *you held*	vous **tîntes**, *you held*	ils **tinrent**, *they held*
venir, *to come*	je **vins**, *I came*	il **vint**, *he came*	nous **vînmes**, *we came*

C. Use of the simple past

The simple past tells about something that began at the past moment under consideration.

Le Roi **parla** et les gens **écoutèrent**.	*The King spoke and the people listened.*
Nous **allâmes** deux par deux vers notre destin.	*We went two by two to meet our fate.*

> *NOTE:* The *imparfait* is used in literary French to describe events whose beginnings are not in focus—just as you use the imparfait in spoken French.

EXERCISE 12-1: Rewrite the following sentences using the passé composé in place of the simple past. Answers and translations are at the end of the chapter.

Example:	Les pèlerins allèrent dans le Moyen-Orient.	*The pilgrims went to the Middle East.*
	Les pèlerins sont allés dans le Moyen-Orient.	*The pilgrims went to the Middle East.*

1. Louis XIV régna au 17ième siècle.
2. Les espions furent attrapés par les soldats du roi.
3. Elle prit toutes les précautions nécessaires.
4. Les musiciens voulurent jouer devant l'assemblée.
5. L'ambassadeur finit sa mission à la cour.
6. Nous répondîmes aussi honnêtement que possible.

7. La princesse eut soudainement des remords.
8. L'armée attaqua la forteresse le lendemain.
9. Nous sûmes que la reine était morte.
10. Les messagers annoncèrent la mauvaise nouvelle.
11. Il mourut sans reprendre conscience.
12. Ils vécurent toute leur vie ensemble.
13. Napoléon fit construire l'Arc de Triomphe.
14. Qui furent ses ministres?
15. Le comte tint sa promesse au roi.
16. La petite fille vit la procession.
17. Nous dûmes remercier notre protecteur.
18. Les invités vinrent nombreux.
19. Les cardinaux choisirent le nouveau Pape.
20. On vendit les biens du baron.

12-2. The Simple Past Perfect

The *simple past perfect* (**passé antérieur**) is used after certain time conjunctions—where you would use the passé surcomposé in spoken French (see Sec. 8-3).

A. Formation of the simple past perfect tense

The simple past perfect uses the simple past of **être** or **avoir** followed by the past participle of the main verb to mean *had* _____ .

Aussitôt qu'il **eut fini**, il annonça les résultats.	*As soon as he had finished, he announced the results.*
Il s'en alla quand il se **fut excusé**.	*He went off when he had excused himself.*

> *NOTE:* The rules for past participle agreement (see Sec. 7-1) apply to the simple past perfect.

Dès qu'elle **se fut mariée**, la Princesse quitta ses parents.	*As soon as she married, the princess left her parents.*

B. Use of the simple past perfect

Use the simple past perfect tense after the following time conjunctions.

quand	*when*	**aussitôt que**	*as soon as*
lorsque	*when*	**après que**	*after*
dès que	*as soon as*		

Lorsqu'il **furent** nés, ils commencèrent à crier.	*When they were born, they began to scream.*

> *REMEMBER:* Like the passé surcomposé, the simple past perfect refers to a singular event and is not used to describe habitual or ongoing actions in the past.

Chaque fois qu'ils **eurent fait** une erreur, ils s'exclamèrent.	*Each time they had made a mistake, they exclaimed out loud.*

EXERCISE 12-2: Supply the appropriate tense of **être** or **avoir** according to whether the event represents a single occurrence or an ongoing situation in the past. Answers and translations are at the end of the chapter.

Example: Quand ils _____ montés à cheval, ils tombaient.	*When they _____ mounted their horses they always fell.*
Quand ils ___étaient___ montés à cheval, ils tombaient.	*When they had mounted their horses, they always fell.*

1. Dès que les révolutionnaires _____ ouvert les portes de la Bastille, les prisonniers se sauvèrent.

2. Tous les matins, quand Napoléon _____ surveillé les travaux, il consultait ses maréchaux.

3. Aussitôt que le Roi se _____ levé, le public dut se lever aussi.

4. Quand Balzac _____ fini un roman, il en commençait tout de suite un autre.

5. Henri IV put monter au pouvoir lorsque ses ennemis _____ été répudiés.

6. Quand les armées _____ chassé les Anglais de France, le peuple se réjouit.

7. Aussitôt que les colonies américaines se _____ déclarées indépendantes, la France les reconnut.

8. Lorsque une croisade _____ annoncée les églises commençaient toutes à demander de l'argent aux fidèles.

9. Les nobles s'arrangeaient pour augmenter les taxes dès que les récoltes _____ été bonnes.

10. Aussitôt que les Anglais _____ brûlé Jeanne d'Arc, elle devint un symbole de patriotisme.

12-3. The Imperfect Subjunctive

The **imperfect subjunctive** is the formal or literary equivalent of the subjunctive mood you use in spoken French (see Sec. 10-1). Unlike the spoken subjunctive, the imperfect subjunctive is always translated by the past or the conditional.

A. Formation of the imperfect subjunctive

The imperfect subjunctive of all verbs is regularly formed by adding the following endings to the stem of the simple past.

Person	Singular	Plural
1st	-sse	-ssions
2nd	-sses	-ssiez
3rd	-ât	-ssent
	-ît	
	-ût	

NOTE: Only the circumflex accent of the third person singular distinguishes the spelling of the imperfect subjunctive from that of the simple past.

Simple past	stem	Imperfect subjunctive
aller, *to go*	alla-	que j'allasse, *that I went* que tu allasses, qu'il allât que nous allassions, que vous allassiez, qu'ils allassent
grandir, *to grow*	grandi-	que je grandisse, *that I grew* que tu grandisses, qu'il grandît que nous grandissions, que vous grandissiez, qu'ils grandissent
perdre, *to lose*	perdi-	que je perdisse, *that I lost* que tu perdisses, qu'elle perdît que nous perdissions, que vous perdissiez, qu'ils perdissent
être, *to be*	fu-	que je fusse, *that I was* que tu fusses, qu'on fût que nous fussions, que vous fussiez, qu'ils fussent

J'aurais voulu **qu'ils** en **fissent** autant.   *I would have liked them to do as much.*

Il n'était pas certain **que les troupes retournassent**.

Nous avions peur **qu'il** (ne) **prît** son temps.

It was not certain that the troops would return.

We were afraid that he would take his time.

B. Use of the imperfect subjunctive

The imperfect subjunctive is the formal or literary equivalent of the spoken subjunctive (see Sec. 10-2).

Spoken French	Literary French	
Il doutait **que nous venions**.	Il doutait **que nous vinssions**.	*He doubted that we would come.*
Tout le monde priait pour **qu'elle revienne**.	Tout le monde priait pour **qu'elle revînt**.	*Everyone was praying for her to return.*

EXERCISE 12-3: Rewrite the following sentences in current, informal French style, changing the simple past and imperfect subjunctive verbs to appropriate conversational forms. Answers and translations are at the end of the chapter.

Example: Il commanda qu'elle fut bannie du royaume.

Il a commandé qu'elle soit bannie du royaume.

He ordered that she be banished from the kingdom.

1. Il n'eût jamais admis son erreur.
2. Les prêtres refusèrent que les impôts fussent diminués.
3. S'il comprenait tout cela il se résignât.
4. Les propriétaires n'étaient pas contents bien qu'ils s'enrichissent.
5. Le capitaine ordonna que les soldats revinssent en arrière.
6. La princesse était contente que son père fit cette célébration.
7. Il fut impossible que nous acceptassions ces conditions.
8. Elle cherchait un mari qui sût faire la guerre.
9. Leurs parents ne permettaient pas qu'ils vécussent ensemble.
10. Il fallut que nous vissions ce spectacle.

12-4. The Pluperfect Subjunctive

The **pluperfect subjunctive** is the literary equivalent of the past subjunctive (see Sec. 10-2).

A. Formation of the pluperfect subjunctive

The pluperfect subjunctive combines the imperfect subjunctive of **être** or **avoir** with the past participle of the main verb—just as the subjunctive of **être** or **avoir** combines with the past participle of the main verb in the spoken subjunctive.

Spoken French	Literary French	
que je **sois retourné**	que je **fusse retourné**	*that I would return*
qu'il **ait fini**	qu'il **eût fini**	*that he would finish*
que tu **te sois assis**	que tu **te fusses assis**	*that you would sit down*

B. Use and meaning of the pluperfect subjunctive

1. In subordinate clauses, the pluperfect subjunctive is the literary equivalent of the past subjunctive and means *had_____*.

Il était content **qu'ils se fussent trompés**.

Tout le monde doutait **que la France eût perdu**.

He was glad that they had made a mistake.

Everybody doubted that France had lost.

2. In main clauses, the pluperfect subjunctive is the literary equivalent of the past conditional and means *would have_____*.

S'il avait gagné nous **eussions célébré**.	*If he had won, we would have celebrated.*
Il **se fût fait** mal s'il était tombé.	*He would have hurt himself if he had fallen.*
Qui l'**eût cru**?	*Who would have believed it?* (affected usage)

EXERCISE 12-4: Rewrite the following sentences in informal, conversational style, replacing the literary tenses by spoken forms. Answers and translations are at the end of the chapter.

Example: S'il s'en était aperçu il eût été enragé.

S'il s'en était aperçu il aurait été enragé.   *If he had noticed it, he would have been angry.*

1. Nous aurions voulu qu'elle eût dit franchement son opinion.
2. Avait-il été certain que vous eussiez rejeté son offre?
3. Si vous nous aviez invités, nous eussions accepté avec plaisir.
4. Elle ne voulait rien entendre, quoiqu'il eût fait tout son possible.
5. L'archevêque douta qu'elle se fût compromise dans l'affaire.

SUMMARY

1. The simple past is a literary tense, which is used on formal occasions and in formal prose to refer to a past action that began at the moment under consideration—where spoken French uses the passé composé.
2. The simple past perfect is used after certain time conjunctions in place of the passé surcomposé to mean *had* _____. It is a perfect tense consisting of the simple past of **être** or **avoir** combined with the past participle of the main verb.
3. The imperfect subjunctive replaces the spoken subjunctive in past or conditional sentences in formal style.
4. The pluperfect subjunctive replaces the past subjunctive in formal style. It is a perfect tense meaning *had* _____. The pluperfect subjunctive is also used in main clauses as the literary equivalent of the past conditional and means *would have* _____.

RAISE YOUR GRADES

The simple past

Rewrite the following sentences in formal style by replacing the passé composé with the simple past. Answers and translations are at the end of the chapter.

Example: Le capitaine les a disciplinés sévèrement.

Le capitaine les disciplina sévèrement.   *The captain disciplined them severely.*

1. J'ai pris la liberté de m'asseoir.
2. Nous avons écrit plusieurs fois au sénateur.
3. Les résultats de cette expérience ont donné des indications positives.
4. L'employé a fait preuve d'une grande intelligence.
5. Ils se sont conduits avec prudence.
6. Les armées du roi ont vaincu les envahisseurs.
7. Les fournisseurs se sont approprié le matériel.
8. Le maire a été élu au conseil départemental.
9. J'ai annoncé les dernières nouvelles.
10. Nous avons dit toute notre pensée.

11. Vous avez eu l'honneur de présenter la médaille.
12. Enfin Malherbe est venu!
13. Le roi a mis la main sur l'épaule du chevalier.
14. Elle est morte avant la guerre.
15. Ils ont vécu ensemble 40 ans.
16. En quelle année est-il né?
17. Ont-ils vu l'Afrique?
18. Elle a bien tenu sa promesse.
19. Ils ont tout dit.
20. J'ai fini cet exercice.

The simple past and the imperfect subjunctive

Rewrite the following sentences in formal style by replacing the passé composé with the simple past, and the subjunctive by the imperfect subjunctive. Answers and translations are at the end of the chapter.

Example: Le comte a insisté que sa femme reste chez elle.

Le comte insista que sa femme restât chez elle. *The count insisted that his wife stay home.*

21. Les paysans avaient peur que les soldats ne reviennent.
22. Nous aimerions que vous nous disiez vos intentions.
23. Notre chef les a honorés bien que ce soient des étrangers.
24. Ce journal a réclamé que le Président révèle les noms.
25. Je n'étais pas sûr qu'il prenne cette affaire en charge.
26. Les soldats sont partis sans que personne les voie.
27. Il chercherait un cheval qui ait l'habitude des batailles.
28. Nous avons refusé de nous rendre à moins qu'ils fassent des concessions.
29. Les maîtres ne se doutaient pas que les esclaves se révoltent.
30. Il n'était pas du tout évident que nous puissions faire face aux événements.

The simple past perfect and the pluperfect subjunctive

Write the formally correct form of the verb **être** or **avoir** in each blank, according to the tenses given in the rest of the sentence. Answers and translations are at the end of the chapter.

31. Le prince lui offrit sa main quand elle _____ révélé ses origines.
32. Les sénateurs avaient bien peur que le président _____ arrangé un compromis derrière leur dos.
33. Dès que les troupes _____ entrées au chateau on ferma le pont-levis.
34. Les messagers partirent sans que les gardes s'en _____ rendu compte.
35. Si l'ennemi avait attaqué nous _____ repoussé l'attaque.

CHAPTER ANSWERS

EXERCISE 12-1:

1. Louis XIV a régné au 17ième siècle. *Louis XIV reigned in the 17th century.*
2. Les espions ont été attrapés par les soldats du roi. *The spies were trapped by the king's soldiers.*
3. Elle a pris toutes les précautions nécessaires. *She took all the necessary precautions.*
4. Les musiciens ont voulu jouer devant l'assemblée. *The musicians wanted to play before the assembly.*
5. L'ambassadeur a fini sa mission à la cour. *The ambassador completed his mission to the court.*
6. Nous avons répondu aussi honnêtement que possible. *We answered as honestly as possible.*
7. La princesse a eu soudainement des remords. *The princess was suddenly filled with remorse.*
8. L'armée a attaqué la forteresse le lendemain. *The army attacked the fortress on Monday.*
9. Nous avons su que la reine était morte. *We knew that the queen was dead.*

10. Les messagers ont annoncé la mauvaise nouvelle. *The messengers announced the bad news.*
11. Il est mort sans reprendre conscience. *He died without regaining consciousness.*
12. Ils ont vécu toute leur vie ensemble. *They lived together all their lives.*
13. Napoléon a fait construire l'Arc de Triomphe. *Napoleon had the Arch of Triumph constructed.*
14. Qui ont été ses ministres? *Who were his ministers?*
15. Le comte a tenu sa promesse au roi. *The count kept his promise to the king.*
16. La petite fille a vu la procession. *The little girl saw the procession.*
17. Nous avons dû remercier notre protecteur. *We had to thank our protector.*
18. Les invités sont venus nombreux. *The guests came in large numbers.*
19. Les cardinaux ont choisi le nouveau Pape. *The cardinals chose the new pope.*
20. On a vendu les biens du baron. *They sold the goods of the baron.*

EXERCISE 12-2:

1. **eurent**   As soon as the revolutionaries had opened the doors of the Bastille, the prisoners escaped.
2. **avait**   Each morning, when Napoleon had surveyed the works, he consulted his marshals.
3. **fut**   As soon as the King stood, the public also had to stand.
4. **avait**   When Balzac had finished a novel, he began another one right away.
5. **eurent**   Henry IV was able to rise to power when his enemies had been repudiated.
6. **eurent**   When the armies had chased the English out of France, the people rejoiced.
7. **furent**   As soon as the American colonies were declared independent, France recognized them.
8. **était**   When a crusade was announced, the churches began to demand money from the faithful.
9. **avaient**   The nobles managed to raise the taxes as soon as the crops were good.
10. **eurent**   As soon as the English burned Joan of Arc, she became a patriotic symbol.

EXERCISE 12-3:

1. Il n'aurait jamais admis son erreur. *He would never have admitted his mistake.*
2. Les prêtres ont refusé que les impôts soient diminués. *The priests refused to lower the taxes.*
3. S'il comprenait tout cela, il se résignerait. *If he understood all this, he would be resigned.*
4. Les propriétaires n'étaient pas contents bien qu'ils s'enrichissent. *The owners were not happy even though they got rich.*
5. Le capitaine a ordonné que les soldats reviennent en arrière. *The captain ordered the soldiers to retreat.*
6. La princesse était contente que son père fasse cette célébration. *The princess was happy that her father put on this celebration.*
7. Il a été impossible que nous acceptions ces conditions. *It was impossible for us to accept those conditions.*
8. Elle cherchait un mari qui sache faire la guerre. *She was looking for a husband who knew how to wage war.*
9. Leurs parents ne permettaient pas qu'ils vivent ensemble. *Their parents did not permit them to live together.*
10. Il a fallu que nous voyions ce spectacle. *It was necessary for us to see that sight.*

EXERCISE 12-4:

1. Nous aurions voulu qu'elle ait dit franchement son opinion. *We would have wanted her to state her opinion frankly.*
2. Avait-il été certain que vous auriez rejeté son offre? *Was he sure that you would have rejected his offer?*
3. Si vous nous aviez invités, nous aurions accepté avec plaisir. *If you would have invited us, we would have accepted with pleasure.*
4. Elle ne voulait rien entendre, quoiqu'il ait fait tout son possible. *She would not hear of it, even though he had done all he could.*
5. L'archevêque a douté qu'elle se soit compromise dans l'affaire. *The archbishop doubted that she would be compromised in the affair.*

RAISE YOUR GRADES

The simple past

1. Je pris la liberté de m'asseoir. *I took the liberty of sitting down.*
2. Nous écrivîmes plusieurs fois au sénateur. *We wrote many times to the senator.*
3. Les résultats de cette expérience donnèrent des indications positives. *The results of this experience gave some positive indications.*
4. L'employé fit preuve d'une grande intelligence. *The employee gave evidence of great intelligence.*
5. Ils se conduisirent avec prudence. *They behaved with care.*
6. Les armées du roi vainquirent les envahisseurs. *The armies of the king conquered the invaders.*

7. Les fournisseurs s'approprièrent le matériel. *The suppliers appropriated the stock.*

8. Le maire fut élu au conseil départemental. *The mayor was elected to the departmental council.*

9. J'annonçai les dernières nouvelles. *I announced the latest news.*

10. Nous dîmes toute notre pensée. *We told all our thoughts.*

11. Vous eûtes l'honneur de présenter la médaille. *You had the honor of presenting the medal.*

12. Enfin Malherbe vint! *Finally Malherbe came!*

13. Le roi mit la main sur l'épaule du chevalier. *The king placed his hand on the shoulder of the knight.*

14. Elle mourut avant la guerre. *She died before the war.*

15. Ils vécurent ensemble 40 ans. *They lived together 40 years.*

16. En quelle année naquit-il? *In what year was he born?*

17. Virent-ils l'Afrique? *Did they see Africa?*

18. Elle tint bien sa promesse. *She kept her promise well.*

19. Ils dirent tout. *They told all.*

20. Je finis cet exercice. *I finished this exercise.*

The simple past and the imperfect subjunctive

21. Les paysans avaient peur que les soldats ne revinssent. *The peasants were afraid that the soldiers would return.*

22. Nous aimerions que vous nous dîtes vos intentions. *We would like you to tell us your intentions.*

23. Notre chef les honora bien que ce fussent des étrangers. *Our chief honored them although they were strangers.*

24. Ce journal réclama que le Président révélât les noms. *That paper claimed that the President revealed the names.*

25. Je n'étais pas sûr qu'il prît cette affaire en charge. *I wasn't sure that he took charge of this affair.*

26. Les soldats partirent sans que personne les vît. *The soldiers left without anyone seeing them.*

27. Il chercherait un cheval qui eût l'habitude des batailles. *He looked for a horse who was used to battles.*

28. Nous refusâmes de nous rendre à moins qu'ils fissent des concessions. *We refused to surrender unless they made some concessions.*

29. Les maîtres ne se doutaient pas que les esclaves se révoltassent. *The masters didn't suspect that the slaves would revolt.*

30. Il n'était pas du tout évident que nous pûmes faire face aux événements. *It was not at all evident that we could save face in the events.*

The simple past and the imperfect subjunctive

31. **eut** *The prince offered her his hand when she revealed her origins.*

32. **eut** *The senators were very much afraid that the president had arranged a compromise behind their backs.*

33. **furent (étaient)** *As soon as the troops had entered the castle, the drawbridge was raised (closed).*

34. **fussent** *The messengers left without the guards being aware of it.*

35. **eussions** *If the enemy had attacked, we would have repulsed the attack.*

UNIT EXAM IV

SUBJUNCTIVE

Answer each question using the phrase in parentheses and the appropriate form of the verb.

1. Vous choisissez des vêtements d'hiver? (Il faut que . . .)

2. Tu corriges tes fautes? (Il est indispensable que . . .)

3. La réunion finit à 10h? (Il est important que . . .)

4. Il a obtenu des billets sans difficulté? (Il est douteux que . . .)

5. Il y a un drugstore aux Champs Elysées? (Je ne suis pas sûr que . . .)

6. Linda vit encore chez ses parents? (Ses amis s'étonnent que . . .)

7. Pierre a envoyé le paquet hier? (Il est essentiel que . . .)

8. La situation était meilleure en 1917? (Je ne suis pas certain . . .)

9. Marie a pu suivre ce cours? (Son frère était content que . . .)

10. On réagit contre le terrorisme? (Les citoyens exigent que . . .)

Complete the following sentences using the appropriate form of the verb in parentheses.

11. Nous voudrions que vous y _____ aussi. (aller)

12. J'étais désolé que votre soeur _____ seule. (partir)

13. Il est dommage qu'ils _____ leur maison le mois dernier. (vendre)

14. Je doute qu'ils _____ aux Etats-Unis en 1980. (revenir)

15. Crois-tu qu'ils _____ sans le consentement de leurs parents? (se marier)

Combine the following pairs of sentences into a single logical sentence, using a coordinating conjunction (**bien que**, **ce que**, **à moins que**, **jusqu'à**, **pourv que**, **quoique**).

16. Nous ferons un pique-nique. Il fait beau.

17. Luc reste à l'hôpital. Sa santé est bonne.

18. Le conférencier a parlé lentement. Nous le comprenons.

19. Vous désirez une nouvelle robe. Vous n'en avez pas besoin.

IDIOMATIC VERB USAGE

Answer the following questions logically, using the time expressions in parentheses plus **il y a**, **il y a . . . que**, or **depuis**.

20. Depuis quand cherchez-vous du travail? (novembre)

21. Quand avez-vous visité Paris pour la première fois? (cinq ans)

22. Depuis combien de temps l'attendiez-vous? (deux heures)

23. Depuis quelle heure l'attendez-vous? (10 heures)

24. Combien de jours y a-t-il qu'il neige? (trois jours)

25. Les Américains sont allés sur la lune? (quelques années)

Answer the questions using the cues in parentheses plus **aller + infinitive, venir de + infinitive,** or **finir par + infinitive**.

26. Quand le programme commencera-t-il? (dans cinq minutes)

27. Les élections présidentielles auront-elles lieu en 1991? (non, en 1992)

28. Pierre est-il enfin arrivé? (oui, à midi)

29. La saison des pluies a-t-elle récemment commencé? (oui, en mai)

Answer the following questions negatively, using a causative construction.

30. Est-ce que tu te coupes les cheveux?

31. Les passagers se servent-ils à manger dans les avions?

32. Louis XIV construisit-il le château de Versailles de ses propres mains?

33. Le Président des Etats-Unis conduit-il sa limousine?

Answer the following questions affirmatively, using the appropriate form of the verb **devoir**.

34. Faut-il que vos parents vendent leur vieille voiture?

35. Aviez-vous l'intention de faire du ski pendant les vacances?

36. Faudrait-il que vous évitiez de tomber?

37. Aurais-tu été obligé de sortir s'il n'avait pas plu?

Answer the following questions using the cues in parentheses and the impersonal pronoun **on**.

38. Est-ce que la salade se mange après le dessert? (non . . . avant)

39. Où les timbres se collent-ils sur une enveloppe? (en haut et à droite)

40. Comment se boit le vin blanc? (frais)

41. Où se trouvent Paris et Lyon? (en France)

LITERARY TENSES

Rewrite each of the following sentences using the appropriate conversational tense.

42. Les autorités obtinrent les documents.

43. La petite princesse pleura la mort de son père.

44. Le chevalier se perdit parce qu'il ne suivit pas la route.

45. Dès que les soldats eurent reçu les ordres, il les exécutèrent.

46. Quand la reine eut tout vérifié, elle mit la main sur l'épaule du page.

47. Après qu'ils eurent assisté à la cérémonie, elles partirent.

48. L'évêque finit son discours avant que la porte ne s'ouvrît.

49. Aussitôt qu'il eut traversé la rivière, l'orage éclata.

50. Les messagers coururent pour que le générale reçût la lettre à temps.

EXAM ANSWERS

Subjunctive

1. Oui, il faut que vous choisissiez des vêtements d'hiver. *Yes, you must choose some winter clothes.*
2. Il est indispensable que tu corriges tes fautes. *It is essential that you correct your errors.*
3. Il est important que la réunion finisse à 10 heures. *It is important that the meeting end by 10:00 A.M.*
4. Il est douteux qu'il ait obtenu des billets sans difficulté. *It is doubtful that he got the tickets without difficulty.*
5. Je ne suis pas sûr qu'il y ait un drugstore aux Champs-Elysées. *I am not sure that there is a drugstore on the Champs-Elysees.*
6. Ses amis s'étonnent que Linda vive encore chez ses parents. *Her friends are surprised that Linda still lives at home.*
7. Il est essentiel que Pierre ait envoyé le paquet hier. *It is essential that Pierre sent the package yesterday.*
8. Je ne suis pas certain que la situation économique ait été meilleure en 1917. *I am not certain that the economic situation was any better in 1917.*
9. Son frère était content que Marie ait pu suivre ce cours. *Her brother was pleased that Marie had been able to take this course.*
10. Les citoyens exigent que l'on réagisse contre le terrorisme. *The citizens demand that there be a reaction against terrorism.*
11. Nous voudrions que vous y alliez aussi. *We would like for you to go, too.*
12. J'étais desolée que votre soeur soit partie seule. *I was sorry that your sister went alone.*
13. Il est dommage qu'ils aient vendu leur maison le mois dernier. *It's too bad that they sold their house last month.*
14. Je doute qu'ils soient revenus aux Etats-Unis en 1980. *I don't think they returned to the United States in 1980.*
15. Crois-tu qu'ils se soient mariés sans le consentement de leurs parents? *Do you believe that they got married (will get married) without their parents' consent?*
16. Nous ferons un pique-nique pourvu qu'il fasse beau. *We will have a picnic if (provided that) the weather is good.*
17. Luc reste à l'hôpital jusqu'à ce que sa santé soit bonne. *Luc is staying in the hospital until he is well.*
18. Le conférencier a parlé lentement pour que nous le comprenions. *The lecturer spoke slowly so that we could understand him.*
19. Vous désirez une nouvelle robe bien que vous n'en ayez pas besoin. *You want a new dress even though you don't need one.*

Idiomatic verb usage

20. Je cherche du travail depuis novembre. *I've been looking for work since November.*
21. J'ai visité Paris pour la première fois il y a cinq ans. (Il y a cinq ans que j'ai visité Paris pour la première fois.) *I visited Paris for the first time five years ago.*
22. Je l'attendais depuis deux heures. *I had been waiting for him for two hours.*
23. Je l'attends depuis 10 heures. *I have been waiting for him since 10:00 A.M.*
24. Il neige depuis trois jours. (Il y a trois jours qu'il neige.) *It's been snowing for three days.*
25. Il y a quelques années que les Américains sont allés sur la lune. *The Americans went to the moon a few years ago.*
26. La programme va commencer dans cinq minutes. *The program will start in five minutes.*
27. Non, les élections présidentielles vont avoir lieu en 1992. *No, the presidential elections will take place in 1992.*
28. Oui, Pierre a fini par arriver à midi. *Yes, Pierre finally arrived at noon.*
29. Oui, la saison des pluies a fini par commencer en mai. *Yes, the rainy season finally started in May.*
30. Non, je me les fais couper. *No, I have it cut.*
31. Non, ils se font servir à manger dans les avions. *No, they get served in an airplane.*
32. Non, Louis XIV a fait construire le Château de Versailles. *No, Louis XIV had the castle of Versailles built.*
33. Non, Le Président des Etats-Unis la fait conduire. *No, the President of the United States has it driven.*
34. Oui, ils doivent vendre leur vieille voiture. *Yes, they had to sell their old car.*
35. Oui, je devais faire du ski pendant les vacances. *Yes, I was supposed to ski during vacation.*
36. Oui, je devrais éviter de tomber. *Yes, I should try not to fall.*
37. Oui, j'aurais dû sortir s'il n'avait pas plu. *Yes, I would have had to go if it had not rained.*
38. Non, on mange la salade avant le fromage. *No, one eats salad before dessert.*
39. On colle les timbres en haut et à droite sur une enveloppe. *You put stamps on the upper right-hand corner of an envelope.*
40. On boit le vin blanc frais. *White wine is drunk chilled.*
41. On trouve Paris et Lyon en France. *Paris and Lyons are in France.*

Literary tense

42. Les autorités ont obtenu les documents. *The authorities obtained the documents.*

43. La petite princesse a pleuré la mort de son père. *The young princess mourned her father's death.*
44. Le chevalier s'est perdu parce qu'il n'a pas suivi la route. *The knight got lost because he didn't follow the road.*
45. Dès que les soldats ont reçu les ordres, ils les ont exécutés. *As soon as the soldiers received their orders, they carried them out.*
46. Quand la reine a eu tout verifié, elle a mis la main sur l'épaule du page. *When the Queen had made sure of everything, she put her hand on the page's shoulder.*

47. Après qu'ils ont eu assisté à la cérémonie, elles sont parties. *After they attended the ceremony, they left.*
48. L'évêque a finit son discours avant que la porte ne s'ouvre. *The Bishop finished his sermon before the door opened.*
49. Aussitôt qu'il a eu traversé la rivière, l'orage a éclaté. *As soon as he had crossed the river, the storm broke.*
50. Les messagers ont couru pour que le général reçoive la lettre à temps. *The messengers ran so that the general might receive the letter in time.*

APPENDIX: Verbs

Conjugation of the verb avoir, to have

Indicative

Present

		Passé composé	
j'ai	*I have, am having*	j'ai eu	*I have had, had*
tu as		tu as eu	
il a		il a eu	
nous avons		nous avons eu	
vous avez		vous avez eu	
ils ont		ils ont eu	

Imparfait

		Pluperfect	
j'avais	*I had, was having*	j'avais eu	*I had had*
tu avais		tu avais eu	
elle avait		elle avait eu	
nous avions		nous avions eu	
vous aviez		vous aviez eu	
elles avaient		elles avaient eu	

Simple past

		Simple past perfect	
j'eus	*I had*	j'eus eu	*I had had*
tu eus		tu eus eu	
il eut		il eut eu	
nous eûmes		nous eûmes eu	
vous eûtes		vous eûtes eu	
ils eurent		ils eurent eu	

Future

		Future perfect	
j'aurai	*I will have*	j'aurai eu	*I will have had*
tu auras		tu auras eu	
elle aura		elle aura eu	
nous aurons		nous aurons eu	
vous aurez		vous aurez eu	
elles auront		elles auront eu	

Conditional

Present conditional

		Past conditional	
j'aurais	*I would have*	j'aurais eu	*I would have had*
tu aurais		tu aurais eu	
il aurait		il aurait eu	
nous aurions		nous aurions eu	
vous auriez		vous auriez eu	
ils auraient		ils auraient eu	

Subjunctive

Present subjunctive

		Perfect subjunctive	
que j'aie	*that I may have*	que j'aie eu	*that I may have had*
que tu aies		que tu aies eu	
qu'elle ait		qu'elle ait eu	
que nous ayons		que nous ayons eu	
que vous ayez		que vous ayez eu	
qu'elles aient		qu'elles aient eu	

Imperfect subjunctive

		Pluperfect subjunctive	
que j'eusse	*that I might have*	que j'eusse eu	*that I might have had*
que tu eusses		que tu eusses eu	
qu'il eût		qu'il eût eu	
que nous eussions		que nous eussions eu	
que vous eussiez		que vous eussiez eu	
qu'ils eussent		qu'ils eussent eu	

Imperative   Present participle   Past participle

aie	*have*	ayant	*having*	eu	*had*
ayons					
ayez					

Conjugation of the verb être, *to be*
Indicative

Present

je suis	*I am, am being*
tu es	
elle est	
nous sommes	
vous êtes	
elles sont	

Passé composé

j'ai été	*I have been, was*
tu as été	
elle a été	
nous avons été	
vous avez été	
elles ont été	

Imparfait

j'étais	*I was, was being*
tu étais	
il était	
nous étions	
vous étiez	
ils étaient	

Pluperfect

j'avais été	*I had been*
tu avais été	
il avait été	
nous avions été	
vous aviez été	
ils avaient été	

Simple past

je fus	*I was*
tu fus	
elle fut	
nous fûmes	
vous fûtes	
elles furent	

Simple past perfect

j'eus été	*I had been*
tu eus été	
elle eut été	
nous eûmes été	
vous eûtes été	
elles eurent été	

Future

je serai	*I will be*
tu seras	
il sera	
nous serons	
vous serez	
ils seront	

Future perfect

j'aurai été	*I will have been*
tu auras été	
il aura été	
nous aurons été	
vous aurez été	
ils auront été	

Conditional

Present conditional

je serais	*I would be*
tu serais	
elle serait	
nous serions	
vous seriez	
elles seraient	

Past conditional

j'aurais été	*I would have been*
tu aurais été	
elle aurait été	
nous aurions été	
vous auriez été	
elles auraient été	

Subjunctive

Present subjunctive

que je sois	*that I may be*
que tu sois	
qu'il soit	
que nous soyons	
que vous soyez	
qu'ils soient	

Perfect subjunctive

que j'aie été	*that I may have been*
que tu aies été	
qu'il ait été	
que nous ayons été	
que vous ayez été	
qu'ils aient été	

Imperfect subjunctive

que je fusse	*that I might be*
que tu fusses	
qu'elle fût	
que nous fussions	
que vous fussiez	
qu'elles fussent	

Pluperfect subjunctive

que j'eusse été	*that I might have been*
que tu eusses été	
qu'elle eût été	
que nous eussions été	
que vous eussiez été	
qu'elles eussent été	

Imperative   *Present participle*   *Past participle*

sois	*be*	étant	*being*	été	*been*
soyons					
soyez					

Conjugation of some common irregular verbs
Aller, *to go*

Indicative

Present		**Passé composé**	
je vais	*I go, am going*	je suis allé(e)	*I have gone, went*
tu vas		tu es allé(e)	
il va		il est allé	
nous allons		nous sommes allés(e)s	
vous allez		vous etes allé(e)(s)	
ils vont		ils sont allés	

Imparfait		**Pluperfect**	
j'allais	*I went, was going*	j'étais allé(e)	*I had gone*
tu allais		tu étais allé(e)	
elle allait		elle était allée	
nous allions		nous étions allé(e)s	
vous alliez		vous étiez allé(e)(s)	
elles allaient		elles étaient allées	

Simple past		**Simple past perfect**	
j'allai	*I went*	je fus allé(e)	*I had gone*
tu allas		tu fus allé(e)	
il alla		il fut allé	
nous allâmes		nous fûmes allé(e)s	
vous allâtes		vous fûtes allé(e)(s)	
ils allèrent		ils furent allés	

Future		**Future perfect**	
j'irai	*I will go*	je serai allé(e)	*I will have gone*
tu iras		tu seras allé(e)	
elle ira		elle sera allée	
nous irons		nous serons allé(e)s	
vous irez		vous serez allé(e)(s)	
elles iront		elles seront allées	

Conditional

Present conditional		**Past conditional**	
j'irais	*I would go*	je serais allé(e)	*I would have gone*
tu irais		tu serais allé(e)	
il irait		il serait allé	
nous irions		nous serions allé(e)s	
vous iriez		vous seriez allé(e)(s)	
ils iriez		ils seraient allés	

Subjunctive

Present subjunctive		**Perfect subjunctive**	
que j'aille	*that I may go*	que je sois allé(e)	*that I may have gone*
que tu ailles		que tu sois allé(e)	
qu'elle aille		que elle soit allée	
que nous allions		que nous soyons allé(e)s	
que vous alliez		que vous soyez allé(e)(s)	
qu'elles aillent		qu'elles soient allées	

Imperfect subjunctive		**Pluperfect subjunctive**	
que j'allasse	*that I might go*	que je fusse allé(e)	*that I might have gone*
que tu allasses		que tu fusses allé(e)	
qu'elle allât		qu'elle fût allée	
que nous allassions		que nous fussions allé(e)s	
que vous allassiez		que vous fussiez allé(e)(s)	
que elles allassent		qu'elles fussent allées	

Imperative		*Present participle*		*Past participle*	
va	*go*	allant	*going*	allé	*went*
allons					
allez					

Boire, *to drink*

Indicative

Present

je bois	*I drink, am drinking*
tu bois	
elle boit	
nous buvons	
vous buvez	
elles buvaient	

Passé composé

j'ai bu	*I have drunk, drank*
tu as bu	
elle a bu	
nous avons bu	
vous avez bu	
elles ont bu	

Imparfait

je buvais	*I drank, was drinking*
tu buvais	
il buvait	
nous buvions	
vous buviez	
ils buvaient	

Pluperfect

j'avais bu	*I had drunk*
tu avais bu	
il avait bu	
nous avions bu	
vous aviez bu	
ils avaient bu	

Simple past

je bus	*I drank*
tu bus	
elle but	
nous bumes	
vous butes	
elles burent	

Simple past perfect

j'eus bu	*I had drunk*
tu eus bu	
elle eut bu	
nous eûmes bu	
vous eûtes bu	
elles eurent bu	

Future

je boirai	*I will drink*
tu boiras	
il boira	
nous boirons	
vous boirez	
ils boiront	

Future perfect

j'aurai bu	*I will have drunk*
tu auras bu	
il aura bu	
nous aurons bu	
vous aurez bu	
ils auront bu	

Conditional

Present conditional

je boirais	*I would drink*
tu boirais	
elle boirait	
nous boirions	
vous boiriez	
elles boiraient	

Past conditional

j'aurais bu	*I would have drunk*
tu aurais bu	
elle aurait bu	
nous aurions bu	
vous auriez bu	
elles auraient bu	

Subjunctive

Present subjunctive

que je boive	*that I may drink*
que tu boives	
qu'il boive	
que nous buvions	
que vous buviez	
qu'ils boivent	

Perfect subjunctive

que j'aie bu	*that I may have drunk*
que tu aies bu	
qu'il ait bu	
que nous ayons bu	
que vous ayez bu	
qu'ils aient bu	

Imperfect subjunctive

que je busse	*that I might drink*
que tu busses	
qu'elle bût	
que nous bussions	
que vous bussiez	
qu'elles bussent	

Pluperfect subjunctive

que j'eusse bu	*that I might have drunk*
que tu eusses bu	
qu'elle eût bu	
que nous eussions bu	
que vous eussiez bu	
qu'elles eussent bu	

Imperative

bois	*drink*
buvons	
buvez	

Present participle

buvant	*drinking*

Past participle

bu	*drank*

Courir, *to run*

Indicative

Present

je cours	*I run, am running*
tu cours	
il court	
nous courons	
vous courez	
ils courent	

Imparfait

je courais	*I ran, was running*
tu courais	
elle courait	
nous courions	
vous couriez	
elles couraient	

Simple past

je courus	*I ran*
tu courus	
il courut	
nous courûmes	
vous courûtes	
ils coururent	

Future

je courrai	*I will run*
tu courras	
elle courra	
nous courrons	
vous courrez	
elles courront	

Passé composé

j'ai couru	*I have run, ran*
tu as couru	
il a couru	
nous avons couru	
vous avez couru	
ils ont couru	

Pluperfect

j'avais couru	*I had run*
tu avais couru	
elle avait couru	
nous avions couru	
vous aviez couru	
elles avaient couru	

Simple past perfect

j'eus couru	*I had run*
tu eus couru	
il eut couru	
nous eûmes couru	
vous eûtes couru	
ils eurent couru	

Future perfect

j'aurai couru	*I will have run*
tu auras couru	
elle aura couru	
nous aurons couru	
vous aurez couru	
elles auront couru	

Conditional

Present conditional

je courrais	*I would run*
tu courrais	
il courrait	
nous courrions	
vous courriez	
ils courraient	

Past conditional

je aurais couru	*I would have run*
tu aurais couru	
il aurait couru	
nous aurions couru	
vous auriez couru	
ils auraient couru	

Subjunctive

Present subjunctive

que je coure	*that I may run*
que tu coures	
qu'elle coure	
que nous courions	
que vous couriez	
qu'elle courent	

Imperfect subjunctive

que je courusse	*that I might run*
que tu courusses	
qu'il courût	
que nous courussions	
que vous courussiez	
qu'ils courussent	

Perfect subjunctive

que j'aie couru	*that I may have run*
que tu aies couru	
qu'elle ait couru	
que nous ayons couru	
que vous ayez couru	
qu'elles aient couru	

Pluperfect subjunctive

que j'eusse couru	*that I might have run*
que tu eusses couru	
qu'il eût couru	
que nous eussions couru	
que vous eussiez couru	
qu'ils eussent couru	

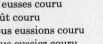

Imperative	*Present participle*	*Past participle*
cours *run*	courant *running*	couru *ran*
courons		
courez		

Craindre, *to fear, be afraid*
Indicative

Present

je crains	*I fear, am afraid*
tu crains	
il craint	
nous craignons	
vous craignez	
ils craignent	

Passé composé

j'ai craint	*I have feared, did fear*
tu as craint	
il a craint	
nous avons craint	
vous avez craint	
ils ont craint	

Imparfait

je craignais	*I was afraid, feared*
tu craignais	
elle craignait	
nous craignions	
vous craigniez	
elles craignaient	

Pluperfect

j'avais craint	*I had feared*
tu avais craint	
elle avait craint	
nous avions craint	
vous aviez craint	
elles avaient craint	

Simple past

je craignis	*I feared*
tu craignis	
il craignit	
nous craignîmes	
vous craignîtes	
ils craignirent	

Simple past perfect

j'eus craint	*I had feared*
tu eus craint	
il eut craint	
nous eûmes craint	
vous eûtes craint	
ils eurent craint	

Future

je craindrai	*I will fear*
tu craindras	
elle craindra	
nous craindrons	
vous craindrez	
elles craindront	

Future perfect

j'aurai craint	*I will have feared*
tu auras craint	
elle aura craint	
nous aurons craint	
vous aurez craint	
elles auront craint	

Conditional

Present conditional

je craindrais	*I would fear*
tu craindrais	
il craindrait	
nous craindrions	
vous craindriez	
ils craindraient	

Past conditional

j'aurais craint	*I would have feared*
tu aurais craint	
il aurait craint	
nous aurions craint	
vous auriez craint	
ils auraient craint	

Subjunctive

Present subjunctive

que je craigne	*that I may fear*
que tu craignes	
qu'elle craigne	
que nous craignions	
que vous craigniez	
qu'elles craignent	

Perfect subjunctive

que j'aie craint	*that I may have feared*
que tu aies craint	
qu'elle ait craint	
que nous ayons craint	
que vous ayez craint	
qu'elles aient craint	

Imperfect subjunctive

que je craignisse	*that I might fear*
que tu craignisses	
qu'il craignît	
que nous craignissions	
que vous craignissiez	
qu'ils craignissent	

Pluperfect subjunctive

que j'eusse craint	*that I might have feared*
que tu eusses craint	
qu'il eût craint	
que nous eussions craint	
que vous eussiez craint	
qu'ils eussent craint	

Imperative ## *Present participle* ## *Past participle*

Imperative		Present participle		Past participle	
crains	*fear*	craignant	*fearing*	craint	*feared*
craignons					
craignez					

Faire, *to make, to do*

Indicative

Present

je fais	*I make, am making*
tu fais	
il fait	
nous faisons	
vous faites	
ils font	

Passé composé

j'ai fait	*I have made, made*
tu as fait	
il a fait	
nous avons fait	
vous avez fait	
ils ont fait	

Imparfait

je faisais	*I made, was making*
tu faisais	
elle faisait	
nous faisions	
vous faisiez	
elles faisaient	

Pluperfect

j'avais fait	*I had made*
tu avais fait	
elle avait fait	
nous avions fait	
vous aviez fait	
elles avaient fait	

Simple past

je fis	*I made*
tu fis	
il fit	
nous fîmes	
vous fîtes	
ils firent	

Simple past perfect

j'eus fait	*I had made*
tu eus fait	
il eut fait	
nous eûmes fait	
vous eûtes fait	
ils eurent fait	

Future

je ferai	*I will make*
tu feras	
elle fera	
nous ferons	
vous ferez	
elles feront	

Future perfect

j'aurai fait	*I will have made*
tu auras fait	
elle aura fait	
nous aurons fait	
vous aurez fait	
elles auront fait	

Conditional

Present conditional

je ferais	*I would make*
tu ferais	
il ferait	
nous ferions	
vous feriez	
ils feraient	

Past conditional

j'aurais fait	*I would have made*
tu aurais fait	
il aurait fait	
nous aurions fait	
vous auriez fait	
ils auraient fait	

Subjunctive

Present subjunctive

que je fasse	*that I may make*
que tu fasses	
qu'elle fasse	
que nous fassions	
que vous fassiez	
qu'elles fassent	

Perfect subjunctive

que j'aie fait	*that I may have made*
que tu aies fait	
qu'elle ait fait	
que nous ayons fait	
que vous ayez fait	
qu'elles aient fait	

Imperfect subjunctive

que je fisse	*that I might make*
que tu fisses	
qu'il fît	
que nous fissions	
que vous fissiez	
qu'ils fissent	

Pluperfect subjunctive

que j'eusse fait	*that I might have made*
que tu eusses fait	
qu'il eût fait	
que nous eussions fait	
que vous eussiez fait	
qu'ils eussent fait	

Imperative

fais	*make, do*
faisons	
faites	

Present participle

faisant   *making, doing*

Past participle

fait   *made, done*

Mourir, *to die*

Indicative

Present

je meurs	*I die, am dying*
tu meurs	
il meurt	
nous mourons	
vous mourez	
ils meurent	

Passé composé

je suis mort(e)	*I am dead*
tu es mort(e)	
il est mort	
nous sommes mort(e)s	
vous etes mort(e)(s)	
ils sont morts	

Imparfait

je mourais	*I died*
tu mourais	
elle mourait	
nous mourions	
vous mouriez	
elles mouraient	

Pluperfect

j'etais mort(e)	*I had died*
tu etais mort(e)	
elle etait morte	
nous etions mort(e)s	
vous etiez mort(e)(s)	
elles etaient mortes	

Simple past

je mourus	*I died*
tu mourus	
il mourut	
nous mourûmes	
vous mourûtes	
ils moururent	

Simple past perfect

je fus mort(e)	*I had died*
tu fus mort(e)	
il fut mort	
nous fûmes mort(e)s	
vous fûtes mort(e)(s)	
ils furent morts	

Future

je mourrai	*I will die*
tu mourras	
elle mourra	
nous mourrons	
vous mourrez	
elles mourront	

Future perfect

je serai mort(e)	*I will have died*
tu seras mort(e)	
elle sera morte	
nous serons mort(e)s	
vous serez mort(e)(s)	
elles seront mortes	

Conditional

Present conditional

je mourrais	*I would die*
tu mourrais	
il mourrait	
nous mourrions	
vous mourriez	
ils mourraient	

Past conditional

je serais mort(e)	*I would have died*
tu serais mort(e)	
il serait mort	
nous serions mort(e)s	
vous seriez mort(e)(s)	
ils seraient morts	

Subjunctive

Present subjunctive

que je meure	*that I may die*
que tu meures	
qu'elle meure	
que nous mourions	
que vous mouriez	
qu'elles meurent	

Perfect subjunctive

que je sois mort(e)	*that I may have died*
que tu sois mort(e)	
qu'elle soit morte	
que nous soyons mort(e)s	
que vous soyez mort(e)(s)	
qu'elles soient mortes	

Imperfect subjunctive

que je mourusse	*that I might die*
que tu mourusses	
qu'il mourût	
que nous mourussions	
que vous mourussiez	
qu'ils mourussent	

Pluperfect subjunctive

que je fusse mort(e)	*that I might have died*
que tu fusses mort(e)	
qu'il fût mort	
que nous fussions mort(e)s	
que vous fussiez mort(e)(s)	
qu'ils fussent morts	

Imperative

meurs	*die*
mourons	
mourez	

Present participle

mourant	*dying*

Past participle

mort	*died*

Ouvrir, *to open*

Indicative

Present

j'ouvre	*I open, am opening*
tu ouvres	
il ouvre	
nous ouvrons	
vous ouvrez	
ils ouvrent	

Passé composé

j'ai ouvert	*I have opened, opened*
tu as ouvert	
il a ouvert	
nous avons ouvert	
vous avez ouvert	
ils ont ouvert	

Imparfait

j'ouvrais	*I opened, was opening*
tu ouvrais	
elle ouvrait	
nous ouvrions	
vous ouvriez	
elles ouvraient	

Pluperfect

j'avais ouvert	*I had opened*
tu avais ouvert	
elle avait ouvert	
nous avions ouvert	
vous aviez ouvert	
elles avaient ouvert	

Simple past

j'ouvris	*I opened*
tu ouvris	
il ouvrit	
nous ouvrîmes	
vous ouvrîtes	
ils ouvrirent	

Simple past-perfect

j'eus ouvert	*I had opened*
tu eus ouvert	
il eut ouvert	
nous eûmes ouvert	
vous eûtes ouvert	
ils eurent ouvert	

Future

j'ouvrirai	*I will open*
tu ouvriras	
elle ouvrira	
nous ouvrirons	
vous ouvrirez	
elles ouvriront	

Future perfect

j'aurai ouvert	*I will have opened*
tu auras ouvert	
elle aura ouvert	
nous aurons ouvert	
vous aurez ouvert	
elles auront ouvert	

Conditional

Present conditional

j'ouvrirais	*I would open*
tu ouvrirais	
il ouvrirait	
nous ouvririons	
vous ouvririez	
ils ouvriraient	

Past conditional

j'aurais ouvert	*I would have opened*
tu aurais ouvert	
il aurait ouvert	
nous aurions ouvert	
vous auriez ouvert	
ils auraient ouvert	

Subjunctive

Present subjunctive

que j'ouvre	*that I may open*
que tu ouvres	
qu'elle ouvre	
que nous ouvrions	
que vous ouvriez	
qu'elles ouvrent	

Perfect subjunctive

que j'aie ouvert	*that I may have opened*
que tu aies ouvert	
qu'elle ait ouvert	
que nous ayons ouvert	
que vous ayez ouvert	
qu'elles aient ouvert	

Imperfect subjunctive

que j'ouvrisse	*that I might open*
que tu ouvrisses	
qu'il ouvrît	
que nous ouvrissions	
que vous ouvrissiez	
qu'ils ouvrissent	

Pluperfect subjunctive

que j'eusse ouvert	*that I might have opened*
que tu eusses ouvert	
qu'il eût ouvert	
que nous eussions ouvert	
que vous eussiez ouvert	
qu'ils eussent ouvert	

Imperative   *Present participle*   *Past participle*

ouvre	*open*	ouvrant	*opening*	ouvert	*opened*
ouvrons					
ouvrez					

Prendre, *to take*

Indicative

Present

je prends	*I take, am taking*
tu prends	
elle prend	
nous prenons	
vous prenez	
elles prennent	

Passé composé

j'ai pris	*I have taken, took*
tu as pris	
elle a pris	
nous avons pris	
vous avez pris	
elles ont pris	

Imparfait

je prenais	*I took, was taking*
tu prenais	
il prenait	
nous prenions	
vous preniez	
ils prenaient	

Pluperfect

j'avais pris	*I had taken*
tu avais pris	
il avait pris	
nous avions pris	
vous aviez pris	
ils avaient pris	

Simple past

je pris	*I took*
tu pris	
elle prit	
nous prîmes	
vous prîtes	
elles prirent	

Simple past perfect

j'eus pris	*I had taken*
tu eus pris	
elle eut pris	
nous eûmes pris	
vous eûtes pris	
elles eurent pris	

Future

je prendrai	*I will take*
tu prendras	
il prendra	
nous prendrons	
vous prendrez	
ils prendront	

Future perfect

j'aurai pris	*I will have taken*
tu auras pris	
il aura pris	
nous aurons pris	
vous aurez pris	
ils auront pris	

Conditional

Present conditional

je prendrais	*I would take*
tu prendrais	
elle prendrait	
nous prendrions	
vous prendriez	
elles prendraient	

Past conditional

j'aurais pris	*I would have taken*
tu aurais pris	
elle aurait pris	
nous aurions pris	
vous auriez pris	
elles auraient pris	

Subjunctive

Present subjunctive

que je prenne	*that I may take*
que tu prennes	
qu'il prenne	
que nous prenions	
que vous preniez	
qu'ils prennent	

Perfect subjunctive

que j'aie pris	*that I may have taken*
que tu aies pris	
qu'il ait pris	
que nous ayons pris	
que vous ayez pris	
qu'ils aient pris	

Imperfect subjunctive

que je prisse	*that I might take*
que tu prisses	
qu'elle prît	
que nous prissions	
que vous prissiez	
qu'elles prissent	

Pluperfect subjunctive

que j'eusse pris	*that I might have taken*
que tu eusses pris	
qu'elle eût pris	
que nous eussions pris	
que vous eussiez pris	
qu'elles eussent pris	

Imperative   *Present participle*   *Past participle*

prends	*take*	prenant	*taking*	pris	*taken*
prenons					
prenez					

Savoir, *to know (how)*

Indicative

Present		**Passé composé**	
je sais	*I know*	j'ai su	*I have known, knew*
tu sais		tu as su	
elle sait		elle a su	
nous savons		nous avons su	
vous savez		vous avez su	
elles savent		elles ont su	

Imparfait		**Pluperfect**	
je savais	*I knew*	j'avais su	*I had known*
tu savais		tu avais su	
il savait		il avait su	
nous savions		nous avions su	
vous saviez		vous aviez su	
ils savaient		ils avaient su	

Simple past		**Simple past perfect**	
je sus	*I knew*	j'eus su	*I had known*
tu sus		tu eus su	
elle sut		elle eut su	
nous sûmes		nous eûmes su	
vous sûtes		vous eûtes su	
elles surent		elles eurent su	

Future		**Future perfect**	
je saurai	*I will know*	j'aurai su	*I will have known*
tu sauras		tu auras su	
il saura		il aura su	
nous saurons		nous aurons su	
vous saurez		vous aurez su	
ils sauront		ils auront su	

Conditional

Present conditional		**Past conditional**	
je saurais	*I would know*	j'aurais su	*I would have known*
tu saurais		tu aurais su	
elle saurait		elle aurait su	
nous saurions		nous aurions su	
vous sauriez		vous auriez su	
elles sauraient		elles auraient su	

Subjunctive

Present subjunctive		**Perfect subjunctive**	
que je sache	*that I may know*	que j'aie su	*that I may have known*
que tu saches		que tu aies su	
qu'il sache		qu'il ait su	
que nous sachions		que nous ayons su	
que vous sachiez		que vous ayez su	
qu'ils sachent		qu'ils aient su	

Imperfect subjunctive		**Pluperfect subjunctive**	
que je susse	*that I might know*	que j'eusse su	*that I might have gone*
que tu susses		que tu eusses su	
qu'elle sût		qu'elle eût su	
que nous sussions		que nous eussions su	
que vous sussiez		que vous eussiez su	
qu'elles sussent		qu'elles eussent su	

Imperative		*Present participle*		*Past participle*	
sache	*know*	sachant	*knowing*	su	*known*
sachons					
sachez					

Venir, *to come*

Indicative

Present		**Passé composé**	
je viens	*I come, am coming*	je suis venu(e)	*I have come, came*
tu viens		tu es venu(e)	
il vient		il est venu	
nous venons		nous sommes venu(e)s	
vous venez		vous êtes venu(e)(s)	
ils viennent		ils sont venus	

Imparfait		**Pluperfect**	
je venais	*I came, was coming*	j'étais venu(e)	*I had come*
tu venais		tu étais venu(e)	
elle venait		elle était venue	
nous venions		nous étions venu(e)s	
vous veniez		vous étiez venu(e)(s)	
elles venaient		elles étaient venues	

Simple past		**Simple past perfect**	
je vins	*I came*	je fus venu(e)	*I had come*
tu vins		tu fus venu(e)	
il vint		il fut venu	
nous vînmes		nous fûmes venu(e)s	
vous vîntes		vous fûtes venu(e)(s)	
ils vinrent		ils furent venus	

Future		**Future perfect**	
je viendrai	*I will come*	je serai venu(e)	*I will have come*
tu viendras		tu seras venu(e)	
elle viendra		elle sera venue	
nous viendrons		nous serons venu(e)s	
vous viendrez		vous serez venu(e)(s)	
elles viendront		elles seront venues	

Conditional

Present conditional		**Past conditional**	
je viendrais	*I would come*	je serais venu(e)	*I would have come*
tu viendrais		tu serais venu(e)	
il viendrait		il serait venu	
nous viendrions		nous serions venu(e)s	
vous viendriez		vous seriez venu(e)(s)	
ils viendraient		ils seraient venus	

Subjunctive

Present subjunctive		**Perfect subjunctive**	
que je vienne	*that I may come*	que je sois venu(e)	*that I may have come*
que tu viennes		que tu sois venu(e)	
qu'elle vienne		qu'elle soit venue	
que nous venions		que nous soyons venu(e)s	
que vous veniez		que vous soyez venu(e)(s)	
qu'elles viennent		qu'elles soient venues	

Imperfect subjunctive		**Pluperfect subjunctive**	
que je vinsse	*that I might come*	que je fusse venu(e)	*that I might have come*
que tu vinsses		que tu fusses venu(e)	
qu'il vînt		qu'il fût venu	
que nous vinssions		que nous fussions venu(e)s	
que vous vinssiez		que vous fussiez venu(e)(s)	
qu'ils vinssent		qu'ils fussent venus	

Imperative		*Present participle*		*Past participle*	
viens	*come*	venant	*coming*	venu	*come*
venons					
venez					

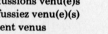

Voir, *to see*

Indicative

Present

je vois	*I see, am seeing*
tu vois	
elle voit	
nous voyons	
vous voyez	
elles voient	

Passé composé

j'ai vu	*I have seen, saw*
tu as vu	
elle a vu	
nous avons vu	
vous avez vu	
elles ont vu	

Imparfait

je voyais	*I saw, was seeing*
tu voyais	
il voyait	
nous voyions	
vous voyiez	
ils voyaient	

Pluperfect

j'avais vu	*I had seen*
tu avais vu	
il avait vu	
nous avions vu	
vous aviez vu	
ils avaient vu	

Simple past

je vis	*I saw*
tu vis	
elle vit	
nous vîmes	
vous vîtes	
elles virent	

Simple past perfect

j'eus vu	*I had seen*
tu eus vu	
elle eut vu	
nous eûmes vu	
vous eûtes vu	
elles eurent vu	

Future

je verrai	*I will see*
tu verras	
il verra	
nous verrons	
vous verrez	
ils verront	

Future perfect

j'aurai vu	*I will have seen*
tu auras vu	
il aura vu	
nous aurons vu	
vous aurez vu	
ils auront vu	

Conditional

Present conditional

je verrais	*I would see*
tu verrais	
elle verrait	
nous verrions	
vous verriez	
elles verraient	

Past conditional

j'aurais vu	*I would have seen*
tu aurais vu	
elle aurait vu	
nous aurions vu	
vous auriez vu	
elles auraient vu	

Subjunctive

Present subjunctive

que je voie	*that I may see*
que tu voies	
qu'il voie	
que nous voyions	
que vous voyiez	
qu'ils voient	

Perfect subjunctive

que j'aie vu	*that I may have seen*
que tu aies vu	
qu'il ait vu	
que nous ayons vu	
que vous ayez vu	
qu'ils aient vu	

Imperfect subjunctive

que je visse	*that I might see*
que tu visses	
qu'elle vît	
que nous vissions	
que vous vissiez	
qu'elles vissent	

Pluperfect subjunctive

que j'eusse vu	*that I might have seen*
que tu eusses vu	
qu'elle eût vu	
que nous eussions vu	
que vous eussiez vu	
qu'elles eussent vu	

Imperative · *Present participle* · *Past participle*

Imperative		*Present participle*		*Past participle*	
vois	*see*	voyant	*seeing*	vu	*seen*
voyons					
voyez					

Some common verbs directly followed by an infinitive:

Verbs of motion: **aller,** *to go;* **courir,** *to run;* **venir,** *to come;* etc.
Verbs of perception: **entendre,** *to hear;* **sentir,** *to feel;* **voir,** *to see;* etc.

affirmer	*to affirm*	espérer	*to hope*
compter	*to count*	faire	*to make, to do*
conduire	*to lead*	laisser	*to let, to allow*
croire	*to believe*	oser	*to dare*
declarer	*to declare*	paraître	*to appear*
désirer	*to desire*	pouvoir	*to be able to, can*
devoir	*to have to, must*	préférer	*to prefer*
dire	*to declare* (used in this sense)	savoir	*to know (how)*
écouter	*to listen*	sembler	*to seem*
envoyer	*to send*	vouloir	*to want, to wish*

Some common verbs followed by à *before an infinitive:*

aider	*to aid, to help*	forcer	*to force*
apprendre	*to learn*	habituer	*to accustom*
arriver	*to arrive, to happen*	hésiter	*to hesitate*
autoriser	*to authorize*	inviter	*to invite*
avoir	*to have*	obliger	*to oblige*
chercher	*to look for, to seek*	renoncer	*to renounce, to give up*
commencer	*to begin*	reussir	*to succeed*
consentir	*to consent, to agree*	servir	*to serve*
continuer	*to continue*	tarder	*to delay*
enseigner	*to teach*	tenir	*to hold*

Some common verbs followed by de *before an infinitive:*

accuser	*to accuse*	mériter	*to merit*
blâmer	*to blame*	négliger	*to neglect*
cesser	*to stop*	offrir	*to offer*
complimenter	*to compliment*	ordonner	*to order, to command*
conseiller	*to advise*	oublier	*to forget*
convenir	*to suit, to arrange*	pardonner	*to pardon*
craindre	*to fear*	permettre	*to permit*
décider	*to decide*	persuader	*to persuade*
defendre	*to defend*	promettre	*to promise*
dire	*to say*	refuser	*to refuse*
écrire	*to write*	regretter	*to regret*
empêcher	*to prevent*	remercier	*to thank*
essayer	*to try*	suggerer	*to suggest*
éviter	*to avoid*	téléphoner	*to telephone*
finir	*to finish*	tenter	*to attempt*

INDEX